CRITICAL DIALOGUES IN SOUTHEAST ASIAN STUDIES

Charles Keyes, Vicente Rafael, and Laurie J. Sears,
Series Editors

Critical Dialogues in Southeast Asian Studies

This series offers perspectives in Southeast Asian Studies that stem from reconsideration of the relationships among scholars, texts, archives, field sites, and subject matter. Volumes in the series feature inquiries into historiography, critical ethnography, colonialism and postcolonialism, nationalism and ethnicity, gender and sexuality, science and technology, politics and society, and literature, drama, and film. A common vision of the series is a belief that area studies scholarship sheds light on shifting contexts and contests over forms of knowing and modes of action that inform cultural politics and shape histories of modernity.

Imagined Ancestries of Vietnamese Communism:
Ton Duc Thang and the Politics of History and Memory
by Christoph Giebel

Beginning to Remember: The Past in the Indonesian Present
edited by Mary S. Zurbuchen

Seditious Histories: Contesting Thai and Southeast Asian Pasts
by Craig J. Reynolds

Knowing Southeast Asian Subjects
edited by Laurie J. Sears

Making Fields of Merit: Buddhist Female Ascetics and Gendered
Orders in Thailand
by Monica Lindberg Falk

Making Fields of Merit

Buddhist Female Ascetics and Gendered Orders in Thailand

Monica Lindberg Falk

University of Washington Press

Seattle

Publication of this book is made possible with the assistance of a grant from the Charles and Jane Keyes Endowment for Books on Southeast Asia, established through the generosity of Charles and Jane Keyes.

Published simultaneously in the United States and Denmark

University of Washington Press
PO Box 50096
Seattle, WA 98145-5096, U.S.A.
www.washington.edu/uwpress

Published in Denmark by NIAS Press
Nordic Institute of Asian Studies
Leifsgade 33, DK-2300 Copenhagen S, Denmark

Library of Congress Cataloging-in-Publication Data

Falk, Monica Lindberg.
     Making fields of merit : Buddhist female ascetics and gendered orders in Thailand / Monica
        Lindberg Falk.
            p. cm. — (Critical dialogues in Southeast Asian studies)
        Originally presented as the author's thesis (doctoral)—Göteborg University, 2002.
        Includes bibliographical references and index.
        ISBN: 978-0-295-98726-2 (pbk. : alk. paper)
        1. Buddhist nuns—Thailand. 2. Women in Buddhism—Thailand.
            3. Buddhist convents—Thailand. 4. Sex role—Religious aspects—
            Buddhism. 5. Women—Thailand—Social conditions. I. Title.
        BQ6160.T4F35 2007
        294.3'65708209593—dc22
                                2007020602

Typeset by NIAS Press
Produced by SRM Production Services Sdn Bhd
and printed in Malaysia
Printed on acid-free paper

All illustrations by Monica Lindberg Falk

Contents

FIGURES

Contents

MAP

TABLES

PRECEPTS AND RULES

Preface

The preparation for the research that resulted in this book begun in 1994 when I went to Thailand to explore the possibility of studying a new Buddhist movement, Phra Dhammakaya, from a gender perspective. My original plans came to a turning point when I visited a forest monastery in Northeastern Thailand. The monk whom I had come to see was not there and the *wat*'s chief monk kindly came and talked with me. We were sitting outdoors under some tall trees, which offered a cool shade in the hot climate. There were no women's quarters at the *wat*. The chief monk admitted that he anticipated a range of difficulties if female ascetics were permitted to live at the *wat*. He explained that it would affect the monks' religious practice negatively and that lay people would not appreciate it if the *wat* was open for female ascetics. During our conversation we came to talk about the female ascetics' situation in Thailand; it turned out that he was well versed in the subject. Our dialogue continued for a couple of hours and before I left, the chief monk wrote two names of women Buddhist scholars on a piece of paper and placed it on the table for me to pick up. The women whom he recommended me to contact were Acaan Chatsumarn Kabilsingh and Acaan Ranjuan.

When I returned to Bangkok I went to see Acaan Chatsumarn at her office at Thammasat University. We talked about the international movement of restoring the female Theravada Buddhist monks' order and about the female ascetics' situation in Thailand. Our discussions convinced me about the importance of paying attention to the female Buddhist ascetics in order to understand gender relations and Buddhism in Thailand. The veneration of the monks and, what I apprehended, the rejection of the Thai female ascetics inspired me to focus my research especially on the *mae chii*s.

It was a *mae chii* in Bangkok who introduced me to Ratburi Samnak Chii; in 1995, I went there for the first time. The *samnak chii* was located in rural area and was much larger than I had anticipated. The ambience at the *samnak chii* was quiet when I visited the first time. The school was closed for the summer holidays and most of the schoolgirls, *dhammacariniis*, had gone home to visit their parents, relatives and friends. I was impressed by the *mae chii*s' gentleness, their discipline and how well organised the *samnak chii* appeared. I selected

Ratburi Samnak Chii as the main field site after visiting several other *samnak chii*s but it took almost two years from my first visit before I came to stay there for a fieldwork period of one year and a half. While living at the *samnak chii* I took part in the daily routines: my interest in and studies of Buddhist philosophy and meditation over the years had prepared me well for participating in ceremonies and meditation sessions.

The fieldwork was carried out in 1997–1998 and was part of my doctoral thesis in Social Anthropology at Göteborg University, Sweden. The title of the thesis was 'Making Fields of Merit: Buddhist Nuns Challenge Gendered Orders in Thailand' (2002). The present book is primarily based on the thesis, but several chapters have been revised, rewritten and updated as a result of generous and professional feedback from friends and colleagues, and many follow-up visits to Thailand.

The result of my in-depth studies is an ethnography of Thai Buddhist women who have renounced the lay world and exchanged their lay identity for monastic life. It examines Buddhist female ascetics' lives and living conditions in contemporary Thailand and explores the processes of change in the *mae chii*s' (Buddhist 'nuns') religious vocation by studying their daily practices, performances and agency through which they are altering their religious position.

Throughout the text, I relate to the wider Buddhist and Thai contexts and the lives and practices of the *mae chii*s at *samnak chii*s, Buddhist 'nunneries', in order to display the complex junction of broad structures of power and socio-cultural meaning on the one hand, and local experiences and agency on the other. However, this study of gender and religious change was primarily conducted at one *samnak chii* in Central Thailand and the *mae chii*s there do not represent all *mae chii*s in the country. My goal has been to illustrate how contemporary *mae chii*s at one particular *samnak chii* are forming their religious identity and authority in relation to the *sangha* and the laity.

The themes of each chapter examine aspects important for understanding Thai Buddhist *mae chii*s' existence and their agency in transforming the bases of their vocation. Certain backgrounds, ethnography and experiences significant for the study will be offered. As a starting point I chose the *mae chii*s' ambiguous position in society where they stand between the lay and the religious realms, without formal authority and recognition as religious persons. Placing the ethnography in a framework requires some historical background and contextualisation in terms of Buddhism and the sex/gender discourses in Thailand. I explore the various linkages that have been made between Buddhism and gender relations in Thai society. I give a brief historical overview of women in Buddhism in order to provide the necessary background for understanding the situation for contemporary Buddhist women. *Mae chii*s often refer to the legacy of the enlightened female monks in early Buddhism and take their starting-point in the teaching about non-self and impermanence that transcend binary gender identities.

The various reasons for becoming a *mae chii* are here related to wider gender discourses in Thai society. Men and women can have different reasons for leaving the lay life, but I argue that women's ordination in Thailand cannot simply be explained as a response to old age, poverty, sickness or 'broken hearts', even though realisation of different kinds of suffering does play a role for women who seek ordination.

A woman who becomes ordained must pass many ritual stages: leaving her family, shaving the head and eye-brows, going through the ordination ceremony, and joining the assembly of *mae chii*s. These stages are used to explain what distinguishes an ordained woman from temporary *mae chii*s (women who stay at a *samnak chii* for a short period of time, typically a week or two) and lay women. The practices at a *samnak chii* and the internalising of the *mae chii*s' monastic code are essential in the process of becoming a *mae chii* and maintaining the religious role. The rules and daily activities are of essential importance for creating, disciplining and maintaining *mae chii*s' religious identity. Their status is influenced by their daily activities. At temples governed by the monks, *mae chii*s' activities are more centred upon the domestic realm even though they have left the worldly life. Their responsibilities do not include religious tasks such as officiating at ceremonies and going on alms rounds, which are the monks' assignments. However, at self-governed *samnak chii*s that are not under the influence of the monks, the role of the *mae chii*s has been broadened and become more analogous to that of the monks.

Education for *mae chii*s is identified as one of the key factors for uplifting the *mae chii*s' religious status. Not all *mae chii*s, however, are interested in education. There are *mae chii*s as well as monks who prefer to dedicate themselves solely to the practice of meditation.

*Mae chii*s struggle for legal recognition and the female monks, *bhikkhuni*s, who are new in the Thai religious field, are also struggling for being recognised in their religious role. *Mae chii*s and *bhikkhuni*s have chosen different ways and strategies to deal with their subordinated position and to achieve formal legitimation as religious persons.

❅ ❅ ❅

Ever since my long fieldwork period, I have stayed in contact with the *mae chii*s. I visit them regularly and follow closely their and other female Buddhist ascetics' struggles in Thai society. Growing numbers of *mae chii*s have tasks similar to the monks' obligations. In areas where *samnak chii* are situated, *mae chii*s are gaining increasing acceptance by and support from the laity and more and more *mae chii*s constitute fields of merit for the lay people today.

A NOTE ON TRANSLITERATION

Thai is a tonal language with a number of vowel and consonant sounds that are not found for instance in English. There is no generally established way of romanising Thai words. In this book, words and phrases in italic typeface are transliterations from standard Thai and rendered phonetically. The transliteration system is a modified version of the Haas convention from 1964 for transcribing Thai. Tonal markings are excluded and diacritics have been kept to an absolute minimum. Place names are spelled as they are usually transliterated on maps. Names and titles are romanised according to established convention, and personal names follow the preferences of the persons concerned (see also p. 255).

Acknowledgements

I am indebted to a large number of people without whom this book would not have been possible. My first thank goes to the Ratburi Samnak Chiis' residents for generously sharing their knowledge, experiences and everyday lives with me. In particular I want to express my deepest thanks to Khun Mae Prathin Kwan-orn, Mae chii Srisalab Upamai and to the late Mae chii Khunying Kanitha Wichiencharoen who helped, supported and sustained me with their wise advice, hospitality and friendship. My gratitude also extends to the Mae Chiis' Institute, to many helpful monks and to all the *mae chii*s whom I met at temples and *samnak chii*s throughout Thailand. I hold deep respect and admiration for their struggle to live a religious life with dignity.

This book is a revised version of my dissertation and the product of several years of research, reflection and dialogue and many people have contributed to shaping my understanding and analyses along the way. Among these I owe special thanks to the teachers and fellow students at the Department of Social Anthropology at Göteborg University for taking interest in my work and for their valuable comments. I am deeply grateful to everyone who generously took time to read and comment on the dissertation and on the manuscript for this book. I would like to express my appreciation especially to Wil Burghoorn. The manuscript has benefited from close readings by Josephine Reynell, Charles F. Keyes, Suwanna Satha-Anand and anonymous reviewers. I also thank the staff at NIAS Press and the University of Washington Press; my special thoughts go to Leena Höskuldsson who did the final editing and saw the book through the whole production phase.

I wish to thank the National Research Council of Thailand for facilitating my work in Thailand and John Butt and his staff at Payap University for guidance and support in the initial stage of my research in Thailand. I am most grateful to my Thai language-teachers and I particularly want to thank Patchara La-eiad-dee and Ning Pongphanga Phongam. My gratitude also extends to many friends in Thailand who offered friendship, advice and practical assistance.

The research project was made possible by financial support from several sources. Generous funding was provided through the Swedish Council for Planning and Coordination of Research (FRN now VR), the Swedish Humanities Research Council (HSFR), Svenska Sällskapet för Geografi och Antropologi (SSAG), Stiftelsen Lars Hiertas minne, Kungliga Hvitfeldtska stipendiestiftelsen, the Swedish School of Advanced Asia Pacific Studies (SSAAPS) and Göteborg University.

Finally, I wish to thank my family, relatives and friends for their unfailing support throughout the years. I am deeply thankful to my husband Bengt-Arne Falk and to my daughter Maria Lindberg who supported me through fieldwork and encouraged me in the process of writing; they sustained my energy and commitment enabling me to bring this project to completion.

Map 0.1 Thailand

CHAPTER ONE

Introduction

Buddhist Female Ascetics in Thai Society

At a quarter to four in the morning Mae chii Somkhit wakes up to the bell ring-ing.[1] The large metal temple bell is hanging on the second floor of the medita-tion hall, *saalaa*, and every morning one of the *mae chii*s wakes up the whole 'nun' community by hitting the big bell with a mallet. The bell sounds loudly over the *samnak chii*'s compound, accompanied by the howling of numerous dogs. It is completely dark outside and the *mae chii*s' rooms light up one by one. *Mae chii* Somkhit gets up from her wooden bed, washes herself, puts on the white *mae chii* dress and fastens her thin outer robe with a pin on her left shoulder. She takes her torch, closes the door, walks to the end of the balcony and puts on her slippers before she goes down the stairs. There is no outdoor light in this area of the *samnak chii* and she needs the torch to see where she puts her foot. While she walks towards the shrine hall she can see light beams from torches as the other *mae chii*s approach the *saalaa*. *Mae chii* Somkhit puts her slippers on the rack outside the *saalaa* building, goes in through the grey metal gate and places the torch on the cupboard inside the door. She turns to the Buddha shrine on the first floor, puts her hands together in a *wai* and bows to the Buddha statue.[2] Quietly she walks upstairs where many *mae chii*s have already gathered. She walks on her knees to her place on the third row of the platform in front of the big Buddha statue. When she passes in front of other *mae chii*s she puts her hands together in a gesture of apology. When she reaches her place she kneels and puts her hands together in a *wai* and bows three times in respect to the Buddha, the Dhamma and the Sangha.[3] Then she sits with her legs under her and waits until the head *mae chii*, Khun Mae, lights the two candles and the three sticks of incense and starts the morning chanting.

This book concerns gender and religion focusing on a little known and am-biguous category of Buddhist female ascetics, *mae chii*s, in Thailand. *Mae chii* and *bhikkhuni* are two categories of Buddhist ascetic women (see Table 1.1). *Bhikkhuni* was introduced during the Buddha's time and *mae chii* is a Thai term used for the largest category of female Thai Buddhist ascetics.

Table 1.1. Thai Buddhist ascetic categories mentioned in the text

Female	Male	Precepts	Status	Admitted to the Thai *sangha*
Bhikkhuni		311	Ordained	No
	Bhikkhu	227	Ordained	Yes
Sikkhamat		10	Ordained	No
Samaneri		10	Ordained, Novice	No
	Samanera	10	Ordained, Novice	Yes
Mae chii		8, 10	Ordained/Ambiguous	No
Siilacarinii		6	*Samanera* aspirant	No
Chii Phraam		8	Lay	No
Dhammacarinii		8	Lay	No
Ubaasikaa		5, 8	Lay	No
	Ubaasok	5, 8	Lay	No

Mae chii Somkhit, mentioned above, is one of about 20,000 or more *mae chii*s who live at temples and *samnak chii*s (*mae chii*s' 'temples') in Thailand.[4] She was one of the visiting *mae chii*s at my main field site, a *samnak chii* in Central Thailand that I shall call Ratburi Samnak Chii. Ratburi Samnak Chii is governed by the *mae chii*s themselves and is independent from monks' temples. This kind of independence is a recent phenomenon in Thailand. Mae chii Somkhit, like many of the visiting *mae chii*s at the *samnak chii*, came from Isaan, the Northeastern part of Thailand. She had spent many years cultivating her mind through intense meditation practice but had never had the opportunity to study. She therefore applied for permission to stay for a period at Ratburi Samnak Chii, where educational facilities are provided for *mae chii*s. Education has been identified as one of the key factors for the Thai Buddhist *mae chii*s' advancement in their religious roles and has, together with Buddhist practice, been of significant importance for the *mae chii*s' legitimacy as religious persons.

The lack of information about the Thai Buddhist *mae chii*s is remarkable and intriguing. The *mae chii*s' invisibility both in literature and on the Thai religious and social scenes stimulated my interest in finding out who these renunciant women are and how they fit into the Thai sex/gender discourses. Very little is known about the background of the *mae chii*s, their lives, under what circumstances they live, the places they live in, and the processes of change that are going on in the *mae chii* communities – questions that this study sets out to explore. Major themes of gender and religion in anthropology will be addressed and studied within a Buddhist *samnak chii* in Central Thailand.

Contemporary Thai *mae chii*s live in a society that has experienced rapid modernisation and economic growth. These processes have affected the society as a whole and the religious sphere is not immune to changes in the secular realm. Thailand is also influenced by the forces of economic and religious globalisation. The globalisation of religion, which includes both the global spread of forms of religion and also local religious identities emerging in response to this is apparent in the Thai religious field.

The *mae chii*s have, since the latter part of the twentieth century, accentuated their religious vocation by refining their practice, upgrading their educational level and drawing a more distinct boundary between themselves and the lay people. In the process, groups of the *mae chii*s have moved away from the monks' temples. The recent decades' growth of self-governed *samnak chii*s and the reports of Thai women's increasing interest in Buddhist monastic life are notable changes in women's behaviour in the spiritual field. This indicates a modification of the restricted male religious and political domains.

From a previously marginalised position in society, groups of *mae chii*s have in recent decades slowly begun to gain increased religious authority. The present anthropological work is concerned with Thai *mae chii*s' agency in the processes of change in their religious vocation.

BUDDHIST PRECEPTS

The sets of Buddhist precepts correspond to the different categories of Buddhist male and female, lay and ordained persons. Buddhist lay people are expected to follow five precepts (overleaf). Four of these constitute basic moral commitments. One, regarding refraining from consuming that (drugs and alcohol) which causes heedlessness, entails an ascetic rather than ethical commitment.

*Mae chii*s observe eight precepts on a permanent basis, and these are the same as those observed by *chii phraam*s and *dhammacarinii*s (overleaf). It is also open for lay people to follow the eight precepts for special occasions such as the Buddhist weekly holy day, *wan phra*. The eight precepts add additional ascetic practices and those who commit to follow the eight precepts, whether for a day or for a longer period, refrain from all sexual activity rather than from wrong conduct in sexual desires as the third precept is understood by lay persons who follow the ordinary five Buddhist precepts. The sixth precept entails not eating any solid food after noon. The seventh precept means avoiding, or keeping one's distance from, entertainments, and avoiding make-up, perfume, jewellery and colourful clothes.

The five Buddhist precepts

1. I undertake the training precept (*sikkha-padam*) to abstain from onslaught on breathing beings.

2. I undertake the training precept to abstain from taking what is not given.

3. I undertake the training precept to abstain from misconduct concerning sense-pleasures.

4. I undertake the training precept to abstain from false speech.

5. I undertake the training precept to abstain from alcoholic drink or drugs that are an opportunity for heedlessness.

Source: Harvey 2000: 67

The eight Buddhist precepts

1. I undertake the training precept (*sikkha-padam*) to abstain from onslaught on breathing beings.

2. I undertake the training precept to abstain from taking what is not given.

3. I undertake the training precept to avoid 'unchaste conduct', *abrahmacariya*, that is sexual activity of any kind.

4. I undertake the training precept to abstain from false speech.

5. I undertake the training precept to abstain from alcoholic drink or drugs that are an opportunity for heedlessness.

6. I undertake the training precept to abstain from eating at an unseasonable time.

7. I undertake the training precept to abstain from seeing dancing, music vocal and instrumental, and shows; from wearing garlands, perfumes and unguents, from finery and adornment.

8. I undertake the training precept to abstain from high or large beds (or seats).

Source: Harvey 2000: 87

Below is an elaboration of what the ten precepts mean that the novice shall avoid doing:

The ten Buddhist precepts

1. Harming living beings by directly killing them, digging the ground or destroying plants or trees.

2. Consuming food or drink (except water) that has not been formally offered; 'corrupting families' by giving small gifts in the hope of receiving abundant alms in return.

3. Actions of a sensual nature, sexual activity of any kind; sleeping in the same dwelling as a woman [if a man], or sitting in a private place with one.

4. False accusations of an offence involving 'defeat', and various other forms of wrong speech, unfriendly behaviour towards a fellow monk and true claims to the laity of having attained higher states. Also, disparaging the lesser rules as vexing, pretending ignorance of a rule, or knowingly concealing a monk's digression from one of the more serious rules.

5. Drinking alcohol.

6. Eating after noon.

7. Unseemly, frivolous behaviour, and going to see an army fighting or on parade.

8. Inappropriate ways of wearing monastic robes: 75 rules in the Theravadin code seek to ensure that the monks (and novices) are graceful and dignified in the way that they wear their robes, walk, move, and collect and eat alms food.

9. Using a high, luxurious bed, or sleeping in the same place as a layman for more than three nights.

10. Receiving, handling or using money in transactions (this does not prevent the acceptance and use of money by a monastery's lay stewards).

Source: Harvey 2000: 94–95

The novice monks observe ten precepts (above), of which eight correspond to those observed by the *mae chii*s and lay people. The *mae chii*s have additional rules either stipulated by the Thai Mae Chiis' Institute or by the temple they are residing at (see Chapter 5). The ten precepts are the same as the eight except that the seventh is split into its two parts, and there is the addition of an undertaking to 'abstain from accepting gold and silver'.

The discipline, *vinaya,* that the ordained commit themselves to is an elaboration mainly of the ascetic rules that ensure that they are not tempted to break one of the fundamental rules constituting violations (*parajika*) that would result in the immediate cessation of their ordained status (to be addressed in Chapters 2 and 5). For a general discussion of monastic discipline, see for example Holt 1999 and Harvey 2000.

*Mae chii*s usually receive eight precepts and it is uncommon for Thai women to receive the ten precepts of novice monks. It is usually monks who secretly give women the ten precepts so as not to upset the *sangha.* However, there are *mae chii*s in Thailand who are openly given the ten precepts. The ordained women at the Asoke group are an example. They are called *sikkhamat* and differ from the *mae chii*s in several respects. The *sikkhamat*s have a unique position since they live in a monastery with monks, they receive the ten precepts and they walk on daily alms rounds. The temple's founder and head monk has placed himself outside the state-controlled *sangha.* This has caused legal troubles for the group and neither the Asoke monks nor the *sikkhamat*s are recognised by the Thai *sangha* (see Chapter 7). Moreover, the possibilities for women to receive *sikkhamat* ordination are limited. A laywoman has to prepare herself for two years in order to be qualified for ordination. However, the number of *sikkhamat*s is restricted to correspond to the number of monks and the rule is that there should not be more than one *sikkhamat* to four monks. If all the Asoke female lay followers were ordained, the number of *sikkhamat*s would exceed the number of monks. Consequently, restrictions mean that it takes several years for women to become *sikkhamat* (Heikkilä-Horn 1996).

GENDER AND RELIGIOUS AGENCY

In the 1990s feminist studies were in the 1990s challenging ideas of single explanations, and differences among women were highlighted. Feminists who had previously concerned themselves with explanations and origins of female subordination retreated from grand theorizing to focus on the great diversity of women's experiences. The post-modern critique caused a shift away from treating women as passive victims of patriarchy to exploring women's competing discourses, strategies of resistance, and own forms of self-representation. Scholars within feminist anthropology combined a historical approach with an attention to the symbolic dimension of representation, discourse, and meaning. They put the construction of gender in relation to systems of power that govern work, resources, mobility, authority, and so forth. This synthetic approach is well represented in works on Southeast Asia that study contested gender meaning in different fields.

As a study on gender and religious change in Thailand, this work concentrates upon female Buddhist ascetics who partake in a gendered religious shift. The *mae chii*s' lives and situation are embedded within a broader social and cultural context and throughout this book their lives as renunciants are related to the demands of lay life. This study takes its departure from the *mae chii*s' viewpoint: the *mae chii*s speak of their lives, their religious quest, the constraints of poverty, their relation to lay people and of their position as women in relation to the men in the religious field.

The focus is on women as agents and their creation of religious space and authority for women. Like Judaism, Christianity and Islam, Buddhism is an overwhelmingly male-created institution dominated by male power structures, and the feminine is frequently associated with the secular. Sered (1999: 206) states that agency is dependent upon social resources, and women's religious agency often increases in situations where men's propagation of woman as a symbol is weakened or absent. In Thailand women's religious agency has progressed at a remarkably slow pace. The symbol of woman as mother is prevalent and contributes to associating women with the secular realm. Keyes (1984) and Whittaker (2002) show how the ideal ways to gain maturity differ for Thai men and women. Women reach maturity in the secular realm by becoming mothers and lying by the fire, and men reach maturity in the religious realm by being ordained as novice monks for a period of time. Keyes argues that motherhood has also been construed as a religious role since women 'nurture' the religion by providing sons who join the *sangha* and offer food on regular basis (ibid.: 230, 233) and states that Thai Buddhist culture does not relegate women to a religiously inferior status relative to men (ibid.: 223). I agree that women are of vital importance for Thai Buddhism but I argue that the Thai *sangha*'s persistence of not opening their doors to women keep female ascetics in a inferior religious status. Rita Gross has identified three general attitudes towards women in Buddhism. She says that the first teaches that female rebirth is a result of negative *kamma*.[5] The second view imagines a Buddha to be male and, therefore, makes male rebirth necessary for women. The third view is that gender is irrelevant for salvation, in the sense that gender is one of the traits of the ego, that needs to be transcended (Gross 1993: 115–117). In Thailand all three attitudes are present and accentuated in various contexts. The third view that says that gender is irrelevant for reaching enlightenment is often expressed by the *mae chii*s. Many of the *mae chii*s that I have interviewed are certain about women's and men's equal capacities to reach the final goal, *nibbana*.

Gender in Thailand is shaped by the popular notion of *kamma*: a female birth is lower than a male birth. Living a celibate, monastic life is considered to be the best way to gain religious merit and reach the Buddhist ultimate goal. In Buddhism, monastic life was originally open to both men and women. Today, however, women in many Buddhist countries face a range of difficulties when they seek ordination. In Thailand, women are refused full ordination as *bhikkhuni*, equivalent to Buddhist monks. The *mae chii*s could be seen as an answer to the lack of the *bhikkhuni* order in Thailand. The denial of women's right to enter into the formal religious domain has created an ambiguous position for *mae chii*s, as falling in-between the lay and the religious realms. They are not part of the prestigious *sangha*, nor do they belong to the lay world since they have given up their lay identity for monastic life. That gives the *mae chii*s a marginalised position in society. However, this study shows that in recent decades the *mae chii*s have begun to take advantage of the indeterminate space between the two statuses and through their own capacity and networking have started to enhance their position and create better circumstances for themselves.

In Thailand gender identity has a fluid character and gender has the capacity to be transgressed (see P. Van Esterik 2000). Gender discourses and the research on 'the third sex' in Thailand form a necessary background and are presented in the chapter discussing the sex/gender orders and discources in Thailand. In the process of becoming a religious specialist and belonging to the religious realm, religious practice and interaction with the lay community are vital. The *mae chii*s' religious agency and performance in the religious field challenge the prevailing notion of women as belonging only to the lay realm. A central theme in this study is the institution of offerings, where the interaction between the *mae chii*s and lay people is explored. In the analyses of meanings and practices of Buddhist offerings (*dana*) gender relations become explicit. Furthermore, the pivotal relationship between the laity and ordained persons through alms-giving ceremonies expresses notions of transcendence from the lay to the religious realm, which imply that the person has become a field of merit for lay people.

In this book I shall address questions about women's agency in the religious field, gender relations in Thai society and the impact of the exclusion of women from the Buddhist *sangha*. Even though I am concentrating on Thai women who have renounced the lay world, this has impacts both on those going forth and on their families left behind. Women's ordination is at once a powerful vehicle for, and an expression of, profound social and personal transformation. Conventionally, Thai women have not been encouraged to be ordained as Thai men have been; yet, over the past two decades more and more women have begun to receive temporary and permanent ordination as *chii phraam* or *mae chii*. In Thailand ordination as novice monk for a period of time before marriage is part of long-standing patterns of masculinity construction (see Keyes 1984, 1986, Kirsch 1985, Tambiah 1970, Whittaker 2002). In contrast, young women's ordination represents a sharp departure from established patterns of female behaviour and notions of appropriate activities for women. Consequently, as women enter new fields of religious practice they confront prevailing understandings of gendered roles and social values. Renunciation highlights points of conflict within existing family relations as well as the ongoing production or reworking of these relationships in new ways. These struggles address not only the individual's circumstances and the needs of particular female ascetics and their families, it also has an impact on more wide-ranging structural and ideological tensions within Thai society as a whole. Women's exclusion from the Buddhist *sangha* has itself been produced by powerful structures of inequality in Thailand. Female ordination engages critical ideological dimensions of women's lack of participation in the formal Thai religious institution.

FEMALE ORDINATION – A CONTESTED ISSUE

Nearly 93 per cent of Thailand's 64 million people identify themselves as Buddhists. Religion is important for Thai identity and part of the logic of their everyday life, even though Buddhist practice varies according to class, age, ethnicity and region. Thai women predominate in daily religious practices and commonly outnumber men in temple activities. However, Thai women who aspire to become ordained usually have to struggle with various difficulties even though they are only seeking *mae chii* ordination rather than that of *bhikkhuni*, as Acaan Chatsumarn Kabilsingh, a well-known female Buddhist scholar, did some years ago.

The *bhikkhuni*s are new in the Thai religious realm and Acaan Chatsumarn was the first Thai woman to receive ordination as *bhikkhuni* in the Theravada tradition. She was ordained as *samaneri bhikkhuni* (novice female monk) by the Sri Lankan clergy in Sri Lanka on 6 February 2001, and adopted the religious name Dhammananda. She received full *bhikkhuni* ordination in Sri Lanka on

9

28 February 2003. However, the Thai *sangha* has not recognised her ordination or her status as a Theravada female monk. Her novice ordination created a sensation and was front-page news in the Thai press. By becoming ordained she had challenged the male Buddhist *sangha*. She said that she had received two main reactions to her ordination. One was admiration, the other was the awkward silence of disapproval (see Chapter 9).

Dhammananda bhikkhuni was previously a professor at Thammasat University in Bangkok where she taught Buddhist philosophy for two decades; she also taught at one of the monks' universities, Maha Chulalongkorn University. Moreover, she has written numerous books in both Thai and English. When I met Acaan Chatsumarn for the first time in 1994 at her office at Thammasat University, I asked her opinion about the prospect of reviving the *bhikkhuni* order in Asia. The order died out in the eleventh century and there has been a longstanding debate about the possibility restoring it. Acaan Chatsumarn said that she believed that it would be possible to re-establish it, but not until in the remote future. However, as early as1988, five Sinhalese women received *bhikkhuni* ordination in Los Angeles, but their ordination was not recognised by the *sangha*s in the Asian countries. In 1996, ten Sinhalese female ascetics became *bhikkhuni*s in Saranath, India. Five years later, in 2001, Acaan Chatsumarn decided to seek novice ordination in Sri Lanka and became the first Theravada *samaneri bhikkhuni* in Thailand. When her two preparatory years as a novice were completed, she was qualified to seek full *bhikkhuni* ordination, which she did in 2003.

A Thai woman who expresses a wish to become a *bhikkhuni* is, by lay people as well as by *mae chii*s, commonly accused of egotism and seen as greedy for status, an undesirable condition considered to be a sign of spiritual weakness. The resistance to female monks in Thailand and people's lack of interest in the *bhikkhuni* issue, at least before Acaan Chatsumarn's ordination, can partly be explained by the fact that it has never been possible to receive *bhikkhuni* ordination in Thailand because the order of female monks never spread there.

Acaan Chatsumarn has worked for a long time for the establishment of the *bhikkhuni* order in Thailand and she is well known among the *mae chii*s. However, during my fieldwork I found that the *mae chii*s, who are the focus of this study, considered the issue of *bhikkhuni* ordination a topic that interested foreigners more than Thais. For several reasons, most *mae chii*s were not especially interested in *bhikkhuni* ordination. Instead the *mae chii*s strive for recognition of their own vocation as ordained persons. Moreover, it has not been uncommon for people to view *bhikkhuni*s as a possible threat to the *sangha.* Some lay women to whom I spoke expressed concerns about the *sangha* being degraded and losing its capacity of being a field of merit for lay people if women entered it. The *mae chii*s who strove to advance their position were careful to point out that they did not aspire to be part of the *sangha.* Although the *sangha* strongly guards its realm from female entry, I actually met more monks than *mae chii*s who were in favour of *bhikkhuni* ordination and some of the monks have even give public support to female *bhikkhuni* ordination.

MEETING WITH A *MAE CHII*

The Thai Buddhist *mae chii*s keep a low profile and are not as visible in society as the monks. I had only met a few *mae chii*s and only spoken briefly with them when I met Mae chii Khunying Kanitha Wichiencharoen in 1995.[6] She was an influential former lawyer who had spent most of her life fighting to protect women from discrimination and exploitation. She was highly respected for her social work and commitment to achieving equal rights for Thai women. In 1993, when Khunying Kanitha was 73 years old, she received *mae chii* ordination in

Figure 1.1. Mae chii Khunying Wichiencharoen sitting in the middle of a group of longstanding *mae chii*s from Northeastern Thailand

Sri Lanka. As with Acaan Chatsumarn's ordination hers did not pass unnoticed. Although it was not criticised in the media, many people found it inappropriate for a woman in her position to become a *mae chii*. Both lay people and *mae chii*s commented on her ordination. At a meeting organised by a university in Bangkok, some well-educated lay women informed me that they thought it was 'unnecessary' for her to become ordained. In their opinion, she could be a pious person without the formal *mae chii* ordination. They considered it more suitable for a woman in her position to be a lay person. The discussion with these women revealed that the *mae chii*s' low social prestige in combination with the prominent *khunying* title, equivalent to the English 'Dame', seemed inconsistent to them. Others referred to the mundane nature of the title and suggested that she should have abandoned the *khunying* title when she became a *mae chii*. Mae chii Khunying Kanitha had no problem with the idea of keeping her title and adding *mae chii* to her name. She had never considered dismissing the title: she explained to me that she had been given the title by the Thai king and it would be wrong to abandon something given by the king.

In contrast to monks, the *mae chii*s keep their lay names after ordination, which is a sign of the Thai *mae chii*s' ambiguous standing. It is not against any of the *mae chii* rules to keep a title. Titles did not bother the other *mae chii*s and they welcomed Mae chii Khunying Kanitha in their community. Her status was not often mentioned by the *mae chii*s, who were more concerned about her spiritual training. Some questioned her choice of establishing a small, what she called, 'nuns' cottage' and staying there together with a few *mae chii*s instead of becoming a member of a *mae chii* community at a temple or a *samnak chii*. Mae chii Khunying Kanitha was aware of the drawbacks of not belonging to an established *samnak chii*s' community, but at the time of her ordination it was difficult for her to live permanently at a *samnak chii*. The Association for the Promotion of the Status of Women, of which she was the founder, still needed her advice and was still dependent on her leadership.

Mae chii Khunying Kanitha was thus a person who was often scrutinised and commented on, especially by lay people. This somewhat controversial *mae chii* was the person who introduced me to the *mae chii*s. I had had contact with her for two years before I started the fieldwork. During preparatory fieldtrips I went with her to conferences and to meetings on gender issues; she introduced me to *samnak chii*s and she put me in contact with the head *mae chii* at Ratburi Samnak Chii that later became my main field site.

CHOOSING A FIELD SITE

I chose Ratburi Samnak Chii as the primary field site for several reasons. Importantly for this study, it was independent of the monks' temples and was well established. It was the fourth *samnak chii* set up by the Thai Mae Chiis' Institute. Furthermore, it was located in Central Thailand where the largest number of *mae chii*s live. The *samnak chii* housed a large community of about a hundred *mae chii*s and schoolgirls of mixed ages. Observation of the *mae chii*s' interaction with lay people was important in order to see in what ways they were accepted as religious specialists by the laity, and I knew from my previous visits that the villagers supported this *samnak chii*. The *mae chii*s went on an alms round every morning, one of the most significant indicators of belonging to the religious realm. Further, the *mae chii*s at the *samnak chii* were invited to various ceremonies at temples, other *samnak chii*s and people's homes.

I spent more than a year living together with the *mae chii*s at the *samnak chii*. The 17 months of fieldwork were carried out in 1997 and 1998 including yearly follow-ups from 1999 until 2002. The research was conducted primarily at Ratburi Samnak Chii, and the *mae chii*s who resided there came from the neighbouring area but also and from other parts of Thailand. I travelled with the *mae chii*s and collected information at *samnak chii*s in other regions, and from temples where monks resided.

Staying at a *samnak chii* in the countryside where hardly anybody spoke English made it crucial to be able to communicate in Thai. During my period of language studies in Bangkok, I chose to stay on the outskirts of the city. This was not the most convenient arrangement since it involved spending three to four hours every weekday travelling on motorbikes and buses back and forth to the school in central Bangkok. But in return it gave me rich opportunities to practise the language and to keep in touch with the *mae chii* communities. The place where I lived belonged to the Association for the Promotion of the Status of Women in Thailand, and Mae chii Khunying Kanitha was at that time still the president of the association. Here I had the chance to meet women from various backgrounds. In the compound there was a range of activities: a gender research institute, a guest house, an emergency shelter, a nursery, a day-care centre, a hospice for women with HIV/AIDS, a gymnasium and the 'mae chii' cottage' headed by Mae chii Khunying Kanitha. The different enterprises that were gathered under the umbrella organisation reflected her various interests and work.

While staying in Bangkok I visited *samnak chii*s and temples and got to know *mae chii*s, lay people and monks from the area. I went together with *mae* *chii*s and lay persons to various events and meditation retreats. I got to know a famous *mae chii* who had recently received the ten Buddhist precepts and I also came in contact with the *mae chii*s at the well-known and respected Mon temple Wat Paknam Phasi Charoen in Bangkok. Wat Paknam has a large *mae chii* department with more than two hundred *mae chii* residents. Some of these were involved in running the school at Ratburi Samnak Chii. There is a close connection between the *mae chii*s from Wat Paknam and the national Thai Mae Chiis' Institute. I got to know some of the *mae chii*s at Wat Paknam well. I travelled with them and stayed with them at Wat Paknam many times during fieldwork. The interviews and talks with them, as well as with *mae chii*s at other temples in Bangkok have been important for understanding *mae chii* life in the capital city, which is special in several ways.

THE SETTING

Ratburi Samnak Chii is located in the Southwest corner of the Central region. This is one of the four geographical zones that Thailand is divided into: the Central region, the Northeastern plateau, Northern Thailand and the Southern region. The *samnak chii* is situated approximately 120 kilometres from Thailand's capital Bangkok, and about 22 kilometres from the provincial capital Ratchaburi. The province has a varied topography with a fertile ground around the basin of the Mae Klong River, where various kinds of crops, vegetables and fruits are cultivated. There are also the high mountain ranges of the Tanawsri Mountains in the west and along the Thai–Burma border. In 1998 Ratchaburi had a population of 819,360 including several ethnic groups. The majority of the population was engaged in agriculture, trade and industry; many worked as labourers.

For administrative purposes, Thailand is divided into eight administrative divisions and subdivided into 76 provinces (*cangwat*) and Ratchaburi is one of the provinces. Each province is further divided into districts (*amphoe*). Ratchaburi has eight districts and the district in which Ratburi Samnak Chii is located is divided into 12 subdistricts (*tambon*) that contain 80 villages (*muubaan*). Ratburi Samnak Chii is situated on the outskirts of a village with a population of 1,160. The village is part of a subdistrict with 10,139 inhabitants. Most of the villagers work in fruit and vegetable gardening and pig breeding.

Geographically Ratchaburi is close to the centralised *sangha* in Bangkok, and this region has a local history of highly revered female renunciants. One well-known and highly respected renunciant from Ratchaburi was Upasika Ki Nanayon (1901–1978). She established a meditation centre for women at Suan

Figure 1.2. The *saalaa* at Ratburi Samnak Chii

Luang Hill in Ratchaburi. Ki Nanayon did not allow men to reside at the centre, and the meditation centre is still a place exclusively for women. Ki Nanayon lived a simple life as renunciant. She was known for her uncompromising style of teaching and her talks and poetry are widely published (Tan Acharn Kor Khao-suan-luang 1991: v–vi). Ki Nanayon's place and her teachings are still equally important for the *mae chii*s today. The relationship between teacher and disciple is essential for the *mae chii*s. Generally they are disciples (*luuksit*) of monks, but female renunciant instructors are significant for the *mae chii*s, and many well respected female *dhamma* teachers have resided at Suan Luang Hill.

Ratburi Samnak Chii was established in 1978 and has expanded continually over its more than two decades of existence. The two *mae chii*s, Mae chii Prathin and Mae chii Sumon had just finished their studies at Magadha University in Bodh Gaya in India when they were invited by the Thai Mae Chiis' Institute to establish a *samnak chii* in Ratchaburi Province. Mae chii Sumon, had completed her PhD and Mae chii Prathin had finished an MA in ancient history. They welcomed the opportunity to start a *samnak chii*, and to found a much needed educational programme for the *mae chii*s. It was a lay woman who had donated land to the Mae Chiis' Institute with the objective of setting up a *samnak chii* (female 'temple'). In 1978, it was fairly rare to find *mae chii* communities outside the administrative structure of the temple. However, the two neighbouring provinces, Ratchaburi and Petchaburi, have had *samnak chii*s run by women renunciates for a long time (Kabilsingh 1991: 65; Tiyavanich 1997: 283). These two provinces have comparatively high numbers of *mae chii*s and, as mentioned above, there are some well-known female *dhamma* and meditation teachers from this region.

In 1997 there were about 50 *mae chii*s, a varying number of *chii phraam*s (temporary ascetic women) and 47 schoolgirls called *dhammacarinii* living at the *samnak chii*. The *dhammacarinii*s studied secondary education and Buddhism at the *samnak chii*'s school. The *samnak chii* opened that school in 1990 and it was the first school ever established by *mae chii*s for girls in Thailand. By contrast, boys have always had the opportunity to get free education at the temple schools. The schoolgirls came from different parts of the country, mostly from poor villages in the Northeastern and Central provinces and they stayed at the *samnak chii* for either two or four years. The school also provided an opportunity for *mae chii*s to acquire higher education and *mae chii*s from all over the country came to live and study at this *samnak chii*.

It was not a novelty for Ratburi Samnak Chii to have a foreigner living among them. At the beginning of my stay there was an American volunteer teaching English at the *samnak chii* school. She had lived there for almost two years and she was very helpful in introducing me to the *mae chii*s and the *samnak chii*. When I arrived she had two and a half months left of her teaching assignment and after that she went back to the United States.

Samnak chii residents can be divided into two distinct categories. The ordained *mae chii*s whose status varies according to the length of their ordainment form one category. The others – *chii phraam*s – also follow the eight precepts, but keep their hair and eyebrows, and only stay temporarily at the *samnak chii*.[7] There are differences in the dress of the two *chii*s. *Mae chii*s wear a white costume consisting of a white blouse, a white *phaasin*, long skirt, and a white cloth draped over the left shoulder. The *chii phraam*s also wear a white blouse and *phaasin*, but they are sewn differently and the *chii phraam*s' outer robe is shorter than that of the *mae chii*s. Spatial arrangements also betray the hierarchy and status differences at the *samnak chii*s. At ceremonies at Ratburi Samnak Chii *mae chii*s sit on a raised platform with the highest ranking *mae chii*s closest to and the newly ordained *mae chii*s furthest from the Buddha statues. The temporary female ascetics, *chii phraam*s and the *dhammacarinii*s sit behind the *mae chii*s but not on the platform, thus demonstrating their lower status.

Everybody who stayed at the *samnak chii* observed the eight Buddhist precepts. I was absorbed into the *chii phraam* category since it would have been inappropriate to stay at the *samnak chii* on a long-term basis as an 'ordinary' lay person. This implied that I followed the same eight precepts as the other residents. I did not shave my hair, and I followed the daily practice with morning chants, meditation and not taking any meals after noon. In the dining hall, I shared a table with the *chii phraam*s and was seated in the same row in the *saalaa*. However, there is a formal ritual that the *chii phraam*s initially perform that I did not do. In the ritual, the *chii phraam*s ask for instructions from the *mae chii*s, declare that they will follow the rules at the *samnak chii* and subordinate themselves to the *mae chii*s' directions. Before leaving the *samnak chii* the *chii phraam*s also perform a short ritual in the *saalaa*.

CONDUCTING FIELDWORK AMONG THE *MAE CHII*S

This book is about the *mae chii*s as I observed them at the Ratburi Samnak Chii in the Southern part of Central Thailand as well as at temples and *samnak chii*s in the Northern and Northeastern parts of Thailand. It has grown out of interactions with groups of *mae chii*s, and my understanding of the *mae chii*s' lives is (partly) built on participatory experience and participatory observation. My choice to study the Thai Buddhist female ascetics was motivated by their agency in the religious field and by recognition of similar processes underway around the world. I wanted to learn as much as possible about the *mae chii*s, their daily lives and about gender and contemporary Buddhism in Thailand.

At the *samnak chii*s, data were collected using mainly participant observation and casual relaxed discussions with the informants. I learned about the life at the Ratburi Samnak Chii by partaking in the daily activities such as meditation, early morning alms rounds, daily communal meals, different kinds of ceremonies at the *samnak chii* and at temples, private homes, and other places for meetings and ceremonies that the *mae chii*s were invited to by other *mae chii*s, monks or lay persons. I gathered insights into *mae chii*s' lives through daily interactions, friendships, informal conversations, and socialising, as well as from recorded interviews. Furthermore, I took part in teaching, training courses, various meetings, work in the gardens, plantations, kitchen, etc.

The advantages of living together with the *mae chii*s were manifold: I would not have been able to get to know the *mae chii*s and their complex situation so fully if I had not lived with them. I followed the *mae chii*s throughout the year and we shared many experiences. Many things that happened at the *samnak* *chii* were unplanned and it would not have been possible to cover them if I had not lived there. There were also events that the *mae chii*s themselves did not find important but which often deepened my understanding of various themes of their lives and situation.

I consider ethnographic knowledge intersubjective and I have attempted to acknowledge my presence where it is relevant to the material. I began the networking process almost two years before I carried out the main coherent part of the fieldwork that lasted 17 months. I commenced the field research in 1997 almost simultaneously with the economic recession that hit first Bangkok and then spread across South-East Asia. The crises put an end to the so-called bubble economy and several decades of economic growth. Thai people experienced the consequences of the crises to various extents. Temples and *samnak chii*s became important places for those who had lost their financial security and looked for advice, consolation and guidance in their lives.

Initially, my status as a white, well-educated, presumably wealthy foreigner from a wealthy country made some of the *mae chii*s shy, reserved and reluctant to talk with me. My entry into Ratburi Samnak Chii, which was facilitated by an introduction from a wealthy, well-educated *mae chii*, made some *mae chii*s curious to know me while others kept a more reserved attitude. But by working side by side and sharing the daily life at the *samnak chii* I gradually came to know the more reserved *mae chii*s. With most *mae chii*s at the *samnak chii*, especially with those who became close friends, points of commonality did emerge and served as a basis for sympathy and communication. During fieldwork I travelled to many provinces in Thailand together with the *mae chii*s, but throughout the fieldwork, Ratburi Samnak Chii constituted the basis for my fieldwork. It was here that I had my room (*kuti*) with a wooden bed, a rack where I kept my books and a desk that I had bought in the small village.

Participating in daily activities was thus a natural way to communicate with the *mae chii*s and the schoolgirls. At Ratburi Samnak Chii, the entire *mae chii*s community met several times a day for ceremonies, meditation practice and at the two daily meals that were eaten together in the dining hall. The *samnak chii* was organised in teams that worked in the kitchen, in the garden, watering plants, cleaning the meditation hall, and so on, and I helped out with these chores. I also assisted the *mae chii*s and the *dhammacarinii*s with their English studies.

The topics of my daily conversations with the *mae chii*s were related to ordinary things. We talked about our lives, families, choices in life and about how they felt as ordained persons. I do not think that I would have got access

Figure 1.3. Khun Mae Prathin Kwan-orn lighting candles at a ceremony in the *saalaa* at Ratburi Samnak Chii

to that kind of information outside the context of everyday life. In the course of my residence at the *samnak chii* I found that the *mae chii*s became increasingly open to me. Sharing the *mae chii*s' daily lives and keeping the *samnak chii* rules were crucial for my contacts with the *mae chii*s. However, I was always and unavoidably a foreigner and more important, my participation was defined from the start as temporary and it was known I would be leaving after about a year.

My experience of doing fieldwork among female ascetics in a community with strict rules of conduct challenged my ability to adapt to a basic way of living under a rigorous discipline. On several occasions during the year my stamina and state of mind were put to the test: once the area was flooded for more than a week and I had one metre of water inside my *kuti* and had to swim inside the *samnak chii*. At another occasion, I was bitten by a dog at the *samnak chii*s' compound. Fortunately the *mae chii*s attributed me with patience and calmness, which are considered positive qualities. The daily schedule framed the life at the *samnak chii* and I understood how indispensable a *samnak chii* is for the *mae chii*s in order to develop an ordained identity. The *mae chii*s met me with great generosity and I felt that I had little to offer them in return for their hospitality. As already mentioned, I helped out at the *samnak chii* with various chores, and with the *mae chiis'* and *dhammacariniis'* English studies. I contributed as generously as possible to the *samnak chii's* funds.

I conducted interviews in order to explore the *mae chiis'* backgrounds, how the *mae chiis* understood themselves, their identity as ordained persons, and how they experienced their situation in relation to the *sangha* and to the lay community. I interviewed more than a hundred *mae chiis*, ranging from 12 to over 80 years of age. Some of them I only met and interviewed once when I was travelling, while others whom I had met in their resident temples or *samnak chiis* in the Northern or Northeastern parts of Thailand, I later met on several occasions at other places of the country when participating in meetings, training courses, meditation retreats, fund raising activities and similar activities. This gave me the opportunity to meet *mae chiis* in different contexts and also to follow up questions and discussions. I met some of the leading *mae chiis* from Central Thailand regularly during fieldwork. Sometimes interviews tended to give an idealised portrayal of *mae chiis'* lives. It was after staying in the field for some time that I came to know more about their actual lives and situation through participant observation and through close friendships.

I collected information about the *mae chiis'* lives both before and after they became ordained. Also, in casual conversations we touched on various themes that covered different aspects of their lives. I also gathered a few full-length life stories from key informants who lived at the *samnak chii*. Life stories provided insights into how individual *mae chiis* experienced, interpreted and expressed their lives and identities over time. Working for more than a year together meant that it was possible to build up a mutual trust: I could get more in-depth understanding of themes in their lives than would have been possible from occasional interviews. I made regular appointments to meet with these *mae chiis* and I met them privately, which was not always the case in other interview situations. Often *mae chiis* other than the interviewee joined in and listened to the interview, which was perfectly normal behaviour. Sometimes an individual interview turned out to be a group interview because of the spectators; this was occasionally better than having a passive audience.

The *mae chiis* paid attention to my choice of study. They appreciated that I was conducting research on them, but at the same time were interested to know why I was interested in studying them since they were continuously neglected in their own society. We discussed differences and similarities between *mae chiis* in different settings. They noticed that I took part in the various activities at the *samnak chii* and they said that they liked that. Some of them were interested in knowing about my family, my husband, daughter and my parents. They said that I 'had merit' (*mii bon*) since I had found their place and was able to stay with them and learn about Buddhism. Most were not especially interested in talking about gender or about their relatively subordinate position *vis-à-vis* the monks. What they were keen to talk about was their religious practice and gradually I came to learn how closely intertwined the issues of gender and ethical practice are for the *mae chii*s. Discussions about restoring the *bhikkhuni* order were brought up by me but never by them. Most had a clear opinion about the *bhikkhuni* issue, and they did not change their view during the course of my fieldwork. However, there are other themes developed in this book that were elaborated by my key informants and constantly addressed during my fieldwork, and they are important to a majority of the *mae chii*s.

Some of the *mae chii*s at Ratburi Samnak Chii came from the nearby provinces. However, many were from other parts of Thailand, with the largest percentage from the Northeastern region. Most of the *mae chii*s visited their home provinces once or twice a year. I was invited to follow the *mae chii*s on their travels back home. I also accompanied those *mae chii*s from whom I had collected life stories to their natal families and to the temples and *samnak chii*s where they had been ordained. I welcomed the opportunity to travel with them because it enriched my research with a more complete picture of *mae chii* lives. By travelling I was also able to compare the socio-cultural contexts in different parts of Thailand and the different conditions under which the *mae chii*s live. We travelled by local means of transport, which took a long time and gave us many hours to talk about their lives and experiences. Usually I went with one or two *mae chii*s at a time. In their home provinces we stayed at the village temple or at the *samnak chii*. We visited the *mae chii*s' families and relatives. I was also introduced to temples and *samnak chii*s and was thus enabled to interview the *mae chii*s living there. In Northeastern areas, many people do not speak Thai; they speak Lao or Khmer and generally the *mae chii*s that I travelled with helped to translate from Lao or Khmer into Central Thai or English.

Most *mae chii*s viewed my interest in studying their community as a sign of its growing progress. My visibility as a foreigner was a valued resource and I was invited to accompany them to many events. My presence as a foreigner was felt by many to increase access to sources of knowledge that could promote the development of the school at the *samnak chii*. To visitors I was often introduced as a teacher, and lay followers came to the *samnak chii* to ask me for English tuition. My interest in the *mae chii*s' lives and my appreciation of their vocation did have implications for my research in some ways. I am aware that in some interviews informants avoided negative aspects and delivered what they thought would be desired answers.

Since the study is primarily based on information collected from personal observation and interviews, consideration of ethical questions is important. I have masked the identity of the informants. A few of them are famous female ascetics and therefore easily recognisable; they have given their permission for me to use their authentic identities.

One aim of this study is to present the experiences of *mae chii*s in Thailand whose voices are rarely heard in debates about social change. I have sought to convey something of the rich experiences and communications that shaped my understanding of the *mae chii*s' lives and situation in Thai society. I have learnt a lot from the *mae chii*s and I have done my best to portray their lives in a spirit true to them.

NOTES

1 The name is fictitious.

2 *Wai* is a gesture of greeting that shows respect. It is made by raising both hands, palms joined and bowing the head.

3 Dhamma is a central Buddhist concept. It can mean the basic constituents of reality, the truth, the teachings of the Buddha. In Thailand, Sangha refers to the assembly of male monks (*bhikkhu*).

4 In 1998 there were 238.416 monks and novices and 14.392 reported *mae chii*s in Thailand. However, the exact numbers of *mae chii*s in Thailand is unknown since they do not always appear on temple records. ('Basic Religious Data'. Data Statistics and Information Section Planning Division, Department of Religious Affairs, Ministry of Education, January 1999.)

5 *Kamma* (Pali): morally relevant actions, intentional actions that result in future states of being. In Thai usage, these are consequences of morally relevant actions of the past, including past lives (Thai *kam*, Sanskrit: *karma*).

6 Mae chii Khunying Kanitha Wichiencharoen died on 13 May 2002.

7 *Chii phraam*s are named after the Brahmin devotees who converted to Buddhism and wore white without shaving (Cook 1981: 44).

CHAPTER TWO

Gender Orders and Gendering Renunciation — Past and Present

Rita M. Gross states that contemporary commentators on the participation of women in Buddhism commonly separate the Buddhist doctrine from the patriarchal norms imbedded in culture. Referring to the core teachings of Buddhism they declare that the 2,500-year-old Buddhist traditions are gender free and gender neutral, perhaps to a greater extent than is the case with any other major religious tradition (Gross 2001: 1). Such a promising basis for gender equality has not meant that women and men have been awarded equal standing or equal opportunities in Buddhist societies. On the contrary, throughout history patriarchal norms have permeated Buddhist institutions. The lack of gender equality in Buddhist institutions has generally been attributed to cultural factors and very little has been done to counteract that cultural influence.

In Thailand, as in most countries, the Buddhist institutions are male dominated. There are prevalent contrasting values and images of Thai women. In certain areas gender seems to carry less significant meaning, and women and men do have the same potential to be acknowledged, whereas in other domains, such as religion and politics, gender is a discriminatory factor. In this chapter, I shall give a brief outline of women's participation in Theravada Buddhism and focus on those aspects of Buddhism and the socio-cultural reality that are important for understanding Thai women's presence in Buddhism.

There are underlying themes related to gender relations in Thailand. One of these are the themes notions of women in Buddhist traditions that show how women were once part of the Buddhist *sangha* but were later excluded from the congregation. This is relevant to contemporary Buddhist ascetics and the issue of *bhikkhuni* ordination. The Thai conceptual models of sex and gender and the debated system of three sexes, are another theme which constitutes a necessary context for further understanding how gender relations and religion are interrelated.

WOMEN'S DECLINE FROM THE BUDDHIST *SANGHA*

Women have been involved with Buddhism from the very beginning of the religion. Horner reports that soon after the Buddha's first sermon in the Deer Park at Isipatana both men and women became lay disciples and the Buddha spoke of the same matters in the same terms to both (Horner 1990: 98). The Buddha created the female order, *bhikkhuni sangha,* in the sixth century BCE, five years after the establishment of the male order, the *bhikkhu sangha.* According to Buddhist legend, Mahapajapati and her sister Mahamaya were both married to the Buddha's father, King Suddhodana. Mahamaya had a son, Siddhatha, who later became the Buddha. Only seven days after he was born, Mahamaya died. His aunt, Mahapajapati, took care of Siddhatha and raised him as her own son. Siddhatha married Yasodhara and had a son, Rahula. However, he left the palace, his wife and son, and did not come back until Mahapajapati was in her late 50s or early 60s. He had then attained enlightenment and reached Buddhahood. Mahapajapati's son Nanda and her grandnephew Rahula had by then also become monks. Her husband King Suddhodana had died and she was now without a family. Many men in the kingdom had become monks and many women were without husbands. A great number of women came to Mahapajapati for advice. Mahapajapati was an influential woman without further worldly obligations. She was surrounded by displaced wives, widows, consorts, dancers, and musicians (Murcott 1991: 14). She turned to the Buddha and asked him to allow women to renounce their homes and enter into the *sangha.* Her request was turned down three times. Then the Buddha went to a place named Vasali. Mahapajapati and hundreds of women shaved their heads, donned saffron robes and walked to Vasali trying to persuade the Buddha to admit them into the *sangha.* The Buddha's disciple Ananda came to Mahapajapati's aid. He also asked the Buddha three times to permit women to renounce the world and the Buddha refused the request each time. Then he changed tactics and asked the Buddha if women were able to realise perfection and become enlightened. The Buddha's answer was yes, and finally Ananda succeeded in persuading the Buddha to allow women to go forth.

The order spread from India to Sri Lanka and developed into the Mahayana tradition in China, spreading further to Vietnam, Korea and Japan. The *bhikkhuni* order disappeared from India sometime after the ninth century. However, it flourished in Sri Lanka until the eleventh century and thereafter both the male and female monks' orders broke down. The male monks' order was later restored with help from Thai and Burmese monks (Goonatilake 1997: 31). According to Barnes, the *bhikkhuni sangha* was probably was brought to Burma in the eleventh century and it is known from stone inscriptions that the female order was still active there until the thirteenth century (Barnes 1996: 271).

The re-establishing of the *bhikkhuni* order has been an issue in Sri Lanka for many decades. The standard argument against reviving *bhikkhuni* ordination is that *bhikkhuni*, according to the Buddhist discipline, have to be ordained by both the *bhikkhu* and *bhikkhuni* orders, and that is not possible since the Theravada *bhikkhuni* lineage disappeared when the order broke down in Sri Lanka. However, there are objections to the notion that the *bhikkhuni* lineage has been broken. Those who argue that the lineage still exists explain that the *bhiksuni* order that remains in the Mahayana tradition in East Asian countries actually originated from Theravada Buddhism.[1] In the fifth century *bhikkhuni* from Sri Lanka travelled to China to establish the *bhikkhuni* order there. Consequently they argue that Mahayana *bhiksuni*s can help ordain and revive the *bhikkhuni* order in the Theravada tradition. The Sri Lankan female ascetics who wanted to revive the Theravada *bhikkhuni* order asked the Mahayana *bhiksuni* to assist them in the dual ordination. In 1996 ten Sri Lankan female ascetics, *dasa sila mata*, received *bhikkhuni* ordination in Sarnath, India and in 1998, 20 *dasa sila mata*s received *bhikkhuni* ordination in Bodh Gaya, India together with 111 women from different countries. Later the same year, the *bhikkhuni* ordination was held in Sri Lanka and the *bhikkhuni* ordination was performed for the first time since the order vanished in the eleventh century. The *bhikkhuni*s are not yet recognised by all the Buddhist denominations in Sri Lanka. However, they are recognised by the Sri Lankan government who issues identity cards that give them the status of *bhikkhuni*s.

ATTITUDES TOWARDS WOMEN IN EARLY BUDDHISM

Numerous writers on Thailand (for example, Khin Thitsa 1980, Tantiwiramanond and Pandey 1987, Kabilsingh 1991, Sivaraksa 1992, Morris 1994) have noted the reluctance to ordain women in the Thai *sangha* and debated the significance of that for the status of women in contemporary Thai society. They are concerned with questions of whether Buddhism is part of the patriarchal suppression of women or not. If Buddhism, like other world religions, exercises such suppression the question is whether that is an intrinsic part of Buddhism or merely a later addition. According to Rita Gross, misogyny, the hatred or fear of women and the feminine, is not widespread in Buddhist texts (Gross 1993: 22). However, the ambiguity of female renunciation seems always to have been present. According to the scriptures, the Buddha was initially hesitant to install an order for women. As mentioned earlier, it was only after several requests from his foster mother, Mahapajapati, and from one of his close disciples, Ananda, that the Buddha reluctantly established the female order, which was instituted five years after the male *bhikkhu* order was established. According to the history, the admission of women into the order was granted on the condition that Mahapajapati should take upon herself the Eight Chief Rules (*garudhamma*) (Table 2.1), which are special rules for women. Mahapajapati accepted the rules and it was clear from the beginning that the female monks were not to be independent of the male monks: they were to be dependent upon them for the proper performance of most of their ceremonies and for the authorisation of all of them (Horner 1990: 118–119). Further, it left the *bhikkhuni* permanently subordinated to the monks.

The Eight Chief Rules, *Gurudhamma*:

1. A female monk must always bow down before a male monk no matter how long she has been a monk.

2. A female monk is not to spend the rainy season in a district where there is no male monk.

3. In order to perform the *Uposatha* ceremony [days for special meetings of the *sangha* and for recitations of the *Patimokkha* rules], the female monks must wait for the male monks to come and deliver the teaching.[2]

4. After the rain's retreat the female monks must hold *Pavarana* [to inquire whether the female monks have committed any fault] with both the male monks and the female monks.

5. A female monk who has been guilty of a serious offence must undergo the *manatta* discipline before both *sangha*s.

6. When a novice has trained for two years in the six precepts, she should seek ordination from both *sangha*s.

7. A female monk is not to revile or abuse a monk under any circumstances.

8. Admonition by female monks of male monks is forbidden, admonition of female monks by male monks is not forbidden.

Finally, after accepting women into the order, the Buddha was said to have complained to Ananda, saying that without women, the 'true' *dhamma* (*saddhamma*) would have lasted a thousand years; now that women were in the order, it would last only 500 years.[3] There is much scholarly debate about the origins of this account. Horner attributes the Buddha's prediction of the decline of the *dhamma* to the monks who edited the sayings ascribed to the Buddha. She says that they would naturally try to minimise the importance which he gave to women and introduce their own misogynist assumptions (Horner 1990: xx, 105). Horner is supported by other scholars who hold the same view about the origin of the misogynist attitudes (see e.g. Barnes 1987: 107; Sponberg 1992: 22; and Gross 1993: 34). However, the statement mentioned above appears in the *vinayas* (disciplinary rules for the monastic community) of every school of Buddhism that exist today, with surprisingly little variation (Blackstone 1998: 38).[4] Further, the origins of the *garudhamma* rules are likewise questioned. However, the rules may have been one of the reasons for the eventual disappearance of the *bhikkhuni* order in India. Falk (1980), Paul (1985), Willis (1985), Horner (1990) and Gross (1993) discuss the impact of the rules. The Buddha's initial reluctance to establish an order for women, the prediction of the decline of the *dhamma* and the institutional subordination contained in the eight rules are still used in the debate about the reinstitution of *bhikkhuni* ordination (see for example Satha-Anand 1999). When I discussed the *bhikkhuni* issue with the *mae chii*s, they commonly referred to the *bhikkhunis*' secondary role in the *sangha* as a negative issue for ordained women.

The initial unwillingness to ordain women was possibly, at least partly, based on women's role in procreation and in maintaining the household. In a society that placed high value on women as mothers, one might expect some opposition to the idea of celibacy for women. Moreover, as in patriarchal societies in general, women were seen as sexually uncontrolled, and were in this setting considered a potential threat to monks' celibacy. Women were sometimes suspected of having opportunistic motives for joining the Order. It was believed that when lay life no longer proved satisfactory, women came to the *sangha*. However, Horner states that in the beginning it was regarded as perfectly respectable for women to enter the homeless life. It was only later that the Order lost that character and became a refuge for the poor, the unsuccessful, the unmarried and the widowed, and the entrants were looked upon as unfortunates who had found life too difficult on account of the fruits of deeds done formerly (Horner 1990: 172).

CONTEMPORARY THERAVADA FEMALE ASCETICS

Thai society has never fulfilled the ideals described in Buddhist doctrine since the *bhikkhuni* order has always been missing. An ideal Buddhist society consists of female and male monks (*bhikkhuni*s and *bhikkhu*s) and female and male lay people (*upasika*s and *upasaka*s) with a distinct boundary between the two groups. Despite the lack of a *bhikkhuni* order, Thai women, like women in other Theravada countries, shave their heads and become renunciants after having received five, eight or ten Buddhist precepts. The female ascetics are named differently in every country. For example in Burma they are called *thila shin* and in Sri Lanka those who have received ten precepts are named *dasa sila mata*. The category of *mae chii* is thus a Thai creation and not found in the old Theravada Buddhist texts. The category of *mae chii* is not the same as *upasika* or *bhikkhuni*. The empty category of fully ordained female ascetics in the Thai *sangha* underscores characteristics in the Thai sex/gender discourses which tie women to the lay domain.

Female renunciants in Buddhist countries are creating categories that distinguish them from lay people. For example, in the early decades of the twentieth century, Sri Lankan women started the *dasa sila mata* movement with female ascetics dressed in ochre robes and observing ten precepts. They created a category in between the eight-precept female ascetics and the *bhikkhuni*s. In Sri Lanka female renunciants had been absent until the early twentieth century (Bartholomeusz 1994: 91 ff.). Women's agency to create a place for themselves in religion was decisive for the project of reviving female ascetics. The *dasa sila mata* established communities and opened schools for young girls. Teaching was a new vocation that the ancient *bhikkhuni*s were not known to have practised. There are *dasa sila mata*s in all the 25 districts of Sri Lanka and they live either in small hermitages or alone. Like female ascetics in the other Theravada countries, the *dasa sila mata*s struggle for educational opportunities and ways to meet their financial needs (Tsomo 1988: 140–144). In 1998, Sri Lanka was the first Theravada country to recognise the *bhikkhuni* order and today it is possible for women to receive full *bhikkhuni* ordination from both female and male monks there. *Bhikkhuni* ordination was once possible in Burma, which is the only country in Southeast Asia that has had a *bhikkhuni sangha*. However, the order vanished in the late thirteenth century and today the Burmese female ascetics only receive eight or ten precepts. The Burmese female ascetics' name, *thila shin*, means 'a person who observes the Buddhist code of morality, one who is virtuous and moral in every way this word would apply' (Kawanami 2000: 87). Like the *mae chii*s in Thailand, the position of the *thila shin*s is ambiguous. They have renounced the lay world and live in temples, yet their ordination is not recognised by the *sangha* and they are therefore in certain circumstances referred to as lay women (ibid. ff.).

Despite the difficulties that women often face in their ordained life, many *mae chii*s develop in their vocation and there are manifold examples of women's great spiritual capacity. There are individual *mae chii*s who are earning public recognition for their activities, most particularly for their meditation skills. The well-known meditation teachers such as Acaan Naeb Mahaniranon (see Kornfield 1996; J. Van Esterik 1996), Ki Nanayon (Tiyavanich 1997) and Acaan Ranjuan (Batchelor 2000) have not asked for *mae chii* ordination. Instead they prefer to keep their lay status. Nevertheless, they shave their heads and follow the same eight precepts as the *mae chii*s. They do not wear the *mae chii*s' dress but usually a black skirt and a white blouse. Further, they do not collect alms in the mornings or officiate at ceremonies or perform other monastic tasks. There are also examples of *mae chii*s who were well known before they became ordained but who continue also to gain respect in their new roles as *mae chii*. These 'public' *mae chii*s are in general well educated and they appear on television programmes as well as in newspapers and magazines. To some extent, they have helped to broaden the picture of *mae chii*s by correcting the stereotyped image that has developed over the years. One of the basic obstacles facing the *mae chii*s is their context-dependent status. In some circumstances they are associated with the lay world and in other situations the religious realm. I found that the *mae chii*s themselves are not ambivalent about their spiritual standing. However, in a culture that draws a distinction between the lay and religious realms, their unclear status has implications for the *mae chii*s' relationships with authorities as well as with the laity.

The *bhikkhuni* issue has not been debated in Thailand as much as in Sri Lanka. During my fieldwork, there were only a few Thai women who had received *bhiksuni* ordination in the Mahayana tradition. The best-known advocate for establishing the *bhikkhuni* order in Thailand was Acaan Chatsumarn Kabilsingh. Her mother, the Venerable Voramai Kabilsingh, was the first Thai woman to receive full *bhiksuni* ordination from both the male and female *sangha*s. She received ordination in the Mahayana tradition in the Dharmagupta lineage in Taiwan in 1971. As mentioned in Chapter 1, Acaan Chatsumarn received ordination as a *samaneri bhikkhuni* (female novice monk) in Sri Lanka in February 2001 and full *bhikkhuni* ordination in February 2003 also in Sri Lanka, becoming the first Theravada female monk in Thailand. In February 2002 a *mae chii* received *samaneri bhikkhuni* ordination in Thailand

and became the first female novice to receive dual ordination in Thailand (discussed in Chapter 9). However, her ordination, like that of the other women, remains unrecognised by the Thai *sangha*.

The *mae chii*s do not generally struggle for *bhikkhuni* ordination. Only a few of the interviewed stated that they would be interested in receiving full ordination if it were possible in Thailand. Most reported that they would rather develop themselves spiritually as *mae chii*s. The fact that the *mae chii*s, who strongly identify with the Theravada tradition, would be ordained by Mahayana male and female monks if they were to receive full ordination, made them hesitant. They were uncertain whether that might imply that they were renouncing the Theravada practice. Most *mae chii*s are particular about following the precepts and they anticipated difficulties in maintaining the more than three hundred precepts (for full ordination), some of which are outmoded and therefore difficult to follow today. The *bhikkhuni* ordination would also subordinate the *mae chii*s to monks and, the *mae chii*s considered this to be a drawback for ordained women.

GENDER DISCOURSES IN THAI SOCIETY

Thai Buddhist cosmology is a vital force in the development of a social hierarchy which posits male members of the *sangha* as supreme moral agents. Buddhism is regularly evoked to account for the position and condition of Thai women. Women are supposedly seen as having less merit, and as having no recognised religious role. Many Thai women are convinced that they carry a heavy load of 'negative karma' due to the simple fact of their sex, and are therefore eager to gain merit to offset it (Kabilsingh 1991: 31).[5] Former deeds, *kamma,* are commonly used to explicate gender, and the idea of rebirth as a woman due to misdeeds in past lives is widespread in Thailand. However this notion is without authority from the Buddhist philosophical texts. Thai women who seek their rights to live a religious life and strive towards uplifting women's position find support for women's spiritual capabilities in the Buddhist scriptures and they are inspired by the narratives of the enlightened *bhikkhuni* and lay women related in the Buddhist teachings as well as in historical tales.

Thai women in history

Among the images of Thai women in history there are women heroines who are highly admired for their courage, strength and cleverness and there are also several women warriors. For example, Queen Srisuriyothai of Ayutthaya

(1548–1569), Khunying Muk and Khunying Jan (1785) who all fought against the Burmese. Another was Khunying Mo who rescued Nakhon Ratchasima from the Lao army. The heroines from the past re-emerge in the present through spirit mediums and have the potential to intervene in contemporary men's and women's lives. Women are also depicted as cunning in finding unorthodox ways to solve problems. For example, the legend of Queen Chamadevi, the Mon leader of Lanna in Northern Thailand, tells us how she counted menstrual blood among her weapons in order to weaken opponents. Women's garments have also been conceptualised as powerful, possessing the capacity to destroy male power. The legend also tells of how Queen Chamadevi confirmed the power of women's polluted lower garments. To avoid marriage and loss of her kingdom, she wove fabric from these into her suitor's hat, rendering him unable to hurl his spear to claim her hand and kingdom (P. Van Esterik 2000: 79).

Power and gender relations also differed over time. For instance, according to Bonsue, women and men were equal in the Kingdom of Sukhothai (Bonsue 1998: 6 in P. Van Esterik 2000: 43). The preserved writings from foreigners' impression of the Kingdom of Siam in the seventeenth century show that Thai women were remarkably visible in society. De La Loubère wrote in 1697 that women managed trade and enjoyed perfect liberty. However, feudal Ayutthaya destroyed the traditional rights of Thai women by codifying Khmer hierarchical laws imposing them over Sukhothai egalitarianism. There are also models that downplay the existence and extent of both gender subordination and slavery in the Ayutthaya period and earlier (P. Van Esterik 2000: 43–44).

Gendered ways to maturity

The distinct separation between the sexually active (lay person) and the sexually inactive (celibate monastic) is fundamental for understanding gender differences in Thai society. According to Thai cultural values the evaluation of women as 'good' and 'bad' depends on their primary duty which is to the family (see Hantrakul 1988; Komin 1992; P. Van Esterik 1996). It is against prescribed gender roles for young, healthy women to leave home for ordained life, and female ordination has traditionally not been encouraged. The notion of Thai women belonging to the mundane realm stands in sharp contrast to boys' ordination, which is celebrated and desirable. Young men become socially mature through a rite of passage – ordination as novice monks. Young women's maturity is not developed through transgressing into the sacred realm; they are tied to the secular and seen to mature through marriage and childbirth. Progression through the different stages in a girl's life as she approaches adulthood is gradual. Marriage marks one change in her status. The birth of a first child, and the custom of 'lying by the fire' after the delivery, confirm her adult role (see Yoddumnern-Attig 1992, Whittaker 2002).

Women in Thai society

Women in Thailand are active in society and especially in the economic sector, which is open to women. However, women's participation in formal politics and religious functions endorsed by the state is almost non-existent: contribution to politics and religion does exist in the informal sphere. Kirsch, for example, highlights the way in which religious views of women's spiritual inferiority could be justified by female prominence in commerce, at the same time as they enhance men's spiritual and social superiority in both religion and politics (Kirsch 1975). Thai women have always worked alongside men and there has been a discussion among scholars about whether Thai women should be regarded as having 'high' status because of their traditional involvement in economic activities or 'low' status because of the notion that they are perceived '*kamm*ically inferior' to men.

Nerida Cook states that prostitution is the most noticeable image that pervades the literature on Thai women (Cook 1998: 250). The amount of attention that Thai prostitution has received in the media is disproportionate but nevertheless important when analysing gender relations in Thailand. There is a huge academic literature on female prostitution in Thailand and possible reasons for women's participation in sex work are debated. The idea that Thai prostitutes are young girls dutifully sacrificing themselves for their rural families has become one of the widely accepted explanations among Thai middle-class and foreign commentators alike (Cook 1998: 264). Mueche (1992: 891) argues that there is a strong cultural continuity in Northern Thai attitudes towards daughters supporting families by prostitution. She suggests that prostitution is for today's daughters what food selling, to supplement family income, was for their mothers' generation. However, Cook points out that by no means all parents allow their daughters to do sex work; in many cases prostitutes disguise their real occupation for fear of their families' disapproval. Also many young women, like young men, migrate to urban areas against their families' wishes. Further, not all sex workers support their families as mentioned above (Cook 1998: 268).

There has been a debate among scholars as to whether men and women enjoy complementary or unequal status in Thai society (see Hanks and Hanks 1963; P. Van Esterik 1996 [1982]; Keyes 1984; Krisch 1982, 1985). There are a variety of other factors that work as markers of social identity and status, such as age, wealth, education and occupational position that in some instances are more significant than gender. The valorisation of maleness and masculinity in Thailand is tempered by a parallel valuing of a range of other status and prestige conferring qualities that can be achieved by both women and the non-masculine male (Jackson 1995). The complex social ranking system of maleness and masculinity are two factors among others that contribute to a person's social standing. If women or non-masculine males exhibit a sufficient number of other status and prestige symbols, such as education, wealth, intelligence, success in their field, dignity and wisdom in old age, then this can be sufficient to grant them an honoured place in Thai society (ibid.). Lucien and Jane Hanks (1963) found that ideals of gender complementarity were current and noted the relatively equal status of men and women in Thailand. They proposed that gender for Thai people was a secondary concern; Nicola Tannenbaum (1999) argues that the conclusion that status and power receive primary consideration is still valid. The image of Thai women's high status has been prevalent throughout the decades and several researchers have held onto the notion of 'equal but different'. Opponents to the former perspective have pointed out that despite high participation in the labour force, Thai women have low representation in fields that would give women influence (Tantiwiramanond and Pandey 1997). Thai women lack political power and they are also under-represented in higher levels of the public service.

Kirsch (1975) argues that Buddhist values provide the basis for understanding the Thai division of labour where women are involved with the economy and men with politics and religion. The volume *Women of Southeast Asia* (P. Van Esterik 1996) contains three articles about Thai women's status in relationship to Buddhism. These articles describe Thai women's linkage with fertility, nurturance and attachment and Thai men with otherworldly power and detachment. Further, in the discussion about women's and men's degrees of attachment to worldly matters, Kirsch (1996) states that in Thailand women are constrained to be more worldly and more attached than men to the realm of desire that hinders the attainment of the Buddhist ultimate goal. Thai moral codes devalue women, rendering them ineligible for ascetic lives and locating them firmly in the world of the sensual as nurturers, mothers providers of sons for the monkhood. Keyes (1984) has countered this view, insisting that a proper reading of Buddhist texts and rituals results in a 'different but equal' view of men and women, rather than a 'superior/inferior' formulation.

Buddhism is by some authors blamed for the subordination of Thai women and is considered to provide a moral framework for men's hierarchical precedence over women. Inequality was the resulting practice, reinforcing the view that Buddhism was more concerned with male hegemony. Khin Thitsa (1980: 7) reasons that the materialistic image of women legitimates prostitution as a place where women can fulfil role expectations as attached to worldly matters.

Ideal male and female gender models

In Thailand celibacy is gendered and does not carry the same meaning for men and women. The difference is not attributed to legal recognition of their ordained status; rather it has to do with prevailing cultural and social values. For Thai men, ordination and the life of a monk are ways to realise their masculine identity. Further, it is desirable that all men be ordained, for at least a short period in life, in order to obtain maturity and transfer merit to their parents. Consequently, Thai men become true males through sexual abstinence, proving that they have control over their sexuality. The monk is depicted as an ideal male who has the strength and qualities to overcome temptations. Most men who become monks or novices do that only for a period of time and the vast majority of men do not remain in the *sangha*. Keyes (1986) has shown that the ideal male is an ex-monk who is a householder.

For Thai women, female identity is not realised by celibacy. In the contrary, women achieve maturity and female identity through marriage and motherhood, which are firmly tied to the secular realm. When a woman decides to reject the female reproductive identity, abandon her home life by assuming a religious identity and become a *mae chii,* she violates social norms of gender. Through celibate practice women transcend the female gender; by exceeding the restraint that is connected with women's reproductive capability they fail to meet the ideals of Thai female gender models. Men can thus realise their masculine identity through ordaining while women abandon their feminine identity through the ordained life.

The ideal male in a Buddhist social order is one who acts in the world while having acquired detachment from worldly passions. The celibate lifestyle for a monk may have provided him with an ultimate challenge to show his potential power by achieving full control over his body and sexual desires, exemplifying his masculine identity to the fullest. The sexual purity of monks is considered as the most distinctive attribute of those who are part of the *sangha*. The incapacity of men to commit themselves to a life in celibacy is the reason most often mentioned as to why men do not continue their lives as monks (Keyes

1986: 83; Tiyavanich 1997: 127–142). Recently several famous monks have been defrocked for violating the precept of celibacy. The *mae chii*s emphasise the importance of celibacy alongside uprooting various forms of attachments and desires. Just as monks have rules that regulate their contact with women, the *mae chii*s have similar rules that restrict their association with men, but the *mae chii*s that I interviewed could not recall any instance when a *mae chii* had been expelled for a sexual offence.

KINSHIP, FAMILY AND MARRIAGE

In Thailand, the community of Buddhist monks is the most culturally celebrated position of authority and value. In spite of the fact that women are excluded from the possibility of being ordained into the monks' community and that they are generally absent from prestigious arenas of political leadership and formal office, the greater equality of women's and men's roles and privileges in Southeast Asia has been contrasted with women's more unequal position in South Asia and East Asia.

Women throughout Southeast Asia are viewed as having 'high status' on the basis that women are usually the ones who deal with money and control family finances, and often become traders (Atkinson and Errington 1990: 4). Thai culture is described as being relatively 'flexible' and tolerant to individual divergences. Thai society is generally noted for more egalitarian gender relations arising from women's roles in finances, land ownership, kinship structures and women's roles in the labour market.

Yet, Thailand is in many ways a highly androcentric society, not least ideologically. Legal codes in the Thai family law in the nineteenth and early twentieth centuries clearly considered women as dependents on their male family members, not free agents (Satha-Anand 2004: 27). In the past, a woman's social status was defined through her husband's position in life. Still there are inequities in the family law that oppress women. For example, infidelity is a ground for divorce if the wife is unfaithful but not if the husband is having affairs, unless he 'honours another woman as his wife'.

Social scientists have described Thai women as having a relatively 'high status' because their central role in the family structure and their late marriage rates are evidence of their relative importance in the family (Phongpaichit and Baker 1996). Women in Northern Thailand had a relatively strong socio-economic position in the agricultural economy. The matrifocal kinship system, which emphasized the authority of mothers and maternal grandmothers, and the fact that women, not men, were the owners of family property, provided Northern Thai women with considerable security in the past (Fongkaew 2002: 148).

The equal inheritance of land by daughters and sons, marriage payments from the groom to the bride's family and the preference for post-marital residence in the wife's home give women access to valuable resources (Hale 1984: 4). The youngest daughter is expected to care for her parents and receives the family house as compensation for her service. However, increasing urbanisation has forced couples to move away from their extended families, and practical considerations often take precedence in deciding who will live where and with whom.

Women are at greater risk than men when entering a marriage, since registrations of double or multiple marriages are widely practised, mostly by men. Prior to 1990 all multiple marriage registrations were legal unless the first wife brought a lawsuit to the civil court to invalidate all the other registered marriages of her husband. All children were recognised as the legal children of the husband. Now, a computerised central marriage registration system based on people's names has been established in Thailand. However, it has not been effective in stopping bigamy since it does not cover the whole country and in many cases it is impossible to check people's marital status because of spelling errors and the large number of people who have identical names (Pruekpongsawalee 2004: 144–145). Thai family law provides two channels for divorce, consensual divorce and judicial divorce. A consensual divorce is unproblematic and the couple can register a divorce in any district office in the country. A judicial divorce is more complicated as the person who seeks a divorce must file a lawsuit according to the ten grounds for divorce. Nine of the ten grounds apply equally to husbands and wives. However, a husband can sue his wife on the grounds of adultery, while a woman cannot use this reason against her husband unless she can prove that her husband has either given maintenance to or has honoured another woman as his wife (ibid.: 143).

Commentators on Southeast Asia often remark that the births of male and female children are equally valued (Atkinson and Errington1990: 4). In contrast to South Asia and East Asia, throughout most of Southeast Asia female children are not a greater financial burden on their parents than male children when they marry. On the contrary, Thai marriage ceremonies involve presenting a brideprice, usually in the form of gold and cash, and marriage might be a survival strategy for Thai families. Whittaker (1999) and Lyttleton (1999) present evidence that brideprice exchanges are increasingly monetary and expensive in Northern and Northeastern Thailand, because of greater dependence on wage labour and cash, and a reduction in agricultural land per family.

Children are under lifelong obligation (*bun khun*) to their parents for their birth, and sons and daughters are expected to repay their debt to their parents in gender-specific ways. A son performs a highly meritorious act for his parents by becoming a Buddhist monk, thereby transferring merit to his parents, particularly his mother. A daughter, barred from monkhood, is expected to be a caretaker of her parents and younger siblings. This caretaking often takes the form of financial support, with professional and wage-earning women sending money to support their parents and siblings (Tantiwiramanond and Pandey 1987).

REPRESENTATIONS OF THE *MAE CHII*S – AMBIGUITY AND INVISIBILITY

Generally, Thai people are ambivalent about women who abandon traditionally accepted social roles, and they do not encourage women to renounce the world. The ideal Thai woman is expected to fulfil the role of wife and mother. Thus *mae chii*s violate cultural norms of gender by abandoning their home lives and renouncing the world. The somewhat negative attitude towards *mae chii*s, together with their ambiguous position as renunciants, has made the role of *mae chii*s' vague and questionable. The authorities, too, treat the *mae chii*s in ambiguous ways. The government supports the monks with free education, free medical care and free or reduced fares for buses and trains. *Mae chii*s do not receive such support from the government on account of their official status as laity. However, their ambiguous position becomes obvious when the same government denies the *mae chii*s the right to vote in public elections on the basis of their renunciation of worldly matters.

The social background of the *mae chii*s has significance for their lives as religious practitioners. Wealth and high social prestige could enhance an individual *mae chii*'s position, but is not enough to ensure acceptance as a religious person, unless combined with religious knowledge and practice. Thus, education and religious practice are crucial for *mae chii*s in their role as ordained persons.

The *mae chii*s are scattered all over the country and their religious practices have not been uniform and there have been variations in ordination procedures and regulations. It was not until 1969 that the Thai Mae Chiis' Institute, *Sathaaban Mae Chii Thai*, was founded. This meant that the *mae chii*s gained a national network and a public representative who could unite the *mae chii*s and work with issues that concerned them (see Chapter 7).

The *mae chii*s do not attract much public attention and they are seldom mentioned in academic works. When they are referred to, they are commonly depicted as elderly, widowed, or as young women who have been ill or suffered some misfortune (see for example P. Van Esterik 1996: 57). Young ordained women tend to be assumed to be destitute or 'broken-hearted' rather than searching for spiritual fulfilment, and the *mae chii*s in general have been seen more or less as 'housekeepers' for the monks at the temples. It is a fact that the *mae chii*s have always been subordinated to monks in the temples. However, the present study shows that the *mae chii*s have diverse backgrounds and are not a homogeneous group: age, social background, educational level, aspirations and motives for receiving ordination vary significantly and inform differences between individual *mae chii*s. Moreover, the study demonstrates that it is significant whether the *mae chii* is a resident at a temple or at a self-governed *samnak chii*. It is also important where in Thailand the *mae chii*s live, since the local variations in temple rules, Buddhist teachings and forms of practice offered have an impact on the *mae chii*'s vocation.

The simplified, degrading, popular picture of Thai women who seek ordination neglects women's spiritual ability and religious reasons for leading an ascetic life. The statement that women seek ordination because of various disabilities implies that the state of female renunciation is seen as a refuge and sign of misfortunes, and women who are capable of living a lay life do not strive for it. These notions are in line with ideas representing women as more worldly and attached than men are. Women's supposed inextricable bonds to the secular world are viewed as signs of women's and men's qualitative difference based on the notion that a female birth is inferior to a male birth. Men, on the other hand, are considered more detached from worldly matters and this legitimises their entrance into the religious realm as ordained persons.

An oft-quoted debate between Thomas A. Kirsch (1996 [1982], 1985) and Charles F. Keyes (1984, 1986) deals with this question of whether women are more attached to worldly things than men. Both take their starting point in Buddhism, but their interpretations of the Buddhist texts differ and they disagree about the notion of women's and men's attachment. Kirsch argues that women are seen as being more related to worldly matters and thereby more attached. He states that women are not associated with *nibbana* and they are prohibited from attaining full ordination into the Buddhist *sangha*. Keyes emphasises the admired role for women as mother and nurturer in Buddhism. He agrees that women as mothers face attachment to their children, particularly to their male children, who will, unlike the daughters, leave home. He foregrounds the structural asymmetry between the sexes, and argues that for women both worldly and spiritual activities can be carried out within the role of 'mother'. In contrast, men must leave the role of householder and be ordained as a monk to fulfil their religious vocation. Sri Dao Ruang holds that in the Thai Buddhist view, women are considered to be more attached to the worldly than are men, partly because of the experiences of childbearing and motherhood. This greater female attachment to the world is one of the reasons commonly given to defend the fact the men may be ordained as monks, but women may not. Yet men are also considered less capable of controlling their sexual desires than women and they are not expected to remain virgins until marriage. In contrast, all women are expected to do so (Sri Dao Ruang 1996: 102).

In my interviews with the *mae chii*s, they say that women through motherhood and responsibility for their family manifest a greater potential for attachment to the world. At the same time they consider women and men to have equal faculties for becoming detached.

The stereotypical assumptions about women's reasons for becoming *mae chii*s reduce and trivialise women's aspirations. The unwillingness to acknowledge that men and women can have the same reasons for renouncing the world further reveals why ordination for women is often perceived to be inappropriate. Men's reasons for entering the monkhood are not doubted. One common reason for men to become monastics is to obtain education. Women have never had the same opportunities to education through the *sangha*. Their spiritual quest has often been doubted and is not seen as a sufficient reason to be ordained and they must justify their decisions to become *mae chii*s.

The *mae chii*s' voices are seldom heard and they could be classified as what Edwin Ardener (1975) calls a *muted group*. Ardener used the concept *mutedness* three decades ago when he called attention to the fact that women are generally given insufficient attention in anthropology. He employs the concept *mutedness* to describe the relationship between dominant and subordinate models of communication. Mutedness is an instrument of exclusion from power and authority. He focuses on situations in which groups can only articulate what they wish to say through, in this case, the dominant male voice.

Mae chiis in the shadows of the monks

Monks are at the centre of the religious sphere in Thailand they are highly venerated and hold an important position in society. The Buddhist temples used to have the most central position in Thai villages, and the monks were educators, sponsors of co-operative work activities, personal and social counsellors and ethical mentors (Swearer 1995: 117). The *mae chiis* do not hold any formal role at the temples and the Thai *mae chiis'* marginal position in the temples and in society is striking, although they have a long history in Thailand and have lived at the temples for centuries. It is difficult to trace their historical development. They may have existed in ancient times, but no records of them survived the Burmese destruction of the capital of Ayudhya in the fifteenth century. The first written evidence of the white-clad, female ascetics appears in the seventeenth century when a French missionary and a German physician who visited Thailand mentioned the female ascetics who lived at the temples (Kabilsingh 1991: 36). Over the centuries there has been silence about them, and their lives and roles in the temples. The impression is that they have lived an obscure life without formal religious assignments. However, Tiyavanich reports that in regional traditions there were prominent women renunciates but their identities and teachings do not appear in official records because they were devoted to meditation rather than scholastic training (Tiyavanich 1997: 281).

In anthropological work on Thailand and monasticism, interest has primarily focused on the relationship between monks and the nation-state or monks and lay donors (see e.g. Bunnag 1973, Hanks 1962, Keyes 1971, Kirsch 1975, 1977, Swearer 1976, Tambiah 1970, 1976 and Terwiel 1976). It was only in the 1980s that scholars started showing interest in the contemporary socio-religious reality of Buddhist women (see e.g. Cook 1981, Keyes 1984, Kirsh 1982, 1985, Tantiwiramanond and Pandey 1987, Khin Thitsa 1983, and J. Van Esterik 1996 [1982] and P. Van Esterik 1996 [1982]). Studies that mention *mae chiis* generally call attention to their subordinate position and the scanty research that is available commonly focuses on themes related to their low position and role in society. Two unpublished MA theses from Mahidol University in Bangkok present comparative studies on *mae chiis'* roles, status and vocation in relation to other religious women. Parichart Suwanbubbha (1983) compares *mae chiis* in Bangkok with Roman Catholic nuns in the same city. She finds that the *mae chiis'* spiritual aspirations do not include social services to the laity. In contrast with the Catholic nuns, the *mae chiis* are not trained to do social work.

Mae chii Yuphin Duangjun (1999) compares *mae chiis* at the temple of Wat Paknam Phasi Charoen in Bangkok with female practioners at Danmahamongkol Meditation Centre in Kanchanaburi province. Her findings demonstrate that the *mae chiis* and the female practitioners have the same motivations as monks for choosing to live a religious life. However, the *mae chiis'* main function at Wat Paknam is to prepare food for the monks. The women who live and practise at Danmahamongkol do not serve the monks and they have the independence to receive support from the laity. In *Thai Women in Buddhism* (1991), Kabilsingh gives a historical perspective on Buddhism and on *mae chii*s in Thailand and devotes a chapter to the *bhikkhuni* movement in Thailand. In the volume, the position of *mae chii*s is contextualised and Kabilsingh brings in several important themes related to women's subordination in Thai society. She states that the *mae chii*s' lack of self-esteem, coupled with negative social attitudes, has resulted in their extremely low status. Marginalised, uneducated, and economically unsupported *mae chii*s are alienated in Thai society.

Very few ethnographic studies exist regarding Thai female ascetics. Exceptions include Nerida Cook's (1981) unpublished master's thesis 'The Position of Nuns in Thai Buddhism: Parameters of Religious Recognition'. She examines *mae chii*s' status and provides an ethnographic description of their life at the well-attended temple Wat Paknam. Cook stresses the *mae chii*s' subordinate position in relation to the monks. However, she portrays them as a heterogeneous group and she sees possibilities for raising their status. Several researchers have identified better education as a key issue for the *mae chii*s. Cook suggests that *mae chii*s could perform an important function in society, but the inadequate educational level of many of them makes them ill-prepared for the role (Cook 1981: 204).

Allan Bessey (1990) relates the *mae chii*s to the modernisation process in Thailand. He agrees with other researchers who consider women's access to secular and religious education as vital for changes to Thai women's roles in society. He believes, however, that influences from other Buddhist countries would be more important in developing the *mae chii*s' role than would, for example, the national Thai Mae Chiis' Institute. Sid Brown's *The Journey of One Buddhist Nun: Even Against the Wind* (2001) presents a life story of an *mae chii* and her various struggles in ordained life. That work focuses on one individual *mae chii* but gives insight into meditation practices and various difficulties that *mae chii*s encounter in their ordained life. Brown notes that the stereotypical picture of the *mae chii* as a poor woman who has lost in love was held by people who had no contact or experiences with *mae chii*s. In contrast, people who contributed to the *mae chii*s' livelihood expressed how impressed they were by their spiritual practice and their contribution to society (Brown 2001: 24–30). I met the same preconceived notions about the *mae chii*s among uninitiated people and the overwhelmingly positive attitudes towards the *mae chii*s among lay people who had actual contact with them.

ALTERNATIVE MODELS – REPRESENTATIONS OF
WOMEN'S SPIRITUAL CAPACITY

In general, Thai *mae chii*s and monks consider the Buddhist texts to be of fundamental importance for their understanding and practice of Buddhism. The Buddhist scriptures are also important for comprehending women's altered standing in Buddhism today. Women have gone from being fully ordained *bhikkhuni* and for centuries being part of the *sangha,* through being excluded from the same congregation and denied ordination to once again having the possibility of receiving *bhikkhuni* ordination. Despite the fact that Thai women are denied entrance to the most venerated realm in society, *mae chii*s express their certainty about women's and men's equal capacities to reach the final goal, *nibbana.* When discussing this subject the *mae chii*s commonly refer to the scriptures regarding women's spiritual capacities and they are encouraged by the Therigatha text that contains narratives of the early enlightened *bhikkhuni*s.

The Therigatha is a text that is part of the Pali canonical scriptures. *Theri* means 'women elders', or 'women who have grown old in knowledge', and *gatha* means 'verse', 'stanza', or 'song' (Murcott 1991: 3). The Therigatha thus contains poems by wise women in Buddhism. The collection of verses is ascribed to the earliest female followers of the Buddha.6 All the authors of the Therigatha are described by the commentary as having attained liberation, i.e., as having become *arahat*s. The Therigatha was passed on orally for six centuries before being written down in the Pali language in Sri Lanka in the first century BCE. The collection is arranged by ascending number of verses per poem and comprises 522 verses compiled into 73 poems; 71 are ascribed to specific almswomen and two are attributed to two groups of followers of Bhikkhuni Patacara, all of them contemporaries of the Buddha (Horner 1990: 162). In his commentary on the Therigatha Dhammapala added a narrative story to each poem. The story included a sketch of that particular woman's life and the circumstances that led her to become a *bhikkhuni.* Dhammapala drew his material from three older commentaries and is considered by modern Therigatha scholars to be quite accurate (Murcott 1991: 6). In the poems, the female monks explain their motivation for entering the order, they also describe their lives and activities, and their thoughts and feelings before and after they entered the religious life.

References to *bhikkhuni*s appear in a number of Buddhist stories, especially those that tell about the formative period of Buddhism. The references are commonly evaluations of the *bhikkhuni*s' spiritual capacities, their role within the community, and descriptions of their activities and spiritual accomplishments.

For example, Bhikkhuni Khema is depicted as the most eminent in wisdom, Nanda was first in meditation, Sona was greatest in energetic effort and Sigala's mother was pre-eminent in faith. The most skilled teacher was Dhammadinna, Patacara was the one who best knew the rules of the discipline and Kisha Gotami established the ascetic practice of wearing coarse robes. Uppalavanna was chief among those with paranormal powers, Sahula was first in clairvoyance and Bhadda Kapilani was best at remembering past lives (Falk 1980: 217). Hence, in the Buddhist canonical sources there are numerous women who had renounced worldly life and reached enlightenment. Of the 71 female monks in the Therigatha, 11 had already reached exceptional stages of advancement in spiritual awareness before becoming ordained, including two, Khema and Sujata, who became fully enlightened even before leaving lay life and reaching the ultimate stage of arahatship (Sharma 1977: 249).

Falk has noted that the stories of the Buddhist lay women are more numerous and often presented in much more positive terms than the stories of the *bhikkhunis* (Falk 1980: 220). Her explanation is that the laity generously provided for the monastics' material needs and laywomen were of vital importance for the *sangha*'s existence. Moreover, laywomen did not constitute a threat to the monastic community since they were considered spiritually inferior to the monks and did not compete with the monks for prestige and influence in the religious community. Further Falk comments that even in stories about outstanding *bhikkhunis*, the focus is often on the deeds that they performed before, not after they had received *bhikkhuni* ordination. She states that it gives the impression that the community was more comfortable with its laywomen than with its *bhikkhunis* and that it probably found the latter's presence an embarrassment (ibid.). Hence the images of women in the Buddhist literature are not unambiguous. However, women in the earliest Buddhist communities seemed to have had prominent and honoured places both as practitioners and teachers. The later history of women in Buddhism is much more mixed. Whereas female patrons and donors remained quite visible, Sponberg notes that the Order of *bhikkhunis* did not appear to have enjoyed the prestige or creativity one might have expected of the successors to the early enlightened *bhikkhunis* (Sponberg 1992: 6–7).

According to the Buddhist doctrine women and men have the same capacity to attain the highest spiritual level, *nibbana*. By so declaring, the Buddha raised the status of women in society. For centuries, the *bhikkhunis* had similar spiritual standing as the male monks, but it is clear that the eight special chief-rules,

garudhamma, (see p. 26), which were the prerequisite to the establishment of
the Order of female monks, subordinated them to the monks.

Sponberg's analysis of the ambiguity expressed towards women in
the early literature identifies four distinct attitudes. He refers to them as
'soteriological inclusiveness', 'institutional androcentrism', 'ascetic misogyny'
and 'soteriological androgyny'. 'Soteriological inclusiveness' confirms that the
female sex is no hindrance to enlightenment, that the path is open to women.
However, inclusiveness does not assert that sex and gender differences do not
exist, but rather that they are soteriologically insignificant (ibid.: 9). 'Institutional
androcentrism' refers to the view that women can pursue a full-time religious
career but only within a regulated institutional structure that preserves male
authority and female subordination (ibid.: 13). 'Ascetic misogyny' is the hostile
abusive attitude toward women, associating women with dangerous sexual
desire and polluting potentials. These views probably originate from pre-
Buddhist traditions (ibid.: 19). Finally 'soteriological androgyny' considers the
goal of Buddhist practice psychologically as a dynamic state of non-dualistic
androgynous integration. The underlying assumption is that gender categories
become irrelevant since all beings, to differing degrees, manifest the full range
of characteristics conventionally identified as gender (ibid.: 24–25).

CELIBACY AND GENDER IDENTITY

According to the Buddhist tradition a person goes through countless rebirths as
both male and female until reaching the level in which gender is transcended. In
Theravada Buddhism, only the lowest levels of birth and rebirth are structured
in gendered terms. Core Buddhist teachings are based on the concepts of
suffering (*dukkha*), non-self (*anatta*), impermanence (*anicca*), and dependent
origination (*paticcasamuppada*). In this framework, the individual has no
ultimately fixed or determinant nature (Sponberg 1992: 10). At the higher
levels of consciousness, there is no male, no female. In the logic of Theravada
Buddhism, we hold false beliefs that there are male and female humans with
separate identities and selves. The concept of 'person' is the conventional truth
of the unenlightened (Collins 1982: 179). *Nibbana*, the permanent extinction
of suffering and the cessation of rebirths, is beyond any consideration of
masculinity and femininity. In order to reach this ultimate goal Buddhism
promotes morals and ethics through *sila* (morality) which is linked to a low
level of consumption and a decrease in materialism, *samadhi* (a peaceful mind
for improving one's behaviour) and *panna* (understanding the nature of things),

and is necessary for perfect development. The best condition for development is the ordained state.

Attachment and clinging are more significant obstacles than self and sexuality in the ideology and practice of Theravada Buddhism. Sex is considered a form of bodily attachment, and sexuality is seen as being an impediment to spiritual progress. In Theravada Buddhism there is a sharp distinction between the ethical expectations placed upon lay people and upon the monastics. Celibacy is mandatory for monks and *mae chii*s; however, lay people are not expected to be sexually abstinent. The vow of celibacy that monks and *mae chii*s take at their ordination involves a general prohibition against all sexual activity (see Chapter 1). In the monks' code of conduct, the *patimokkha,* the most severe grades of sanction, *parajika,* entail expulsion from the order. The first of those four rules that carries this penalty concerns monks who engage in sexual intercourse (Nanamoli 1992: 66).

When a person asks for Buddhist ordination in the Thai *sangha,* sex and gender identity are of crucial importance. Not all men fulfil the conditions necessary for becoming a monk. The candidate must be male and the *kathoey* (transgender males) are not admitted into the *sangha* due to their non-male gender identity. Similarly, women are excluded due to their sex. Further, the candidate must not have a criminal record and not have committed any offence to the Buddhist *sangha* when previously being ordained as a monk (Vajirananavarorasa 1989: 3). Some important features of the ordained person in Thailand are that he collects alms, has Buddhist knowledge, officiates at ceremonies and practises meditation.

Women also go through an ordination ceremony when they leave lay life and become *mae chii*s. Ordinations of monks and novices are often, although not necessarily, elaborate public ceremonies, while *mae chii*s receive their precepts in smaller settings (to be discussed in Chapter 4). The Thai Mae Chiis' Institute has formulated a list of requirements for ordination as a *mae chii,* among them that the candidate must be a woman, not be pregnant or caring for a baby, be in good health, be free from debt and have no addiction to drugs. Moreover, she must not hold a criminal record or be disabled. The process of initiation is for women as well as for men a break with their lay identity. The shaving of the head, a new name and honorific title, the monastic robe, the disciplined living in temples or *samnak chii*s are all markers of their new belonging.

Keyes (1986: 85–86) asserts that after a male has been ordained as novice or a monk he assumes a new gender identity, one that is neither male nor female. Further, he declares that the *sangha* gender identity is not based on biological sexual attributes, nor is it a consequence of a physical mutilation. Instead, it is acquired through the monastic discipline that makes it possible to transcend sexuality. Keyes states that this discipline is applicable only to males in the Theravada tradition, which reflects a religious perspective that views maleness and femaleness very differently. Further he declares that 'whatever significance female renunciation may have had at the time when an order of *bhikkhuni* existed in India or Sri Lanka (but never in Southeast Asia), no Northern Thai woman nor any other woman in the Theravadin societies of Southeast Asia can alter her gender identity by ordination' (ibid.: 86). It is true that no *bhikkhuni sangha* was ever established in Southeast Asia except in Burma (see Barnes 1996: 271). However, during the centuries when the *sangha* was open for women, I presume that the *sangha* gender was applicable also to women who became ordained and lived monastic lives. I have found that contemporary Thai women who become ordained, even though their ordination is not recognised by the authorities, assume an identity based on their celibate and disciplined monastic lifestyle and recognised and attributed by lay people.

A SYSTEM OF THREE SEXES AND THE IDEAL OF NO SEX

Thailand has a rich indigenous history of complex patterns of sexuality and gender. The word used to differentiate sexed or gendered being is *phet*. According to Peter Jackson there have traditionally been three categories of *phet* in Thailand, masculine men, feminine women and the *kathoeys*. The term *kathoey* may be derived from a pre-Ankorian Khmer verb which meant 'to be other/different' (Jackson 1995: 193–194). This notion of three human sexes appears to have remained prevalent in Thailand up until this century. The notion is reflected in the early twentieth-century Thai colloquial expression for *kathoey* as the third sex, *phet thii saam*. Sinnott argues that this is a relatively new term and was probably introduced through Western sexology (Sinnott 2004: 6). Some contemporary emic Thai accounts describe *kathoey* in terms of Thai cultural conceptions which continue to describe them as a distinctive sex, who occupy a middle ground between male/masculine and female/feminine (Jackson 1995: 194). The contemporary *kathoey* is a transgender male, but is said to historically have been a possibility for both men and women and to have existed alongside normative masculine and feminine identities (Jackson and Cook 1999: 3–4; Jackson and Sullivan 1999: 4–6).

Rosalind Morris (1994) describes two radically different sex/gender models in Thai society; the traditional model described above with a trinity of three sexes and a more recent order of four sexualities that is structured around Western notions of binary genders. Jackson (Jackson and Sullivan 1999: 5; Jackson and Cook 1999: 233) has stated that he is sceptical about Morris's suggestion that the new Thai identities reflect the emergence of a new discourse of sexuality. He argues that indigenous discourses have resisted the formation of a domain of sexuality distinct from gender. He says: 'All Thai discourses continue to be framed in terms of the indigenous category of *phet,* a notion that incorporates sexual difference (male vs. female), gender difference (masculine vs. feminine) and sexuality (heterosexual vs. homosexual) within a single discursive regime' (Jackson and Sullivan 1999: 5). Further, Jackson states that Thai discourses have not borrowed, the Western 'gay'/'straight' binary. The term 'gay' has been borrowed but it has been reinscribed within a gender discourse beside 'man', *kathoey* and 'woman', rather than constructed in opposition to a category of heterosexuality (ibid.). Sinnott, who has studied female same-sex relationships in Thailand, follows Jackson and convincingly argues that the borrowed terms *thôôm* and *dii,* for female homosexuals, are incorporated into the Thai discourse and their identities are hybridizations of local gendered categories (Sinnott 2004: 27).

The Thai system of three has, according to Morris, the capacity to implicitly escape from biological essentialism and may even shore up the absolutist claims for genetic and morphological duality. The third term acts as an aporia in the conceptual framework. Morris further points out that it is not *kinds* of sexual identities but a system of sexual and gendered identities (Morris 1994: 26). She refers to historical texts and finds support for the assumption that Thai sexual and gendered identities are incompatible with Western binary models, explaining that because of the radically different notions of body and personhood that define Thai and Western sex/gender systems. In contemporary Western societies *kathoey*s would encompass both transsexuals and transvestites. They are born as men and they remake themselves in the image of women (ibid.: 23). The number of translations usually offered for *kathoey* really reflects a scarcity of concepts for the biologically irreducible third category implied here.

In order to trace the cosmological origin of the system of three sexes, Rosalind Morris refers to some origin legends. She draws on examples from Northern and Northeastern Thailand. The legends tell about the universe emerging from non-being through the intermingling of cold and hot air, these being dimensions of nothingness as well as the principles of inactivity and activity, respectively. Shortly thereafter, a female being emerges from the earth. Later, a male being is born of fire. Together, they populate the world, and from the four elements – earth, fire, water, and wind – they conjure 'three sexes': female, hermaphrodite, and male (Morris 1994: 20). Although it emerges from a context of a binary model, the sexual trinity is central and fundamental to the origin of humanity. Humanity is correlated with a triadic logic and Morris says that the interpretation of the sexual trinity is problematic, the more so because the text provides no description of the various sexes. The intersexed person fades in and out of the narrative, coupling with both the female and the male, and is referred to as both father and mother by the children of their unions. The binarity is thus absent and in that text, the intersexed does not undermine oppositions between male and female but constitutes the third point in the triad in which there can be no single antithesis. Nor can the intersexed be seen as a secondary identity. Rather, it possesses the same ontological status as the male and female characters: he/she is substantial, possesses an identity and is a self-same self. Tannenbaum (1999) has raised objections to Morris's uses of anecdotal and textual evidence and her failure to provide any indication for the relevance of texts to everyday gender constructions. Sinnott argues that the binary of Thai/Western as a descriptive categorization of sexual and gender forms fails to account for these complex interactions between local understandings of sex and gender, and transformations brought about by intense interaction with Western or global forces. Therefore she applies the concept of *hybridity* to examine the processes of how local gendered categories blend and interact with other cultural discourses (Sinnott 2004: 27–28, 35).

Kathoeys, who are the most visible signifiers of the tripartite system, are a very real part of the contemporary social landscape in Thailand. Today the *kathoey* is construed in a male idiom, where the tripartite system permits maleness in two modes, as masculinity and femininity. The *kathoey* is thus not only a man with a female wrapping; a *kathoey* is a *kathoey* with or without makeup. Men, women, and *kathoeys* all agree that this potential is preordained from birth (Morris 1994: 24). The fact that *kathoeys* today are a class of males is underscored by the fact that the so-called third sex, *phet thii saam*, or *kathoey*, is not used for women who dress and behave like men. They are called *thôôm*, a word derived from the English word 'tomboy', which would indicate that this is a recent gender category. *Thôôm* or tomboy denotes a masculine acting lesbian, while *dii* from 'lady' denotes a feminine lesbian. Sinnott explains that *thôôms* and *diis* are new in that there were no such categories exactly like them in the past, although the basic components, female masculinity and recognised forms of female homosexuality, existed (Sinnott 2004: 39).

I met several *thôôm*s and *dii*s at the place where I lived in Bangkok. Some of them worked for the Association for the Promotion of the Status of Women and others stayed at the Emergency Home. However, it was unusual for the *thôôm*s to display their *thôôm* identity at a *samnak chii*.

Lay women frequently came to the *samnak chii* and received *chii phraam* ordination. They commonly stayed for a couple of days or weeks and spent their time meditating and studying Buddhism. One morning in the dining hall there was a *chii phraam* who differed from the other temporary female ascetics at the *samnak chii*. She did not wear the *chii phraams'* dress, but instead wore a white shirt and white long trousers. Her hair was cut short and I noticed when I sat down beside her that she wore quite a large wristwatch. I did not have a chance to speak with her that morning since we always ate in silence and directly after breakfast I left for Bangkok. A *mae chii* from Ratburi Samnak Chii and I had planned to go on a four-day study trip to Trat province together with a group of *mae chii*s and monks whom we were to meet in the capital. On the bus I asked the *mae chii* that I travelled with if she knew the new *chii phraam* who sat at my table that morning. She answered that other *mae chii*s had told her that she had once been a *mae chii*. I asked about her dress and my companion told me that she was a *thôôm*. As we drew onto the Petchakasem Road to Bangkok, we continued talking about same-sex relationships and Buddhist ordination. The *mae chii* said that it was no problem to let *thôôm*s become ordained as *chii phraam*s because they stayed at the *samnak chii* only for a short time. To become a *mae chii*, she said, was more difficult. She only remembered one *thôôm* who had received *mae chii* ordination. She had been at Ratburi Samnak Chii when my companion first arrived there and the woman had been ordained *kae bun* (ordination in order to fulfil a vow). She said that the *mae chii* had been exactly like a man. But she hastened to say that it was no problem having her at the *samnak chii* and she was there for a limited period of a couple of months. I asked if she knew any *kathoey* who had been ordained. She told that there were two *kathoey*s from her home village who had gone to Chiang Mai and received monks' ordination at a temple there. She explained that they could not reveal that they were *kathoey*s, because in that case the *sangha* would not have accepted them.

Nancy Falk suggests that Buddhism recognises differences between male and female, as with other varieties of human difference, as products of humans' essentially fallen state and is in accordance with the workings of *kamma*. As a person works toward spiritual perfection the consequences of falling, including sexual differentiation, tend to drop away. This means essentially that the process of spiritual development, in which the renunciants' vocation represents a relatively advanced step, tends to nullify sexual identification and limitations. This ideal of convergence of the sexes is reflected in the ordained persons' identical clothes, as well as in their virtually identical spiritual paths and disciplines (Falk 1980: 220–221).

Buddhist texts imply that sex is irrelevant for reaching Buddhahood. Those who grasp the teaching of Emptiness understand that sex difference is illusory. In several sutras in the Mahayana tradition there are narratives of females changing their bodies into male ones in order to prove that a woman can become a Buddha (Barnes 1987: 119–121). For example, there is a dialogue between a monk and a female *bodhisattva* in one of the sutras. The monk asks the *bodhisattva* why she has not changed her sex and she answers that there are no innate characteristics of the female sex. To make her point she changes the monk into a female and herself into a male. Generally, high-stage *bodhisattva*s and Buddhas are portrayed as male or as androgynous (Havnevik 1990: 30). The change of sex is itself only illusion and there is no attaining enlightenment as a woman or a man, merely a mode of being that is genderless (Barnes 1987: 120). Further, the Mahayana sutras demonstrate dramatically that a man who clings to his maleness is not an enlightened being, and the woman who does not worry about changing her sex is genuinely enlightened (ibid.: 121).

Diana Paul (1985) claims that female deities entered the Mahayana pantheon at the end of the fourth century. The celestial Bodhisattva Avalokitesvara appeared as the female Kuan-Yin in China. Kuan-Yin was portrayed as a white-clad woman who helped women in childbirth and sailors at sea. Kuan-Yin was introduced to China at the same time as Tantrism, in around 600–700. Paul stresses that as late as the eighth century, Kuan-Yin male images were also present in China. Therefore, Kuan-Yin is to be perceived as asexual or androgynous, rather than purely female (Paul 1985: 249–252, 285).

GENDER PERFORMATIVITY

I would now like to bring in the concept of performativity (Butler 1999: 171–180), which will facilitate an understanding of how *mae chiis'* gender identity is empowered by their practice. The theory of performativity offers the possibility of reworking gender and shifting its meanings through the repetition of performance. Gender performativity is about doing, but also about an individual's relation to gender, sexuality, sex and the body through the symbolic. Gender performativity is concerned both with how one enacts a gender within a specific set of regulatory practices and of the disjunction between the exclusive categories of the sex/gender discourses and the actuality of ambiguity and multiplicity in the way gender is enacted and subjectivities are formed.

The human body is the site where subjects are constructed, it marks the intersection of the social and symbolic. Further, the boundary between sex and gender has proven unstable and sex classification is not enough to determine gender categorisation, which has been shown by the work on third sex and transsexuals. Rosalind Morris states that the Thai sex/gender system is a system in which bodies exist less as the locus and origin of consciousness than as an iconic ground or symbolic potential, which is realised through everyday practices (Morris 1994: 25). For example, *kathoeys* have developed into signifying men who appropriate female form without becoming women and without ceasing to be men. The categories *thôôm* and *dii* have developed through intense cultural interaction and exchange and are simultaneously unquestionably Thai (Sinnott 2004: 39).

By seeing gender as a process of becoming and acquiring an identity, we focus on the 'doing' of gender rather than the 'being'. In Chapter 5 I shall describe how the *mae chiis*' identity is constituted through their daily practices. In the following chapters, I shall continue to explore how their position and identity evolve. Religious practices signifying that a person belongs to the religious realm (*lokuttara*) were previously carried out by monks in Thailand. Therefore, *mae chiis* did not, for example, walk on alms rounds in the mornings, nor commonly studied Buddhist philosophy or officiated at ceremonies since these are indicators of renunciants who belong to the non-lay realm. A *lokuttara* person is dependent on the members of the *lokiya* (lay realm) for material support. The assembly of monks provides a field of religious merit for secular people. They are dependent on one another, and this complementarity provides the basis for Buddhism in Thailand. Since most of the *mae chiis* live at temples where they are not entitled to perform duties that are restricted to monks, it is still quite unusual that they carry out monks' assignments. However, in areas where self-governed *samnak chiis* are situated, *mae chiis* are gaining increasing acceptance by and support from the laity. The following chapters examine their agency and the prerequisites required for contemporary *mae chiis* to become fields of merit for lay people.

NOTES

1   *Bhiksuni* is Sanskrit and used in the Mahayana tradition; *Bhikkhuni* is Pali and used in the Theravada tradition.

2   *Patimokkha* (Pali): Monks' disciplinary code of 227 precepts.

3   These numbers are not to be taken litterally, but simply as meaning 'over a long time'. The story is found in many places in Buddhist literature, for example in Cullavagga 10. 1–3.

4   The *vinaya-pitaka* is the first of the three *pitaka*s or 'baskets' of scriptures. The *vinaya-pitaka* is the 'discipline' text, i.e. its contents are concerned principally with rules governing the life of the Buddha and Sangha – male and female monks (Ling 1981: 194).

5   *Karma* (Sanskrit) *kamma* (Pali). The Buddhist concept of *kamma* means moral or immoral actions and it is important to point out that it never means the result of action (Nyantiloka 1972: 130). However, the popular understanding of *kamma* does not follow the ideal understanding of the concept.

6   Siddhattha Gotama, the historical Buddha, is by the Theravadin reckoned to have lived between 560 and 480 BCE. Mahayana maintains that his dates were 460–380 BCE. Both traditions agree that he lived for 80 years (Murcott 1991: 3).

CHAPTER THREE

Themes of Going Forth

Renouncing lay life is, for most Thai women, not easily achieved. The ideal Thai woman is a dutiful daughter who is expected to marry and become a caring wife and a self-sacrificing mother. Despite the many difficulties met on the way towards an ordained life, many Thai women wish to become *mae chii*s. Since young women commonly have to struggle for the opportunity to become ordained, their spiritual conviction is usually strong and although some of them describe suffering and misfortune in their lives, their spiritual motives of being ordained should not be downplayed. Young, healthy, unmarried women who want to become *mae chii*s generally have to convince their parents to give their permission. Most of the interviewed *mae chii*s, who had become ordained at a young age, had experienced resistance from their families. They said that their parents would have preferred them to get married instead of ordaining. Ordination is a normal part of Thai men's life since a man is considered to gain maturity through ordination and a son's ordination is believed to transfer merit to the parents and this is of particular value to the mother. Consequently, men's ordination is highly prized, whereas women who leave the lay life deviate from Thai cultural values, which hold that daughters should care for their parents in all ways possible. Women who become *mae chii*s abandon their families and their choice is felt as a loss by some parents.

Gavin Jones (1997) reports that dramatic changes in non-marriage patterns have taken place in Southeast and East Asia. The rates of non-marriage in some of the large cities of the region are among the highest in the world (ibid.: 113). Today, more and more middle-class Thai women choose to stay single and if a woman can acquire social status on her own, marriage is no longer as important as it used to be. Better education and financial opportunities have made it possible for women in Thailand to view marriage as one possible choice in their lives and not an absolute goal. It is possible for well-educated *mae chii*s or those with financial assets to live a single life and most *mae chii*s that I interviewed had not become ordained in order to escape from marriage. They said that they could have lived a single life even if they had not become ordained.

The idea that lay life entails difficulties, suffering and negative bonds to life through marriage and child-rearing is a major theme in *mae chiis'* stories about their reasons for ordaining. This theme seems to cut across socio-economic circumstances. The lay life is commonly depicted by the *mae chiis* as boring. Poverty, sickness vows, and lack of access to education are popular reasons cited by lay people for why some women choose to become *mae chiis*. These motives could be part of both women's and men's decision to become ordained, but they are seldom the principal reasons. They are too reductionist and do not correspond with the reasons that women themselves proffer for their choice. Being poor is actually a hindrance for ordination since women commonly must pay for electricity, water and personal expenses at the temple; sickness is a disqualifying factor for ordination. The ordained life as a *mae chii* is arduous and it would be very difficult to put up with the demanding life if *mae chiis* were not highly motivated. However, poverty and sickness are by some *mae chiis* interpreted as 'lack of merit' and are in that sense a driving force for some women to become a *mae chii* or a *chii phraam* with the object of improving their *kammic* status. In such cases they usually save up before ordination or find a sponsor, e.g. among relatives. Those who have been ill receive ordination when they have recovered from their sicknesses.

Many of the *mae chiis* who had been ordained at a young age stated that they had previously longed to become *mae chiis* and live a spiritual life. Several of them declared that they had wanted to become ordained as soon as they realised that it was possible for women to live a religious life. Lay life did not attract these women and they usually expressed an absolute lack of interest in getting married. Prior to their ordinations, these young women had often developed a deep faith in Buddhism through listening to Buddhist radio programmes, reading Buddhist books and listening to monks at the temples.

In order to reflect the variety of reasons of seeking a religious life and to look at the *mae chiis'* different backgrounds, I have chosen to relate a number of their stories. Some of these narratives seemingly correspond with the stereotypical picture of why Thai women become *mae chiis*, while others differ radically from the prejudiced views of why women become ordained. Most of the *mae chiis* who appear in this chapter have been in the ordained state for many years and their notions and narratives are of course influenced by their religious lives. Their interpretations may have changed over the years and become woven into the *mae chiis'* discourse concerning why women seek ordination. However, my intention has been to present *mae chiis'* personal reasons for renouncing the world. I have also met many of their relatives and friends who confirmed their narratives.

REALISING SUFFERING

The principal reasons for seeking ordination were to realise the basic Buddhist truths about suffering (*dukkha*), and to gain the opportunity to attain enlightenment (*nibbana*) through ordained practice. My informants, Mae chii Lek and Mae chii Noy both stated that their main reason for becoming ordained was that the ordained life would provide a way to liberation.

Mae chi Lek became ordained when she was 21, 27 years prior to my meeting with her in 1997. Her life before ordination could be considered as poor and unfortunate a perfect example of the widespread, stereotyped notion of a destitute. However, she looked upon her life as quite ordinary, and considered her childhood happy. The events important for her decision to live an ordained life had to do with encountering different forms of suffering. Mae chi Lek was born in the Northeastern Thailand, in a village close to the Cambodian border. Her mother died when she was born and she was adopted by a foster family when she was three months old. Her family lived under the same circumstances as other families in the village. Like most of the girls, she studied only up to primary school level. After finishing the four years of compulsory education she worked in the fields, herded buffaloes and helped out with various chores at home.

Mae chii Lek considered some events and experiences in her childhood to have had particular importance for her interest in the spiritual side of life. She related a period when she was 13 and had gone with her natal brother and her foster brother to work in the fields in Saraburi province. There is a famous Buddha's footprint in Phra Buddhabat that was close to where they were working. Every half moon there was a pilgrimage festival. Many crippled people went there to play music and seek opportunities to acquire some money. There were also many beggars. Mae chii Lek said that she felt sad when she saw all the suffering people. She and her friend, who was a few years older and worked at the same place, visited the festival every evening. She said that there were so many things to see. There were music, movies, exhibitions and plenty of things to buy. One day when they were at home somebody called her friend's name and said that there had been a car accident on the road. It was a young boy Mae chii Lek's age who had died. She said that the sight of the dead body made a deep impression on her. The boy had been travelling in a tricycle-taxi (*saamlôô*) when a car hit him. He was already dead when Mae chii Lek and her friend saw him lying on the road. His stomach was torn up and they saw his intestines. His skull was cracked and they could also see his brain. Mae chii Lek said: 'I felt very afraid, very afraid. My friend and I went to the festival every day. We walked to the festival and we used to pass in front of cars and buses and we usually went home by *saamlôô*. I thought that it could have been me lying there dead on the road.'

The Buddha's footprint was located in the middle of the ordination hall of the temple and people went there to pay respect to the footprint and to ring the bell. Mae chii Lek also bowed and showed respect to the footprint and rang the bell when she visited the temple. She recalled that during that time she thought that she had 'thick sin' (*baap naa*).[1] She had met some people whom she called 'Thai people'; they came from Central Thailand, and had said that her mother had died because of her and that she therefore had 'thick sin'. She said:

> In my village we only spoke the Khmer language. People never said I had 'thick sin'; on the contrary they said I had merit [*mii bun*]. They said that I was a meritorious person. They said I had merit because I could survive despite my mother's death. They also said I had survived because my real father was richer than my foster family, and therefore they did not mind bringing me up. If I had been born in a poor family I would probably have died. In my village they never blamed me for my mother's death.

Mae chii Lek was concerned about her 'status of merit' and she reflected upon her earlier disobedient behaviour and started to act in ways that would hopefully give her merit. She said that she wanted to repay her mother and father because she was indebted to them. When she came back to her village her foster mother noticed the change in her and was very pleased that she had become so gentle and helpful.

Mae chii Lek also referred to events that happened in her village as important for awakening her interest in developing her mind. One day when we were sitting and talking in her room she said: 'Today I shall tell you why I started to meditate. It was because of a ghost.' She recounted that she was about 15 years old and she had been at home almost a year when the rainy season came with unusually heavy rains. The area became flooded and the men had to build a temporary bridge over the river. On one occasion they were transporting seedlings of rice on a cart, which was pulled by a bull. The current was very strong and several people helped to push the cart. A young woman, seven or eight months' pregnant, was also helping transport the seedlings. When they were at the middle of the bridge, the bridge broke down, and the pregnant woman fell into the water. The current carried her away and the villagers could not find her. The whole village searched without finding her body. Mae chii Lek remembered that the villagers were terrified because some people reported seeing the dead woman's naked ghost. Finally a monk, who was skilled in meditation, was invited to the village. He told them where to look and the woman's body was found. The monk later said that she had drowned in the river because she had poisoned a lot of fish in a previous lifetime. Her body was brought back to the village. They had a ceremony and cremated her. The funeral was conducted in the conventional manner. Mae chii Lek said: 'Everyone came to the funeral and showed their respect. However, we did something wrong. She had died a violent death and was not in peace.'

After the funeral several unexpected deaths took place in the village. One man who had an extramarital affair was shot and beaten to death by the woman's husband. Mae chii Lek herded buffaloes close to the place where the killing took place. She said that she heard the man scream and the killing made her terribly afraid. The murdered man's body was also cremated according to the village custom. Mae chii Lek said that it was very difficult to cremate him and the villagers told her that it was always difficult to cremate a person who had much 'sin' (*baap*). However, the deaths did not stop: shortly afterwards two young boys died. One drowned in a pool and the other one in the river. Mae chii Lek's close friend's mother also died unexpectedly. She had given birth to a baby, and when the baby was one month old, Mae chii Lek said the ghost passed behind her friend's mother. She became severely ill and died soon afterwards. Then there was a young boy who went missing. The villagers searched for him and finally found him drowned in a well.

Mae chii Lek said that the whole village was terrified by all the deaths. They knew that they had to do something, but they did not know what they could do to prevent the ghost from haunting. Finally, they invited seven monks to the village. They built several shrines and the monks surrounded the village with thread. The monks stayed for seven days and chanted every morning and evening and walked around the village and sprinkled water. They conducted ceremonies and performed the daily chanting. After that the deaths ceased. However, her friend who had lost her mother was inconsolable. She cried constantly. Mae chii Lek said that everybody felt pity for her. At her mother's funeral there was a person who used to be a monk and had later become a lay meditation teacher. He volunteered to teach her to meditate. Later, Mae chii Lek's friend told her that she had seen her mother in her mind when she meditated. Her friend had called her mother *'mae, mae'*, but her mother was not interested in her, and did not even look at her. Mae chii Lek said that after her friend had 'met her mother' she could 'let it go' and her friend was not that sad anymore. She said that her friend became calm and she looked very bright after she had begun meditating. Mae chii Lek was impressed by her appearance and decided to start practising meditation as well. She talked with her friend's meditation teacher and he suggested that she should go to the temple and ask for meditation instruction from the monks, which she did.

Mae chii Noy is 20 years younger than Mae chii Lek. They are both from Isaan, the Northeastern part of Thailand, but from different provinces. When Mae chii Noy was a child she used to go to the temple. She liked to be there, helping out with different chores and listening to the monks giving talks about the Buddha, his former lives, and about what life is all about. The temple was not far away from her home and she went there almost every day. She said that it was *rôôn*, ('hot') at home and sometimes she felt that she could not stand being there, and she even went to sleep in the temple's *saalaa*.[2] Mae chii Noy said that she did not understand why they had to suffer so much. When she asked her mother, she used to answer that suffering is *thammadaa* (common, normal), that suffering is part of life, but Mae chii Noy said when she was a child she could not understand what her mother meant.

Mae chii Noy related much of the suffering that she experienced as a child to her family's difficult situation. Her father had left them when she was four. Her mother had been married once before and Mae chii Noy had three older siblings. Their father had died and her mother got remarried to Mae chii Noy's father. Mae chii Noy looked sad when she told that her father had three stepchildren and three children of his own when he left them to live with another woman, a second wife (*mia nôôy*). Mae chii Noy's family did not hear from him for many years. He did not send any money or letters. Her mother had a very hard time supporting and taking care of her six children. One day he came back without warning. He just appeared outside their house where Mae chii Noy and her younger brother were playing. They did not recognise their father and ran away, hiding from what they thought was a stranger. Mae chii Noy said that her father cried when they ran away from him. He was hurt that they had forgotten that he was their father.

Her father moved in with them again and a year later Mae chii Noy had a new sister. She said that she watched her mother giving birth and she thought that it was terrible. The delivery took place in the kitchen area. She saw her mother squat on a low table, holding onto a towel that hung from a roof beam and she heard her mother crying and crying. After the baby was born she said there was blood everywhere. The experience frightened her greatly. She said: 'Hearing my mother having so much pain was as if I had been cut by a knife. It was terrible.' Later when her sister gave birth, she could not bear to stay at home and hear her screaming. She found it too painful and she went to the temple and stayed there. Mae chii Noy said that when she was a child she often pondered over why women had to give birth while men did not. She said that she thought that it was *naakliat* (ugly, despicable). She decided early that she did not want to give birth and have a family and she did not want to live a lay life which consisted only of problems and suffering. This was in sharp contrast with the calm and peaceful life in the temple. She strove to achieve a peaceful life like that.

When Mae chii Noy's father moved in to live with them he promised that he would not leave with another woman again. If he left it would be to become a monk. The family stayed together for a couple of years, but it did not work out. With permission from his wife, he received ordination as a monk. Before he left the house, Mae chii Noy heard him accusing her mother of things that she knew were not true. Mae chii Noy said that after what she had seen, she felt that most men seemed to escape responsibility if they could. When her father left home, she said that she did not understand why he should abandon them again. She thought that he did not like them anymore. She said: 'I was so disappointed in him and I wanted to become ordained to see what he had chosen over us. But that was just a thought. I did not know then that it was possible for women to become ordained. I had never seen a *mae chii*.'

THE WAY TO FREEDOM

To be free (*isara*) and not restricted by being locked up in a marriage were motives that *mae chii*s offered for receiving ordination. They saw marriage as a hindrance to achieving the ultimate goal and they often referred to experiences of lay life as empty and boring.

Mae chii Noy said that she wanted a peaceful life, without all the troubles of married life. She had seen her mother, her sisters and other women struggle alone with raising children, always short of money. She said that she never dreamt of having a family of her own and ending up with a life like that of her mother's. She said, too, that she was bored with just eating, working, sleeping, eating, working, sleeping. When Mae chii Noy's father left for the monkhood, she had completed primary school and wanted to continue at secondary school, but her mother could not afford it. Instead she had to both work and take care of her siblings. She helped her mother to run a grocery store and for four years she also sold fried food from a vehicle at different places in the village. When she was about 15, her responsibilities for her family grew because her older siblings had established their own families, leaving her to care for the younger ones. Later she also took care of her older siblings' two children.

Thai girls are taught that virginity is of crucial importance and for 'good' Thai women, monogamy is the only acceptable practice. Mae chii Noy said that she was impressed by the Buddhist teaching that taught that if one wants to be free from defilement one needs to live in celibacy. Further, she stated that it is only through celibacy that one can gain freedom from birth, old age, sickness and death. There is no restriction for women who have been married to receive ordination as *mae chii*s. However most *mae chii*s that I interviewed expressed the importance of virginity (that was the same as never been married). Virgin *mae chii*s treasured the fact that their bodies were intact and their lack of experience of married life seemed to give them an informal higher status. They stated that they wanted to be *borisut* (clean, innocent) and to live a 'clean life'. When a longstanding *mae chii* was about to go abroad to study, she told me that she was not concerned about the studies, language difficulties or things like that. She worried about her virginity and she was afraid of being raped.

From an early age, Mae chii Noy kept away from any contact with males. When her schoolmates talked about marrying and having boyfriends Mae chii Noy had other aspirations for life and thought that her friends would not understand if she told them and she was therefore silent. She did not look at boys, and in order not to encourage young men to speak with her she avoided answering those who tried to chat with her. There were some young men who were interested in marrying her, but she told her mother that she would run away if her mother tried to make her marry.

Mae chii Noy turned her attention towards the temple. She had learnt to meditate in the temple and she practised walking meditation early every morning. When she was 15, she took up the practice of wearing white and observing the eight precepts, first on holy days and later permanently. The eight precepts (see pp. XX) contain the five lay precepts, which are to abstain from killing, stealing, sexual misconduct, lying and intoxicants, together with being celibate, taking no meal after noon, not beautifying oneself, not listening to music and not sleeping on thick mattresses. Mae chii Noy followed an even stricter regime of eating only once a day. She also made a shrine at home where she led evening chanting with her family and friends. Also, on the Buddhist holy day (*wan phra*) people came to their house and Mae chii Noy led the chanting. She said that her brothers and other people asked her teasingly why she did not seek ordination at a temple since she was not interested in getting married. Seeking ordination was what she wished to do and when she was 17, she told her mother that she wanted to become ordained. Although her mother was a devout Buddhist, she cried initially and said that she wanted her to stay at home and help her instead. At the same time she understood her desire and finally gave her consent.

Mae chii Lek too was more interested in seeking harmony in the temple than getting married. She did not, however, express the same aversion for lay life as Mae chii Noy did, but she said that she had always been more interested in developing spiritually than living a lay life. She told that there had been a young man who had proposed to her when she was about 18 years old. He was a couple of years older than she was, and was a monk at the temple where she went every day to donate food. Mae chii Lek was not aware of his affection until he left the monkhood and his relatives came and asked Mae chii Lek's mother for permission for him to marry her. At first, her mother agreed to the proposition, but when she understood that her daughter was terrified she left the decision to Mae chii Lek herself. Mae chii Lek said: 'At first I was not fond of him, and I certainly did not like him following me. However, gradually my mind became weak and I felt that I liked him.' But she was not sure if she wanted to get married. She broke up with him when she had to go to another province and take care of her mother who had fallen ill there. The young man went back to the temple and received ordination again. When she returned to the village, he left the monkhood. He was persistent and once again he came to her house and proposed to her. Mae chii Lek said: 'I did not marry him because I was not certain about marriage. Always when I thought about being married my mind became troubled.' Later, when she received *mae chii* ordination, he was ordained for a third time. He started to study and went to high school. When he had finished his education, he left the monkhood and took a job with Bangkok Bank. He married and had three children. Mae chii Lek said with a smile: 'If we had married when he proposed to me, we would certainly have been farmers. He would not have had the possibility to study. So, because of me he has a good life now. He is rich.'

GLIMPSES OF TRANQUILLITY

In Thailand, the practice of meditation is considered appropriate for *mae chii*s and the temples offer meditation instruction to both the laity and the clergy.

Meditation constitutes a lay-oriented and a less prestigious activity. Further, the practice of meditation is seen as a personal vocation necessary for gaining Buddhist insights but divorced from the knowledge achieved through books. It is considered easier to practise meditation than to study Buddhism (*dhamma*) through books, and the latter is therefore regarded as suitable for monks.

Many *mae chii*s told me that they had become inspired to meditate and live a pure life in celibacy by reading and listening to famous monks' teachings. They felt that these teachings transcended gender differences, and they were therefore encouraged to seek ordination in spite of the fact that they were women. Mae chii Noy said that she was about 10 or 11 years old when she saw a *mae chii* for the first time. It was in her village. The *mae chii* got off the bus. Mae chii Noy did not speak with her, but she said that she became extremely happy when she saw her in her white dress because she understood it was possible for women to become ordained. She was 16 when she went to a temple together with her mother to receive lay ordination for one week. They received ordination as what is today commonly called *chii phraam,* a form of temporary ordination that does not include shaving the head. Mae chii Noy related that during those seven days that she spent in the temple, she felt real happiness for the first time. She said she had wanted her heart to be cool (*jen*) because caring for children made her heart unpleasantly hot (*rôôn*). At the temple, she found peace and became cool. The place where they stayed was a quiet and serious meditation temple. She explained that at temples, the clergy carry out similar tasks to those that people do outside the temple, but they do these differently, mindfully. Monks and *mae chii*s train their minds while working. Before she became ordained, she had listened to sermons about the way to be free from suffering, but she had been in doubt as to whether it was true or not. She said that the seven days at the temple confirmed that this was the way and she became confident that the practice would free her from suffering.

Life at temples and *samnak chii*s is highly determined and repetitive. Following the training rules enables monks and *mae chii*s to concentrate on developing their consciousness. The objective is to discover the three fundamental features of life: suffering, impermanence, and egolessness (*dukkha, anicca* and *anatta*). Practising, working, walking, eating, standing, etc. are done in silence and very slowly in order to develop mindfulness. As Mae chii Noy noted above, life in the temple is not a suspension of everyday life; it is to go deeper into it, to reveal the conditions of human existence – 'everyday life is heightened'. The practitioners try to understand and extinguish suffering, and accept impermanence and egolessness as traits of human life.

PARENTS' REACTIONS TO DAUGHTERS' ORDINATION

In the temple, Mae chii Noy learned to be much calmer and when she returned home she felt good. She said that her suffering was reduced; it had left her heart and also her body. Something had changed. She thought that if she had good merit (*mii bun*), that if she was virtuous, she would probably be granted the chance to become ordained again. She continued to work hard, and after some time she started to feel 'hot' as before. The coolness did not last, and she was not content. She said that she went to temples and donated some money and that satisfied her sometimes. She talked with her mother about her wish to become ordained. Her mother cried and said that she would be alone with all the work if she left. But Mae chii Noy said she could not live there any more. Her mother told her that it was possible to reach *niphaan* directly (*trong*) if a person did enough good deeds.[3] Mae chii Noy said she was not interested in that. She had listened to the monks and they said that it was necessary to exterminate *kilet* (moral defilement) first.[4] Finally her mother gave her permission and she went to visit her father at the temple for his permission and advice.

Mae chii Lek, too, had a close relative who was a monk and supported her *mae chii* ordination. Her elder brother had been a monk since he was young and Mae chii Lek used to tell her mother that if her brother would come and fetch her elder sister for ordination, Mae chii Lek would go with them. Mae chii Lek wanted to become a *mae chii,* but when she asked her mother's permission, she answered: 'Then you have to cut yourself into two parts: one part for me and one part for your brother.' Her mother did not give her consent. Mae chii Lek felt that it was useless trying to persuade her.

Mae chii Lek said that performing good deeds and creating religious merit was most important for her. She had shaved her head one time before she received ordination. She was in her early teens when she took a vow that consisted of shaving. She did this privately and did not receive *mae chii* ordination at the temple. It was fulfilment of the vow that she had made to the Buddha and she said she had felt shy having a shaved head but that she had had to do it because she had vowed to.[5]

Mae chii Lek was 21 when she decided to go to Bangkok to find a job. At that time, her elder brother was a monk at a temple in Bangkok. When he learnt that his sister was looking for a job in Bangkok, he volunteered to introduce her to what he said was 'the best work you could get'. He knew that she used to be a keen meditator and he brought her to a temple with a large *mae chii* section in order to seek ordination as a *mae chii.* That was not the kind of work she had had in mind when she went to Bangkok. However, she appreciated meditation and she decided to follow her brother's suggestion and became a *mae chii*. She did not ask for her mother's permission. Mae chii Lek was not ordained at the same temple as her brother, but he had arranged for a longstanding *mae chii* to be his sister's guardian.

Some of the *mae chii*s who appear in this chapter have foster backgrounds. Foster children in Thailand are not reported as being treated badly by their foster parents. The *mae chii*s who had been fostered did not complain or say that their foster parents had mistreated them. They told me that the fact that they had lost their parents had had an impact on how they at times had interpreted their lives. One said that she did not feel the same obligations to her foster parents as she would have felt to her biological parents. Those *mae chii*s said that when they were young they had thought about their *kamm*ic status and wondered whether being without parents was a sign of a non-meritorious state. However, it had not been easier for foster children to get their foster parents' consent for ordination, and some foster parents viewed their foster daughter's ordination as a failure personal as parents.

Many of the *mae chii*s that I have met reported that their parents had only reluctantly given their consent for the ordination. There are also *mae chii*s whose parents did not approve of their daughters' ordination. *Mae chii*s find many different strategies for dealing with their families' rejections. Mae chii Maalii said she had a strong desire to live a spiritual life. She was 25 years old when I met her and she lived in a *samnak chii* in Isaan. Her parents had not given their consent to her ordination and she told me how she had accomplished her wish to become a *mae chii* despite her family's refusal. Mae chii Maalii had become ordained in Chiang Mai province in the Northern part of Thailand when she was 17 years old (1990) and had been a *mae chii* for eight years when I met her. Before ordination, she lived with her parents and younger brother in a province in Isaan. She said she began reading Buddhist books because she wanted to understand *dhamma*. She went regularly to the temple and a highly revered monk at her village temple, whom she referred to as Luang Phôô, said to her that it was only by taking the precepts and practice that a person could understand *dhamma*. She knew no *mae chii* before she became ordained herself. She had seen some old *mae chii*s though and, despite her young age, she said that she wanted to be like them. She said that married life seemed to be so unhappy and she had no desire to get married.

However, Mae chii Maalii's parents did not grant their permission and the head monk of the temple would not ordain her without her parents' consent. She told me that eight years earlier she went with her aunt to visit some relatives in Lampang province in Northern Thailand. Her aunt returned home, but Mae chii Maalii did not go with her. She saw her chance to receive ordination and travelled alone to a famous monk's temple in Chiang Mai and asked for ordination there. The monk wanted to know if her parents had given their permission. She said that she lied and answered that they had, although her parents in fact knew nothing. After three months, some people from Lampang came to visit the temple in Chiang Mai where she was staying. They asked her where she came from, and it turned out that they knew her relatives in Lampang. When they returned home they contacted her relatives who called her parents. Mae chii Maalii's parents travelled immediately to Chiang Mai. She said they cried and wanted her to go back home with them. She explained that she did not want to go back to lay life, and later they gave their permission for her to stay in the temple for two years and then return home. However, she did not go back home. Mae chii Maalii was firm in her decision. She explained that since she had made the decision to become ordained with great care, she had no intention of changing her mind and living a lay life.

Becoming ordained without the consent of one's parents, husband or wife violates the prescribed rules for both monks and *mae chii*s. A *mae chii* from Central Thailand, who was 21 years old when I met her and had been ordained for six years, said she had initially obeyed her parents when they refused to give their permission for her ordination. She said that when she was a young girl she had had two main interests: playing and meditating. She started to meditate when she was ten years old and she said she enjoyed the calm feeling. She did not study Buddhism at school but often went with her family to the temple and learned about Buddhism by listening to the monks. She said that she used to give food to the monks every day and she often walked to the temple without her family. One day, a monk asked her if she wanted to become a *nak buat* (become ordained). When she told her parents, they said: 'If you do this we will not come and visit you, you will not be our relative any more.' She said she did not understand why her parents were against it or why they said this. Her parents' refusal implied that she could not become ordained right away, as she would have preferred. She stayed in the temple and instead of receiving *mae chii* ordination, she received temporary lay ordination as a *chii phraam*, which her parents accepted.

Her parents never gave their approval. She did not want to go against her family and her solution to the dilemma was to leave the decision about ordination to the head monk. The head monk talked with her parents, but they did not change their minds. However, later she was ordained in the temple without the parents' consent. By letting the head monk take responsibility for her ordination, despite the fact that her parents had not given their approval, she said that she overcame the feeling of having violated her parents' decision. She said: 'Still, I think my family has not fully accepted that I have chosen this life. Right now I do not want to change my life, I do not want to marry, I want to continue my life as a *mae chii*.'

For many Thai women it is unthinkable to go against their parents' decisions. A *mae chii* who was 63 years old when I met her at a temple in Isaan decided to do her duty as a daughter as long as her parents were alive. She waited until they had died before seeking ordination and by this time she was 51 years old. She never married, but worked as a dressmaker and took care of her parents. She said that her parents would never have accepted her ordination. She felt she was free when they had passed away and she could finally live the life she wanted. However, it cost her the relationship with her brothers and sisters. She almost lost contact with them because they disapproved of her ordination and did not understand the religious life she had chosen.

A 36-year-old *mae chii* who was a former teacher at a college decided to become ordained after being a lay follower and meditation practitioner at a temple. She said that the reason why she started to meditate many years previously was that she was concerned about her father's *winjaan* (spirit). She wanted to be able to connect with this. Although she never succeeded in communicating with her dead father, meditation calmed her and she felt happier. She continued to meditate every day and she also started to stay in the temple overnight. On weekdays she went to work at 8 o'clock every morning and she lived like that for eight months. She wanted to extinguish suffering, to cut worldly ties; she wanted to become ordained.

She went to stay in a *samnak chii* for a short period of intense meditation practice. After staying there only three days, she asked the leading *mae chii* for ordination. The leading *mae chii* considered this as being too hasty and refused her request. At the same time another young woman, who also wanted to become ordained, had come to the *samnak chii* and they decided to go together and see the head monk at the nearby temple and ask him for ordination. He agreed and took the initiative to meet with her relatives and talk with them. At first her mother did not give her permission. Nor did her siblings approve. Nevertheless, she had made up her mind and she had started to cut her hair before she resigned from her job as a teacher. She said: 'Cutting my hair was an unambiguous sign that I was serious in my intentions. My mother fainted when she saw my short hair. Finally they gave their permission, and I became ordained.'

However, not all parents are against their daughters' wishes to become ordained. I met a few *mae chii*s who told me that their parents had actually suggested that they should become ordained. One *mae chii* from a province close to Bangkok said that by becoming ordained she had fulfilled her father's wish. She never married but became ordained when she was 22 years old. She was 47 when I met her. She came from a middle–class family in the Bangkok area and was the third child in a family of six sisters. Her family had property, and she also had some income from her family's business. Her financial situation had made it possible for her to study, and she had recently completed a university degree. She became ordained at a temple, and lived periodically at *samnak chii*s. Her sisters became *chii phraam* now and then, but she was the only *mae chii*. She said it was her father who told her to become a *mae chii*. He had deep faith in Buddhism and not having any sons, asked her to become a *mae chii*. Her father passed away two years before I met her. He became ordained late in life and stayed 11 years in the monkhood. Her mother was still alive, but the *mae chii* said she had always been closer to her father.

CUTTING FAMILY TIES

Earlier in this chapter I gave examples that showed how young women are not usually subjected to a demand to become ordained and are not expected to renounce the world. Women who become *mae chii*s abandon their families and the expectations laid upon them as women. Female ordination deviates from Thai cultural values, which hold that daughters should care for their parents in all ways possible, and in this sense women's ordination violates society's sense of order and young girls are generally discouraged by their families from becoming *mae chii*s. Today it is common, especially in the urban areas, for well-educated women who earn their own living to choose to live a single life. They are not considered to violate the prescribed gender rules by not marrying as long as they take care of and support their families when needed. This is one important difference between lay unmarried women and *mae chii*s.

In several cases ordained relatives played an important role in young women's lives when they wanted to become ordained. A 29-year-old *mae chii* at Ratburi Samnak Chii who was ordained at the *samnak chii* when she was only 13 years old is one example of someone introduced to religious life by a close relative. This *mae chii* was doing her 16th *phansaa* (rain retreat as ordained) when I met her. She was born in the province in which the *samnak chii* is located, had finished primary school in the provincial capital and had studied at secondary level at the *samnak chii*. In the city she had gone to primary school at a monastery. She said the school was located at the temple but was run by lay people and was open to both boys and girls. Girls are not allowed to go to temple schools, and the *mae chii* explained that the school had been a temple school but was turned into a public school run by lay people.

Her grandmother was a longstanding *mae chii,* who had moved to stay at Ratburi Samnak Chii. In the holidays, her grandmother invited her to come and stay with her. She said she experienced the atmosphere at the *samnak chii* as quiet, and she liked it. She helped with the construction work there and with the plantations. When the holiday was over her parents came and asked her to come home and continue studying, but she did not want to leave the *samnak chii.* Her mother was not against the idea that she should become ordained, but she thought she was too young and said that she could be a *mae chii* later, after she had finished school. But she liked living at the *samnak chii* and wanted to stay. Her grandmother approved and finally her parents agreed to let her live at the *samnak chii* and become ordained. The *mae chii* said her grandmother taught her everything: the Pali language, meditation, how to do the walking meditation, etc. She said that she had never wanted a married life and she recalled some neighbours who were always arguing. She did not like that. Her own family was quite harmonious before her ordination, but afterwards her father took a second wife (*mia nôôy*).

The problem with the irresponsibility of husbands and of their having more than one wife was often brought up in discussions with lay women and *mae chii*s. Despite Thai women's strong position in the family, patriarchal values dominate legal codes. For example, until recently it was not illegal for a man to have more than one wife, adultery is a ground for divorce only for the husband and rape is legally defined as a crime only committed by a man against a woman other than his wife (Klausner 1997).

Temples function as refuges for both women and men. The deaths of her husband and some family members preceded one woman's ordination. She was 68 years old when I met her at a big temple in Isaan. She had become ordained when she was 34, together with her 14-year-old daughter. It is unusual for both mother and daughter to receive ordination at the same time. They still lived at the same place and the mother was now the head of the *mae chii* section. Before their ordination they lived about 2 kilometres from the temple. They used to visit the temple and the mother knew the teaching monk and she had faith in Buddhism.

The family had gone through many difficulties and before they received ordination several close relatives had died. The mother told me that she had had a son who died when he was a year old. Her parents, her sister and her husband died within a short period of time. Finally, she said: 'It was only my daughter and myself left.' She used to go to the temple and listen to the head monk teaching. She said that he explained about life and death and the uncertainty of when a person's life is over. She started to study Buddhism at the temple and said that she reflected deeply over the three characteristics of life, *dukkha, anicca, anatta.*[6] She realised that everything has to be born and that nothing is permanent. Suffering is *thammadaa,* which means that it is normal and a common part of life. She explained to me that we should strive to become detached and thereby avoid grief or illness. Her faith in Buddhism and desire to meditate and learn about the realities of life made her life easier to bear. Since she was poor and lacked family, staying in the temple gave her a form of social security that would have been difficult for her to obtain in lay life.

One of the most distinguished, longstanding *mae chii*s at Ratburi Samnak Chii was Mae chii Ning, a 55-year-old originally from Isaan. She had studied at the university and had been a teacher for many years. Besides other subjects she also taught the Pali language. She became ordained when she was 24. She considered her father's death, when she was 9 years old, to be one of the most important events in her life. She was the youngest child in the family. She had one older brother who was a monk and vice-abbot at a large temple in Bangkok. He had died five years prior to my meeting with Mae chii Ning. She said that she was not very close to her brother. He was much older than she and became more like a father who felt responsibility for her. Mae chii Ning finished primary school in Isaan and after her father's death her mother remarried, and when she was 11 years old she was sent to live with a family in Bangkok. In Bangkok, she lived with her foster mother and her children and she also went to school there. She finished secondary school but had no chance to continue studying immediately after that. The family chose instead to support her brother's continued education. Her foster mother was a pharmacist and went to work every weekday and Mae chii Ning took care of the household duties. In the mornings, she had to cook and send the children to school. Then she had to cook food for her brother who was a monk. She said that she was doing the same thing every day and she found it tremendously boring.

Her foster mother got married, when Mae chii Ning was 16 and Mae chii Ning had then started to work at home with sewing. During this period she studied English at the YMCA in Bangkok. Mae chii Ning said that she suggested that she should do some kind of domestic work, but her brother did not think that it was safe for her and was afraid that something bad would happen to her. Then she wanted to study dressmaking, but her foster mother did not allow her to. Instead, her foster mother bought fabrics and clothes that she could copy so she could learn by herself. Mae chii Ning said: 'One day when I was sitting sewing I saw a bird fall dead down from the ceiling. I thought, I will become like that. I am going to die like the bird that had died. I felt that my life was meaningless and I had to do something.' She made up her mind and told her foster mother that she wanted to be a *mae chii*. Her foster mother said she felt very sad about her request. Luang phi, her brother, asked her foster mother to give her permission since he thought that she would never manage to remain a *mae chii* for long – she liked to eat, roam around and spend money. Mae chii Ning said: 'My brother did not know my mind. I felt sad when the children told me what my brother had said to my foster mother about me.' Marriage was never a choice that she considered attractive and she never aspired to have a life like her mother's. Mae chii Ning said that her mother had so many children and when Mae chii Ning had moved to Bangkok she did not miss home at all. In six years, she only went home once. She recalled that her real mother tried to arrange a marriage for her just before she was ordained. Her mother had a Chinese friend who had two children, a daughter and a son, and they wanted Mae chii Ning to marry the son. Mae chii Ning turned down the proposition and became ordained instead and has now been a *mae chii* for 31 years.

OVERCOMING SICKNESS

For some women ordination provides a way to overcome sickness, or change an unwholesome lifestyle. Health problems were one of the factors motivating the following two *mae chii*s to become ordained. However, temples and *samnak chii*s do not normally serve as a refuge for sick people. The monastic rules in fact prohibit people with mental or physical disorders from seeking ordination. These two *mae chii*s had recovered from their sicknesses when I met them, and were in good health. They had their permanent residence at temples, and were visiting *mae chii*s at Ratburi Samnak Chii while they were studying. The younger was Mae chii Yupin. She was 24 years old and had been ordained since she was 14. The other, Mae chii Amara, was almost 20 years older and had only been a *mae chii* for five years. They were both from Northeastern Thailand, but not from the same province. Each had five brothers and sisters and neither of them had any close relatives who were ordained.

Mae chii Yupin became ordained after finishing primary school. She said that she told her mother that she wanted to become ordained and her mother had no objection to her daughter's suggestion and went with her to the famous monk Luang Phôô Thet. Luang Phôô accepted her, but before she received formal ordination she had to stay in the monastery for a probation period of two months. During that period she shaved her hair and wore a black skirt and white blouse. She enjoyed the monastic life from the very beginning. She liked to be shaved since it made her feel clean. Mae chii Yupin had been severely ill before she became ordained. It was an illness that resembled malaria and she said that she thought she was going to die. She said that her main reason for becoming ordained was that she wanted to accumulate merit. While she was sick and nearly dying she was concerned about her lack of merit and worried about what would happen to her with no stores of merit. When she recovered from her illness, she felt depressed and she thought that ordination would help her state of mind. After a short time at the monastery she said she felt happier and stronger and became more energetic.

A lay devotee, an *upasika,* who cooked food for Luang Phôô at the monastery, castigated Mae chii Yupin for becoming ordained without having any financial assets. The *upasika* considered that it would have been better if she had waited until she had worked and saved money for ordained life. However, Mae chii Yupin said thatshe still felt happy that she had been ordained early in life and now she even had the chance to study in order to deepen her practice. She said that she never had thoughts of marrying and having children because she assumed that that kind of life would be unsatisfactory. She explained to me that through marriage one becomes attached and when one has children the attachment is even greater. Mae chii Yupin speculated that it was probably all the suffering in her own family that made her turn away from that kind of life. She claimed that she was bored by all the problems of lay life. Her family had once had the economic capacity to secure a good life for its members. They had a small business, fields and cows. But her mother had to close the business when Mae chii Yupin's older brother stole money from the firm. Her father also liked to drink and gamble and he eventually destroyed the family's financial stability. She said she felt sorry for both her mother and her father. She also told me that her father had many wives and this further undermined good family life. Before he married Mae chii Yupin's mother he had taken a Vietnamese wife and they had five children. After marrying her mother, he had several mistresses. Her father had died four years prior to our meeting of a liver disease caused by his drinking. At the end of his life, Mae chii Yupin went home and took care of him. She played Buddhist tapes for him and taught him how to meditate. He told her that if he survived his illness he would like to be a *phao khaow* (a pious lay person, who follows the eight precepts and dresses in white). Every morning he asked his wife to prepare offerings to the monks. Mae chii Yupin thought that the status of his mind improved during the last period of his life.

Mae chii Amara decided to become ordained when she was 36 years old. She had completed only four years of primary education before she became a *mae chii*. After finishing primary school, she worked in farming (*tham rai*) and after that she worked as an unskilled labourer in many different occupations. When she lived in her home province she stayed with her father as long as he was alive and later she stayed with her older sister. Mae chii Amara did not go to the temple often when she was young. She said she sometimes went there to play. Her knowledge of Buddhism was very vague and she said she became a *mae chii* because her father had told her to do good things.

Mae chii Amara went to Bangkok to work when she was 26. It was a long way from home, but she said that her parents never worried about her because she had always been like a man and they were confident that she could manage and take care of herself. She did not get involved with men and she only had female friends. Before she went to the capital, she met some Chinese people from Bangkok whom she liked and admired for their diligence and capacity to work hard. When she arrived in the city they employed her to sell grilled ducks and pork and to work with groceries and vegetables. However, despite her hard work she had nothing left. It was just a question of eating and spending and there was nothing left in the end.

Mae chii Amara recalled that long ago when she was young she went to work in Rayong province. An agent had come to her province in Isaan to recruit people to work. Mae chii Amara was taken on to work with sugarcanes, which was a very heavy work and she received only 35 baht a day. No food was provided so they also had to pay for their meals. Something that made a deep impression on her during this period was a group of *mae chii*s who used to stand on a hill at 4 o'clock in the morning reciting *metta* (loving kindness). She heard the recitation and she said she was deeply affected by it: it went straight to her heart. Mae chii Amara said that this experience returned to her later in life.

Like most of the *mae chii*s whom I interviewed, Mae chii Amara was of the opinion that marriage and children were constraining. She wanted freedom and she wanted to be independent. However, before she became ordained she abused alcohol. She started to drink when she was a teenager. Finally, her body could take no more drinking and she had to stop. It was her sister who begged her to stop, but Mae chii Amara told her it was impossible for her to quit though, with great determination, she finally managed. She also used to smoke and had similar difficulties in stopping. Mae chii Amara said that before she became ordained she used to listen to a song about *dhamma,* and said to herself: 'I cannot be a monk, but at least I can be a *mae chii.* My sister helped me to the temple, and introduced me to Khun Mae, the head *chii,* who accepted me.'

FULFILLING VOWS

Reasons such as vow fulfilment or making merit for family members or relatives are also among the motives that *mae chii*s give for their ordination. Today, it is quite rare for women to become *mae chii*s in order to fulfil a vow and it is more common that they become ordained temporarily, staying at the temple as *chii phraam*. Nevertheless, there are some women who fulfil vows by becoming ordained, and they usually decide beforehand how long they will remain in the ordained state. A 37-year-old woman came to Ratburi Samnak Chii in February 1998 in order to become ordained and stay at the *samnak chii* for about three weeks. She was married and had two children, a girl who was ten and a boy who was seven years old. She came from a nearby province and both her husband and she worked with growing fruits and vegetables. Almost 20 years earlier, when she was 17, she had made a vow to a venerated monk that she would become ordained if she was cured from an fever-illness that made her life miserable. Before going to the temple she had consulted a doctor but had felt no improvement. She therefore turned to the temple and made a vow to the old monk. She said: 'I folded my hands and said: "If I become well from my sickness I shall become ordained."' She was cured, but she did not fulfil her vow. In January 1998 she became sick in the same way again. 'One night I dreamt about a crocodile, which came to my house. I asked some old people what the dream meant. They said the crocodile had come to remind me about the vow.' Their house was at the *klong* (canal) and she dreamt that the crocodile came swimming there. She decided immediately to become ordained and went to visit a monk at the village temple for advice about where to do it. He told her that Ratburi Samnak Chii was a good place. She said: 'I could have been a *chii phraam,* but when I made the vow there was no such thing as temporary *mae chii*s, there were no *chii phraam*. When I made the vow I said that I would become ordained, and shave and do everything if I got better.'

Before becoming ordained, she went together with her husband to Ratburi Samnak Chii to consult Khun Mae about her ordination. She praised her husband and said that he was a fine man (*khun dii*) who always spoke nicely, never quarrelled and was never rude. He had once been ordained for two years and would have stayed in the monkhood but had to disrobe because his parents were indebted and he had to work and help them out financially. She discussed the matter with her husband and decided not to become ordained close to their home because their children would come and see her and she did not think that was a good idea. She said: 'For example, as a *mae chii* I cannot touch my son. He is only seven years old, and that would be difficult for him to understand.' She had selected Ratburi Samnak Chii over some other places because of the standard of practice. She had heard of other places where the *mae chii*s did not chant and did not practise alms rounds and she appreciated that Ratburi Samnak Chii upheld strict monastic conduct.

I did not meet many *mae chii*s at *samnak chii*s who had become ordained in order to fulfil vows. However, at a temple in Isaan I met one 55-year-old *mae chii* who had become ordained because she had made a vow to the Buddha. She told me that she had been working in Israel for 18 years when her relatives in Thailand informed her that her father was seriously ill, probably dying. She phoned her father every evening and talked with him. She said: 'I was so concerned about his health, I took a vow to the Buddha, and promised to become ordained and become a *mae chii* for one year if my father survived.' Her father recovered and when I met her he was 85 years old. She planned to go back to Israel and continue working when she had completed her year as a *mae chii*.

ACCESS TO STUDY

To gain access to education is a common reason why young men seek ordination. However, the *sangha* has never offered women education. Today, a few *samnak chii*s offer girls free secondary education but it is not necessary for the girls to become ordained. Some of the resident *mae chii*s at Ratburi Samnak Chii mentioned education as one of several reasons for their ordination. They often stressed a desire to live a peaceful life without the suffering and difficulties they perceived in lay life. Mae chii Siriporn and I lived in the same building at the *samnak chii*. She had studied up to secondary level at the *samnak chii* and was now studying at the Open University. She was 33 years old and had become ordained at Ratburi Samnak Chii eight years earlier. She said that she had always wanted to study but when she was 12 and finished primary school it was not possible for her to continue. Instead she stayed at home and helped her mother. She explained that she had six younger brothers and sisters and there was so much work to do at home. So she helped her mother in the kitchen, took care of her siblings and helped her father with work in the garden. She said: 'I would have liked to continue studying, but my family could not afford it. I did not want to disturb my parents with my education. I always thought of my parents and siblings first, and not of myself. My parents were not in good health and I felt that I had to help them. If I had not become a *mae chii* I would not have had the chance to continue studying.' Mae chii Siriporn came from the province in which Ratburi Samnak Chii was located. Her parents worked with gardening and pig breeding. She said that she had never aspired to marry and have children. She knew how hard lay life could be and she said she was bored with taking care of her five younger siblings.

Several of Mae chii Siriporn's family members had experiences of ordained life. Her father had been a monk before he married and a brother was ordained for the second time though he had recently decided to leave the monkhood. Her mother had been a *chii phraam* once in order to fulfil a vow she had made when she was ill. Mae chii Siriporn did not know about Ratburi Samnak Chii until her father told her about it. Her father's sister had been ordained at Ratburi Samnak Chii and when Mae chii Siriporn learnt of this she went to see her. Before her ordination, Mae chii Siriporn practised meditation and visited temples that arranged retreats. She participated in several seven- and ten-day retreats at temples with intensive Buddhist practice. She also read books about meditation and listened to Buddhist radio programmes and followed the monk's meditation instructions over the radio. She said: 'At that time I only knew about sitting meditation. When I came here the first time I took the precepts and stayed just one day. I was introduced to a type of meditation that I had not practised before, and I learnt how to practise walking meditation, which was new to me. I was very impressed by the *mae chii*s and this place, and I was surprised that the *samnak chii* also offered meditation instructions. I had not expected that.'

RELEASED FROM FAMILY DUTIES

I have interviewed numbers of *mae chii*s who were well educated, had secure incomes and good health before they became ordained. Even these *mae chii*s, who had been well-to-do before ordination, had been discontented with secular life. As with most of the *mae chii*s I talked to, they mentioned a desire to be free and not locked up in a marriage as one of their motives for seeking ordination. They also said they had experienced lay life as empty and boring and referred to basic Buddhist truths about the conditions of life, such as suffering (*dukkha*) and their wish to attain enlightenment (*nibbana*), as the principal reasons for seeking ordination.

At a *samnak chii* in which about 12 *mae chii*s resided, I met a 38-year-old *mae chii* who had been ordained for six years. She had graduated from a university in Bangkok, spoke English and had a well-paid job in Bangkok before she was ordained. Her family was Sino-Thai and she had nine brothers and sisters. However, when she was born her parents gave her away to an aunt who only had one son and she said she had suffered much from that. She had never discussed this with her family, but she had always wondered why they had given her away, and why they could not keep her when they kept all the other nine children. She said she loved her foster parents and when her foster father died she missed him very much. After her foster father's death her brother went to America, and later her foster mother followed him. She had tried to persuade her foster mother to come back to Thailand, but she preferred to stay with her son. The *mae chii* explained that it was when her brother said that the mother was his and that she could not take her away from him, that she felt as if a chain was broken. She said:

> I was not connected anymore. I felt *isara* (freedom). Now I could do what I wanted. You know, here in Thailand we have to take care of our parents, we have to look after them – I was free. I had done my best. It took a very long time for me, I was nearly 30 years old, until I understood: *tham cai* – follow your heart. Suddenly when I was meditating in the forest in the Chiang Mai area in the mountains of Doi Inthanon, I realised: 'Do your duty.' I was doing my duty. I did not have to do their duties. I have always believed that it is best to be single. You know when a man is interested in a woman, he takes the woman's hand and looks at her lines in her palm, and then he takes all of her, and she is not free anymore.

She had previously been a businesswoman at an export company working seven days a week, often long hours. She said she liked it, but after five years she started to ask herself why she was working so hard. It was not for money and not for a position and she felt that something was lacking. A friend gave her a book written by the famous monk Buddhadasa. She started to read, but did not understand it. However, she became interested in Buddhadasa's teaching and went to see him at his place, Suan Mokh, in Southern Thailand. She followed the meditation sessions and listened to the teachings. 'There were so many words I did not understand. I had hundreds of words on my list that were new to me. I talked with Buddhadasa and he asked what kind of suffering I had. I said I had suffering inside. Outside things were OK. But inside I had suffering. After this first weekend at Suan Mokh I had to go back to Bangkok to work. Buddhadasa gave me lots of books and I read and read. Gradually I became more convinced that I wanted to live my life as a *mae chii*.'

Another well-educated and wealthy *mae chii* became ordained when she was 49 and had been ordained for six years when I met her. She was from Bangkok and had been a professor at one of the large universities in the capital. She had also written a couple of books about Buddhism. Her attitudes towards *mae chii*s had earlier been negative, and she said that she looked upon their lives as tragic. However, she had practised Buddhism since childhood and before becoming ordained she was a lay follower of a Buddhist monk in the Mahayana tradition, whom she also supported financially. A turning point for her was when she discovered that he did not follow the monastic precepts. That disappointment drove her to study Buddhism more independently, which also led her into contact with *mae chii*s.

She was born during the Second World War and had two sisters. The family lived in Southern Bangkok; the mother had a shop and the father was a doctor (pharmacist). Her parents considered education important for their daughters and the three sisters completed university studies. They travelled abroad and the *mae chii* had lived in the United States.

The *mae chii* said she did not know any *mae chii*s before she became ordained. Many years ago one of her sisters shaved her head and she really thought her sister had gone mad. She felt ashamed of her and did not want to speak with her. Then she decided to shave her own head because she said that she wanted to experience how she would react when people looked down upon her, but to her surprise that never happened. No one treated her with contempt. People respected her even as a *mae chii*. She recalled that her colleagues, friends and people around her advised her not to shave because of the low status *mae chii*s have and they could not understand why she wanted to do it. She mentioned an additional important reason why she had sought ordination and that was the traffic in Bangkok combined with being afraid of death. Her health was weak and she had become ill. She tried various ways to overcome her fear. However, she said it was superficial, she was only clinging onto something.

Finally, she decided that she wanted to live at a *samnak chii* and her sister and she made a list of 28 *samnak*s (both independent *samnak chii*s and *mae chii*s' departments at temples) that they would visit in order to choose one place for her to live in. They had visited 18 places when they came to a forest *samnak chii* located in Isaan. At that time there was no road to the *samnak chii* and its location was difficult to approach. The *samnak chii* consisted of only a few buildings, meditation huts (*kuti*s) and the *saalaa*. She remembered that when they arrived, Luang Mae, the head *mae chii*, came quickly to greet them. They talked and when her sister asked which place she wanted to see next, she told her that she had found the place where she wanted to live. However, first she had to build a house to live in and they went back to Bangkok and contacted an architect who made the drawings for the *kuti*. She said it took three months to build it. They phoned her when the *kuti* was ready, and she left Bangkok. She had now been at the *samnak chii* for six years and despite her being a Bangkokian with no experience of the forest, she found it surprisingly easy to adjust to life as a *mae chii*.

Mae chii Khunying Kanitha, who was mentioned in Chapter 1, became ordained in October 1993 when she was 73. She said that she had had this idea of becoming a *mae chii* for 50 years. When she was a child she studied in a Catholic convent school in Bangkok and she was very impressed by the Catholic nuns. She said that her mother was a good, religious person and always took her to the Buddhist temple. She grew accustomed to the temple, but she did not really study Buddhism. She remembered seeing the *mae chii*s cooking and doing domestic chores in the temple and compared them to the Catholic nuns in the convent who had access to higher education. She thought that the *mae chii*s should have the same opportunity. After she graduated from the Catholic school, she studied law for five years. Then she went abroad and studied three more years before she went back to Thailand and started her career at the Ministry of Foreign Affairs. She met her husband, married, and had three children. Mae chii Khunying Kanitha said: 'I had warned my husband before we married that one day, when I had fulfilled my duties, I would enter religious life as a *mae chii*.'

Mae chii Khunying Kanitha said that her mother had inspired her to become a *mae chii* and they had actually planned that they should be *mae chii*s together in a monastery. However, when her mother was old she went alone to live in a temple. Unfortunately, she had a fall in the temple and had to be brought back home and never had a second chance to receive ordination. Mae chii Khunying Kanitha had a busy life with many assignments; but when she was 72, she told her husband and children that the time had come for her ordination. Her husband was understanding and had no objections, but her children resisted the idea. Therefore she postponed the ordination one year. In 1993, she was ordained in Sri Lanka. She said that she discussed the International Women's Buddhist conference to be held in Sri Lanka with Acaan Chatsumarn who suggested that she could be ordained there, which she did.

*Mae chii*s who become ordained late in life usually after fulfilling their duties to their families commonly describe lay life as unsatisfying. Before becoming ordained, most of those that I spoke to had supported the Buddhist clergy for a long time. One *mae chii* from Northeastern Thailand, who had been married and had five children, became ordained when she was over 50 and had been a *mae chii* for almost 20 years when I met her. She said she had taken care of her children alone since her husband died when her youngest was six years old. She had long owned a factory, which one of her sons was now taking care of. She said: 'Before I became ordained, my daily life was working, eating, working, working, sleeping. Eating, eating and getting fat.' She said she did not know anything about Buddhism at that time. She went to the *wat* (temple) to make *tham bun* (meritorious offerings). She said she felt bored and over two and a half years she donated a lot of money. Her goal was to reach *nibbana,* although she said she did not understand anything about *nibbana.* Before ordination, she viewed *mae chii*s as beggars. After ordination she said: 'I should be a good monk. *Mae chii*s can do the same things as monks. However, *thudong* practice is very dangerous for women. In that case women must practice in groups. My goal is to reach *niphaan.*'

In order to broaden the stereotypical picture of contemporary *mae chii*s and their lives before ordination, I have related a number of *mae chii*s' stories, where they reveal their reasons for seeking a life in celibacy. Men's motives for becoming monks are generally not questioned. Their ordination is highly desirable, and young men are expected to become monks for at least a few months before they marry. Women's motives for becoming *mae chii*s are, contrary to those of men, often doubted and reduced to signs of misfortune. These conceptions reflect the reluctance to accept women as ordained persons, and these stereotypical notions have been perpetuated even by Western scholars.

To live in accordance with the strict monastic regime of fasting and hard work that many *mae chii*s perform requires stamina and deep faith in the spiritual goal. My findings do not support the simplified picture of Thai women as seeking ordination as 'old and poor' or 'young and sick' that Van Esterik gives in the oft cited article: 'Lay women in Theravada Buddhism' (P. Van Esterik 1996: 49, 57). There are usually combinations of reasons why women wish to live an ordained life. Economic circumstances must also be favourable to enable a Thai woman to live an ordained life. Several of my informants stated that they wanted to pursue a pure and spiritual life, and that marriage would be an obstacle to this goal. Most of the *mae chii*s describe married life as one filled with suffering. Marriage is frequently portrayed as spiritually unproductive, and it does not meet the *mae chiis'* aspirations in life. There are unfavourable socio-economic factors that may account for the fact that some Thai women choose to become *mae chii*s. However, there are numerous *mae chii*s who have no such difficulties, who are well educated and well-off and could no doubt have managed quite well fending for themselves as lay women.

Most of my informants maintained that their ordination was motivated by the suffering inherent in lay life, and their preference for living a spiritual life. One might ask what in fact constitutes a 'pure' motivation for becoming a monk or a *mae chii*. Most of the *mae chii*s mentioned in this chapter could have chosen alternative ways of life. However, for them it was highly meaningful to become a *mae chii* in order to embark on the path to *nibbana*.

NOTES

1   *Baap* signifies demerit.

2   In Thai 'hot' is a negative expression describing something unharmonious, filled with the aggressive temper and anxiety that upset the mind and make life unpleasant. At that temple the *saalaa* was a building on stilts without walls where the monks were presented with their meals, held ceremonies and gave speeches to the laity.

3   *Niphaan* is the Thai term for *nibbana* (Pali) which means the permanent extinction of suffering.

4   Moral defilements, *kilet,* such as greed and attachment.

5   Becoming a *mae chii* in fulfilment of a vow is called *buat kaebun*. The reason for the vow might be to overcome some difficulty such as one's or one's relative's illness, an examination and so on.

6   *Dukkha* (Pali) means suffering, dissatisfaction of conditioned existence, stress, conflict, pain. *Anicca* (Pali) means impermanency of things which is the rising, passing and changing of things or the disappearance of things that have become arisen.

7   *Anatta* (Pali) means 'not-self', non-ego, egolessness, impersonality.

CHAPTER FOUR

Transcending the Lay Realm

Thai female ordination, *nak buat chii,* is often private in contrast with men's more public ceremonies. In Thai, ordination is called *buat,* which originates from the Pali word *pabbajja,* and means going forth into the 'homeless life'. Going forth implies giving up lay life and letting go of all belongings, family relationship, these ways of eating, dressing, speaking, thinking and even feeling that are normal in lay life. To be an ordained person involves being under the guidance of and receiving ongoing training from one's preceptor. The practice is designed to free a person from greed, delusion, hatred and attachment until finally the ultimate state of enlightenment is reached. Consequently, ordination is not the final goal but the beginning of a process of physical and spiritual development.

There are great expectations associated with young Thai men's initiation into the Buddhist monkhood. Their ceremonies are usually grand and attract much attention. By contrast, Thai women's ordination into the Buddhist female ordained state is not commonly celebrated. The differences in attitudes towards male and female ordinations betray the Thai sex/gender order, which has thus far only promoted male ordination. Spiritually, the Buddhist practice and ultimate goal are the same for both sexes. Socially, however, Buddhist ordination serves different goals and often contains different meanings for women and men. Young men who pass through the Buddhist initiatory process are transformed into mature adults. They are, in the Thai idiom, 'ripe' (*suk*) for marriage, and few men remain to devote their lives to the religion and become permanent monks.

Keyes notes that while a man must reject his nature (that is, his sexuality) in order to pursue the path, a woman must first realise her nature as a prerequisite to her embarking on the path. A woman's 'nature' is to become a mother and she becomes detached by sacrificing her son to the Buddhist *sangha* (Keyes 1984: 229). Consequently, manhood and maturity are gained through celibacy and monkhood, whereas womanhood is gained through motherhood. A male rejects sexuality and becomes a mature man; a female who chooses celibacy loses the possibility of becoming a mature woman.

There are both similarities and differences between male and female ordination. *Mae chii* ordination is sometimes compared with novice ordination, probably because of the similarities in their numbers of precepts, and of the novice's inferior standing at the monastery. A novice monk and a *mae chii* have thus considerably fewer precepts than male monks (*bhikkhu*) and female monks (*bhikkhuni*). *Bhikkhu*s observe 227 precepts and *bhikkhuni*s observe 311 precepts. The novice monks obey ten precepts and most *mae chii*s observe eight, as may lay people do on special holy days such as *wan phra*. However, both novice monks and *mae chii*s must also follow the 75 rules (the *sekhiya* rules) that are included in the monks' training rules and govern every aspect of daily activities and behaviour. The 75 training rules are an additional support and a guide to help the ordained to regulate their lives (to be discussed in Chapter 5). The *sekhiya* rules are commonly described as merely dealing with social etiquette and politeness. For *mae chii*s, the rules have a deeper meaning and the *sekhiya* rules are important for their ordained identity. As Holt points out, the *sekhiya* rules demonstrate that the discipline of one's inward state is of the utmost importance for the spiritual life of the renunciants (Holt 1999: 102). On account of the novice monks' inferior position at the temples, they are excluded from the decision-making meetings of the *sangha* and they are not allowed to attend the final part of the monks' ordination ceremony (*upasampada*). Nor are they allowed to join the monks when the *Patimokkha* is recited.

ORDINATION IN RELATION TO THE PARENT–CHILD RELATIONSHIP

In Thailand men do not become ordained for life, and they can therefore go in and out of the *sangha*. Customarily, it is only those young men who join the order for the first time in their lives who do so in an elaborate public manner. Many of the differences between the novices' and the *mae chii*s' ordinations rest upon the different social implications that the female ordination and the young men's novice ordination have.

The bonds that sons and daughters have to their parents change through the ordination, but the changes are gendered. All children have a moral debt of gratitude to their parents for raising them. The *bun khun* obligation of repaying debts is commonly met by a son through his ordination, by which he creates and ritually transfers merit to his parents, and especially to his mother. However, a daughter is not expected to repay her debts through ordination. Instead, she is expected to help and support her parents and siblings.

The great appreciation of male ordination and the importance of the mother–son relationship are highlighted in a text from Northern Thailand, *Anisong buat* 'Blessings of Ordination' which is often read by a newly ordained monk at the end of the ordination ceremony (Keyes 1986: 80–81). It consists of a myth that tells of the great merit gained by a mother who allows her son to become a novice. The story is assumed to have been told by the Buddha himself when he lived near Savatthi. According to the legend, there was a young man, who wanted to be a monk. However, his parents held false beliefs, and his father in particular was a hunter and a cruel man who had no faith in the *dhamma*. His parents did not give him permission to become a monk. The young man became very dispirited and started to fast. After seven days, his mother could no longer stand the sight of her son wasting away and she gave him permission to be ordained. The son was happy and asked his mother to take him to a learned monk for ordination. He then became a novice monk and his mother continued about her everyday tasks. One day while in the woods gathering firewood, she grew tired and stopped to take a rest. She fell asleep, and while sleeping she was visited by a servant of Yama, the Lord of Hell. He asked her if she had made any acts of merit while in the human world. When she responded that she had not, the servant of Yama tied her up and told her he would take her to hell. When she saw the flames of hell, she said that they had the same beautiful yellow colour as her son's robes when he entered the *sangha*.

Lord Yama consulted the documents and found that the woman had committed actions of demerit by holding to false views. He struck her mouth three times with a piece of wood and then took her and cast her towards hell. Just at that moment, there appeared a beautiful golden lotus as big as a cartwheel that spread out to catch her. Seeing her protected from the fires of hell, Lord Yama was truly amazed. He brought her back and said that he could not understand, since the documents showed that she had acted demeritoriously and he had tried to place her in hell, but she had not suffered. He asked if she had done any meritorious acts in her lifetime. She answered that she had neither done any act of merit nor observed any of the moral precepts while in the human world. She said she had one jewel-like son who entered the *sangha* and he had become a novice monk and intended to receive higher ordination and become a *bhikkhu*. The woman was returned to the human world where she then reported what had happened to her son. The son realised that having gone forth as a novice, he was able to show compassion and help his mother. Then, he thought, he would become a monk in order to help his father.

While the myth also tells of how following ordination as a monk permitted the monk to transfer merit to his father, the key relationship is clearly that of mother and son. The myth underscores what has in fact happened in the ritual: the son goes forth, leaves his mother-centred home, and enters the Buddhist brotherhood. By doing this, the son fulfils his filial obligations by transferring merit to his parents, especially to his mother. This is a reward for their parenting that is precious beyond material measure.

I have interviewed *mae chii*s who have received *mae chii* ordination at the request of their families, but this is rare. However, all *mae chii*s that I have talked with have claimed that their parents gain merit from their daughters' ordination. Although becoming a *mae chii* is not considered a daughter's duty, a daughter's central place in the family and the expectations made of them to be an asset as well as their own reliance on their native families becomes evident when they want to become ordained. Women's ordination evokes strong emotions both within the candidates and their parents. By becoming ordained, the young woman leaves her family, perhaps forever, which is a more definitive action than it is for a male novice who will usually return home after a settled period of time. Mothers' different attitudes towards sons' and daughters' ordination are clearly displayed. The novice monks' mothers that I met have been very proud of their sons' ordinations. The mothers of the *mae chii*s, however, often expressed ambiguous feelings about their daughters' ordination and usually said they felt it was a loss.

TWO STAGES OF ORDINATION

The ordination ceremony for males to become fully ordained monks (*bhikkhu*) consists of two stages. The first stage transforms the candidate into a novice monk (*samanera*) and those under the age of 20 can only receive novice ordination. This first stage is called *pabbajja*, which literally marks departure from the lay world into the 'homeless life'. The second stage is known as the *upasampada* and transforms the novice into a *bhikkhu*. *Bhikkhuni* ordination also contains two stages, the *pabbajja* and the *upasampada;* however there is an additional ordained form for women, which I shall deal with below.

The rite of the novice monks' ordination re-enacts a myth that recalls the Buddha's own renunciation of the world in order to seek enlightenment. The myth tells how Prince Siddhatha left the palace one night after a magnificent party. He left his sleeping wife and infant son, flew across the river on his horse, Kanthaka, then stopped at a spot where he cut his hair and exchanged his regal costume for the plain robes of an ascetic. Then, with an alms bowl in hand, he set off to find the way to achieve ultimate transcendence of worldly desire. Like Prince Siddhatha, every man and woman is considered to have the potential to exercise the same act of will, thereby renouncing the world and setting out on a course that will eventually lead to the attainment of enlightenment, *nibbana* (Keyes 1986: 74).

The Buddha's son, Rahula, became the very first novice monk. After Rahula became a novice, the Buddha's father became distressed that he had lost first his son and then his grandson to the mendicant way of life. He asked the Buddha to allow boys to become ordained as novices only if they had their parents' permission. The Buddha agreed and made it an offence for any monk to ordain a boy as a novice without the parents' permission. The rule still stands today and is valid for both boys and girls.

A boy's ordination ritual is a costly event and money to cover the expenses for the ceremony is often collected from relatives, friends and neighbours. The performance of the novice ordination ceremony varies according to the families' social position and where in the country it is held. There are stipulated rules about how the ordination should be conducted and differences in performance do not alter the core ritual elements of that. The first phase of the ritual starts on the day before the actual ordination. In Northern Thailand, the novice candidates are usually dressed in finery, resembling Prince Siddhatha in his lay state (Keyes 1986: 75). When the candidate moves any distance during the day, he is expected to ride on a horse, the equivalent of Kanthaka. In practice, horses are rarely available, so a vehicle of any kind or even the back of a man often provide suitable substitutes. Several rituals usually take place at the house of the main sponsors, usually the parents. The ordinant's head is shaved and monks are customarily invited to chant. Sometimes a lay specialist takes over and performs other kinds of rituals. Often there is music and dancing throughout the night. On the day of the ordination, the ordinant is dressed in white and led in procession to the monastery. In front of the procession there are usually musicians and some older members of the community. The spatial organisation is important; *dana* is central, since participating in these rituals is considered to be of high meritorious value. The main sponsors lead the procession and carry the robes, bowl and ritual fan for the ordinant. Under the shade of an umbrella comes the aspirant novice monk. He is carried by friends, or riding on a horseback, or travelling in an open truck or just is walking. At the rear, people carry various offerings for the novice monk. The ordinant takes official leave of his parents inside the temple. The boy's head and eyebrows are shaved before he requests the ten novice precepts from the monk. These are as follows (see also Chapter 1):

The ten novice precepts

I undertake the rule of training to refrain from:

Taking life,

Taking what is not given,

Being unchaste,

Speaking falsely,

Taking distilled and fermented intoxicants or drugs,

Taking food at the wrong time,

Dancing, singing, playing music and seeing shows,

Using flowers, perfumes and cosmetics for beautifying and adorning the body,

Using high and luxurious sleeping places and seats,

Accepting gold and silver (i.e. money).

The *pabbajja* ceremony includes requesting and repeating the ten precepts and it turns the boy into a novice monk. The ordination ritual carries an immense amount of beneficial *kamma* for the main sponsors, who are usually the parents, and this is reflected in the great care with which the 'pouring water ritual' (*rodnaam*) is performed immediately after the ordination. While the monks chant, the newly ordained pours water as a sign of transferring merit to his parents and kin; the parents themselves enact the same rite to impart some of the merit that they have acquired to their dead parents and other ancestors (Tambiah 1970: 106, Terwiel 1994: 200).

The novice ordination ceremony is usually short and during the ceremony the boy changes into the robes of a novice. After the ceremony, the new novice makes a small offering to the monk, and the parents pay their respects by bowing not only to the monk but also to their son, the new novice, since he has now been elevated to a higher social position than their own.

The requisites of a monk are three sets of robes, an umbrella, a monk's bowl, a pair of slippers, a lamp, a razor and a water strainer.[1] These are symbols of the renunciants' ascetic living. The novice's robes are the same as those of a monk;

an underrobe or waist-cloth held up by a cord belt, a thin 'waistcoat' which covers his chest, and the outer robe. The novice does not wear the additional robe (*sanghati*), which is folded into a long rectangle and draped over the monk's left shoulder during monastic ceremonies.

ADMISSION TO THE FEMALE *SANGHA*

The reluctant attitude towards women's ordination has a long history and was also experienced by the founder of the first order of Buddhist renunciants, Mahapajapati Gotami (see Chapter 2). She was the Buddha's aunt and foster mother and she met with considerable resistance when she requested ordination for women. It is tempting to compare the difficulties that women once had gaining entry into the *sangha* with the hardship women still face. Young women today often have difficulties in securing their parents' consent. Often, they have to travel far away to find a suitable place to receive ordination and they also often have difficulties in financing their ordained life.

There is one form of ordination that is solely for women and it is called *sikkhamana*. The *sikkhamana* originated later than the other forms of ordination and was instigated after a *bhikkhuni* was found to be pregnant and was driven out of the *sangha* for transgressing the rule of sexual relationships. However, the *bhikkhuni* had asked for ordination without knowing that she was pregnant. In order to make sure that this situation would not occur in the future, a period of two years training as a *sikkhamana* was introduced for women. A *sikkhamana* has to observe the six *anudhamma*s which are the first six precepts in the ten precepts for novices. Kabilsingh emphasises that a *sikkhamana* is considered having a training level higher than novice monks even though the *sikkhamana* receives only six precepts. That is because the *sikkhamana* is a preparatory stage prior to receiving higher ordination, which differs from the novices. If the receiving *sikkhamana* during the two years' training should transgress any one of the precepts, she has to start all over again (Kabilsingh 1998: 13). When the *sikkhamana* has observed the six *anudhamma*s for two years she can approach her *pavattini* (*bhikkhuni* preceptor) to arrange for higher ordination, *upasampadaa* (Horner 1990: 138–139).

A so-called dual ordination is required for the ordination of *bhikkhuni*. The preceptor for the higher ordination must have 12 years standing as a *bhikkhuni*, be learned, and appointed by the *sangha*. That contrasts with the requirement that a preceptor for monks should have been ordained for ten years (Holt 1999: 114–115). After the ceremony, which is led by the *bhikkhuni,* the aspirant asks for ordination from the monks' *sangha*. This must be done on the same day. Men do not need the *bhikkhuni sangha* for their ordination. It is only women who are requested to ask for the two *sanghas*. The explanation given for the necessity of 'dual ordination' for *bhikkhuni* is as follows. In ancient times, the female aspirant renunciant did not have to ask the *bhikkhuni sangha* for ordination. She only needed to approach the *bhikkhu sangha*, but when she asked for ordination she had to answer various questions to check whether there were any obstacles to her becoming fully ordained. The set of intimate questions put to the women were asked by the assembly of monks, and the aspirant was often so shy that she could not answer. It was therefore often unclear to the *bhikkhu sangha* whether she was free from these obstacles or not, and under these circumstances the ordination procedure could not be continued. In order to solve the problem, it was decided that the special 11 questions put to the female aspirant renunciants should be asked by the *bhikkhuni* (ibid.: 140–142). Therefore the initial part of the ordination, to question the female aspirant, is done only among the *bhikkhuni sangha*, and it can even be done outside the *sima* boundary. After the questions have been answered, the *bhikkhuni sangha* recommends the aspirant for full ordination, and the *bhikkhu sangha* completes the procedure.

At the ordination ceremony, the candidate has to answer 24 questions. There are 16 disqualification questions, which are divided into 11 questions concerned with gynaecological deformities and five with diseases. The questions about the five diseases – leprosy, boils, eczema, consumption, and epilepsy are the same for women and men. Further questions are: Are you a human being? Are you a female? (And in the case of the male candidate, Are you a male?) Are you a free woman? Are you free from all debts? Are you a king's servant? Have you obtained permission from your parents? (Or in the case of a woman, ...parents or husband) Are you over 20 years of age? Have you got your bowls and robes? What is your name? Who is your proposer? (Horner 1990: 145–153).

> In order to qualify the female candidate 'must not be of furious temperament, nor grief-stricken, nor pregnant, nor a householder, nor without female characteristics, nor with both female and male characteristics, nor with mixed female and male characteristics, nor currently menstruous, nor non-menstruous, nor of doubtful sexual characteristics, nor a corrupter of monks, nor a slayer of mother, father or *arahat* [enlightened person], nor producing blood or wicked thoughts in the presence of a Tathagata, nor a heretic, nor a thief, nor a flag destroyer, nor a thieflike inhabitant, nor one who has been made to live apart from monks and nuns, nor one who has been expelled from a monastic order'. (Paul 1985: 90)

There are explicit prohibitions upon eunuchs entering the *sangha;* monks must be capable of performing sexually, while controlling completely the desire to do so. The ordination process, Keyes argues, transforms those who undergo it into a new gender identity that transcends sex. The gender of the renunciant does not result from a biological sexual attribute, nor is it, he adds, 'a consequence of physical mutilation' (Keyes 1986: 85–87, 93). It is essential that the male candidate is sexually competent, implying that the candidate is equipped with all the faculties that he is later required to 'give up'. Also ordained women should have the capacity to perform sexually while keeping sexual desire in check. A female renunciant should be fertile, although her fertility must be controlled (Lang 1995: 36). The gynaecological questions put to the female candidates have no corresponding formulations in the initiation ceremony of male candidates. However, the 32 characteristic marks of a Buddha's body specify that a Buddha's penis is drawn inwards or enclosed with a sheath. 'The sheathed penis', Nancy Barnes suggests, 'symbolizes that his genital virility is controlled and contained and is replaced by his oral "virility" ' (Barnes (Schuster) 1987: 259, n. 11). For all ordained, the *mae chii*s included, it is important to control the mental organ which controls sexual responsiveness.

In the *mae chii*s' ordination procedure, the candidates are not questioned on their sexual ability. They are asked whether they are free women, free from pregnancy, debts and not in royal service. They must be fit to lead a homeless life and free from the types of diseases listed for the *bhikkhu* and *bhikkhuni* candidates. Today, HIV/AIDS has been added to the list of diseases that disqualify women from receiving *mae chii* ordination.

FINANCIAL CONSTRAINTS

Men who seek ordination are not asked about their financial position but for women financial assets are an important prerequisite for their lives as *mae chii*s. *Mae chii*s will face difficulties if they do not have savings of their own or receive financial support from lay persons. In some temples, older *mae chii*s function as guardians for younger *mae chii*s to whom the younger *mae chii*s can turn in times of need. In temples like Wat Paknam, *mae chii*s without economic means work in the kitchen, and this is often necessary for newly ordained *mae chii*s if they live at a temple. The support of lay people is not taken for granted by *mae chii*s as it is for monks. Some *mae chii*s told me that they had planned their ordination and worked for years, saving up money for their ordained lives. Many that I interviewed said that it was almost impossible to become ordained without economic assets or financial support from relatives or other lay people. However, today, with the increasing numbers of independent *samnak chii*s and greater support from lay people, the *mae chii*s' financial situation has to some extent improved. Even so, most Thai *mae chii*s live under economic strain, lacking the governmental support that monks receive.

Spiritual training is required for entering the *bhikkhu* and *bhikkhuni* orders, but since both *bhikkhu* and *bhikkhuni* live homeless lives supported by the laity, their financial standing is not a qualifying question. Many *mae chii*s had difficulties in finding financial support. One example was Mae chii Noy, whom we met in Chapter 3. She had wanted to become ordained since she was very young and she followed the eight precepts for a couple of years before she finally received ordination. At that time, her father was a monk at a temple in another village. When she went to see him, they had not been in touch for some time. She needed his approval for her ordination and she also turned to him for advice. There were a large number of monks at her father's temple, but there was only one *mae chii* and she spent most of her time in the kitchen. In this part of Thailand it was not common for women to become ordained and Mae chii Noy had only seen a few *mae chii*s, and she had never spoken to any of them. Nor was her father familiar with the situation of a *mae chii*. He knew the *mae chii* at his temple, and he explained to his daughter that the life of the *mae chii*s was not like the life of a monk. *Mae chii*s at temples did not usually officiate at public ceremonies, they spent much time in the kitchen, though they did practise meditation since that was considered suitable for *mae chii*s. Her father recommended that she become ordained at a meditation temple that he knew of near Bangkok. He accompanied her to the temple and introduced her to the head of the *mae chii*s' department. The head *mae chii* informed Mae chii Noy and her father about the prerequisites for women's ordination and they became aware of the financial difficulties that women face when they seek ordination. Mae chii Noy said:

> We did not know about the situation for *mae chii*s at temples. I had only a small amount of money when we left Isaan. The head *mae chii* asked me about my financial position. I told her I did not have any savings, and she informed me that I needed at least 500 Baht per month to stay at the temple. Novices and monks did not have to pay, but *mae chii*s did. I did not know what to do. The head *mae chii* said I could stay as a *phraam* for one week. My father suggested that I should go back home, start working and saving up money. I did not want to go back home straight away and I therefore decided to stay at the temple for

seven days. My father left and promised to return for me within a week. I really desired a celibate life. I wanted to become ordained, but I did not know how to realise that.

Mae chii Noy stayed at the temple and received temporary ordination as a *chii phraam*. She meditated and followed the ceremonies at the temple. One day she met a visiting *mae chii* who had heard that she wanted to become ordained but could not meet the economic requirements. The *mae chii* was in charge of a small *samnak chii* and she offered to support Mae chii Noy if she agreed to help to take care of two relatives who stayed at the *samnak chii*. This was an opportunity for Mae chii Noy to fulfil her dream and she accepted the offer. She was happy that she would be able to receive ordination, but when she recalled her ordination ceremony she expressed grief over her poverty which meant she was unable to fulfil the act of reciprocity that is anticipated at ordination ceremonies. She said:

> I received ordination before I went to the *samnak chii*. My relatives could not attend the ceremony because it was far away from my village. I did not have any money. I could not donate anything to the monks who conducted the ceremony. I felt so bad about not having anything to give. I still feel sad when I think about that. But I was very fortunate to have the chance to become ordained. I felt happy and grateful to Khun Mae who gave me the opportunity. There is a big difference between temporary ordination and becoming ordained and shaving properly. Living with eight precepts as a *phraam*, and living with the eight precepts as a *mae chii* are not the same thing, even if the precepts are the same. Before I became a *mae chii*, I followed the eight precepts at home for two years. I worried a lot about my family, I thought of my mother, siblings and nieces. I was always concerned about their wellbeing. After I received ordination I did not worry about them anymore. Everything changed. It was as if they were not my family in the same way as before. When I became ordained I got a new family, and a new chance. It was like being born again, getting a new life. Shaving makes a big difference.[2]

Mae chii Noy and other *mae chii*s stated that it was almost impossible to become ordained without economic assets of their own or financial support from relatives or other lay people. This speaks against the assumption that poverty is one of the most important reasons why women seek ordination. Mae chii Noy came from one of the poorest provinces in the Northeast, and she was the only woman from her village who had become ordained. She mentioned spiritual reasons for becoming ordained but not poverty. On the contrary, poverty is a great obstacle for women who want to receive ordination and live an ordained life.

MAE CHII ORDINATION

The ordination of *mae chii*s is not lavish and the cost is commonly covered by the family or the *mae chii* herself. By contrast with the celebrations held for male novice ordination, *mae chii* ordination is not celebrated and there is no party the day before. Usually, one or a few monks will officiate at a *mae chii* ordination ceremony at a temple, and only a small group of people gather. Ideally, the female candidate's parents and relatives are present on the day. Many of the interviewed *mae chii*s who had been ordained at temples had gone through the ritual without any of their family members attending the ceremony. There are also differences between the female ordination ceremonies held at a temple and held at a *samnak chii*. At self-governed *samnak chii*s the ceremony has developed into a more public event. At least five monks are usually invited and both monks and *mae chii*s usually officiate. Family members and other lay people attend the ceremony.

The *mae chii*s did not usually go into detail about their own ordination ceremonies. They often said that it was a simple ceremony and only a small gathering. Although the *mae chii* ordination ritual is not a big public event, it is one of the most important moments in an ordained woman's life. It was common for the *mae chii*s whom I interviewed to say that they experienced their ordination as the death of themselves as lay persons. They said it was like being born again (*koet iik krang*) and that they had acquired a new chance in life. In Buddhism, death is the most important *rite of passage* (Tambiah 1970: 179). Death and birth are seen as interlinked processes that may be described as a doorway that one goes in an out of. Walpola Rahula explains that the difference between death and birth is only a 'thought moment': the last thought moment in this life conditions the first thought moment in the so-called next life, which, in fact, is the continuity of the same series. During this life too, one thought moment conditions the next thought moment (Rahula 1978[1959]: 34).

There are variations in the *mae chii* ordination ceremonies. The different phases that are explicitly marked in the novice initiation are also found in the *mae chii* ordination ritual but they are not as elaborate. At Ratburi Samnak Chii, at least five monks and five *mae chii*s officiate at the *mae chii* ordination ceremony. Monks used to be invited from nearby temples, but if the aspirant wishes, the head *mae chii* at the *samnak chii* can be the preceptor, and in this case no monks are invited. The qualification questions and preparations are performed by the *mae chii*s at the *samnak chii*. The ordination ceremony starts in the *saalaa* with the *mae chii* aspirant ritually asking her parents and relatives for forgiveness by passing a *phaan* (a plated tray) with flowers to each person.

Each person receives the tray and utters words of forgiveness and then gives it back to the aspirant. Then follows the shaving of the woman's head and eye brows and Khun Mae gives the *mae chii* robes to the candidate. Once her head is shaved and she is dressed in the *mae chii* robe, the ceremony continues with the *mae chii* taking 'refuge in the triple gem': the Buddha, the *dhamma*, and the *sangha*. Then the aspirant asks in Pali for the eight precepts from the *upachaa,* the preceptor (a monk qualified to be in charge of ordinations), after which the monks are presented with candles, incense, flowers and envelopes with money.3 Thereafter the monks end their part of the ceremony with chanting. Then the woman receives the ordination from a group of five *mae chiis* and commits herself to follow the *mae chiis*' training rules. The *mae chiis*, too, receive a donation, though the sum of money is smaller than that to the monks. Following this the *mae chiis* end the whole ceremony with chanting.

A *mae chii* ordination ritual that was held at a *samnak chii* in the Northeastern part of Thailand resembles the ceremony at Ratburi Samnak Chii. Both *samnak chiis* are members of The Thai Mae Chiis' Institute which has made an outline of how the ordination ceremony for *mae chiis* should be performed, although there is room for individual variations. One of the *mae chii* candidates in the following ordination ritual was Nok, a 13-year-old girl from Northeastern Thailand. She had recently finished the compulsory six years of primary school and wanted to continue studying. However, her family could not afford the school fees, and the free secondary education offered at Ratburi Samnak Chii was the only chance for Nok to continue her schooling. At Ratburi Samnak Chii, girls do not have to become ordained in order to study so Nok could have studied without becoming ordained. But she wanted to become a *mae chii* and she chose to shave her head and live according to a more restrict regime than most of her schoolmates at the *samnak chii*. Her family members had discussed Nok's ordination back and forth for almost a year. Finally they had decided to agree to Nok's request. It was planned that Nok should become ordained at a *samnak chii* in Isaan before going to Ratburi Samnak Chii where the age limit was 14. Ratburi Samnak Chii would, however, admit *mae chiis* below the age of 14 who had been ordained elsewhere.

There were two other women who received ordination at the same time as Nok. They came originally from Bangkok, had university degrees, and had lived with the eight Buddhist precepts for several years. One of them was in her 30s and the other was about 55. In this case, none of the three candidates lived at the *samnak chii* where they were going to be ordained. They received ordination at the same ceremony after which the two older women went back

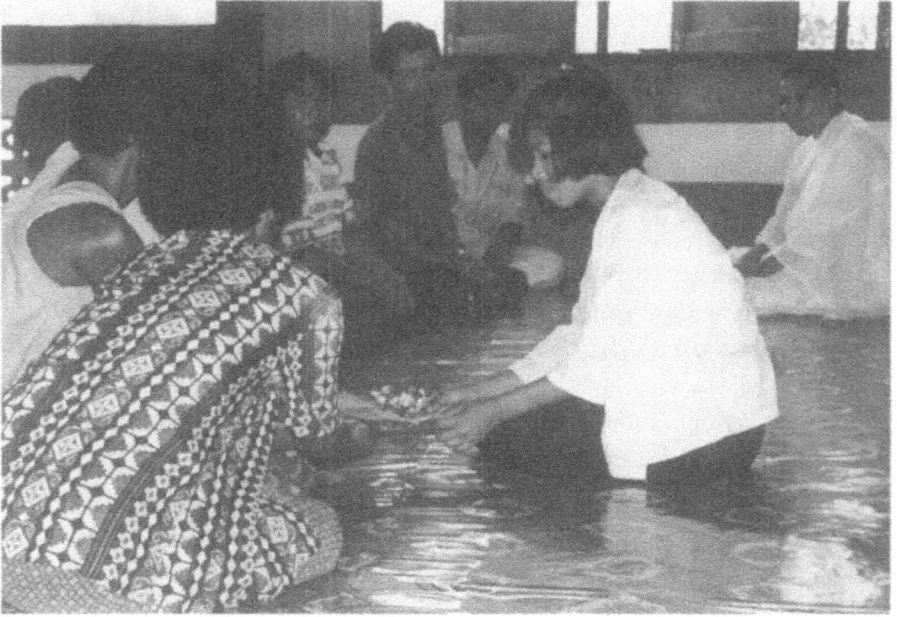

Figure 4.1. A *mae chii* aspirant ritually asking her parents and relatives for forgiveness before ordination

to their old *samnak chii* in the same province. Nok had travelled from a distant province and after the ordination ceremony she went with the big gathering from her village to Ratburi Samnak Chii.

The head *mae chii*, Khun Mae, had made agreements with five monks from temples in the area to officiate at the ceremony; also five *mae chii*s were invited. Khun Mae had made all the arrangements for food and the other items required for the ordination. I had followed the planning of Nok's ordination for about six months. There were discussions at Ratburi Samnak Chii concerning her young age and the difficulties that she might face in adjusting to ordained life. I also visited Nok's village where her family was discussing whether they should give their consent for her ordination. Finally they agreed to her proposal and I was invited by Nok's relatives and by Khun Mae to participate in the ordination ceremony. I travelled to the Northeast of Thailand a couple of days before the ordination ceremony took place. On the ordination day the bell rang before four o'clock in the morning as is usual at temples and *samnak chii*s. The day started like all other days with chanting and meditation followed by an alms round in the village. A few hours later some women from the village came to help out in the kitchen. Nok's mother, stepfather, sister, grandmother, aunts, cousins, and neighbours were busy preparing for the ceremony. Khun Mae talked with Nok, asked her the qualification questions and instructed her in the proceedings of the ceremony.

The ceremony started at nine o'clock at the indoor *saalaa* where the daily chantings were held. Nok wore a blue sarong-like wrapped skirt (*phaasin*) and a white blouse. The *mae chii*s and Nok's relatives, friends and neighbours sat in front of the Buddha statue. Khun Mae and Nok sat closest to it. Nok lit a candle and incense in front of the Buddha and bowed three times. She then turned around and faced her relatives. She had a *phaan* with flowers and she kneeled in front of every person and handed over the *phaan* and asked them for forgiveness for any wrongdoings she had committed. They repeated the words of forgiveness and gave the *phaan* back to Nok. When this was finished, the shaving procedure began. Nok sat on a chair and her relatives lined up in front of her. Her mother started to cut some of her hair which was then put in a bowl with water. Then her grandmother cut some, her stepfather was the next person to cut, and then every lay person cut some of her hair. Then Khun Mae recited a Pali text and started to shave her head, whereupon another *mae chii* took over; her aunt a *mae chii* herself finished the shaving. This part of the ceremony was emotional and Nok was in tears, but people around her laughed as Thai people usually do when somebody cries in public. Nok's mother ended this phase of the ceremony by taking the bowl with the hair and putting it under a tree at the outskirts of the *samnak chii*.

After the shaving ceremony, Nok and Khun Mae went and sat in front of the Buddha statue once again. Khun Mae handed over the white *mae chii* robe to Nok. Nok donned the *mae chii*'s dress and went to the open *saalaa*. The five monks and the invited *mae chii*s had arrived and the monks were sitting on the Buddha image's left side. The five *mae chii*s sat on the images' right side along the long side. The oldest of the three *mae chii* aspirants opened the ceremony by lightening a candle and incense. A *phaan* with flowers, a special bundle of candles and incense (*thuupthianphae*) and an envelope with money were first presented to the Buddha and then to the monk who was the preceptor. Then the candidates asked the preceptor for the *mae chii* precepts. The candidates recited three times: *Namo tassa bhagavato arahato samma sambuddhassa* ('Reverence to the Lord who is worthy and fully awakened'). Then they took refuge in the triple gem (*Buddha, Dhamma, Sangha*). The preceptor held the fan in front of his face and gave the candidates the eight precepts. After the aspirants had received the precepts by repeating them, the monks recited Buddhist texts. The ceremony continued with the five *mae chii*s chanting Buddhist texts in Pali. At the end of the ceremony, the newly ordained *mae chii*s gave flowers, money and offerings to the five monks and five *mae chii*s. The monks were offered lotus flowers and the *mae chii*s orchids. The offerings were various items to be used by the *mae chii*s and monks in their daily lives. The sum of money was the same for monks and *mae chii*s. The ordination ritual was completed and Nok and the other two *mae chii*s were now properly ordained and had entered the ordained state.

The parents and relatives did not pour any water to transfer merits as was done in the male novice ordination ceremony in the Northern Thailand; instead water was poured over the *mae chii*s' hands in order to wish them success in the ordained life. This is a Thai custom practised at various ceremonies and occasions. However, it was the first time that I had encountered this practice at a Buddhist ordination ceremony. The monks poured water first, and after them the *mae chii*s and then parents, relatives and friends. That ended the ceremony and everybody then went to the indoor *saalaa* for lunch. Usually monks eat first, but on this occasion, because of shortage of time we all ate at the same time. We were, however, divided into three groups and sat on three different mats. The monks were seated on the one closest to the Buddha image, then came the *mae chii*s and finally the lay people on the third mat.

GENDERED ORDINATION

The diverse ordination performances for men and women reveal the differences in the social significance and cultural meaning of ordination in Thailand. For women the *mae chii* ordination is not about a transition from one phase of life into another. It is rather a break off from ongoing life and the start of a completely new way of life. In the ritual, the female candidate breaks with her former lay life and lay identity and becomes an ordained person. She formally says farewell to her relatives and friends. The begging of forgiveness for any acts committed intentionally or unintentionally and that may have been offensive to her superiors, her parents and relatives also marks the end of her lay belonging. Once she has entered the *mae chii* community, she can no longer act in the lay manner, and it is no longer possible for her to correct previous offences to others. When the candidates have asked for the precepts and the preceptor, usually a monk, has given the precepts, the *mae chii* formally belongs to the community of *mae chii*s. The shaving of the head is the peak of the ceremony that is concerned with leaving the lay realm. Shaving the head signifies a rite of separation, a turning away from the heat of sensual desire toward the coolness

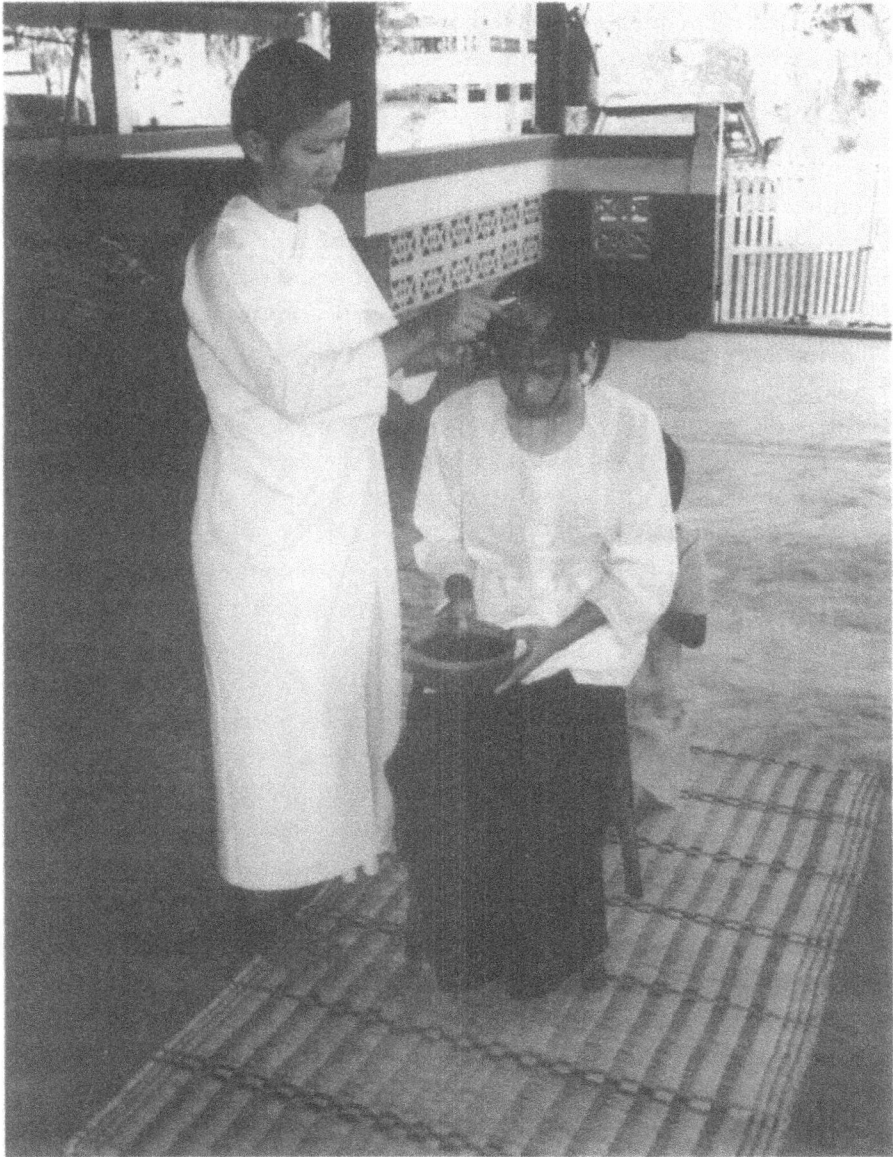

Figure 4.2. Shaving of a young *mae chii* aspirant's head

of *nibbana* (Lang 1995: 33). Shaving the head is said to cool the body; the intention of turning the mind away from the sensual objects in this world cools the mind. When the shaving is finished, the white robes are handed over to the candidate, usually by the *mae chii* who is highest in rank. In Nok's case it was not her parents but other *mae chii*s who had donated *mae chii* robes to her. Her family and friends donated the alms bowl and other items needed for ordained life.

Where the ordination takes place also betrays men's and women's respective positions. Ordinations for novices are usually conducted in the image hall or ordination hall of a temple. Ordinations of monks must take place within a consecrated space, a building called *bot* or *uposatha* set apart from other buildings in a temple by stone markers (*sima*). It is normally taboo in Northern Thailand for women to enter an ordination hall, *bot*, but not in the Central Thailand. However, in Northern Thailand sometimes mothers and older female relatives of the candidates are allowed to sit just inside the entrance to the ordination hall. According to local notions, women are considered to represent a threat to the disciplinary purity of the *sangha,* although the taboo against women entering an ordination hall has no Buddhist charter and is not observed in Central Thailand (Keyes 1986: 77). In 2004, the Khon Kaen Senator Rabriabrat Pongpanit challenged the prohibition banning women from entering 'sacred areas' in temples in Northern Thailand. She was refused entrance to a pagoda with a sacred relic in Chiang Mai area and she stated that it was against women's rights in Clause 30 of the Thai Constitution. An intensive debate about this issue followed in radio programmes, newspapers and on television. The senator, who was a member of the Senate Committee on Women, Youth and the Aged Affairs, was accused of showing disrespect for Buddhist beliefs and for the Northern Thai, Lanna, custom. On 7 July a large gathering of men and women, young and elderly, teachers and monks from Chiang Mai area signed a petition to have the senator dismissed from her political posts. They demanded an apology and the senator extended a public apology to the Chiang Mai residents for aggravating and interfering with their traditions and beliefs. The senator also received a death threat for having asked the National Buddhist Office to clarify why many Northern temples impose a ban on women to enter inner sanctums housing Buddhist relics, as she was concerned that it might violate an equal rights clause in the 1997 constitution. The senator remained on her political posts, the issue was discussed at Thai universities and at meetings organised by NGOs working with gender issues, but women are still denied entry to the sacred areas in the Northern Thai temples.

In Central Thailand, women are not forbidden to enter the *bot* building and in Bangkok it is not uncommon for *mae chii*s to chant together with the monks in the *bot*. A *bot* is not found at *samnak chii*s and ordination of *mae chii*s is usually held in the *saalaa*, the image hall of the temple and the *samnak chii*. Further, the *mae chii*s do not don saffron robes like the monks but are ordained in white. White signifies their observation of abstinence, but white can also be seen as a lay colour. Lay women and men who observe the eight precepts on *wan phra* may wear white. White symbolises purity and in Buddhist terms it implies abstinence from indulging in sensual pleasures. White is further the traditional colour of mourning, also of purity for participants in various rituals. The *mae chii*s expressed no ambiguity about their white dress. They said that they saw the white robe as a symbol of their pure (*borisut*) state, and did not connect white with any liminal position. The suggestion made by P. Van Esterik, that white should connote a liminal state, comes from the comparison between male and female ordination where male ordinants don plain white robes for a brief time in the middle of the ritual, and from the association of white with the laity (see P. Van Esterik 1996: 57). After the male novice candidates have been wearing the white robes, they put on saffron robes and enter into the *sangha* community. The saffron colour stands for maturity. Maturity is what they should be striving towards while in the monkhood. Their shaven heads, their robes, their religious names, their precepts and new status are all reminders of their new standing and obligations towards the monks' community and towards the laity, including their parents. While monks are associated with maturity, *mae chii*s are associated with purity. Maturity may also be connected with wisdom, education and power, and purity with moral behaviour. *Mae chii*s keep their lay names as *mae chii*s. However, their shaved heads, white robes, and Buddhist precepts are all markers of their ordained state.

The male ordination ritual follows the steps in the ritual that Van Gennep (1960) calls *rites de passage*. He distinguishes three major phases: separation (preliminal), transition (liminal) and incorporation (postliminal). On the basis of the ritualised action of passage rites, Van Gennep treats societies as if they were rooms separated by doorways or passageways. Transition from one social status (or 'room') to the next requires means for negotiating them, namely rites of passage (Grimes 1996: 529). In Thailand, both men and women go through the rite of passage leading from one position in lay society into the religious realm and, for most men, back into lay life. For men the '*sangha* room' is open and gives those who pass through it an elevated position in the lay world; however, that 'room' is closed for Thai women. Women have been knocking on the locked door to the *sangha* and invoking women's equal right to be part of the congregation. Entry for women would give them religious legitimacy, but their efforts have hitherto been in vain. However, the *mae chii*s have not aspired to be part of the *sangha* but instead, with assistance from lay people, have created a parallel female religious realm outside the male *sangha*.

The phases of the ordination ritual may be interpreted differently, depending on what objectives the renunciation fulfils. Ordination does not mean the same thing for novices, who commonly spend a fixed period of time as novice monks and then return to lay life, as for those men whose ambition is to stay permanently in the monkhood. As already mentioned, novice ordination serves at least two important social objectives for young Thai men. One is maturity, which they are considered to gain through ordination, and the other is the demonstration of filial piety towards their parents. Mothers in particular gain much merit through their sons' ordination. Thus, neither the status of monk, nor the ambition to attain *nibbana,* are final goals for these young men. The aim is rather to accomplish their obligation and re-enter the lay world. The period that they spend in the temple may be understood as a liminal phase, and returning to lay life as the completion of the novice ritual. However, for those men who become ordained in order to remain in the monkhood, the ritual is completed when they are admitted into the *sangha.*

Young, unmarried women who become *mae chii*s have chosen a deviant path in life by abandoning their prescribed vocations as wives and mothers, while men become fit for married life through monkhood. Further, men usually stay in their home villages and become monks at temples close to home. They often have friends who become ordained at the same time, whereas women usually have to leave their villages and move far away. This implies that women have to adjust themselves to their new lives as *mae chii*s among other *mae chii*s and lay people who are strangers.

The proposed *sangha* gender mentioned in Chapter 2 is acquired through renunciation and the practice of celibacy. Keyes (1986: 86) states that a person acquires *sangha* gender through a uniquely human endeavour whereby one subjects oneself to a 'discipline' that makes it possible to transcend 'natural' sexuality and that this discipline is applicable only to males in the Theravadin tradition (ibid.: 85). I suggest, however, that although women are excluded from the *sangha* on the institutional level, this does not mean that they cannot acquire an identity similar to the male *sangha* gender identity through the same practice of renunciation and celibacy in *mae chii*s' monastic communities. On the spiritual level the *sangha* gender is for both sexes and both men and women are considered to have the capacity to reach the highest spiritual goal. However, on the socio-cultural level, ordination commonly carries different meanings for men and women.

Ordained persons develop a gender identity based on renunciation and a celibate lifestyle, and the ordained gender is based on the individual's identity as an ordained person who belongs to the religious realm. Their *'sangha* gender identity' becomes strengthened when it is confirmed by the laity's legitimising of them as a field of merit. The *mae chii*s whom I interviewed had often had experiences of being *chii phraam*s before they received *mae chii* ordination, but they assured me that receiving *mae chii* ordination implied an entirely new becoming and a new belonging. As ordained women they were no longer expected to fulfil the prescribed gender norms as nurturers and mothers. The female sex disqualifies Thai women from entrance into the *sangha*, but their sex does not disqualify them from attaining an ordained identity based on their spiritual transcendence into the religious realm. However, a *'sangha* gender identity' needs confirmation from the lay community.

NOTES

1 According to the text, however, he should only possess eight articles: alms bowl, three robes, a belt, a razor, a needle and a water strainer.

2 For *mae chii*s, shaving the head signifies a rite of separation from the lay life and a turning away from the heat of sensual desire.

3 According to their rules, monks are not allowed to handle money and money donated to them should be taken care of by the monastery's lay attendants. However, today this precept is often violated since monks sometimes have to handle money.

CHAPTER FIVE

Mae Chii Communities and the Making of a Mae Chii

The ritual of ordination and subsequent monastic life both make a distinction between the lay and religious realms and also generate a hierarchical form of unity in the ordained community. Being ordained is the first step on the religious path after which the process of internalising the monastic code begins. In order to uphold monastic life, the three Buddhist practices – *samadhi* (concentration), *panna* (wisdom) and *sila* (moral conduct) are essential. Of these, moral conduct is said to be the foundation upon which the other two rest. The *mae chii*s at Ratburi Samnak Chii learn morality by studying Buddhist texts, upholding the Buddhist precepts and following the *mae chii* rules.

The *mae chii*s' training at Ratburi Samnak Chii is characterised by their regulated life and shapes their *sangha* gender identity. The restricted life shows that the training involves the whole person and comprises the *mae chii*s' minds as well as their outer appearance, their conduct in relationship to other monastics and lay people. Moreover, the place where the *mae chii*s live is of significance for their ability to develop spiritually. A *mae chii* can choose to live at a temple where monks also reside or at a self-governed *samnak chii* with solely female inhabitants. The differences between the two places of abode affect the *mae chii*s' lives and religious roles and the differences in spiritual status between *mae chii*s at temples and *mae chii*s at *samnak chii*s. Purity and pollution practices have developed in co-ordination with the stratification of Buddhist societies and are further explored in this chapter.

SAMNAK CHII – A WOMEN-ONLY RELIGIOUS SPACE

At many temples in Thailand the *mae chii*s live in separate communities (*samnak chii*) within the temples' administrative structure. This is in accordance with traditional Theravada practice, where the living quarters of male and female renunciants are separated from one another. Most of the *samnak chii*s in Thailand belong to temples and the temples are owned by the *sangha*. Since Thai *mae chii*s do not fall under the *sangha*'s administration, it has been possible for the *mae chii*s to establish their own communities. However, it is only in the last decades that *samnak chii*s independent of temples have increased in number. Some *samnak chii*s are built on land owned by the *mae chii*s or their families. Commonly, lay people initiate the foundation of *samnak chii*s by donating land for the specific purpose of establishing a *samnak chii*.

A *samnak chii* is generally modelled upon the structure of a Buddhist temple, but it does not contain all the buildings that a temple usually consists of. Thai Buddhist temples may differ in terms of architecture and size, but inside the temples' boundaries there are usually several basic structures. These are: a *saalaa* where ceremonies and also other gatherings take place and which is open for both laity and renunciants; a *vihara*, which is used by the monks for various religious services and where laity may also join; an *uboosot*, which is used primarily by the monks for ordination ceremonies and other monks' ceremonies. The *uboosot* is a building that is erected on consecrated ground and surrounded by *sima* stones. There is also a *chedi*, or *stupa*, which is a bell-shaped tower containing relics, and there is lodging for monks and *mae chii*s that may be a dormitory-like building or individual huts, *kuti*.

The main building at a *samnak chii* is usually the *saalaa* where ceremonies and many other activities take place. *Samnak chii*s do not have structures such as *vihara* or *uboosot*. Some *samnak chii*s have *chedi* and all *samnak chii*s have huts or dormitory-like buildings for the *mae chii*s. Many temples have a crematorium, but that is not found at *samnak chii*s. Both temples and *smnak chii*s usually have a special showcase with the many volumes of the Tipitaka, the Buddhist canon. Likewise a *bodhi* tree (the tree under which the Buddha became enlightened) is usually found on the temple grounds and at *samnak chii*s. There is often a school building at temples, and a few *samnak chii*s have more recently also built schools.

An important difference between a *samnak chii* and a temple is that *samnak chii*s lack some of the significant and sacred structures that are present at temples. Since temples include these particular buildings, which cannot be transformed into lay structures, they do not risk degeneration into lay places. The ordination hall, *uboosot*, surrounded with *sima* stones, is one example of a sacred building that is never found in a *samnak chii*'s compound. A *samnak chii*'s standing as a monastic place cannot therefore rely on its buildings, but is dependent on the order maintained and on the *mae chii*s' daily activities. How life is carried on at the *samnak chii* is thus essential in making the *samnak chii* into a religious place. Daily chantings and Buddhist practice are important for the *mae chiis'* status but also for the *samnak chii*'s authenticity as a suitable abode for monastics. The *mae chii*s whom I spoke to declared that the Buddhist chants constitute the backbone of their daily practice. They claimed that a place that houses *mae chii*s who do not uphold the morning and evening chants is not considered to be a monastic place, and is not suitable as a dwelling for *mae chii*s.

According to the *mae chiis'* rules, a *mae chii* should not live together with lay people. It is considered important that *mae chii*s live together in order to accomplish the ordained life's aims of moral and spiritual development. The Thai Mae Chiis' Institute has stipulated that a *samnak chii* must house at least three *mae chii*s in order to be acknowledged as a *samnak chii*. However, a *samnak chii* is not a monastic place solely because *mae chii*s live there; as is clear from the above, the *mae chii* practices are of crucial importance. Following the monastic code and upholding the monastic schedule are minimum demands.

Consequently, *samnak chii*s have the potential to be ambiguous in ways that temples do not, and a *samnak chii* could easily turn into a lay place if religious practices are not upheld. The indispensable practices of morning and evening chants are performed every day at Ratburi Samnak Chii. The morning chanting ceremony begins at 4 o'clock and is followed by meditation; the evening chants are held at 7 o'clock, and there are never any exceptions from this schedule. The routines of morning and evening chants are likewise highly important for individual *mae chii* practice, which I realised when I travelled with the *mae chii*s. They proved to be scrupulous about keeping their daily routines of chants and meditation even when they were outside the *samnak chii*. The *mae chiis'* ordained status demands that they uphold religious practice. The practices confirm their non-lay identity, which I presume would otherwise be called into question.

Ratburi Samnak Chii is a large *samnak chii* with about 50 *mae chii*s and more than a hundred live there altogether. The boundary between the lay and the ordained realms is also maintained inside the *samnak chii*. The three categories, *mae chii, chii phraam* and *dhammacarinii* hold different positions. The most crucial distinction is between the *mae chii*s who are permanently ordained and the other two categories. This corresponds to the boundary between the lay and the ordained realms. However, there are also differences between those who are temporally ordained (*chii phraam*s) and the schoolgirls (*dhammacarinii*s). Both follow the eight precepts but have more of a lay status. Their different positions are based mainly on age since the *dhammacariniis* in most cases are younger than the *chii phraam*s. In the category of *mae chii*, the hierarchical differences rest basically on the number of years spent in the ordained state (*phansaa*) and on their educational level. The *mae chiis*' ages varied from 13 to more than 70. Some *mae chii*s were the same age as the *dhammacariniis*; however, they were not allowed to spend much time together because of the rule that says that lay persons and *mae chii*s should be kept apart. The *mae chii*s are, for example, not allowed to visit the *dhammacariniis*' quarters and likewise the *dhammacariniis* should not visit the *mae chiis*' dwellings.

The hierarchical differences of the members at the *samnak chii* are displayed and maintained throughout daily practice. It finds expression in the sitting arrangements in the *saalaa* and in the dining hall, where the *mae chii*s live in the *samnak chii*, whom they are together with, what kind of chores they are engaged in, and so forth. Since this order permeates daily life so much, the members of the community are continuously reminded of their roles and positions. The *mae chiis*' standing *vis-à-vis* the laity is also confirmed daily through their relationship with the households who offer food every morning at the alms round.

The *saalaa* is the most revered place at the *samnak chii*. It was one of the first buildings to be constructed at Ratburi Samnak Chii and it is the first building one sees when entering the compound. Several Buddha statues are placed in the *saalaa* on the second floor and the *mae chii*s treat the images with great respect. In front of the Buddha statues there is a platform covered by a red carpet where *mae chii*s and monks sit when they visit the *samnak chii*. The platform is a special space, reserved solely for the ordained. The *mae chii*s always wear their outer robe when they sit on the platform. They never walk on their feet on the platform but do it on their knees. They never turn their backs to the Buddha statues but walk backwards on their knees. They always bow, show respect to the Buddha, the Dhamma and the Sangha and before they sit down and they do the same thing before they leave the platform.

The *mae chiis*', *chii phraams*', *dhammacariniis*' and lay people's positions are differentiated in the *saalaa*. The *mae chii*s sit according to their years in the ordained state. However, spatially, it is both a horizontal and a vertical organisation. Most of the *mae chii*s sit on the same level, directly on the mat on the raised platform. The *dhammacariniis* and the *chii phraam*s sit below and behind the *mae chiis*' platform. Khun Mae, the head *mae chii*, has the most prestigious place closest to the Buddha statue, and she sits on a white cushion which makes her position vertically higher than most of the other *mae chii*s.

Other long-standing *mae chii*s who hold high positions in the *samnak chii* sit beside her. Their elevated positions are marked by white cushions. There are a few other *mae chii*s whose positions are also raised. Their cushions are brown and their status depends on the number of years they have been ordained and the level of religious and secular education. A newly ordained *mae chii* has the lowest position, and she has her seat behind all the others, farthest from the Buddha statue, and closest to the *chii phraam*s, and the *dhammacarinii*s. Lay people who follow the five precepts sit behind those who observe the eight precepts.

Among the *mae chii*s', status differences are most noticeable between 'ordinary' *mae chii*s and the *mae chii*s who have high education and are addressed as *acaan*, 'professor'. A *mae chii* who has only been ordained for few years but is highly educated may enjoy higher status than a long-standing *mae chii* without higher education. I also noticed that virgin *mae chii*s, those who have not been married, seem to be held in higher esteem than those who have a marital life behind.

FEMALE SPACE AND CONTESTED CONCEPTIONS OF POLLUTION

It is interesting to explore whether a sacred place with only female inhabitants requires special rules of conduct that have to do with the female body and its supposedly degrading capacities. I understand purity and pollution as relational and highly gendered concepts. Meanings of pollution express understandings of women's relationships with men and their social and moral status. Kim Gutschow (2004: 199) stresses that purity and pollution are less a matter of fixed categories than of a strategic relationship of two terms. Like sacred and secular, purity and pollution offer collective representations, which can maintain and subvert social authority. The two categories imply a symbolic system of local morality and cosmic justice.

In Mary Douglas's (1966) framework on the symbolic anthropology of purity and pollution, women's menstrual blood may be regarded as a substance 'out of place' in that it transgresses the boundaries of the body. Thai discourse on purity and pollution is strongly gendered. The female body is conceived as leaky and ambiguous, unlike the male body that is both unambiguous and bounded. Pimpawun Boonmongkon states that in Thai society, the female genital organ is considered to be inferior, polluted, taboo, ugly, and hidden – compared to the male genital organ that is considered to be superior and symbolically related to prosperity and wealth. The last point is demonstrated by the common practice of Thai shopkeepers and restaurant owners of keeping a wooden carved penis together with their money for the purpose of bringing good luck in business (Boonmongkon 2004: 242).

Shigeharu Tanabe states that menstrual blood is considered a 'polluted and morally degraded entity' in Thailand (Tanabe 1991: 188). The notion of the uncleanness of menstruation is linked to the concepts of the power of women to pollute men and sacred objects. For fear of women's power to pollute and defile, restrictions are placed on women so that men and sacred objects charged with protective power do not deplete their power through contact with women's bodies. Menses are thought to neutralise men's supernatural strength, their sexual potency and their mental-emotional integrity. Men are therefore careful to avoid contact with women's lower garments, which are always washed and hung out to dry separately because of their potential as pollutants. The perception that women's bodily substances are polluting is often cited as a fact on contributing to the subordination of women.

Women's bodies are understood to embody both dangerous substances and potent forces of fertility. This power is concentrated in female genitalia and bodily secretions such as menstrual blood. Sexual relations are avoided during menstruation. Women's underwear and skirts should not come into contact with men, especially their heads. Women are careful to hang these items below waist level and in a discrete location to avoid men accidentally walking under the washing line.

Menstruation carries both negative and positive meanings, and menstrual blood is primarily a positive sign of maturity, fertility and strength. Paradoxically, then, the presence of menstrual blood is a sign both of female defilement and the powers of female fertility.

According to Kabilsingh, the low value attached to female bodies, and the assumption that female bodily processes are polluting and destructive of male power, emerges from Brahmanism, not Buddhism (Kabilsingh 1988: 10–11). The source of these ideas about pollution are said to be the Brahmanic beliefs and practices of the Ayutthaya period (1351–1767), when Brahmanic rituals were used to produce magical charms and amulets to protect soldiers during battle. The charms were believed to become ineffective when they came in contact with menstrual blood or menstruating women (P. Van Esterik 2000: 78). However, researchers have pointed out that Thai women have internalised the notions that women are polluting to the monastic order (Tantiwiramanond and Pandey 1987: 140; Terwiel 1994: 78, 99, 243).

The lay women that I met did not share a unified view about how women should act in relation to menstruation and visits to Buddhist temples. Some avoided going to the temple while menstruating, others went there but were strict about not using the lavatory at the temple, whereas yet others did not restrict themselves to any special behaviour.

Menstruation is viewed as a monthly cleansing of impurities from a woman's body. Andrea Whittaker's ethnography from Northeastern Thailand shows that women are particular about not blocking the flow of menstrual blood and her informants said that they prefer to wear two *phasins* (skirts) and stay at home when menstruating, and they would only wear pads if they had to go out to the market (Whittaker 2000: 72–73).

According to the Thai traditional medicine's discourses, all secretion from women's genital organs is polluted and seen as negative, but the links to fertility and motherhood are positive. These discourses are complex and contradictory and, as mentioned above, simultaneously indicate both positive and negative values of a woman's body.

After childbirth a woman's stomach is believed to be full of bad blood, which is perceived as a dangerous fluid that poisons the womb. Confinement of 'lying by the fire' is practised traditionally to drain the postpartum woman's womb. It makes the womb dry and helps the womb revert to its proper position. Today not many postpartum women practise 'lying by the fire'. They consider it as inconvenient and out-of-date. However, the beliefs of dangerous fluid inside the womb after giving birth are still strong (Chirawatkul 2004: 219).

In Thailand, the disciplining of female sexuality is normally strictly controlled. In contrast, such discipline and constraints are least exercised on elderly, postmenopausal women who are seen as asexual. They are granted power and freedom in society, and they can become outspoken in the public sphere, participating in temple activities and being highly influential in matters of kinship (ibid.: 222).

Kim Gutschow shows in her study of Buddhist ascetic women in Zangskar that unlike the upper-caste Hindu culture, which forbids women from cooking while menstruating, Zangskari women perform their regular household chores during their menstrual periods. In Zangskar, all women must avoid village and household altars and temples while menstruating. Even women who may have ceased to menstruate or are celibate remain excluded from certain religious places of power in the landscape. Kim Gutschow says that whether this is due to pre-Buddhist notions of sacrality or the advent of Buddhist patriarchy is difficult to tell (Gutschow 2004: 209).

At Ratburi Samnak Chii there were no prohibiting rules for *mae chii*s who were menstruating. The weekly cleaning of the Buddha statues in the *saalaa* could, for example, be carried out by *mae chii*s regardless of which phase of their menstrual cycle they were. However, there were restrictions concerning waste pads. The rules at the *samnak chii* are specific about never throwing pads away together with other refuse. Instead, they are thrown in a special, deep hole in the ground on the outskirts of the *mae chii*s' compound. The hole is covered by sheet metal mainly to protect it from the dogs and the waste is not burnt but kept in the ground.

Ratburi Samnak Chii is a female space and the *mae chii*s who live there did not show any concern about the conceptions of the inherent pollution of the female principle. While Thai men fear menstruation because of its danger to them, women are less concerned with their polluting status and are more concerned with the weakening effects of menstruation upon their energy and strength (Whittaker 2000: 71). The *mae chii*s at the *samnak chii* were not restricted in their actions because they were women as they would have been at a temple with male monks. Pollution was seldom discussed. The *mae chii*s were more preoccupied with thoughts of *kamma* and about performing according to the Buddhist precepts. That could be explained by the facts that they lived at a place with only female inhabitants and that the comprehensive theory of purity and pollution is subsumed by the doctrine of *kamma*.

WAN PHRA – DAY OF REFLECTION

Monastic places need support and legitimacy from the laity. Lay people often go to different temples and *samnak chii*s on special religious occasions as well as for the weekly *wan phra*[1]. *Wan phra,* the Buddhist Sabbath, occurs four times per lunar month, and is considered to be an auspicious day for merit-making (*tham bun*). I noticed that the *mae chii*s received larger donations of food on their alms round at *wan phra.* Lay people also offered flowers, incense and candles to them, and this was not usually done on ordinary weekdays. At temples and *samnak chii*s, sermons are usually delivered in the mornings and in the evenings, and lay people come to receive the five precepts and the blessings from the monks. *Wan phra* is also the day for engaging in religious activities that are not normal for everyday life. People come to temples and *samnak chii*s to meditate and listen to *dhamma* talks. Some pious Thai lay people even dress in white and stay at a monastic place and observe the eight Buddhist precepts and practise meditation for a day.

In Thailand there are ample opportunities to listen to Buddhist sermons on radio and TV. It is also possible to receive the Buddhist precepts on the radio. In the morning of *wan phra* the national radio broadcasts *dhamma* talks given by monks. At Ratburi Samnak Chii these talks are listened to in the *saalaa*. All *mae chii*s, *chii phraam*s and *dhammacarinii*s meet at eight o'clock in the morning for a gathering that usually takes about two and a half to three hours. The *dhammacarinii*s, who are dressed in white blouses and grey skirts on weekdays, wear white on *wan phra*. In the *saalaa*, flowers and some money are offered. The radio programme starts with the national anthem and before the monk delivers the sermon he gives the eight Buddhist precepts. The *mae chii*s, *chii phraam*s and *dhammacarinii*s receive the precepts and recite after the monk. While listening to *dhamma* talks, everyone sits in a respectful position with their legs folded under them and their hands folded in front of them in a *wai*. When the monk finishes his preaching, the radio is turned off and the ceremony is concluded by chanting performed by the assembly in the *saalaa*.

One of the *mae chii*s, using a microphone, then reads some sets of rules from 'The Mae Chiis' Handbook'. The assignment to read the rules in the *saalaa* rotates among the *mae chii*s and Khun Mae decides which sets of rules are to be read. When the *mae chii* finishes reading, the gathering proceeds with one senior *dhammacarinii* reading the 19 special rules for the *dhammacarinii*s. Finally, Khun Mae gives a talk. Her speeches at *wan phra* could be characterised as applied *dhamma* talk. She weaves Buddhist knowledge into experiences and incidents in everyday life. The topics she chooses to talk about often relate to the *mae chii*s' and the *dhammacarinii*s' lives at the *samnak chii*. She manages to speak both to the very young *dhammacarinii*s and to the long-standing *mae chii*s and her clear statements of moral behaviour combined with her mild, motherly attitude create a compassionate atmosphere. *Wan phra* is the day on which the whole *mae chii* community is gathered and therefore Khun Mae also takes the opportunity to inform them about the coming week's plans and events.

Wan phra is dedicated to meditation and reflection and the practices are more elaborate than on weekdays. For example, the chantings are in both Pali and Thai, the monastic rules are read out loud, the eight precepts are received formally. Every fourth *wan phra* is full moon and the *mae chii*s shave their heads and eyebrows. At *wan phra* there is no teaching of secular subjects at the school, the laity come to pay respects to the *mae chii*s, offer meals and other necessities to the *samnak chii*. That is done on weekdays as well, but *wan phra* is considered to be an auspicious day for special donations.

Since the school is closed, the *dhammacarinii*s have some free time after lunch and before the afternoon's meditation session. They often get permission to go outside the *samnak chii*. Despite the hot weather in the middle of the day, they walk a couple of kilometres to the centre of the village. They stroll around at the market and enjoy being free from schoolwork and other chores for a few hours. The *mae chii*s, however, spend the time at the *samnak chii*. Lay people come for temporary ordination and stay overnight. Others come and donate lunch to the *mae chii* community, and some come to meditate and listen to the afternoon's *dhamma* talk.

A VISIT TO *MAE CHII*S AT A FOREST MONASTERY

At the end of March 1998 I visited a large, well-reputed forest monastery that belonged to the Mahaanikai order and was located in the Northeastern Thailand. I went there together with three *mae chii*s. Two of them lived at Ratburi Samnak Chii and one came from a neighbouring province in Isaan. None of us knew anybody at the forest temple and before entering the *mae chii*s' department we had to register with the monk secretary at the monks' office. At this monastery, the *mae chii*s' activities outside the monastery were restricted. The sharp separation between the monks and *mae chii*s was betrayed by the secretary monk's ignorance of the *mae chii*s at the temple. He had been a monk at this temple for more than 30 years, and he was in charge of keeping the monastery's records. To my surprise, he did not know the name of the head *mae chii*, who had lived at his temple for 34 years and he said he would not recognise her if he saw her. He, like the rest of the monks, had never been inside the *mae chii*s' department.

After going through the registration procedure we walked to the *mae chii*s' area and inside the gate were warmly welcomed by the head *mae chii*. She invited us to stay overnight in a *kuti* on stilts, built by disciples from Bangkok. There were 45 *mae chii*s residing permanently at the monastery, and six *chii phraam*s who were staying for shorter periods of time. After bathing, washing clothes, meditating and listening to a *dhamma* talk on tape by the former abbot Luang Phôô, I and a group of seven *mae chii*s gathered outside a *kuti* to talk about the *mae chii*s' lives at this particular monastery.

Throughout our conversation the *mae chii*s referred to Luang Phôô's teachings which they considered essential to them. Luang Phôô had established the department for *mae chii*s when his mother was old. The *mae chii*s said that it was because of her that he allowed *mae chii*s to stay at the monastery. His mother became a *mae chii* at the monastery for 20 years and lived there until she died.

At the *mae chiis'* ordination at this temple there was only one monk present and the women commonly received the precepts from the head monk at the monastery. The *mae chiis* said that earlier there were more older *mae chiis* there and the *mae chiis* whom I spoke to complained that most of the old *mae chiis* were not any more very strict in their practice. However, more young women were now receiving *mae chii* ordination and also more women were coming to the monastery to receive temporary ordination as *chii phraams*. The *mae chiis* mentioned that some of them had come to the monastery in order to sort out their problems. Some practised in order to prepare themselves mentally and to accumulate merit before starting university studies. They had usually finished high school and came before their entrance exams. Some who sought temporary ordination were dedicated *dhamma* practitioners, and there were also those who came to the *samnak chii* just for a vacation. Some women had been *mae chiis* there before and came back for a temporary visit.

The monastery accepted *mae chiis* who had been ordained at other places, but they had to follow the rules at this *mae chiis'* department; they were not allowed to spread practices and ideas that they had learnt elsewhere. The *mae chiis* said that there were more rules at the *samnak chii* at present than previously. Luang Phôô had written the 21 rules of conduct which were read out loud in the *saalaa*, twice a month, similar to the monks' *uboosot*.[2] The *mae chiis* had a committee of five leading *mae chiis*, who held meetings regularly, and if someone had committed some misdeed they discussed it at the meeting.

No *mae chii* at this *samnak chii* was a member of the Thai Mae Chiis' Institute. They said that they receive invitations to the Institute's meetings in Bangkok, but they had so far never been granted permission by the head monk to go to the meetings. The reasons that the abbot gave for not letting them attend the meetings were that it was too far away and that the *mae chiis* were not familiar with Bangkok. The *mae chiis* knew about the proposed law for *mae chiis* (to be discussed in Chapter 9) because the Thai Mae Chiis' Institute had sent the proposal to them for their comments. The *mae chiis* were willing to accept it, they had discussed it with the abbot and he had said: 'Let them do it.'

These *mae chiis* did not have identity cards like those issued by the Thai Mae Chiis' Institute. As long as they stayed at the monastery, they did not need such a card. However, the lack of identification documents that could prove their ordained status was very inconvenient when they went to other places. One of the *mae chiis* recounted: 'Not long ago a *mae chii* from here visited Khon Khaen. She became ill and when she went to the hospital her identity was thoroughly investigated. At the hospital they did not believe that she was a *mae chii.* They thought she was a fake *mae chii* because she did not have a *mae chii* ID card.'

However, as long as they stayed at the *samnak chii,* the *mae chii*s were taken care of by the monastery, they received help with medical care and the hospital provided them with free medicine. They said: 'Everybody is treated the same here. It does not matter if you are poor or rich.' They also said that they did not need much money. Sometimes lay people came and donated money and relatives also supported them. They explained that the *mae chii*s at this monastery had never practised going on alms round and stressed that the monks and *mae chii*s were not close. They also informed me that it does not look good if monks and *mae chii*s went together. They thought that it was perhaps not safe for *mae chii*s to walk on alms rounds. The villagers offered a lot of food to the monastery and they did not therefore need to spend much time cooking but could instead concentrate on their Buddhist practice. All of them agreed that it was a suitable place for them to practise and they appreciated that the monastery did not sell any amulets or other religious things. They said: 'This place is pure (*borisut*).'

Neither Luang Phôô nor the present abbot taught the *mae chii*s individually. The *mae chii*s said that Luang Phôô's teaching was for everybody. The speeches were played in the *saalaa,* and they could hear them all over the monastery. The *mae chii*s were convinced that Luang Phôô had had a telepathic mind. They said that he knew what was going on and used to teach about the things that they needed. When they had problems, Luang Phôô solved them. Khun Mae remembered that 'he always knew what I was struggling with. For example when I tried very hard to practise sitting-walking meditation, I felt that I could not concentrate. In the afternoon he talked about not being occupied with the results of the practice because then we would not improve.'

The *mae chii*s at this monastery stated without reservation that it was possible for women to reach the final goal, *nibbana.* They were not allowed to get formal Buddhist education; they could study books by themselves, but not in class and not together in groups, although they were allowed to teach each other. If they had any problems of understanding the texts, the abbot came and advised them. The *mae chii*s taught lay people privately, but not in a class. Nor did Luang Phôô allow them to practise *thudong* alone. Sometimes the *mae chii*s travelled to other places and 'practised under the umbrella', *thudong* practice. They were allowed to practise at branch monasteries. Wherever they went, they never went alone but always together with other *mae chii*s.

The *mae chii*s followed the monastic routines with early morning chanting and meditation. Before seven o'clock, they walked barefoot to the big *mae* *chii* dining hall. There the *mae chii*s and *chii phraam*s sat on wooden benches without backrests with their legs folded under them. There was then silence as everybody waited for the bell to ring. The food was already on a table, but nobody would begin until the bell rang signalling that the monks, who had eaten in a separate building, had finished their meal. The monks would eat first, then the *mae chii*s and after them the temporary *mae chii*s. The lay people had to wait until the ordained community had eaten. This was the only *mae chii* community that I visited at which the *mae chii*s did not recite before having their meal. The explanation offered was that the food had already been recited over by the monks.

I asked a leading *mae chii* at the Thai Mae Chiis' Institute to comment on the reasons for abbots not allowing the *mae chii*s to become members of the Thai Mae Chiis' Institute. She confirmed that many abbots prohibit *mae chii*s from becoming members and she said that they were afraid of losing the control over the *mae chii*s. For example, the Thai Mae Chiis' Institute encourages *mae chii*s to study and some abbots are not in favour of that. The Institute has also drawn up rules that forbid *mae chii*s to engage in lay activities that would hamper their spiritual development and blur their religious standing, but some abbots, she felt, do not realise the importance of the regulation and consider all this unnecessary. She said that there were abbots who wanted their *mae chii*s to clean and cook at the temples and only to practise meditation. Further, she noted that if the *mae chii*s do not study then they cannot know how they should practise. Although *mae chii*s want to reach *nibbana,* they often believe that only men can attain that level. That belief is without foundation in the Buddhist doctrine, and if the *mae chii*s start studying they will understand that women are also capable of reaching *nibbana,* and they will gain wisdom. Another reason for the reported reluctance of some abbots is that they have developed their own teachings and do not want the *mae chii*s to learn anything else.

MAE CHII – A HETEROGENEOUS CATEGORY

The lay people that I interviewed were of the opinion that there were differences between *mae chii*s at temples and those at self-governed *samnak chii*s. The lesser respect afforded to *mae chii*s at temples was attributed to their presumed lack of knowledge of Buddhism, lack of Buddhist training, failure to keep the precepts or follow the *mae chii*s' rules. There are many examples to contradict this stereotypical idea. However, their lack of educational opportunities and guidance in Buddhist training are well known obstacles for Thai *mae chii*s (see

P. Van Esterik 2000: 74–77). The contention that *mae chii*s at *samnak chii*s had better conditions for their monastic training than those at temples held true for those living in the area where Ratburi Samnak Chii is located.

The differences within the category of *mae chii* were expressed in various ways. The distinctions between *mae chii*s at *samnak chii*s and at temples were highlighted at alms giving rituals. Also the authorities and the *mae chii*s themselves drew distinctions between *mae chii*s, usually on the basis of their educational and spiritual levels. The difficulty of conceiving them as a homogeneous group was very evident at events at which monks and *mae chii*s performed. Several annual, communal gatherings are held in Thai villages. One of these events is the celebration of the King's birthday, also named Father's Day (*wan phôô*). The King's seventieth birthday was celebrated on 5 of December 1997. In early November that year, Ratchaburi Province experienced an unusually heavy flood. Normally, floods affect the *samnak chii* during the rainy season, but not to the extreme extent of that year. Many of the rooms in the *samnak chii* were flooded with one metre of water. The *saalaa,* the dining hall and other buildings in the *samnak chii* compound were also flooded. The *mae chii*s made rafts and tried to save as much as they could from their plantations. Quantities of vegetables and fruit were ruined. About a week after the water had subsided, lay people began visiting the *samnak chii* to offer food and other necessities. The leaders of the district (*amphoe*) also made an official visit and offered donations. Soon afterwards the *samnak chii* received a formal invitation to participate in the *wan phôô*'s communal alms round in the village. It was the first time that the *mae chii*s had been invited together with the monks from the temples in the area. The *mae chii*s regarded the invitation as a recognition of their religious vocation.

At six o'clock in the morning ten *mae chii*s went to the ceremony. The event was held outdoors, on a road near the train station. There were several local governmental buildings in that area. The ten *mae chii*s who were going to perform the alms round went separately in a pick-up truck. The *chii phraam*s and *dhammacarinii*s travelled together in another car.

While waiting for the function to begin, the *mae chii*s and the monks sat inside a fenced area outside one of the official buildings. The *dhammacarinii*s and myself waited outside the building where tables were already sat up on both sides of the road. A few lay people had arrived when we came and more and more people filled the area over the following half-hour. The lay people were dressed up and brought baskets with items that they were going to donate. They brought food and other things that monks and *mae chii*s need in their daily lives and they piled their goods on the tables. Cooked rice and curries, which are given on the daily alms round, are not donated on special occasions like this.

After a while, I noticed two *mae chii*s from one of the village temples who had come to make a donation to the monks. They had brought two silver-plated rice bowls one filled with boiled eggs and the other with packages of juices. They occupied one of the tables closest to where the alms round would start, and they were to be first to give alms to the monks. Later a *chii phraam* arrived and took a place beside the two *mae chii*s. As people gathered, music blared from loudspeakers and now and then the organisers announced the time for the function to start. People were talking and laughing and the atmosphere was joyful.

The ceremony started with the monks followed by the assembly reciting *Namo tassa...* three times.[3] Thereafter followed the three refuges to the Buddha, Dhamma and Sangha, which were also recited three times. After that, on behalf of all the laity, a male lay person asked the monk for the five lay precepts: '*Mayam bhante tisaranena saha panca silani yacama.*' The monk gave the precepts and the lay people received them one by one by reciting after the monk. Then the monks began the alms round, walking in the middle of the road. People were standing on both sides and they filled the monks' bowls as they passed. The two old *mae chii*s donated their eggs and packages of juices to the monks. When the Ratburi *mae chii*s came walking in the line after the monks with their alms bowls in front of them, the two temple *mae chii*s seemed perplexed. They had obviously not expected any *mae chii*s to walk in the line and they did not have any eggs or juices left. They looked at each other and then they took their empty silver-plated rice buckets, and went to the end of the line of the Ratburi *mae chii*s. Uninvited, they joined the alms round with their rice buckets as alms bowls in front of them and lay people filled them with alms.

The Ratburi *mae chii*s were treated as monks at this event; they were invited to the function, they sat in the same area as the monks while waiting for the performance to start, they walked in the same line, although behind the monks and carrying their alms bowls. The lay people treated the *mae chii*s and the monks similarly. However, the two *mae chii*s who initially came to donate to the monks were not treated in the same way. When they walked in the line as alms persons, lay people offered alms to them but did not kneel down or raise their hands in respect as they had done with the monks and the Ratburi *mae chii*s.

LIVING AT A *SAMNAK CHII*

A *mae chii*'s life at a self-governed *samnak chii* differs in several respects from life at a temple where monks also reside. *Mae chii*s at temples do not have the authority to officiate at ceremonies. *Mae chii*s at *samnak chii*s, however, conduct ceremonies similar to those of the monks. At temples, *mae chii*s are usually responsible for the kitchen, while the monks alone perform the alms round. At *samnak chii*s, *mae chii*s cook food as well, but they also go on alms rounds in the mornings, which in my study has proved to have an important impact on *mae chii*s' identity as ordained persons.

*Mae chii*s at the *samnak chii*s that I visited followed the religious tradition of morning and evening chants, meditation practice and Buddhist studies. Supporting the monastic community is highly valued and seen as an important, meritorious deed in Thai society. Since the *mae chii*s who live at temples are not usually considered to be alms persons and 'fields of merit', the villagers support the *mae chii*s only indirectly through the monks. The lay people give alms to the monks, who later distribute food to the *mae chii*s.

By receiving ordination, women choose to live a celibate, single life and by living at a *samnak chii* they also choose a life in a female community without any male influence. *Mae chii*s who come to live at a *samnak chii* have usually favoured this over the option of living at a temple. The *mae chii*s at Ratburi Samnak Chii commonly said that living at a *samnak chii* gave them greater freedom to develop in their religious role and more time and opportunity to study and to practise. They declared that their religious vocation was taken seriously at the *samnak chii* and they considered this important. It was important to them that they were entitled to perform in their religious role in relation to lay people.

Actually the *mae chii*s at *samnak chii*s have to work hard, often even harder than the *mae chii*s at temples since they cannot rely on the laity to the same extent as monks and *mae chii*s at temples. Despite the hard work, the *mae chii*s valued their self-reliance and benefits from growing in their religious role. Most of the *mae chii*s at *samnak chii*s had been ordained at temples and had experiences of living both at temples and at *samnak chii*s and they often said that they felt free at the *samnak chii* with no monks around. The *mae chii*s who had been ordained at Ratburi Samnak Chii said that they found living in a *mae chii* community more appropriate than living at a temple with monks. In their opinion, monks and *mae chii*s should practise separately.

ADJUSTING TO THE ORDAINED STATE

To lead a proper ordained life is something that is regarded as having to be learned, trained for and grown into. Women who aspire to ordination are recommended first to receive the eight Buddhist precepts and become a *chii phraam* at a *samnak chii* or temple. A *mae chii* who was 24 years old when I interviewed her had, at her own request, received ordination after finishing primary school. When I met her she had already been a *mae chii* for ten years. She recounted that she had had to stay at the temple for two months before she was formally ordained, as this was the custom at that particular temple. During the training period, her head was shaved, but she was not allowed to wear white. She wore a black skirt and a white blouse. The custom of having a training period before receiving ordination is a common practice at temples and *samnak chii*s. However, the length of the training period varies and in some cases women become ordained without this period of training. Normally, these are women who were already familiar with the temple or *samnak chii* that they had chosen for their ordination, and had prepared themselves by regular visits to monastic places. Some of my informants told me that they had spent several years visiting temples at weekends before they became ordained. They felt that

Figure 5.1. Inside a *mae chii*'s *kuti* at Ratburi Samnak Chii

Figure 5.2. *Mae chii*s at Ratburi Samnak Chii working on the land

Figure 5.3. A *mae chii* washing clothes outside her *kuti* at Ratburi Samnak Chii

they had gradually grown into the monastic lifestyle by staying in close contact with the temples.

*Mae chii*s did not generally say that they had experienced great hardships when adjusting to the ordained state. This could be explained by the fact that many women had had a long period of preparation for their ordained life. While waiting for the opportunity to become ordained, they had often lived in a semi-ascetic state. A *mae chii* in Northeastern Thailand, who had planned for her ordained life over a couple of years, said that before ordination she had spent the weekends at temples and received temporary ordination. Consequently, she had had a long preparation period. When she finally had enough savings for ordained life, she was also mentally well prepared for the monastic vocation. She said that her immediate feeling after she had shaved and donned the white robe was that she had been ordained for a long time, and the laity I met in her village recalled that she had performed like a long-standing *mae chii* from the start.

Young women who became ordained at Ratburi Samnak Chii usually kept a low profile and stayed in the background. However, the speed at which they adjusted to monastic life varied from individual to individual. Some of them acted with great confidence and gave an impression of being content with

Figure 5.4. *Mae chii*s making charcoal at Ratburi Samnak Chii

their new identity, while others took on a more expectant attitude. Several *dhammacariniis* became ordained after having finished their studies at the *samnak chii* school. Even though they had lived with the eight precepts at the *samnak chii* for up to four years and were familiar with the life of a *mae chii*, they said that it made a big difference actually to become one.

At the *samnak chii* the *mae chiis* often gathered in smaller groups and normally worked together in pairs. Usually those who had the same standing at the *samnak chii*, had been ordained at the same time or came from the same part of Thailand worked together and accompanied each other when they were outside the *samnak chii*. They were not permitted to be alone outside the *samnak chii*, and there was a rule saying that the *mae chiis* were not allowed to leave the *samnak chii* without permission from one of the superior *mae chiis*.

DAILY LIFE AT RATBURI SAMNAK CHII

Generally, all monastic places follow almost the same daily schedule. The fixed routines are part of, and a basis for, the ritualisation of daily life. At Ratburi Samnak Chii, chanting, meditation and Buddhist studies are important daily activities. However, the *mae chiis* have many assignments to attend to, and they carry out most of the tasks without any help from lay people. Ratburi Samnak Chii is organised in teams. Cooking, cleaning and other domestic chores are rotated. The *mae chiis* who study at the secondary school at the *samnak chii* have lessons five days a week. Some study individually at the Open Universities and can devote a couple of hours each day to their studies.

At the *samnak chii*, there are several daily collective performances that express the monastic code. One example is the alms round which is performed every morning. This is a ritual performance and will be addressed in Chapter 6. Collecting alms is solely for *mae chiis* and may not include either *chii phraams*, *dhammacariniis* or lay people. The alms round is an expressive act that communicates reciprocity between the lay and ordained communities. Collecting alms has a great impact on the *mae chiis'* ordained identity, and many told me that it had strengthened their Buddhist practice.

The *mae chiis* have two meals a day. Both are before noon. The ascetic practice of not eating anything after 12 o'clock until sunrise the next morning must be followed by all Thai monastics. Eating at the *samnak chii* is ritualised and ceremonial and the meals, together with the schedule of chanting, meditation

The *mae chii*s' daily schedule at Ratburi Samnak Chii	
3.45	Wake up bell
4.00	Chanting and meditation
5.30	Alms round
7.00	Breakfast
8.00	National anthem. Chanting (for *mae chii*s who study)
9.00	The schoolday starts (for *mae chii*s who study or teach)
11.00	Lunch
13.00	The schoolday continues (for *mae chii*s who study or teach)
16.00	Chanting. Presentation of a Buddhist text
17.00	Gardening, watering plants, work in the kitchen
19.00	Meditation and chanting
21.00	Rest

and alms rounds, form daily peaks of condensed spiritual expressions. The ritualised eating also emphasises and marks the *mae chii*s' ordained identity.

At Ratburi Samnak Chii, the meals are held in the dining hall. The *mae chii*s eat at the same time as *chii phraam*s and *dhammacarinii*s, but they do not sit at the same tables.4 The dining hall is furnished with tables and red metal stools. The *mae chii*s and *chii phraam*s sit four to six at a table and the 50 *dhammacarinii*s sit together at two long tables. On the wall above the *dhammacarinii*s' tables hangs a large picture of Khun Mae. The tables are covered with tablecloths of plastic, and yellow or blue plastic shades protect the food bowls that are placed on the tables before the *mae chii*s arrive.

The meals are considered events of spiritual importance. A sign of their significance is that the *mae chii*s always wear their outer robe, *phaa*, in the dining hall. This outer robe is not sewn in the same elaborate fashion as a monk's outer robe. The *mae chii*'s white robe symbolises purity and morality. They always wear the *phaa* in the *saalaa*, when they conduct religious performances, when they teach, when they greet visitors and when they are outside the *samnak chii*. It is important that the *mae chii*s' robes are clean, ironed and worn as prescribed in the Mae Chiis' Handbook. The *mae chii*s explained that the reason that they are so strict about their outer appearance is because this forms part of their moral training. They stressed the importance of being *riabrôôy*, which means to be neat, tidy, in good shape and in good order but it also means to be polite and well-mannered.

The meals as well as other ceremonies at the *samnak chii* share an underlying scheme of classification and hierarchy. The seating arrangements in the dining hall follow the same spatial order as in the *saalaa*. The head *mae chii* and other long-standing *mae chii*s sit closest to the *saalaa* building, and *chii phraam*s and *dhammacarinii*s sit further away. The different categories at the *samnak chii* are kept apart and if there are lay people visiting they sit at separate tables. When men visit, they have a table of their own. The *mae chii*s' higher position is not vertically marked as in the *saalaa*; however the high-ranking *mae chii*s have chairs with backrests, and eat on china plates and have rice and drinking water on the table. The other *mae chii*s serve themselves rice from the big basins of rice from the morning alms round, which is placed in the kitchen. The *mae chii*s, *chii phraam*s and *dhammacarinii*s eat on enamel plates and fetch clean

Figure 5.5. *Dhammacarinii*s having lunch at Ratburi Samnak Chii

drinking water from either a newly installed water purification reservoir that was donated by lay followers from Bangkok and stands inside the dining hall, or from the old big water tank outside the building.

Five minutes before the meal starts, a *mae chii* rings the bell outside the dining hall. The *mae chii*s stop whatever they are doing, put on their outer robes and walk to the dining hall. Inside the dining hall the meal starts with the *mae chii* of highest rank striking a small bell placed on her table. She is the one who leads the chanting. Everybody sits with their hands folded and chants words of reflection over the food and transfers merit to the donors. When the chanting is finished, the *mae chii*s and *chii phraam*s place their hands in their knees while the *dhammacarinii*s still have their hands folded in a *wai*. They continue with a special recitation that expresses thankfulness to the *mae chii*s, their parents and other people who support, teach and take care of them.

When the recitations have died away, the dining hall is silent. Nobody speaks around the tables. The *mae chii* strikes the bell again and this time it signals that everybody may start eating. There is silence throughout the meal and all concentrate on eating mindfully. If someone has to rise from the table during the meal, they fold their hands in a *wai* before doing so and they do the same thing before they start eating again. When the meal is finished they do not have to wait for others to finish. They rise individually and if it is the morning meal, they put the red stools under the tables or, if it is the day's last meal at 11 o'clock, pile them up on top of each other. The remaining food from the first meal stays on the tables covered by the shades until the next meal. The leftover food is eaten at the 11 o'clock meal together with some newly prepared dishes. The *mae chii*s wash their own plates, glasses, forks and spoons; however the *dhammacarinii*s are encouraged to volunteer and take over the washing up from the *mae chii*s.

The *mae chii*s' meals are distinct from conventional eating. They follow the pattern of monastic meals at Thai temples and are as such a reiteration of a centuries-old tradition. The meals at the *samnak chii* simultaneously communicate a conventional monastic ritual and women's unconventional role in religious leadership.

In the village, the *mae chii*s' performances are carefully observed by the laity. If any of the *mae chii*s behaves inappropriately, lay people complain to the head *mae chii*. During fieldwork, I assumed that the emphasis laid upon the *mae chii*s' behaviour and actions was partly a reflection of their lack of legal standing as religious persons. The *mae chii*s' position outside the Thai *sangha* makes their role as religious specialists uncertain. If they do not live up to the standard, they risk falling into lay status. Maintaining and refining their training is therefore of great importance and shaved heads and white robes are not sufficient to ensure the *mae chii*s' authority. Their knowledge, strict behaviour and non-lay performance are important for their identity as ascetics and for their religious standing.

THE *MAE CHIIS'* RULES

While living at Ratburi Samnak Chii, I found that the *mae chiis* are particular about following the *mae chii* code. They consider that their own as well as the *mae chii* community's standing rests on their own performances. They stated that observing the rules was both important for themselves and for the laity, claiming that they had responsibilities towards the laity, that unworthy behaviour might cause people to lose faith. This is in line with Buddhist teaching about monks' behaviour.[5] I noticed that *mae chiis'* behaviour was indeed under strict observance by the lay people, and was often commented on. The villagers who supported Ratburi Samnak Chii usually expressed admiration for the *mae chiis*. They said that they respected them for their strict living, their exemplary conduct and for their work with the Dhammacarinii School.

The *mae chii* rules were introduced in order to facilitate and control moral discipline, *sila*. Originally *sila* was a very broad concept, incorporating all aspects of the Buddhist Eightfold Path. Over time, however, it came to refer to ethical conduct as determined by certain guidelines of moral behaviour and to the life of purity, identified particularly with the monastics. Eventually, the concept narrowed even further to specifically denote the rules of the *patimokkha*, the monastic codes of discipline.[6] *Sila* became a paradigm for conducting the spiritual life of the community of monks and *mae chiis*. The concept was elaborated in the *vinaya* texts, which describe the permissible and desirable conduct of a Buddhist renunciant. The *vinaya* texts explain the precepts with narratives to show how they arose and how they are to be understood. Although these contextual materials may have been added later or created to illustrate the rule, they show a human and practical side of the rules and they reveal the attitudes and ideals of the early *sangha*.

The *mae chiis'* rules are found in 'The handbook of the Thai mae chii' (*Rabiab patibat khôông sathaaban mae chii thai haeng pratheet thai*) which, among other things, is the *mae chiis'* guidebook for righteous living. The handbook was published by the Thai Mae Chiis' Institute in 1975. Every *mae chii* at Ratburi Samnak Chii is familiar with it. It is used at the ordination ceremonies and it is also used every week at *wan phra,* the Buddhist observance day. It is widely circulated and used by *mae chiis* all over the country, just as the *Patimokkha* is used by the monks. It contains a description of the Thai Mae Chiis' Institute's administrative organisation and training rules for the *mae chiis*. The ordination procedure is described in it and the preceptor's and *mae chii* candidate's minimal qualifications are laid down. The ordination for *chii phraams* (the handbook uses the Pali word '*upasika*') is described as well as the de-robing procedures. Both *mae chii*s and *chii phraam*s observe the same eight Buddhist precepts, which are elaborated in the Handbook. The eight-precept observance that is formally recited at *wan phra* is as follows:

The eight-precept observance

1. *Panatipata veramani sikkhapadam samadiyami.*
   I request the training rule to refrain from the taking of life as well as from ordering others to kill.

2. *Adinnadana veramani sikkhapadam samadiyami.*
   I request the training rule to refrain from stealing as well as from ordering others to steal.

3. *Abrahmacariya veramani sikkhapadam samadiyami.*
   I request the training rule to refrain from unchaste behaviour which is an obstacle to the Brahma faring.

4. *Musavada veramani sikkhapadam samadiyami.*
   I request the training rule to refrain from false speech.

5. *Sura-meraya-majja-pamadatthana veramani sikkhapadam samadiyami.*
   I request the training rule to refrain from distilled and fermented intoxicants which cause carelessness.

6. *Vikala-bhojana veramani sikkhapadam samadiyami.*
   I request the training rule to refrain from eating at the wrong time, the wrong time being from noon to the dawn of the next day.

7. *Nacca-gita-vadita-visuka-dassana mala-gandha-vilepanadharana-mandana- vibhusanatthana veramani sikkhapadam samadiyami.*
   I request the training rule to refrain from dancing, singing, music and seeing entertainments which are stumbling blocks to wholesomeness and to refrain from wearing garlands, using perfumes and beautifying the body with cosmetics.

8. *Uccasayana-mahasayana veramani sikkhapadam samadiyami.*
   I request the training rule to refrain from sitting and lying down on seats and beds with legs over the limit, on large seats and beds, from using intricate or detailed bed coverings.

Source: Somdet Phra Buddhaghosacariya 1992[7]

Besides the eight-precept observance, the handbook also contains discipline rules and detailed training rules concerning proper behaviour for both *mae chii* and *chii phraam*. Punishment for breaking the disciplinary rules is also described in the document. The mildest correction is a reminder of the rule by the head *mae chii* and the most severe is to unfrock the *mae chii* and reclaim her

Figure 5.6. A woman lighting candles before asking the head *mae chii* for the *chii phram*'s precepts

mae chii identity card. The handbook says that punishment should be decided upon by a committee of *mae chii*s. There are disciplinary rules also for the *chii phraam*s; these rules are not as comprehensive as the *mae chiis'* rules, but breaking them means that the *chii phraam* must leave the *samnak chii* and her *chii phraam* state.

According to the Mae Chiis' handbook every *mae chii* has to practise the *sekiyadhamma,* which consists of the 75 training rules for monastics. The *sekhiya* rules are in the sixth section of the *Patimokkha* and are to be studied by *bhikkhus*, *bhikkhunis* and novices (Kabilsingh 1984: 133). The *sekhiya* rules may be taken as a manual of manners proper for monastics. Researchers have commonly referred to the *sekhiyas* as matters of social etiquette and politeness. In contrast, John Holt claims that these rules are outward reflections of the inner state of a monastic's mental condition (Holt 1999: 101–103). He says that the bodily and verbal expressions must be co-ordinated by a thoughtful readiness that is the result of the disciplined mental culture and a thoughtful expression is required by every *sekhiya* determination (ibid. 103).

According to Kabilsingh (1984), there are grounds to believe that some of the *sekhiya* rules are among the oldest rules of the *Patimokkha*. The *sekhiya* rules for *bhikkhunis* are the same set of rules in both content and numbers as the *bhikkhus'* rules, and the *mae chiis* use the same *sekhiya* rules. The rules are divided according to subject into four groups: etiquette in dress and behaviour when in inhabited areas; etiquette in accepting and eating alms food; etiquette when teaching the *dhamma*; and etiquette in urinating, defecating and spitting. The rules do not impose a direct penalty, they simply say that it is a form of training to be observed.

Further, the handbook states that *mae chiis* should pay attention to the seven sexual intercourse fetters, *methunasamyojana,* in order to maintain a life of chastity. *Mae chiis* should also follow six rules of *saraniyadhamma*. These rules deal with conciliation, communal harmony, and the virtues of living together, and are also important for monks.

Moreover, the *mae chiis'* rules command that a *mae chii* shave her hair and eyebrows at least once a month at full moon. Shaving is the strongest marker of leaving the lay world. The distinctive dress that monastics wear is also a clear indicator of their religious belonging. The proper dress codes for *mae chiis* and *chii phraams* differ and are shown in detail by drawings in the handbook. The rules give clear instructions about how the correct *mae chii* robe and their outer appearance should be. The Mae Chiis' Institute has decided that all *mae chiis* shall wear the same kind of dress, with round neck and long sleeves. *Chii phraams* also wear a white dress; these are, however, distinguished from the *mae chiis'* dresses by the way they are sewn. *Chii phraams* do not wear a long outer robe, *phaa;* their outer robe is short. There are also rules that further differentiate the *mae chiis* from the laity by way of dressing. It is, for example, against the rules to wear a bra, and at the *samnak chii* they are allowed to wear a cap to protect them from the sun, but a cap is not permitted at other places. Instead, an umbrella in a subdued colour is permitted, but two persons may not walk under one umbrella. Shoes must have low heals and be in suitable colours, and their *yaam,* the traditional textile bag used by monks and *mae chii*s, must be white. They are not allowed to have any thread around their neck, nor can they use any kind of beautification or watch around their wrists, no long nails, and so on.

Maintaining the distinction between the lay and ordained realms also includes the different activities that the laity and the monastics are supposed to carry out. Special chores that are closely associated with the lay realm, such as childcare, are forbidden. Children under the age of seven are not allowed to stay at *samnak chii*. *Mae chii*s should not embrace or hug a child, and if children visit the *samnak chii,* the handbook says that they have to be controlled so they do not disturb other people. Boys are not allowed to stay at the *samnak chii* at all, no matter what age they are. There is a rule saying that *mae chii*s should not be close to any men, monks or novices even if they are their relatives. Further, they should never as individuals, be alone with men, including monks, or they should meet them at places where other people can see them and listen to their conversation. After 7 o'clock in the evening *mae chii*s are forbidden to receive visitors or meet with people outside the *samnak chii.*

Vocations that are explicitly mentioned in the handbook as improper for *mae chii*s are for example: to deal with fortune telling, to carry out massage, to perform miracles, to become possessed, to play games or lotteries. *Mae chii*s are also forbidden to perform a task for another person for a payment, serve or work for lay people, engage in anything commercial, collect donations if they are not for a specific purpose, give collecting envelopes to people who are not their relatives.

BECOMING FIELDS OF MERIT

Developing an ordained identity permeates the *mae chii*s' whole existence. Exploring their daily life reveals that becoming a religious person is to a great extent a bodily process. The training for the ordained life has commonly started before ordination, and after ordination the training intensifies. The objective of the training is thus to embody the *mae chii*s' rules, which involve both the body and the mind. The body becomes the vehicle in the process of becoming a *lokuttara* person and is the *mae chii*s' engagement with the world to which they communicate their ordained identity. The process involves also incorporation into a dominant symbolic order that conveys that the ordained, celibate identity is preferably male and not in line with the female sex/gender identity. Shaving is the strongest marker of crossing the boundary between the lay and the religious

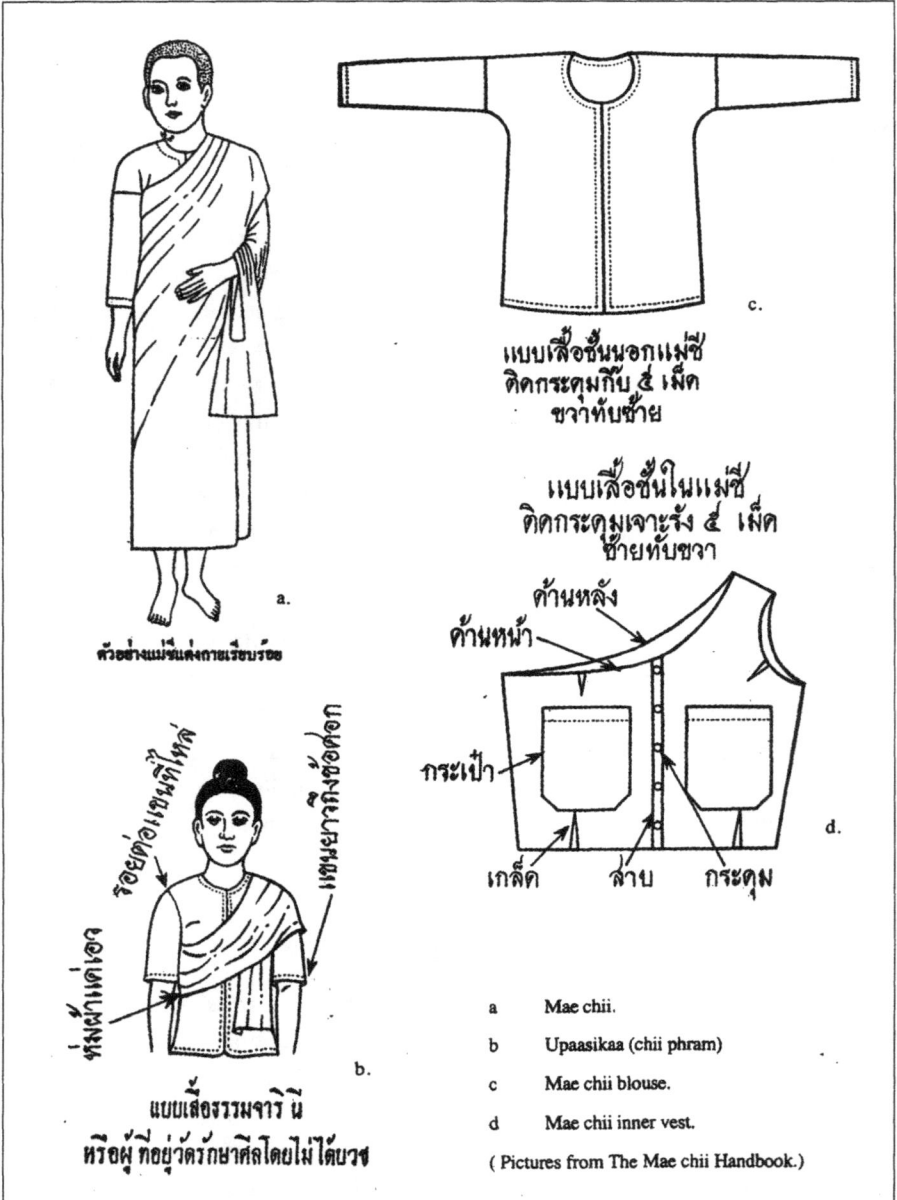

แบบเสื้อชั้นนอกแม่ชี
ติดกระดุมกิ๊บ ๕ เม็ด
ขวาทับซ้าย

แบบเสื้อชั้นในแม่ชี
ติดกระดุมเจาะรัง ๕ เม็ด
ซ้ายทับขวา

ด้านหลัง
ด้านหน้า
กระเป๋า
เกล็ด   สาบ   กระดุม

ตัวอย่างแม่ชีแต่งกายเรียบร้อย

แบบเสื้อธรรมจาริ นี
หรือผู้ ทอยู่วัดรักษาศีลโดยไม่ได้บวช

a	Mae chii.
b	Upaasikaa (chii phram)
c	Mae chii blouse.
d	Mae chii inner vest.
(Pictures from The Mae chii Handbook.)	

Figure 5.7. *Mae chii* and *chii phram*. Drawings from the *Mae chiis' Handbook*

realms. The shaved head serves as a constant reminder for the individual *mae chii* of the potentials of the ordained state and also of the dominant norms of the religious vocation.

Butler's employment of 'performativity' is useful when analysing the possibility of moving beyond the understanding of the construction of gender identity as a one-sided process of determination, seeing it instead as a more open process of repetition. The *mae chiis'* strict and detailed rules, which actually are similar to the monks' code, of how they shall walk, sit, talk, eat, and so on, denote both a process of profound corporeal inscription and an instability at the core of the dominant gender norms, which says that this practice is solely for ordained male persons.

Performativity communicates both the cultural susceptibility of the 'performed' gender identity and the performances' deep impact by reinscribing upon the body. The idea of performativity does not refer to a voluntarist process of performance so much as a 'forced reiteration of norms' in the sense of a compulsory and constraining heterosexuality that impels and sustains gender identity (Butler 1993: 94). In Thailand, gender is characterized as fluid, and gender norms are not perceived as unsurpassable boundaries. However, developing a '*sangha* identity' requires ordination, and legal access to the *sangha* is only open to heterosexual males. The heterosexual norm is challenged by *kathoeys, toms, dees* and, I suggest, to some extent also by female ascetics who receive ordination and take on the celibate life that in Thailand is reserved for men.

Change seems to be possible partly because of the instability of the symbolic and discursive structures. The necessity for performative reiteration of symbolic performances is revealed in the *mae chiis'* daily chanting ceremonies, to which they attach crucial importance and consider indispensable for upholding their ordained identity. The alms round in the morning is one of the most important performative acts that signifies the ordained persons belonging to the *lokuttara* realm. As already mentioned there are *mae chii*s at temples with monks who are not permitted to perform the alms round in contrast to *mae chii*s at self-governed *samnak chii*s who do perform the alms round. Here the performative highlights how restraints are constructed but also the gaps for gender subjectivity which open space for agency. When explaining their exclusion from the performance of the alms round, the *mae chii*s emphasize the historicity of the structures that have developed in Thailand. Even though *mae chii*s do not in general aspire to become *bhikkhuni*, they refer to the enlightened *bhikkhuni*s at the Buddha's time in order to prove women's equal spiritual capacity.

Agency is, as explained by Butler, a sedimented effect of reiterative or ritualized practices (Butler 1999: 178). The symbolic norms of celibacy and the ordained rules are for the *mae chii*s repeatedly inscribed upon the body, and living through these norms permits the emergence of a stable bodily ego as an ordained *lokuttara* person. The performative construction of gender identity causes agency in that the identificatory processes, through which norms are materialised, permits the stabilization of a subject who is capable of resisting those norms. A process of resistance takes place primarily at the boundaries of the corporeal norm, in the domains of 'excluded and delegitimated' sex (ibid.: 162–163). The partial and sometimes conflictual identifications made by those who are excluded from a regime can result in a destabilising process of resignification in which symbolic norms are subversively used to articulate identities. The *mae chii* practices and identity as *lokuttara* persons are one example of such a resignification process.

The meditation practice is in line with the traditional *mae chii* role as female ascetic and perceived as a suitable practice. Nevertheless, the intensive periods of meditation retreats are of outmost importance for the *mae chii*s in ordained identity and heighten their practice of embodying the rules and training the mind.

MEDITATION AND NETWORKING

There has been a long-standing debate in the Thai *sangha* about whether monastics, both male and female, should emphasise the study of Buddhist scriptures or concentrate on gaining Buddhist wisdom solely through practising meditation. At many temples, studies are primarily reserved for the monks and there are temples that strictly forbid the *mae chii*s to study. Ratburi Samnak Chii has an educational profile and there are always numbers of visiting *mae chii*s who live at the *samnak chii* for a limited period of time in order to study.

At Ratburi Samnak Chii, the *mae chii*s study both secular and religious subjects and they also have daily training in reading, memorising and reciting chants. The *mae chii*s learn to recite sermons used in various rituals that are important for their public performances in the village. Every religious occasion at the temple requires chanting by the monastics. The *mae chii*s are often invited to chant at the nearby temples, for example at funerals and at people's homes at house blessing rituals. At the *samnak chii*, there are regularly chants (*suatmon*) recited by the *mae chii*s at collective merit-making rituals. The laity usually participate in these ceremonies at the *samnak chii* or at locations outside the *samnak chii* where *mae chii*s are invited to hold ceremonies. These activities are typical vocations that Thai village monks engage in. To perform these ceremonies requires specific knowledge that not all *mae chii*s possess.

Figure 5.8. Meditation retreat at Ratburi Samnak Chii

The *mae chii*s at Ratburi Samnak Chii practise meditation according to a daily schedule. At certain periods during the year meditation is particularly in focus, on the meditation retreats. I participated in a meditation retreat that started on 4 January 1998. It is common in Thailand that temples and *samnak chii*s organise training periods of meditation and Buddhist studies. At Ratburi Samnak Chii a meditation retreat was held at least once a year. The five-day retreat started on the full moon of the second lunar month. The day before the full moon day, a donation ceremony (*phaphaa*) was organised at the *samnak chii*. This is a public event that attracts a large gathering. At Ratburi Samnak Chii there are two main *phaphaa*s every year, a large one in August and a smaller one in January. These events are commonly well attended by local people as well as by people from Bangkok who come in cars and rented buses. Monks are also invited to the *phaphaa*. I shall elaborate on these events in Chapter 6.

The land on the outskirts of the *samnak chii*, where the meditation retreat is located, is used exclusively as a meditation site. About seven years ago, the Ratburi Samnak Chii planted trees in the area to give the meditators shade and for support of the wooden sticks that are used for hanging the big umbrellas (*krot*). A couple of years later a cement house with bathrooms was built. Three white meditation *kutis* on stilts were constructed on the site. Nobody lives permanently in these houses. They were designed for *mae chiis* who want to live in solitude and meditate for a period of time.

Preparation for the retreat started as early as mid-December, a month before the retreat opened. The heaviest work was to clear the land on the fringe of the *samnak chii*'s compound from grass and brushwood. The *mae chiis* and the schoolgirls worked hard with pickaxes and sickles until the ground was free from vegetation. The mowed grass was then laid out to dry in the sun and the brushwood was made into charcoal in the *samnak chii*'s charcoal stack.

The retreat was located outdoors. The whole *mae chii* community moved out from their permanent rooms and slept on mats under big umbrellas with mosquito nets. An outdoor *saalaa* was also set up, protected by a huge plastic roof supported by steel poles. A large piece of wine-red velvet drapery was placed behind the shrine with a Buddha statue. A clock hung on the drapery and flowers were placed on both sides of the Buddha statue and there were candles and incense in front of it.

The outdoor *saalaa* was used for chants and *dhamma* talks; the meals were also eaten; there. The dried grass was put on the ground to make a flat foundation on which bast and plastic mats were laid out. The *mae chiis* had placed two big wooden chairs in the open *saalaa*. One was decorated with carved dragon heads in gold, red and green and the other was without decorations. The first one was used when invited monks came and gave *dhamma* talks and the other when *mae chiis* gave Buddhist talks.

The retreat started on full-moon day and the *wan phra* ceremony was held in the outdoor *saalaa*. The ceremony followed the usual routine for conducting the observance. At the retreat, meditation was emphasised and Khun Mae's speech on the opening morning was about the benefit and importance of meditation. After she finished her talk, one of the leading *mae chiis* gave instructions in sitting and walking meditation techniques. The practices of *sila* (morality) and of *samadhi* (meditation) were interwoven, and awareness of moral discipline was to be sharpened by meditation practice.

The retreat was open to monastics from other temples and *samnak chiis* and also to lay people who received temporary ordination as *chii phraams*, or *phu khaows*, i.e. male practitioners with the eight precepts. Most of the participants stayed all five days, but it was possible to join the retreat for only a couple of days. At the meditation site, the boundary between *mae chiis* and temporary ordained persons was maintained. Men and women also stayed in separate areas. The *mae chiis* and *chii phraams* had their umbrellas in one part of the area but in different sections, the *dhammacariniis* stayed in another section and the men were placed at the edge of the meditation site.

The schedule at the retreat at Ratburi Samnak Chii	
4.00	Morning chanting
7.00	Breakfast
9.00	Dhamma talk
11.00	Lunch
14.00	Dhamma talk
16.00	Chanting
19.00	Evening chanting
21.00	Rest

At the retreat, the morning bell rang at 3.30 in the morning. At that time, it was silent and still dark. The *mae chiis* had brought sound equipment to the meditation site and the chanting was heard over the whole area. In the mornings and early evenings tapes were played with stories from the Buddha's life. A very soft and gentle voice told the stories and there were background sounds with pouring water from waterfalls, birds singing, and so on. Buddhist tapes like these are usually played at retreats and they create a special atmosphere.

Alms rounds were not performed during the retreat. Instead villagers came to the *samnak chii* and offered food. Lay people could also host a meal and feed the whole meditating community; this was considered to render the donor much merit. Before meals, the *mae chiis* and the other meditators lined up and walked barefoot, as if on an alms round, to the *saalaa*.

Khun Mae and another *mae chii* who was a well-known meditation teacher gave meditation instructions. Sitting and walking meditation were practised from the early morning until the evening. Bodily movements were to be carried out as mindfully as possible and a minimum of talking was recommended. The participants sat meditating on mats under open umbrellas with the mosquito nets tied in knots above their heads. There was space for individual meditation paths used for walking meditation. Some meditation sessions were performed collectively, but most of the time the practice was done individually.

At the retreat monks and *mae chiis* delivered daily Buddhist talks. The speakers came from various temples and *samnak chiis*, although *mae chiis* from Ratburi Samnak Chii also gave speeches. The topics dealt with Buddhist practice, and meditation was focused upon in most of the speeches. Listening to Buddhist teachings is considered to bring religious merit even to the ordained community. Money was collected among the listeners as acts of *dana,* religious giving, and of gratitude to the monks and *mae chii*s for their teachings. 'Money trees' were made by fastening the collected 20 and 50 baht notes on sticks and then arranging them as a tree. After the talk, a robe, incense, candles, flowers and money in an envelope were donated to the speaker. Most of the speakers donated the money further to Ratburi Samnak Chii. According to their rules, monks are not allowed to handle money. There is no rule that forbids *mae chii*s from dealing with money, although there are *mae chii*s who avoid handling it.

A retreat is a collective event in which meditation, which is considered an individual vocation, is in focus. Organising a retreat demands much planning and work. The *mae chii*s considered retreats to be of great importance. The *mae chii*s and also the *dhammacarinii*s spoke of the retreat as one of the highlights of the year. The *mae chii*s said that they welcomed the opportunity to sleep outdoors, to live more simply than usual, to listen to *dhamma* talks and have more time for meditation. However, the retreats were not a complete withdrawal from communication with other people. I found that the meditation retreats played an important role for networking among the monastics. Retreats are held at almost every *samnak chii* and temple throughout the year and *mae chii*s and monks invite each other to come and meditate, give instruction and give *dhamma* talks. Some of the *mae chii*s from Ratburi Samnak Chii were often engaged as teachers at other monastic places.

LEAVING THE ORDAINED STATE

Certain breaches of the monastic rules carry the penalty of expulsion. For monks these are the four *parajika*s, the breaking of the rules regarding celibacy, stealing, killing and boasting about supernatural power. For the *bhikkhuni*s there are eight *parajika*s. The first four are shared with the monks and are more serious than the others. The *parajika* rules 5–8 deal with contact with males and hiding the fact that another *bhikkhuni* has committed a *parajika* offence (Kabilsingh 1984: 51–56).[8]

Breaking other precepts or rules results in a heavy penalty without expulsion and, for some, a lighter penalty. The *bhikkhu*s have 13 rules named 'sanghadisesa' and the *bhikkhuni*s have 17. The *bhikkhu*s and *bhikkhuni*s share seven of the rules in this section (ibid.: 58). Breaking the first nine of these immediately entails a transgression. However the last rules in this section may be broken up to three times before the rules are considered transgressed (The Buddhist Monastic Code 1993: 111). Interestingly, the first four *sanghadisesa* rules for *bhikkhu*s are similar to the *bhikkhunis'* last section of *parajika* rules.[9] For *bhikkhu*s this set of rules is classified under *sanghadisesa,* which implies that breaking them is not viewed as seriously as it is for the *bhikkhuni*s since their rules are classified under *parajika* (Kabilsingh 2000).

Instances of monks breaking the rules and thereby being expelled from the *sangha* are not uncommon in Thailand. The *mae chiis'* rules for expulsion and penalty follow the first four *parajika*s; however, it is rare that *mae chii*s are forced to leave the ordained state.

Most *mae chii*s who leave the ordained state do so at their own request. Like monks and novices, *mae chii*s must formally resign (*suk*) before they return to lay life. The procedure for leaving the *mae chiis'* state is a simple ceremony, involving formal giving up the eight precepts in the presence of monks or *mae chii*s and formally receiving the five precepts. At Ratburi, no monks are invited to this ceremony. While I stayed at Ratburi Samnak Chii, several *mae chii*s left the ordained state. Some of them had decided in advance that they would be a *mae chii* for a limited period of time. Others had various reasons for leaving. The first reason that almost every *mae chii* gave when asked was that they had to help their parents. Many *mae chii*s were under pressure from parents to return to lay life.

Mae chii Ooy was one of the first *mae chii*s that I met when I came to Ratburi Samnak Chii. She had been a *mae chii* for six years when she decided to return to lay life. She had planned to go to Bangkok to work and help her mother financially and at the same time continue studying at the Open University. One Saturday evening, Mae chii Ooy had made a flower garland (*puang maalay*) which she brought to Khun Mae's house and told her that she wanted to leave the ordained state. Khun Mae talked with her for two hours and wanted her to think it over carefully. Mae chii Ooy was determined and did not change her mind. The following Monday was *wan phra* and when the morning ceremonies and talks were finished, Mae chii Ooy brought a *phaan* with flower garland, candles and incense and walked on her knees to the first row where Khun Mae and the other high-ranking *mae chii*s were seated. She bowed to the *mae chii*s and handed over the *phaan* and asked formally to be allowed to leave the Samnak Chii for lay life. Her request was accepted and the *mae chii* gave the *phaan* back to Mae chii Ooy. Usually *mae chii*s hold the ceremony of leaving the ordained state at the same temple or *samnak chii* where they were ordained. Mae chii Ooy had been ordained at Ratburi Samnak Chii and therefore the ceremony had to be performed there. Khun Mae asked when she had planned to *suk* and her answer was on Thursday. Khun Mae uttered: 'Another four pure days' (*iik sii wan borisut*).

The ceremony was held at 6 o'clock on Thursday morning. Mae chii Ooy had prepared a *phaan* with an envelope with money, candles, incense and a beautiful flower garland with white and red flowers. Mae chii Ooy had not invited any of the other *mae chii*s to the ceremony. Only Khun Mae, Mae chii Ooy and myself were present in the *saalaa*. The ceremony started with Mae chii Ooy bowing in respect to Khun Mae. She gave the *phaan* to Khun Mae who took it and placed it at the Buddha shrine. Mae chii Ooy lit the two candles at the Buddhist shrine and she also lit three incense sticks. She then bowed three times and took refuge in the Buddha, Dhamma and Sangha. Khun Mae recited in Pali and Mae chii Ooy asked for the five precepts. Khun Mae gave them and Mae chii Ooy recited them. She bowed three times and Khun Mae took off her outer robe. Mae chii Ooy bowed in front of Khun Mae and she was now a lay person. Khun Mae spoke privately with Ooy. She explained the five precepts and how she could live a good lay life by observing them. Khun Mae wished her good luck and recited in Pali with her hands in a *wai*. Ooy bowed again, Khun Mae put out the candles and the ceremony was over.

> Ooy was unusually silent that morning. She walked to every shrine at the *samnak chii* and lit incense. She put on blue jeans and a white blouse and started to wash her *mae chii* clothes that she would then give to other *mae chii*s at the *samnak chii*. She did not eat any breakfast that morning. She said that she was not hungry. She cleaned her room and packed her things. Later that day she left for her mother's house in a province in the South of Thailand and on Sunday the same week she went to Bangkok to find a job.

In a society where women receive ordination with the intention of being ordained for life, as in the Tibetan tradition, disrobing is considered extremely unfortunate and shameful (Havnevik 1990: 191). That is in contrast to Thai society, where women can ordain for a short period of time and leaving the ordained state is not seen as dishonourable even if the aim had originally been to be a *mae chii* for life. The *mae chii*s at Ratburi Samnak Chii did not discuss Mae chii Ooy's decision to leave. They knew her reasons for disrobing and they did not try to persuade her to change her mind. I got the impression that they felt sorry for her. They agreed that she had to help her mother and they said that she made the right decision. When somebody leaves the *mae chii* state, a common and popular expression is that her 'store of merits' is finished.

NOTES

1   *Wan phra,* literally means 'monk's day'.

2   *Uboosot* days, every full and new moon. On these days monks recite the *patimok,* the monks' disciplinary code of 227 precepts, in the *uboosot* (ordination hall) also called *bot.*

3   That can be translated as: 'Reverence to the Lord who is worthy and fully awakened.'

4   At temples that I visited *mae chiis* had to wait until the monks and novices had finished their meals.

5   As the Buddha pointed out: 'These monks (newly ordained) wear the robes inappropriately, they move in the village for food with no proper manner, they approach people not at the right time, ... these blameworthy behaviours cause people who have faith to lose faith, people who do not have faith not to have faith...' (Tipitaka Vol 4, p. 138).

6   The *Patimokkha,* a set of monastic rules, is the binding force of the *sangha,* the community of male and female monastics. There is also a *Bhikkhuni Patimokkha,* the monastic rules for female Buddhist monks, which is also a part of the oldest Buddhist text, *vinaya pitaka,* the monastic disciplines.

7   The precepts are written in Pali and in the Mae Chiis' handbook they are translated into Thai. The translation into English that I use is from Wat Bowonniwet, which is the temple at which the Thai Mae Chiis' Institute is located.

8   *Parajika* numbers 5–8 are as follows: do not enjoy the touching of men; do not hide the fact that another *bhikkhuni* has committed a *Parajika* offence; do not keep companay with a monk expelled from the *sangha*; do not make appointments to see men alone.

9   The *bhikkhus'* sanghadisesa numbers 1–4 are: do not permit ejaculation; do not touch a female body; do not take pleasure in speaking to women sensuously; do not lure women verbally to satisfy your sexual desire.

CHAPTER SIX

Gender and the Fields of Merit

In Thailand, merit making (*tham bun*), or acts of generosity, plays a central role in people's religious practices. The phrase *tham bun* is generally used to refer to a wide range of good deeds and acts of generosity that are considered to improve a person's *kamm*ic status. To be generous is thus understood to carry beneficial *kamma*. The doctrine of *kamma* assures a person that each good deed will have its reward, if not in this life, then in later existence. Merit makers often share the merit earned with their family, relatives and with all living beings. Water is used as a vehicle to transfer merit symbolically.

Some people i.e. those who have a store of good *kamma* are considered to 'have merit' (*mii bun*). Monks who are renowned for their virtuosity in meditation or for their learning are believed to have merit. Those who hold legitimate power are also assumed to be persons who have merit. Merit is sought by lay people because it is presumed that merit, the consequence of moral acts, will effect a reduction in suffering.

There are ample opportunities for people in Thailand to make merit. Lay people can make a range of meritorious offerings, from the giving of food in the morning to the monastics to donating large sums of money for the construction of sanctuary buildings. Temples and *samnak chii*s regularly administer various kinds of donation ceremonies. Ordination, listening to Buddhist sermons and meditation are also ways of making merit. The most oft-cited form of merit making is offering food to the monks in the morning. The virtue of generosity and merit-making practices is commonly portrayed through women giving food to male monks. The gendered portrait of women giving and monks receiving has begun to change in relation to the emergence of *samnak chii*s independent of temples. As mentioned earlier, the custom of *mae chii*s performing alms rounds has started to become prevalent through initiatives from lay people who, in various ways, have contributed to the establishment of *samnak chii*s.

Merit is a complex concept and is considered dependent on the purity of the actors' intentions. The roles of the recipients and the donors as well as what is given are of significance. Ideally, however, the focus of giving should be on the development of the donor's mind. The recipient of the offerings is significant for the quality of the merit that the alms (*dana*) will entail. High-quality merit is considered to require recipients who are separated from the lay realm and who through strict living constitute a 'field of merit'. Giving to monks who belong to a *sangha* is traditionally considered to be the most meritorious form of giving. Giving to *mae chii*s, who are formally not part of a *sangha*, does not therefore give the best results. This raises the question of whether giving to the *mae chii*s is motivated by pity or by respect, a question that will be explored in this chapter (see Table 6.1).

Table 6.1: Monks' and *mae chii*s' positions as 'fields of merit' in *dana* ceremonies

	Daily alms round	*Thôôt kathin*	*Thôôt phaapaa*
*Mae chii*s at self-governed *samnak chii*s	Yes	No	Yes
*Mae chii*s at monks' temples	No	No	No
Monks	Yes	Yes	Yes

DANA VERSUS GIFTS

Giving alms (*dana*) is the benevolent action of giving mainly food, drink and other requisites of life, while generosity (*caga*) is the charitable disposition to do good to others. The main purpose of giving *dana* is, according to the Buddhist doctrine, to get rid of one's attachment to things in this world and to be free from greed (*lobha*). The Buddhist *dana* should not be mistaken for a gift. *Dana* implies no reciprocity and what alms may legitimately be given and accepted is carefully defined and categorised. Monastics must accept alms from all, with no distinction of wealth or status.[1] *Dana* theoretically involves what Tambiah (1970) has called 'a double negation of reciprocity'. The monk stands as a model of nonreciprocity and is not supposed to return anything in exchange for the alms. The layman, for his part, theoretically expects nothing from the monk in direct return for his alms since the merit attached to alms does not derive from the monk himself. *Dana* should be received without destroying it by reciprocity.

Even showing gratitude would return the alms to the giver. The puzzle is that if what defines *dana* is its difference from the object of exchange, then any form of reciprocity or return to the giver destroys the *dana* precisely by turning it into an object of exchange. It is, therefore important how to receive *dana* without destroying it, since even gratitude would return the alms to the giver and compromise its gratuitous character. Even to refuse it, is to acknowledge it and so, in a sense, give a return. *Dana* must be given without obligation or duty, in order to differentiate it from exchange.

Consequently, *dana* to the ordained community should never be returned in equivalent material form. Whatever the theory, monks and laymen are undoubtedly thrown, through the medium of *dana*, into a highly ritualised and necessary interaction. In practice, as often observed, this model appears to be readily displaced by a simple pattern of reciprocity whereby offerings are given to monks in reward for their participation in various merit-making ritual occasions and other services. Moreover monks are also giving to the lay community, and the teaching of *dhamma* (*dhammadana*) is conceived as the greatest *dana* of all and is given by monks to lay people.

Bowie (1998) noticed that villagers in Northern Thailand generally use the phrase '*tham bun*' to refer to a wide range of good deeds or good actions, regardless of institutional setting. She gives a picture of villagers performing the ideal giving that implies that the donor focuses on his mind. She says that the villagers practise similar treatment towards both monks and beggars. She compares the act of donating food to monks with giving food to beggars and offers an account of the beggars and the donors' actions. She describes the beggar standing quietly just inside the gate, face downcast, while the donors remove their shoes, hold the bowl above their heads before pouring the rice into the bag of the beggar. But, before he leaves, she says, the beggar raises his hands in a *wai*, which is a gesture of respect and gratitude and mumbles a blessing (ibid.: 471). Here, I suggest, is a significant difference between the behaviour of the renunciant and the beggar. There is no usual reciprocity involved in giving to members of the religious community, but gifts to ordinary people demand gratitude. The donor, after giving alms to the renunciant, commonly kneels down and raises his hands in a *wai*. This is not done after giving to a beggar. The monks' non-reciprocal performances displays independence and superiority, the beggars' acts of reciprocity show their subordination.

Gombrich discusses two kinds of giving according to Buddhist thinking. One is giving with thoughts of worship, which is motivated by respect, and the other one is with thoughts of doing favours, motivated by pity. The former is exemplified by *dana* to the *sangha,* the latter by a gift to a beggar. For both, the accompanying thoughts are all-important, but the former is superior, i.e. it brings more merit. Merit varies with the virtue of the recipient, but only insofar as that virtue is known to the giver: if the monk practises secret vices this does not diminish the merit. Someone practising the supreme quality of giving, like Vessantara (see below), gives to everyone, regardless of his or her virtue, but for obtaining the best results one should find out about the recipient beforehand (Gombrich 1971: 290).

THE PERFECTION OF GENEROSITY

The Vessantara story and the other two legends mentioned below are stories about the Buddha's previous lives. They are called 'Jataka tales' and are in a collection of 547 stories about the Buddha's earlier existences. [2] The collection of Jataka tales has a flavour of regional Buddhism and is not in focus in the modern state Buddhism, which instead emphasises events in the latest Buddha's life (Tiyavanich 1997). The Jataka stories are commonly accepted as stories told by the Buddha or his disciples. However, many scholars assume that the Jataka were originally folk tales that subsequently came to be identified as stories of the Buddha's former lives (Keyes 1987: 181). Of all birth-stories, the *dasa-jataka* the last ten before the birth of Gotama Buddha are deemed the most important. Each of these is said to show how the Buddha-to-be acquired one of the ten transcendent virtues that were essential preconditions for his becoming the Buddha. The list of the ten perfections (*parami*) is: generosity, virtue, renunciation, discernment, energy/persistence, patience/forbearence, thankfulness, determination, good will and equanimity.

The last legend of Prince Vessantara is considered to be the most important, and has attained the greatest popularity among Theravada Buddhists. That legend is a natural point of departure for understanding the ideal of generosity in Thai society. For Thai people the Vessantara story is said to provide moral models, important social relationships between rulers and subjects, parents and children, husbands and wives as well as world-renouncers and laity (ibid.). According to the legend, Prince Vessantara was a *bodhisatta* and as such he was non-attached and gave offerings that would be impossible for ordinary people to give. [3] He gave freely the parts of his body, his children, his wife, and even his own life. The legend of Bodhisatta King Sivi tells that he plucked out both his eyes with his hands and gave them to a blind old man. That was considered a remarkable *dana*. Another legend tells of a Bodhisatta taking birth as a wise hare. The hare jumped into a fire after inviting a famished Brahmin to eat him roasted. It is said that because of the purity of the Bodhisatta's mind the fire did not hurt him as it burned his flesh. In relating the story, the Buddha said that the fire had calmed the hare and brought him peace as if it had been cool water, because of the perfection of *dana* (Jootla 1990: 15–17).

The Vessantara tale is widely known throughout Thailand. Thai children read the story at school. The legend is often presented in the form of a sermon, and told at major festivals, and it is also dramatised in theatre and film. This story might, together with two other texts, the Phra Malai and the Trai Phum, be termed 'key' texts of Thai cosmology (Keyes 1987: 181). It is believed that if one can listen to the whole sermon of the Vessantara story in one day, the great merit earned will enable the person to be born in the next Buddha's lifetime. This tradition is still practised in urban Bangkok and in rural Thailand.

Vessantara was a prince born in the kingdom of Sivi at the foot of the Himalayas. He was born clean with his eyes open and spoke immediately and said to his mother that he wanted to give a gift. His mother gave him a purse with a thousand gold coins, which he distributed. He was also given an auspicious white elephant, which ensured rainfall and became a treasure of the kingdom. By the time Prince Vessantara was 16 he married Maddi, a young woman of highest rank. They had two children: a boy and a girl. Vessantara became well known for his generous mind. When a neighbouring, rival kingdom suffered from drought, a group of Brahmins came and asked Vessantara for his auspicious white elephant, Vessantara gave it without hesitation. Although Vessantara was known for his generosity and gave everything people asked for, this gift was too much for the people in his kingdom. They could not accept that the favourable elephant was given away, and turned to Vessantara's father and asked him to banish his son from the country. Reluctantly the king followed the will of his people and the next day Vessantara, Maddi and their two children left the kingdom for a life in exile in the jungle.

Vessantara continued to give: on the outskirts of the town he first gave away his horses, and then his chariot in which they had travelled. Vessantara and his family had to walk and finally they reached Crooked Mountain where they started to live as hermits in two leaf huts. In a nearby kingdom lived a Brahmin called Jujaka. He had heard about Vessantara's generous mind and went to Crooked Mountain and asked Vessantara to give his two children as slaves to him and his young wife, Amittatapana. Vessantara gave without hesitation, but he suggested that they should not leave until Maddi arrived from the forest. The Brahmin anticipated difficulties if they waited for Maddi and he decided to leave promptly. Vessantara watched his children and the Brahmin leaving and he saw the Brahmin binding their hands with a creeper, and beating them with the ends of the creeper so badly that the skin broke and blood flowed. Overwhelming grief rose up in Vessantara and he went into the leaf hut and wept bitterly.

At first Vessantara did not tell Maddi that he had given their children away. After hours of searching for the children Maddi was beside herself with grief and fell unconscious. When she woke up Vessantara told her that he had given the children as slaves to a Brahmin and he said: 'Look to me, Maddi, not to the children. Do not grieve too much. Be happy with me, Maddi, for children are the very best gift.' Maddi replied: 'I am glad for you, my lord; children are the very best gift'. (Gombrich and Cone 1977: 74)

The lord of the gods, Sakka, was now afraid that somebody would come and ask for Maddi. Therefore Sakka decided to appear in the guise of a Brahmin and ask for Maddi. As usual Vessantara gave without hesitation. Then Sakka left Maddi with Vessantara and said: 'I leave her with you, but as you have given her to me, you cannot give her to any other'. (ibid.: 78)

When Jujaka and the two children came to the Kingdom of Sivi, the children's grandfather, the king of Sivi, redeemed the children from slavery by paying Jujaka the children's ransom. The king also gave Jujaka a palace and plenty of food, but not long afterwards the greedy Brahmin died of overeating. The king decided it was time to get Vessantara and Maddi back home. Vessantara received back his children and the kingdom, including the white elephant.

The virtue of generosity is thus the main theme in the Vessantara story. I found the Vessantara story much loved and often referred to by the *mae chii*s and it seemed to constitute a paradigm of generosity. One *mae chii*, who was about 30 years old and had been ordained for 12 years when I interviewed her, said that she identified strongly with the children in the story when she was a child. The *mae chii*'s father had left the family. She said that she could not understand why he did not stay with them. She was hurt and felt that he deserted the family. In relation to talking about her father leaving the family she recalled the Vessantara story and said:

While I was a child I went to the temple almost every day. I liked to be there listening to the monks giving talks and I enjoyed the Jataka stories. I used to cry when I listened to the story of *Phra Vesendorn*. He gave away everything, he was not attached. He even gave his children and his wife. In those days I found it difficult to understand how a person could be so generous and I felt terribly sorry for the children. Now I understand his supreme sacrifice and excellent generosity.

The responses that I received from the *mae chii*s, interpreting the Vessantara Jataka, displayed an ideal understanding of the tale. The *mae chii*s saw nothing wrong in Vessantara's giving away his children and wife. They understood his actions as *dana* and explained to me that Vessantara did love his family and therefore giving away his children and wife was painful to him. The *mae chii*s focused on Vessantara, and not on Maddi. The important distinction for them appeared to be between the lay and the ordained status. Vessantara was regarded as ordained. He always giving up what he had, always renouncing. The women in the story exemplified the troublesome lay life of attachment, which the *mae chii*s had left. They did not give Maddi much attention, although she was highly appreciated, especially in her role as mother. The role of mother and nurturer, guided by compassion, is exceptionally revered in Thai society.[4] Vessantara practised the perfection of giving and non-attachment. His acts of *dana* could perhaps be compared to what Emerson calls a 'true gift'. A 'true gift' must be a gift of one's self, it must be something painful to give. He says that rings and other jewels are not gifts, but apologies for gifts. 'The only gift is a portion of thyself. Thou must bleed for me' (Schrift 1997: 26). This comparision shows a fundamental difference between 'true gift' and *dana*. *Dana* should be given without any pain and with the ideal mental state of being non-attached to worldly matters.

THE ALMS ROUND AT RATBURI SAMNAK CHII

Dana is thus not analogous to an exchange of gifts between friends or equals. On the contrary, *dana* involves the donor's acknowledgement of the recipient's superiority. The alms round (*binthabaat*) is a manifestation of the significant relationship between lay people and the monastics. The practice of the alms round is not expandable to include lay people; it is specifically a vocation for renunciants, performed only by those who constitute a field of merit. At temples, alms rounds are strictly for monks. At *samnak chii*s like Ratburi Samnak Chii the performance of the alms round has proved to be expandable to include the *mae chii*s. The lay people, who request that the *mae chii*s collect alms in the morning, thus legitimise the *mae chii*s as a field of merit. I argue that the interaction between *mae chii*s and the laity in the daily alms round shows that the *mae chii*s have actualised the potential of their ordained position. *Dana* to the *mae chii*s is motivated by respect. *Dana* is important as a confirmation of renunciation. The lay person plays as important a role as the renunciant by continually reaffirming both the connection and disconnection between monks and laymen. Many Thai people start the day by giving their first spoon of rice to the ordained community. Support from the laity is essential for upholding

Figure 6.1. *Mae chii*s from Ratburi Samnak Chii on their daily alms round

the monks' and *mae chii*s' lives as monastics. Giving alms is often a collective act, performed by villagers in the vicinity of a *samnak chii* or a temple. Offering food to monks and *mae chii*s in the morning is done individually, and by giving only a small portion of rice the donor also thinks of neighbours and other people who would then have a chance to offer food to the renunciants and thereby make merit.

At Ratburi Samnak Chii the *mae chii*s have been performing alms rounds for nearly two decades. They began collecting alms in the morning in response to the requests of lay people who lived in the vicinity of the *samnak chii*. The first morning when I followed the *mae chii*s on their alms round was *wan koon*, the day before the holy Buddhist day (*wan phra*) in August 1997. The school was closed for these two days, but the days started as all other days with the bell ringing at 3.45 in the morning. Then followed chanting and meditation sessions in the meditation hall.

Every morning about 15 *mae chii*s from Ratburi Samnak Chii walk barefoot, carrying their white alms bowls in front of them, collecting rice and side dishes from about 75 households in the neighbourhood. They walk in silence and the interaction between the donor and receiver has a ritual pattern, which defines it as a religious act. When the *mae chii*s come to a house, they stand quietly with their eyes downcast. Before giving the rice the lay people remove their shoes as a sign of respect, they lift the rice bowl above their heads, and put rice in each *mae chii*'s bowl. Upon completing this they usually kneel down and raise their hands in respect. During the offering the *mae chii*s are completely silent, they do not look directly at the donor and they walk away quietly.

At temples it is common that a young temple boy (*dek wat*) or a male lay person helps monks to carry alms on their alms round. At Ratburi Samnak Chii the schoolgirls (*dhammacariniis*) fulfil the function of temple boys and they follow a rotating schedule. Two *dhammacariniis* go together with each group of *mae chii*s. The *mae chii*s have been invited by individual households to collect food. In order to visit the donors the *mae chii*s walk in three directions. The shortest round is on narrow gravel roads near the *samnak chii*. The two other rounds are longer. One group of *mae chii*s goes to the market and the other group, which has the longest way to walk, crosses the main road and goes into a densely built-up area.

About half past five, when the morning chants and meditation are finished, the *mae chii*s and the *dhammacariniis* gather outside the *saalaa*. The girls chat sitting close together on their heels, with the yellow plastic buckets beside them. Those *mae chii*s who have already arrived, stand with their white bowls in their arms waiting for the other *mae chii*s to come. While waiting I strolled along the balustrade, which encircled the *saalaa*. Inside, the schoolgirls had started sweeping the floor. I heard them singing. The light in the *saalaa* contrasted sharply with the black night outside.

The *mae chii*s wore their white dresses with their outer robes. The schoolgirls had grey skirts and white blouses and I was dressed in the white *chii phraam* dress. Monks and *mae chii*s always walk barefoot when they collect alms. It is a continuation of the practice since the Buddha's time. Shoes were not among the requisites for *bhikkhu*s or *bhikkhuni*s. The lay people also remove their shoes when they give food to show respect. At Ratburi Samnak Chii everybody who helped carry the alms had to walk barefoot.

At half-past five, the *mae chii*s opened the big green metal gates, which were always locked at night. The group that went to the market left the *samnak chii* first, then the *mae chii*s who walked the longest distance. I followed the last group of seven *mae chii*s who walked the shortest round. After leaving the *samnak chii* we turned to the left and headed north. A schoolgirl and I walked at the end of the line. The *mae chii*s walked fast and it was sometimes difficult for me to walk barefoot on the small gravel roads.

Figure 6.2. A lay woman offers alms to *mae chii*s in a village in Isaan

Outside the first house two women stood waiting for the *mae chii*s. Each of them had a bowl of rice in her hands. The *mae chii*s lined up in front of the house. They had their eyes downcast, and before giving the rice the women removed their slippers, lifted the rice bowls above their heads and then they put a big spoon of rice in every *mae chii*'s bowl. The women had also made a side dish that was put in a bowl and placed on the gatepost. It was the schoolgirl's and my task to take care of what the lay people gave besides rice. For that purpose we had brought buckets and a practical multi-compartmental layered food container called *pintoo*. The *pintoo* consisted of a number of buckets placed upon each other and kept together with a metal-stand and a handle. The schoolgirl put the *pintoo* buckets into the big plastic bucket that I carried and filled one *pintoo* bucket with the curry that the women had donated. We had to do everything very quietly and without speaking. The *mae chii*s did not utter a word and before we left the laywomen knelt down and raised their hands in a gesture of respect (*wai*). The *mae chii*s stood with their eyes downcast and did not respond in any way to the lay person.

In the next house there was one woman who gave rice and a side dish. We repeated the procedure with the *pintoo* buckets. Then we turned into a narrow pebbly road and approached two traditional Thai wooden teak-houses on stilts. They were beautifully located beside a lotus pond. One woman outside each of the houses was waiting for the *mae chii*s. They gave rice and side dishes. Before we left they knelt down and paid respect to the *mae chii*s. A man dressed in black came out from one of the houses. He glanced at us, got into a car and drove away. We turned around and continued walking on the narrow, pebbly road. A woman and a man were waiting for the alms round outside the nest house. They also gave rice and a side dish. Then we turned and walked to the big road again. A young man stood waiting outside the gates to his house. He gave rice and he had two bowls with deep-fried fish. He gave one of the bowls with fish to the *mae chii*s. After giving, he made a high *wai* in respect to the *mae chii*s. When we left that house we met monks walking on their alms round. The *mae chii*s stopped walking and stood still with their eyes downcast until the monks had passed us on the other side of the road. The monks went to the house that we just had left and the young man donated rice and the other bowl with deep-fried fish to the monks. I could not see any difference in the way he acted towards the monks or the *mae chii*s.

We turned to the right and walked on another small road. It had begun to get light and the scenery was beautiful. The air was still fresh and the dark brown houses and the area with its many ponds took on a special shimmer in the early morning. The *mae chii*s collected alms from 12 more houses that morning. Some had put the side dishes in small plastic bags. Commonly they put the bags in the *mae chii*s' bowls, whereupon we took the bags and put them into the plastic buckets. That morning the *mae chii*s also got bananas, other fruits, sweets, bottled water and juices. The *pintoo* buckets were only for keeping cooked dishes. When we arrived at one of the last houses on the alms round we had no empty buckets left. The man donated omelettes and my companion turned one of the lids and put the omelettes on it. The girl giggled quietly; I imagine because it is not correct to do this, but it saved the situation. We had one house left and I wondered where we should put the side dish from that house. The schoolgirl did not seem to worry, she probably knew that the woman in that house usually only gave rice, as she did that morning, too.[5]

When the *mae chii*s had collected food from the last house we were not far away from the *samnak chii*. We walked a few hundred metres on the main road with cars passing us at high speed. We had walked for about an hour and the alms round was completed. The schoolgirl carried the *pintoo*; I carried the yellow plastic bucket in one hand and large bag with bananas in the other. The *mae chii*s' bowls were almost filled with rice. Back at the *samnak chii* we went directly to the kitchen. The *mae chii*s emptied their bowls in big basins and we put the side dishes on a big table in the kitchen. The *mae chii*s who worked in the kitchen decided on which tables in the dining hall the different dishes should be placed. The *pintoo* buckets were then placed on the tables and covered by the plastic shades.

That morning our group collected alms from 18 households. At ten houses the donors were women and at eight houses men gave alms to the *mae chii*s. During fieldwork I joined the alms round in all three directions regularly. The alms round to the market and the longest round used to collect alms from about 25 households each. The donors were both men and women and the numbers of women were slightly greater than of men.

THE LAY DONORS

Both the lay people and monastics that I interviewed expressed strong feelings about alms giving. The *mae chii*s often recalled thoughts and memories from their childhood of giving alms to the monks. They talked about how their family used to cook food in the morning and donate to the monks. They said that giving created feelings of contentment and happiness. The *mae chii*s declared that collecting alms had a personal meaning for them – that they felt proud of being ordained. They said that the interaction with the laity was important for their practice. They felt a greater sense of responsibility towards lay people and said that it deepened their practice and their identity as ordained persons. They also claimed that the alms round demanded that they practise even more seriously and maintain excellent behaviour in order to be worthy of their position as religious alms persons.

The *mae chii*s who lived at Ratburi Samnak Chii came from different places in Thailand. Those who had been ordained and lived at temples had not practised alms rounds before they came to Ratburi Samnak Chii. One *mae chii*, who was 24 years old and ordained at a temple in the Northeastern Thailand ten years previously, told me about her experiences of going on alms rounds:

Khun Mae asked me when I arrived at the *samnak chii* if I had ever performed alms rounds. I told her I had not, because the *mae chii*s at my temple do not go on alms rounds, it is only the monks who do that. Khun Mae invited me to go. She did not force me. I could decide by myself when I wanted to go. I prepared myself for two days before I decided to try. I found it very difficult in the beginning to walk the long distance barefoot at the same time as holding the bowl in a steady position in front of me. Now I do not find it difficult at all and I walk the longest round. The feeling when people give is so profound. When people give we have to practise more, to be worthy of the donation, because they have faith in us. It is very important for *mae chii*s to perform alms rounds. It makes us autonomous. It is also important for the community, so the lay people have the chance to get merit, because the 'good *mae chii*s' are a field of merit.

Often lay people who gave alms in the morning to the *mae chii*s also gave to the monks. They said that it was equally meritorious giving to *mae chii*s and to monks. They stated that the important thing was how well the *mae chii*s and the monks kept their precepts and practised Buddhism. Alms were considered to be purified by the receiver's virtue and alms would be even purer if the renunciant, before accepting alms, gave the lay people the five precepts (*panca-sila*). Alms should be given with faith. Alms must be well prepared, given at the proper time, be given without greed – nothing should be expected in return, and not be given to belittle other persons or to show off one's own importance (Egerton 1990: 27). Further, the donor should be happy at the thought of giving, and should be satisfied after the offering is made. Absence of greed before, during or after the offering makes *dana* truly great. The recipients should be free from lust, hatred and delusion, or they should have embarked on a course of training for the elimination of these mental defilements (De Silva 1990: 34).

Khun Ning was one of the lay donors who offered food to the *mae chii*s every morning. I visited her one afternoon to interview her about giving donations to *mae chii*s. Khun Ning was 75 years old and lived in a traditional Thai teak house on stilts, not very far from the *samnak chii*. We sat talking in the shade under the house. One of her daughters and her son's wife sat chopping vegetables, and her young grandson was playing on the ground. Khun Ning had lived in that house for about 50 years. She moved there together with her husband after they had married. They had seven children, four sons and three daughters.

Khun Ning talked appreciatively about her husband who had passed away two years earlier. She said he had been a 'very good person' (*khun dii maak*): he did not smoke, he did not drink and he appreciated the *mae chii*s and their work. Khun Ning's husband had held a leading position in the village and he had helped the *mae chii*s to construct buildings at the *samnak chii*. Khun Ning and her husband bought their land from a wealthy woman who lived in the area. She was one of two well-to-do women who had owned land there and they later donated land to the *mae chii*s in order to set up a *samnak chii*. One of them also donated the big Buddha statue that is placed inside the *saalaa* at the *samnak chii*. The two women did not live in the village anymore. One of them had moved to Bangkok, and the other lived at a temple in a nearby province. Khun Ning said that both of them wanted to make merit and they preferred to give to the *mae chii*s.

Some *samnak chii*s were established on land owned by the *mae chii*s themselves or their families. Generally, the foundation of *samnak chii*s was instigated by lay people, who donated land, gave financial support and often also assisted in erecting buildings at *samnak chii* compounds. Donating land, giving financial support and assisting an ordained community whose members live according to the Buddhist precepts are examples of meritorious activities that are considered to render the donor much merit.

Khun Ning remembered when the first two *mae chii*s, Khun Mae Sumon and Khun Mae Prathin were invited to start building the *samnak chii*. They were the first *mae chii*s to arrive and soon afterwards two more *mae chii*s joined them. In the beginning there were only these four *mae chii*s who lived at the *samnak chii*. Khun Ning could not recall any *mae chii*s going on alms rounds in the village before Ratburi Samnak Chii was established. When the *mae chii*s first settled there were not many people who offered food to them. Those who had donated land and invited the *mae chii*s to establish the *samnak chii* gave to them. When people saw the results of their work they gradually started to donate to them. Khun Ning had always given food in the morning to the monks, and when the *mae chii*s sat up the *samnak chii* she started to offer food to them each day. She said that she had faith in the *mae chii*s because they were strict (*khreng*) and rigorously observant of the precepts. Over the years, she had continued to donate to temples. This year she had gone to fund-raising ceremonies (*phaapaa*) at four temples and she said that she had donated to more temples than that.

It was important for Khun Ning to give alms (*tak bat*) every morning. She said that if she did not do it she did not feel happy. She claimed that she had the same intention when she put rice in a *mae chii*'s bowl as in a monk's bowl and that the merit was the same. She told me that after she had given food she always recited while pouring water from one container to another (*rodnaam*), and she dedicated the merit to her sons, daughters and all her relatives. She said: 'I want them to be happy. I do not know if it helps, but I do it every day.'

The custom of pouring water after having performed an act of generosity in order to spread the merit is known from the Buddha's time. In mural paintings at temples picturing the Buddha's life there is one scene where Mara, the symbolic king of evil and temptation who mustered his forces in an effort to prevent the Buddha from achieving Buddhahood, attacks the Buddha. The

Buddha calls the Goddess of Earth Nang Thoranii to bear witness to his right to enlightenment through the accumulated virtue of many previous lives. The Goddess of Earth appears and drowns the forces of Mara by wringing the water from her hair that she had collected every time the Buddha performed an act of virtuous generosity. The tremendous amount of water represents the innumerable times that the Buddha dispensed charity and alms in his former lives. The act of *dana* was indicated by pouring water upon the hands of the receiver, spreading water from one vessel to another, and thus upon the Earth.

The water symbolises a river, which fills the ocean, and a wholesome deed is so plentiful that it can also be shared with others. The 'sharing' of one's wholesome deeds with others is another form of generosity. This does not mean that other people can receive the results of one's good deeds. People receive the results of the deeds that they have done themselves. Sharing wholesomeness with others means that the good deeds can be the condition for the arousal of beneficial consciousness in others, also in beings in other planes of existence (Van Gorkom 1990: 55–56).

Khun Wimon lived on the longest alms round. She gave food to the *mae chii*s every morning and one morning when I walked with the *mae chii*s I made an appointment to visit her in the afternoon for an interview. She lived with her family in a modern white house built on the ground surrounded by a big fence and metal gates. She was 40 years old, married and had two sons. Her husband grew fruit, and she helped him when he needed her on the farm. However, most of the time she worked with the chicken and egg production that she had set up in an area at the back of their house. It was a small-scale enterprise and she said that she strove to run it as ecologically as possible. The chickens were not in cages, she did not use any chemicals, and she had her own compost.

Khun Wimon was born in the village and her parents did not live far from her house. She said that she helped the *mae chii*s to raise funds for constructions at the *samnak chii*. Her husband had helped with building the first house at the *samnak chii*. She said that the *mae chii*s at Ratburi Samnak Chii lived a strict monastic life and were very well mannered (*riabrôôy maak*). Further, she stated that she was not interested in *mae chii*s at temples. She considered them ignorant in their role as ordained persons and said: 'They are still greedy.' She preferred to give alms to the *mae chii*s at Ratburi Samnak Chii because she found them stricter than the monks. She told me that on one occasion she had donated 50,000 baht: 40,000 to the *mae chii*s and 10,000 to the monks. We were sitting and talking in the shade outside her house when she went inside and fetched a big, framed picture from the donation ceremony. I recognised it. It was one of the ceremonies the Thai Mae Chiis' Institute regularly organises at the royal temple Wat Bowonniwet for donations. They are usually held on the opening day, the 7th of April, of their annual meeting. The picture showed one of the royal princesses and Khun Wimon who was accepting a blessed gift from the princesse's hand in recognition of her large contribution.

Khun Wimon said she had given food to the monks since she was a child. Now she gave alms to the *mae chiis* every day. She stated that the merit rendered by giving to the *mae chiis* and giving to the monks was the same. She also always transferred the merit earned and she performed the same ceremony after giving to the *mae chiis* as she did when she gave to the monks. She said that the merit was dependent on the monks' and the *mae chiis*' practice. She declared that if a monk did not follow the rules and uphold moral conduct there was no merit even though he wore the monk's robe.

In the early mornings, outside Khun Wimon's house, usually Khun Sombon stood and waited for the *mae chiis*' alms round. His house was on a small road behind Khun Wimon's and he preferred to go there and offer to the *mae chiis*. Khun Sombon usually got up at 5 o'clock in the morning and steamed rice. When the rice was ready, he put it in a silver-plated basin and walked to the food stall close to Khun Wimon's house. He bought some curries in plastic bags and when the *mae chiis* came on their alms round he offered rice and curries to them. He said he felt happiness (*khwaamsuk*) when he gave, and had he not had that feeling he would not have continued giving. Every morning after he had given he used to *rodnaam,* and he dedicated the merit to his relatives, to his mother and father. He explained that water was used for transferring merit and that the water was considered pure. Water, he said, was like the mind, it spread and could easily go anywhere.

Khun Sombon was 55 years old and worked as a driver. He had separated from his wife 15 years earlier, and was now living alone. He had two children, a boy and a girl. His son was a teacher and after finishing his studies he had been a novice monk for one rainy season. His daughter was 19 and had recently finished her vocational studies. Khun Sombon gave alms to the *maechiis* every morning when he was not travelling. During the rainy season (*vassa*) he also gave to the monks, but only during the rains; the remaining nine months he only gave to the *mae chiis*. One reason was that the *mae chiis* did not get as much support as the monks did. He said that the monks had more food and money than they needed. Another reason was the *mae chiis*' strict training, which he appreciated. He said their practice was vital for his willingness to give. Had their practice not been excellent, he would not have donated to them. He considered the Ratburi Samnak Chii stricter than other places and he honoured that. He added that the *mae chii*s had Buddhist knowledge, sympathy for other people (*metta songsaan*) and a generous mind.

The lay donors presented above donated food daily to the *mae chii*s and they all lived along the *mae chii*s' longest alms round. Beside the highway, not far away from the *samnak chii*, there was an ice factory which the *mae chii*s passed every day on their alms round. The owner was Khun Malii and she donated a big sack of ice every day to the *samnak chii* which was delivered before the meal at 11 o'clock. Khun Malii was a businesswoman with many assignments and I had arranged an appointment with her at her office that was located in one of the houses on the main road in the village. Khun Malii was married and about 65 years old. She was born in the province town and when she married, 46 years ago, she moved to the village where Ratburi Samnak Chii is located.

Khun Malii said that she first visited Ratburi Samnak Chii while Khun Mae Sumon was still alive. She told that at that time the *mae chii*s did everything themselves. They grew vegetables, fruit and also rice in the *samnak chii* compound. The *mae chii*s also cooked their own food. Khun Malii said that the *mae chii*s followed the rules strictly and that their Buddhist training was excellent. She remembered that when the *mae chii*s opened the school and she saw the children who studied there she felt that she wanted to help them more. Since then she had visit the *samnak chii* often. She said she used to ask Khun Mae what they needed and make a donation according to their requirements.

Khun Malii did not give alms in monks' or *mae chii*s' bowls every day. She said that she was very busy and did not have time to prepare food in the morning. However, at special functions she would give food to both monks and *mae chii*s. Khun Malii and her family regularly hosted meals at Ratburi Samnak Chii. When I asked whether offering to *mae chii*s or monks rendered different merit, she replied that the merit was the same no matter which one the donor gave to. If the donor had good intentions, the merit would be the same, but she emphasised that there was a difference between *mae chii*s who lived at *samnak chii*s and those who lived at temples. She explained that the *mae chii*s at *samnak chii*s were superior because of their better training and they were rigorous about following the rules and their precepts, whereas the *mae chii*s at temples were not.

DANA FROM MONKS TO MAE CHIIS

Terwiel points out that the practice of donating is not reserved solely to laymen: a monk accumulates beneficial *kamma* in the same manner every time he gives a book or an amulet to a layman or to a fellow monk (Terwiel 1994: 192). There are ample examples of monks donating to *mae chiis*. At alms rounds with the Ratburi *mae chiis* I witnessed monks giving from their alms bowls to the *mae chiis'* bowls. Many of the buildings at Ratburi Samnak Chii had been constructed by financial means from a monk's lay followers from Bangkok. I met *mae chiis* from Isaan who studied in Central Thailand and were financially supported by monks from Isaan. There is nothing unusual about monks and *mae chiis* giving *dana* to other monastics or to lay people. However, *bhikkhu* are prohibited from receiving alms offered by *bhikkhuni*. That is found in *Patidesaniya*, which is one section in the Patimokkha. The Buddha laid down that rule for the *bhikkhu* in order to protect the *bhikkhuni* from being taken advantage of (Kabilsingh 1998: 25–26).

Monks support *samnak chiis* in various ways. I visited a *samnak chii* in Isaan that was financially supported by a monk. The *mae chiis* stressed that the monk was careful about whom he gave donations to. The *mae chiis* further explained that he did not donate to everybody who was in need of support. On the contrary, he would only give if they were worthy recipients. For that reason he tested the *mae chiis'* Buddhist knowledge and inquired about their practice. Later he had taken on the assignment to become their teacher monk and supervisor. Teaching Buddhism is also an act of generosity, and listening to Buddhist teachings is considered to yield religious merit.

Not all *mae chiis*, however, had the support from monks. I met *mae chiis* who reported severe difficulties when they wanted to leave the temple where they lived and set up a *samnak chii*. This was initially the situation also for the *mae chiis* at the *samnak chii* mentioned above. At first, some monks in the village had been against the establishment of a *samnak chii*. However, there were other monks who approved of the *mae chiis'* vocation. Some of those who were in favour of a *samnak chii* donated alms bowls to the *mae chiis*. The *mae chiis* who received the alms bowls interpreted the monks' donation as a legitimation of their practice and recognition of them as religious alms persons.

In general, however, there was no opposition between temples and *samnak chiis*. The *mae chiis* did not intend and were in no position to confront the monks. They considered it of great value for the *samnak chii* to have support from monks. I found that *samnak chiis* and temples often co-operated when needed. The monks from neighbouring temples were invited to Ratburi Samnak Chii on special occasions. The temples also invited the *mae chii*s to certain ceremonies. On a few occasions during my fieldwork, Ratburi Samnak Chii hosted meals at the village temples. At these events the *mae chii*s prepared the food at the *samnak chii* and brought it to the temple. There was individual variation of how engaged the *mae chii*s were in activities that concerned interaction with the monks. Many *mae chii*s offered food to the monks on special occasions. However, some did not participate in alms giving activities related to monks.

DONATING PROPER THINGS AT THE PROPER TIME

The *mae chii*s and the monks carry out many similar duties; however there are restrictions on the *mae chii*s' performances as religious persons. The ceremonies *thôôt kathin* and *thôôt phaapaa* presented in this chapter aim to illustrate monks' and *mae chii*s' positions in two ceremonial contexts, both involving lay people.[6] In contrast to the alms round, the robe offering ceremony (*thôôt kathin*) is an example of a ritual that is performed solely by monks with higher ordination. *Thôôt kathin* is thus not held at *samnak chii*s but is nevertheless an important event for most *mae chii*s. The 'fund-raising' ceremony (*thôôt phaapaa*) is not as prestigious as the robe-offering ceremony and is held regularly at temples as well as at *samnak chii*s. Performances of meritorious offerings display not only differences between monks, *mae chii*s and lay people but they also illuminate processes of change within the category of religious persons and within the category of *mae chii*.

It is common that lay people come to Ratburi Samnak Chii in order to make merit (*tham bun*) by giving *dana* and offering a meal to the *mae chii*s, *chii phraam*s and *dhammacarinii*s. Lay people contact the *samnak chii* in advance and decide together with the head *mae chii* a suitable date for the donation based on practicality and auspiciousness. The lay donors were commonly present in the dining hall during the ceremony held prior to the meal. On these occasions, the assembly of *mae chii*s, *chii phraam*s and the *dhammacarinii*s perform the regular chants as well as special chants in both Thai and Pali. During the special chants everybody turns to face the laity who sit and pour water from one brass vessel into another, in order to transfer merit. Afterwards they bring the bowl with water outside and pour it on the ground under a tree.

During the rainy period of my fieldwork, there were hosted meals followed by special chants (*haiphôôn*) almost every day. When the lenten season was over (*ok phansaa*), the numbers of offered meals decreased considerably, and in the following 30 days (the *kathin* period), there were almost no groups of lay people hosting meals at the *samnak chii*.

THÔÔT KATHIN

The robe-offering ceremony originates from the time of the Buddha. When the monks were wanderers and the Buddhist year was divided into two parts. During nine months the monks might wander about, living in the woods or at a monastery, but for the remaining three months, residence in a monastery was obligatory (Tambiah 1970: 70). The end of the rainy season was marked by a ceremony called *pavarana*, at which the monks asked one another to pardon any offences that might have been committed. Immediately after that, the *kathin* ceremony was held, which consisted of the distribution of robes by lay donors to the monks for their use in the year commencing with the retreat. Over time the temporary residence changed into permanent residence, and the rainy season retreat (*vassa*) itself has become a marked phase of retreat and intensified religious activity in the routine life of monastic communities (ibid.).

The *kathin* period falls at the end of the rainy season retreat in mid-October. During that period, lay people donate new robes to Buddhist monks and this provides one of the major opportunities for the laity to earn merit from generous actions. The *kathin* offerings take place during the month immediately following the full moon *uposatha* ceremony in October. The *kathin* ceremony generally lasts between one and three days and involves *dana* of food, clothing and other necessities to the monks.

According to Tambiah (1970), the cycle of Buddhist temple rites in Thailand is closely interwoven with the village economy, which is based on the cycle of rice cultivation. The period preceding the *kathin* ceremony is the monastics' retreat period. The retreat coincides with the rainy season and it is said that it was the Buddha who prescribed the retreat for monks so that they would not crush or destroy vegetable life and small creatures during their travels in the rainy season. The retreat corresponds to the season of the heaviest rains, which impregnate the rice goddess, Lady Koosok (Davies 1984: 181). According to the legend, Lady Koosok is said to be 'pregnant', that is to say that the rice begins to form heads, at about the end of the *vassa*. Tambiah has pointed out that the intensified asceticism of the monks during *vassa* is linked to the growth of the rice and to the assurance of adequate rainfall to fertilize the rice (Tambiah 1970: 155–156). By the time of the *kathin* festivals, the rice is considered 'pregnant', and the monks' duty is finished. Ideally, during the three months of *vassa* no ordination should take place and no monk should leave the order and resume lay status. Lay persons, too, keep special *vassa* observances. It is, for example, not recommended to hold house warming and wedding rituals during that period (Davies 1984: 181).

The merit earned by donating *kathin* robes to the *sangha* is considered to be of especially high value. Offering *kathin* robes does not include offering robes to the *mae chii*s. The robes offered were solely for monks with high ordination. The literal meaning of the Pali word *kathina* is 'frame'. Originally monks would take the cloth received on this day, stretch it on a frame (much like a quilting frame) and work jointly to stitch the pieces together (Swearer 1995: 180). Unlike other meritorious deeds, the offering of *kathin* alms can only be done within 30 days: from the full moon day of October to the full moon day of November. The monks who accept a *kathina* robe must have received the higher ordination and have observed the rains retreat for three months. Commonly, the donors offer the robes to the *sangha* and not to individual monks, where, according to the disciplinary rules, there must be at least five higher ordained monks to receive the *kathin* robe. Each temple can receive robes only once, and for many temples this is the major event in the whole year.

MAE CHII AND KATHIN OFFERINGS

The *mae chii*s' position – outside the *sangha* and below monks – is highlighted during the *kathin* period. The robe-offering ceremonies are not expandable to include the *mae chii*s. Nor are the *mae chii*s at Ratburi Samnak Chii recipients of *kathin* offerings. On the contrary, the *kathin* period is important for individual *mae chii*s as donors. The *mae chii*s sometimes act as vehicles for lay people to present offerings to the *sangha*.

The *kathin* period is a time for travel for lay people and also for the *mae chii*s. However, the head at Ratburi Samnak Chii does not encourage the *mae chii*s to travel, and some express hesitation about participating in the 'merit-making trips'. However, those who can afford to travel and are interested in making merit through offering to the *sangha* visit temples and partake in *kathin* ceremonies. Some *mae chii*s travel together in small groups. Typically, however, several people plan the trip, rent a bus and recruit friends to come along. Passengers pay a fare for the bus trip and contribute to a merit fund, which is offered to the temple or *samnak chii*. Lay people arrange such trips regularly around significant Buddhist ceremonies, usually without any *mae chii* participating.

The *kathin* offering is generally a collective giving and although nearly every family in a community is involved in the preparation of food and other material gifts offered to the monks at a particular monastery, the principal donor may come from another village, town or region. This custom stems from the traditional view that greater merit accrues when the identity of the donor is unknown to the *sangha* (Swearer 1995: 23).

In November 1997, I was invited to go on a journey with a group of *mae chii*s and lay people to the North of Thailand for *kathin* donations. The trip was initiated by one of the leading *mae chii*s at Ratburi Samnak Chii and had been planned for several months. The lay people in the village had donated robes, money and various things for the monks so that they could further donate the offerings to a specific village temple in the North of Thailand.

The trip was originally planned to take place at the beginning of November, but it was postponed more than two weeks because of a huge flood that affected the Central and Southern parts of Thailand that year and made it impossible to travel. When we were finally able to go, it was a few days after the *kathin* period had finished. This was considered disadvantageous meritoriously and the participants were sad about it. However, the temple had been contacted and they wanted the *mae chii*s to carry out the journey even though it was overdue. The *mae chii*s knew monks and *mae chii*s throughout the country and they assisted each other in times of need. They said that they had chosen to donate *kathin* offerings to that particular temple in Northern Thailand because they knew the monks and *mae chii*s there and they were aware of the difficult financial situation of the school.

We started the more than 900-kilometre journey at 4.30 in the morning, of 23 November. We travelled in two pick-up trucks. *Mae chii*s and lay people went in both vehicles and some of us sat on the hard benches on the pick-up's platform. One car was loaded with all the offerings to the temple and the other vehicle carried the food we needed on the journey. We stopped for breakfast at 7 o'clock and lunch at 11 o'clock. We travelled from Ratchaburi through the outskirts of Bangkok through Don Muang, Nakhon Sawan, Suphanburi, Phitsamulok, Uttaridit and Tak, and in the late afternoon, after more than 12 hours' journey, we arrived in the mountainous area Doy Thao in Chiang Mai district.

We went directly to the temple where the headmaster of the village school and a *mae chii* welcomed us. The villagers had gathered on the temple grounds and they offered us lime juice to drink. The laity had prepared for the donation ceremony and we unloaded all the things that we had brought. A symbolically important offering presented to the monastic order at this time is a 'tree' with money and other offerings. The villagers had made quite a large tree and attached banknotes, and various things used by the monks like soap, tooth paste, towels and garlic. The *mae chii*s laid an ochre cloth (*phaa*) on the tree, symbolising the monks' robe.

The village temple was small with about five resident monks and only a few *mae chii*s. The *mae chii* who welcomed us was a visiting *mae chii* who resided permanently at a big temple in Bangkok. The school was closely connected to the temple and was located in the temple area. When the resident monks had arrived, we went into the ceremonial hall. The monks sat on a raised platform beside the Buddha image and faced the *mae chii*s and the laity. The ceremony started with our leading *mae chii* lighting the two candles and incense before the principal Buddha image. The *mae chii*s and laity recited and the assembly took refuge to the Buddha, the Dhamma and the Sangha. Then the *mae chii* asked the monks for the eight precepts and the abbot held the ceremonial fan in front of his face and gave the precepts. The leading *mae chii* then presented the robes and an envelope with the collected money to the head monk. The money was a donation to the school but was given to the abbot who later passed it on to the school. After the abbot had received the robes and the envelope he once again used his fan. He rose from the platform, shielded his face with the fan, walked to the tree and fetched the robe. As he did this, the assembly sat with their hands folded in a respectful *wai* position. The abbot returned to his seat on the platform and our group, both *mae chii*s and lay people, presented the other offerings to the monks. Finally the monks and novices chanted 'tham bun blessings' to the *mae chii*s and laity, followed by chants by the *mae chii*s.

The money that accompanied the *kathin* alms had thus gone from the laity in Ratburi district, through the *mae chii*s, to the monks who passed it on to the village school. *Dana* that passed through the monastics was considered to carry much more merit (*bun*) than if the lay people in Ratburi had donated it directly to the school.

We did not spend the night in Doy Thao. As mentioned above, the *mae chii*s have a well-functioning network and they know *mae chii*s all over the country and when they travel they usually stay at *samnak chii*s or temples with a *mae chii* section. This time they had been invited to stay at a *samnak chii* in another part of Chiang Mai district. The head *mae chii* at that *samnak chii* was a friend of one of the *mae chii*s from Ratburi Samnak Chii and they had known each other for many years. This small *samnak chii* was beautifully located not far from Doi Inthanon, the highest point in Thailand. Over the following days we visited *mae chii*s at temples and *samnak chii*s in the area and we also went to Doi Inthanon. For most of the participants it was the first time they had visited that area and part of the attraction of participating was the experience of travelling and seeing new places. On our way back to Ratburi Samnak Chii we also stopped at the *samnak chii* with the Dhammacarinii School in Lamphun district. At all of these places offerings were central. The visiting *mae chii*s offered food or other things for the *mae chiis'* daily use and they received offerings like plants and vegetables to bring back to Ratburi Samnak Chii.

ROBE OFFERINGS TO *MAE CHII*S

According to the Buddhist scriptures, the *bhikkhuni*s were not excluded from the *kathin* ceremony and they were presented with the same offerings as the monks (Horner 1990: 331). The only temple or *samnak chii* that I came across during fieldwork that organised robe offering ceremonies for women was Wat Song Dharmakalyani, which was the female monk Bhiksuni Voramai Kabilsingh's temple in Nakhom Pathom province.[7] She was the first Thai woman to receive full *bhiksuni* ordination in the Dharmagupta ordination lineage. It goes back to the Dharmagupta sect, which was one of the earliest Buddhist schools. Today the ordination lineage belongs to the Mahayana tradition but it is closely related to the Theravada tradition and the precepts are similar. Bhiksuni Voramai Kabilsingh received *bhiksuni* ordination in Taiwan in 1971. Before her *bhiksuni* ordination she had been a *mae chii* for 15 years (Kabilsingh 1991: 49, 52). Wat Song Dharmakalyani conducts the *kathin* ceremony annually and the ceremony is carried out together with a three-day blessing ceremony of herbal medicine. First they make the herbal medicine and then they chant the Medicine Buddha gatha 108 times. The chant (*gata*) is taken from Bhaisajyaguruvaidulyaprabha Sutra. They have kept up this tradition of the blessing of herbal medicine since 1985 and the medicine is offered to everybody who visits the temple during the *thôôt kathin*.

I went to the *kathin* ceremony at Wat Song Dharmakalyani on 2 November 1997. Venerable Ta Tao, which is Voramai Kabilsingh's ordained name, was 89 years old and had been ill for a few years and was bedridden at that time. There were no more *bhiksuni* at the temple and her daughter, Acaan Chatsumarn, was in charge of the activities at the temple. Throughout the *kathin* day, Bhiksuni Ta Tao lay on a bed in the *saalaa* on the first floor. Because of her sickness they had made a special air-conditioned room of glass for her to stay in. She wore a yellow robe and lay down on a bed most of the time. A nurse helped her to sit up when people came to pay respect to her. The ceremony started at one o'clock in the afternoon and was held in the ceremony hall on the second floor. The *bhiksuni* was connected with the ceremony via a white sacred thread (*sai sin*) that was stretched between the *bhiksuni*'s bed and the second floor where the ceremony was held.

In the ceremony hall the donations were displayed and there were four big 'money trees'. No monks were present and Acaan Chatsumarn conducted the ceremony dressed in white. Four quite old *mae chii*s lived at the temple and they participated in the ceremony. They did not hold prominent positions at the temple and during the ceremony they mingled with the lay people and were even seated behind the laity. Acaan Chatsumarn started the event by giving an annual report of the temple's activities and after that she gave a Buddhist speech. Then robes, fans and bowls were passed around so that everybody could touch the offerings. The temple donated Buddha statues to some schools and other associations. Then Acaan Chatsumarn led a meditation session. She concluded the ceremony by sprinkling water over the assembly and on the way out from the ceremony hall everybody was given two specially blessed oranges.

During the *kathin* period the same year, a group of *mae chii*s from Ratburi Samnak Chii went to make offerings to a temple in Isaan. The temple they went to was the permanent residence of one of the visiting *mae chii*s and they went to present robes and other offerings to the *mae chii*s at their section. When the *mae chii*s returned to Ratburi Samnak Chii they showed pictures taken at the ceremony when they offered the white *mae chii* robes wrapped with pink ribbons, and other alms to the *mae chii*s. They told me that only *mae chii*s had participated in the robe presenting ceremony. The *mae chii* who had initiated the trip said that she did it in order to honour her *mae chii* and other longstanding *mae chii*s at her temple. At Ratburi Samnak Chii *mae chii*s were offered robes on several occasions, and robes could be presented at any time during the year. The *kathin* period was usually not selected for special donations to *mae chii*s and there was no big ceremony at Ratburi Samnak Chii during the period.

THÔÔT PHAAPAA CEREMONY

Phaapaa and *kathin* ceremonies have some similar traits. However, there are also differences, and one is that the *phaapaa* can be held at any time of the year. *Phaapaa* is organised to raise funds, and the donations are considered to yield the donors religious merit. Ratburi Samnak Chii organises *phaapaa* twice a year – one large *phaapaa* in the end of August and a smaller one in January before the yearly meditation retreat begins (see Chapter 5). The words *'phaa paa'* are Thai and mean forest robe. Presenting offerings in a tree is also part of the *phaapaa* ritual and commonly recognised in Thailand as a very formal deed. It is often seen as related to the concept of heavenly plants such as the mythological wishing 'tree' (*kapparukkha*) which reputedly yields any object that individuals may wish for. Usually, the money trees are carried to the monastery where the fund-raising festival is held and the people who carry the money are received with great respect. At temples the amount of money on the tree is publicly announced and recorded so that when a similar occasion is held in the monastery whose community made this *dana*, a deputation can be sent with an offering not markedly greater, but certainly not less. Consequently, the array of tree offerings that accumulates during a fundraising ceremony reveals part of the network of formal obligations between different communities in a wide region (Terwiel 1994: 213).

The *phaapaa* at Ratburi Samnak Chii commonly attracts people from the vicinity, and from nearby provinces; a large number of people also come from Bangkok. In 1998 the small *phaapaa* took place on 4 January. It was Sunday and the day before *wan phra*. Early in the morning local sellers of herbal medicine, dried fruits, vegetables and other goods arrived at the *samnak chii* and displayed their wares in the *samnak chii*'s compound. The *mae chiis* had put a large table covered with pink fabric in front of the main entrance to the *saalaa*. The table was decorated with artificial flowers and there was one large silver-plated bowl on a stand for lay people to put their donations in. A longstanding *chii phraam* and a lay woman were sitting at the table and they registered people's donations and wrote receipts. Registrations of donations and receipts were always written when people donated money to the *samnak chii*. Sometimes the donors' names and how much they had donated were displayed in the *saalaa* building. There was no procession with people walking to the *samnak chiis* with 'money trees'. Instead, people donated money and the banknotes were later made into money trees. The trees were placed in yellow plastic buckets and the buckets were filled with small packages of washing powder, soap, canned food and other offerings to the *mae chiis*. In every money tree there was also one monk's robe.

The daily giving of food to the monastics is a ritualised performance and done in silence, the anonymous giving described as an ideal at the *kathin* offering and the offerings at the *phaapaa* events are the same regardless of whether the offerings are for *mae chiis* or for monks. The practice of giving receipts and displaying the donors' names is commonly done when people give donations for specific purposes such as constructing buildings. It is important both for temples and *samnak chiis* to keep financial records in order to avoid being accused of economic irregularities, which would undermine their religious authority.

The *phaapaa* ceremonies at Ratburi Samnak Chii started at 1 pm. Nine monks were invited from the village temple. When monks conduct ceremonies at the *samnak chii*, they and *mae chii*s sit facing each other. On this occasion, both monks and *mae chii*s sat on the platform. The monks had their place on the right side of the Buddha statue and the *mae chii*s sat on statue's left side. The monks sat on brown cushions i.e. higher than the *mae chii*s. The *mae chii*s sat on the red carpet and did not use their cushions when monks were present. The monks were offered flowers, incense, a candle, some money in envelopes and a robe.

An important part of the *phaapaa* at Ratburi Samnak Chii was to transfer merit to others. Inside the *saalaa* on the right hand side beside the Buddha statue, the *mae chii*s had put some small tables and arranged ten photographs of people who had been important for the *samnak chii*. One picture was of the former head *mae chii*, Khun Mae Sumon, who had passed away after living at the *samnak chii* for a couple of years. The other photographs were also of deceased persons. There were pictures of *mae chii*s and of male and female lay people. A sacred cotton thread (*sai sin*) was fastened onto the large Buddha statue and was attached to one corner of each of the ten pictures. At the ceremony, the monks sat with their hands in a *wai* position and held the thread between their index finger and thumb as they chanted. The *mae chii*s, however, did not hold the thread. After the monks had recited Buddhist texts, the highest ranked monk used the fan in front of his face and fetched the robes from the 'money trees'. Then followed ritual chants and blessings by both monks and *mae chii*s. The ceremony was concluded with speeches by some of the *samnak chii*'s leading *mae chii*s.

Monks were always invited to important ceremonies that included lay people. Some *mae chii*s claimed that it was unnecessary to invite monks since they could perform the ceremonies themselves and the merit earned by the laity would be the same. However, most of the *mae chii*s preferred to invite monks and regarded it as important for the lay people that monks were also present since they were considered to increase the merit.

After the ceremonies, lay people were invited to eat. The *mae chii*s and lay people alike had prepared food in large quantities. A large roof was erected over the area between the *saalaa* and the dining hall. Tables and chairs had been brought outside and the food was served in the outdoor room made for the occasion. It was a joyful event. Many of the visitors were people who came to every *phaapaa* that the *samnak chii* organises and many of the lay people knew each other. Most of the participants who came in rented buses from Bangkok and other places returned in the afternoon. Several *mae chii*s from other temples and *samnak chii*s, and also some lay people stayed at the *samnak chii* in order to participate in the retreat that started the following day.

Merit-making travel such as the *thôôt kathin* and *thôôt phaapaa* trips have a combination of spiritual and worldly purposes. Besides acting in the most prestigious arena of Thai social and moral order by making merit for the monastics, the trips also offer opportunities for worldly entertainment. These journeys usually include sightseeing attractions like visiting Thailand's highest peak, Doi Inthanon, a waterfall, a famous temple, national park, cave or dam. People from all social spheres participate in merit making journeys. Also migrant workers in Bangkok and other places organise *thôôt phaapaa* trips. Usually migrants from the same area travel to their home villages. These trips allow them to return home and fulfil their obligations as good village daughters and sons and also to exercise their modern (*thansamay*) identity (see Mills 1999: 138–146).

MAE CHII – FIELDS OF MERIT

Dana to the members of the *sangha* are thus deemed to be most meritorious, but giving to fellow lay people also renders beneficial *kamma*. Therefore a person acquires merit by giving alms to beggars and by donating to charitable institutions. As stated earlier, the act of giving that is considered to confer merit upon laymen is made by the donors themselves. Ideally, giving should be done with a proper attitude of selflessness and detachment, with no expressed regard for the alms' *karm*ic outcome. The value of the offering is determined by how it is given: i.e. in the proper way and with the proper state of mind. These ideals were familiar to the lay people whom I interviewed; however, they explained that they were also relevant to offering to a worthy recipient.

The question of whether donations to *mae chii*s are motivated by pity or by respect is important when analysing the relationship between *mae chii*s and lay people. I met people in Bangkok and Chiang Mai, the two largest cities in Thailand, who did not have any contact with *mae chii*s, and who said that to give alms to a *mae chii* was like to give alms to a beggar. In the 1970s, *mae chii*s who went on alms rounds were regarded as beggars (Cook 1981: 206). I interviewed longstanding *mae chii*s who told that there had been problems with women who donned white robes and shaved their heads in order to get financial benefits. The problem with false *mae chii*s had been worst in Bangkok and other provincial centres. This issue was one of the first tasks that the Thai Mae Chiis' Institute had to deal with when it was established in 1969 (to be discussed in Chapter 7). One *mae chii* informant told me that many years, ago she had often approached fake *mae chii*s begging at a market in Bangkok. She used to ask them for the name of their preceptor (*upachaa*) and which temple they belonged to. When they could not answer these questions, she condemned their behaviour and explained how much demerit (*baap*) they created by their actions. If they did not stop pretending to be *mae chii*s they were reported to the police. The difficulty of controlling the false *mae chii*s was that when they were arrested by the police, they insisted that they were ordained and to arrest them and make them go hungry was an act of demerit. That argument seemed to discourage effectively some of the police in their duties because they were afraid of involving themselves in demerit (*klua baap*) (Cook 1981: 206). Since the Thai Mae Chiis' Institute began issuing special identity cards for *mae chii*s, the problem of identifying fake *mae chii*s has been minimised.

One important factor when making offerings to renunciants is time. According to the monastic rules, cooked food must be given and consumed before noon. However, food may be given to beggars at any time of the day. The reasons offered for considering some *mae chii*s to be lay beggars rather than religious persons included the fact that they did not observe the proper alms round conventions and conducted 'alms rounds' at incorrect times. The idea that *mae chii*s conducting alms rounds were seen as beggars meant that the Thai Mae Chiis' Institute initially discouraged them from doing it. Cook noticed that the practice was severely frowned upon if not carried out strictly in the manner of the monks (ibid.).

The *mae chii*s at Ratburi Samnak Chii are particular about following the monastic code strictly. Their manners prove to be of great significance for their relationship with the laity and the lay people also evaluate the *mae chii*s' performance. The *mae chii*s act as monks during alms rounds, without any sign of reciprocity. The interaction between the laity and the *mae chii*s is the same as the interaction between lay people and monks – offering is motivated by respect, and communicates and confirms a vertical relation between the laity and the ordained.

NOTES

1   Only as an exeptional measure of reprobation does the *vinaya* provide the possibility of refusing *dana* by overturning the alms bowl.

2   *Jataka* in Pali, *Chadok* in Thai.

3   *Bodhisatta* is a future Buddha, one who aspires to be a Buddha.

4   See the short story 'Matsii' in which the female writer tries to justify a 'Maddi' character's rejection of her children (Sri Dao Ruang 1996: 95–103).

5 Everyone who whishes to give should have the opportunity. Any food should be accepted apart from the flesh of forbidden animals – including man, dog, tiger, bear – and apart from meat or fish which is seen, heard or suspected to have been killed specially for the renunciant (Bhikkhu Khantipalo 1964).

6 *Thôôt kathin* in Thai, *kathina* in Pali.

7 Bhiksuni Voramai Kabilsingh lived to be 95. She died on 23 June, 2003.

$\mathcal{A}$ $\mathcal{R}$*eligious* $\mathcal{F}$*ield in* $\mathcal{T}$*ransition*

The past century entailed considerable political, economic and religious changes in Thailand. During that period a process of centralisation of the *sangha* took place. This implied that the boundary around the *sangha* became more formalised and less permeable for women. During the last part of the century, when Thailand experienced rapid economic growth, institutional Buddhism weakened and new Buddhist trends emerged. The declining importance of the central Buddhist hierarchy, the intense media coverage of moral scandals and corruption among sections of the *sangha* encouraged a decentralisation of religiosity and the growth of personality-focused religious movements. The *mae chii*s operate outside the institutional structure of Buddhism. They have created and refined their religious roles and communities and have in recent decades attracted more supporters than before. The fact that the *mae chii*s are excluded from the *sangha* has not prevented events occurring among monks from influencing the *mae chii*s as religious persons. This chapter focuses on circumstances and directions in the Thai Buddhist realm that have relevance for understanding the *mae chii*s' position in relation to the *sangha* and to the laity and provides a background to the ongoing changes in the *mae chii*s' roles and of their communities.

REFORMING THE THAI MONKS' ORDERS

In the early nineteenth century, Thailand – or Siam, as the country was known until 1939 – consisted of several more or less independent kingdoms. Thailand never fell under colonial rule as did the neighbouring countries during the second half of the nineteenth century. In the kingdoms, religious practices and customs varied considerably. There were, for example, as many as 18 lineages (*nikai*) of Buddhist monks in Chiang Mai alone (Tiyavanich 1997: 5).

A new lineage, which was considered a reform movement, was created in Bangkok in the third decade of the nineteenth century. The founder was Prince

Mongkut, a Buddhist monk who was inspired by the strict discipline observed by the monks in a Mon temple in Bangkok (ibid.: 6). He called the lineage 'Thammayut', meaning the order adhering to the *dhamma*. Prince Mongkut left the monks' order and became king in 1851.[1] The Thammayut order established that education through Buddhist scriptures and commentaries should be the foundation for Buddhist knowledge, and traditional practices were downplayed. The reformist monks proposed that the Buddha's teaching (*dhamma*) should be rigorously followed. In the same line, ethical actions based on a strict following of the monastic code of conduct (*vinaya*) were considered more important than ritual practice. Mongkut introduced a new style of wearing robes, new ordination rituals, new pronunciation of the Pali language, new temple routines and new religious days to observe. Mongkut was convinced that true religion was a matter of doctrine and belief and those local stories about demons, gods, miracles, magic, rituals and exorcism had nothing to do with Buddhism (ibid.: 6–7). Mongkut also accepted the Christian missionaries' views that traditional Buddhism was too superstitious. Tiyavanich suggests that Mongkut and the Siamese elite sought to prove to Western missionaries that Buddhism was compatible with science and could support intellectual study and learning. They published books on Buddhism and adopted a rationalist mode of discourse for theological debates with Christians (ibid.: 7). The Thammayutnikai was therefore in opposition to other Buddhist orders in Thailand (referred to as Mahaanikai) and the Thammayut order would likely not have survived without its close relationship with the Thai monarchy.

The head monastery for the Thammayut order is the royal temple Wat Bowonniwet in Bangkok. King Chulalongkorn's half-brother, Prince Wachirayan, the abbot of Wat Bowonniwet, was appointed as head of the Thammayut order. The Thammayut order was formed into an administrative elite, which provided a focal point for royal control over the monkhood. The order attracted high-ranking monks, but also rural monks, especially in the Northeastern part of Thailand (Jackson 1989: 66–67). It was the Thammayutnikai that stimulated the emergence of modern forest monasticism in the Northeastern region (Keyes 1999a: 9).

The revolution in June 1932 ended the absolute monarchy in Thailand and transformed it into a constitutional monarchy. The king had no longer actual power to rule and that created a lasting crisis of legitimacy (Tambiah 1976: 472–514). The decrease in prestige of the Thai monarchy also affected the Thammayut order. Moreover, the relationship between religion and political order in Thailand changed fundamentally after the trauma of the political crisis of the mid-1970s.

Up until the late 1960s or early 1970s Thai governments were highly suspicious of forest-dwelling monks who emphasised meditation practice over scriptural learning and who had withdrawn from the bounds of established authority. They considered forest monks to be obstacles to national development and to the progress of religion (Tiyavanich 1997: 241). They were often suspected of supporting communism. From the 1970s onwards, however, the royal family began visiting some of the forest-monk Man's disciples. Jim L. Taylor underscores the historical nexus of monks and the king and states that the intense interest in charismatic forest monks was related to the paralellism between the vitality of these monks and the king. The latter, as 'the righteous ruler', provided the right conditions for the *sangha* to thrive within the conglomerating kingdom (Taylor 1993: 217). He explains that the 1970s fervid interest in forest monks by the nation's rich and powerful coincides with a period of intense domestic insecurity, particularly emanating from the Northeast, and the need for a unifying and legitimating ideology (ibid.: 2). In the 1970s and 1980s, considerable publicity was given to the forest-dwelling monks and they became well known nation-wide. Increasing numbers of people began to turn to these monks to receive their blessing, amulets or for help in various mundane matters. Within less than a century, wandering monks had risen from the bottom of the national *sangha* hierarchy to the top, and from being despised as vagabonds (by urban elite) to being venerated as saints (ibid.: 288).

The emergence of various Buddhist movements has generated tensions and conflicts between the governing elite and followers of particular Buddhist movements, but also between different followings (Keyes 1999a: 1). The *sangha* has endeavoured to streamline the many regional monastic traditions. Swearer comments that the bureaucratisation and centralisation of the *sangha* and the standardisation of Buddhist thought and practice had a deadening effect on mainstream Buddhism in Thailand (Swearer 1999: 202). Doctrinal Buddhism is less equipped to deal with the rapid changes in society than popular Thai religiosity, which has a closer relationship with people and answers to their spiritual needs.

However, the actions against fragmentation of the *sangha* have not always been successful, and there have always been monks who have been against the decrees from the centralised *sangha*. The distinctions between putting emphasis on knowledge gained from studies of texts and that gained from practising mindfulness through meditation is still important. One consequence of putting preference on study over practice is that it devalued lay asceticism, and led to a decline in women's prestige in religious communities. Tiyavanich reports that in regional traditions there used to be prominent women renunciates, and there is evidence that teachers of regional Buddhist traditions held female ascetics in high esteem (Tiyavanich 1997: 280–281). The so-called fragmentation of Buddhism in Thailand today could be seen as yet another expression of how the multifaceted Buddhism in Thailand has always existed.

THE *SANGHA* ACTS

In creating a modern Thai state the Bangkok authorities strove towards unifying both the language and the religion (Tiyavanich 1997: 8). The three Sangha Acts of 1902, 1941 and 1962 dealt with clerical conduct and administration. As part of the process of national integration, King Chulalongkorn decreed the first Sangha Act in 1902. For the first time, the Thai *sangha* administrative authority was centralised in a Council of Elders, *Mahatherasamakhom*. It was headed by the *Sangharaat* and four senior regional Sangha governors and four deputy regional Sangha governors were appointed. The Act led to a reform of the administrative structure of the *sangha* that paralleled the reforms of the secular bureaucracy. The implementation of the Sangha Act included a revision of Buddhist textbooks in order to adjust them to a doctrinal orthodox interpretation of the Buddhist teaching. Through the 1902 Sangha Act, Bangkok's control over the *sangha* was strengthened, and regional interpretations and practices of Buddhism were rejected (Jackson 1989: 69). In 1941 it was replaced by a Sangha Act with a more democratically modelled administration. Representatives from the large Mahaanikai order were proportionately admitted into the Mahatherasamakhom, which actually gave them a majority on the council. Authority was also given to a wider section of skilled monks. The majority of representatives from the Mahaanikai order created a conflict between the orders and this made the administration ineffective (ibid.: 78). The third Sangha Act of 1962 verified the independence of Thammayut and Mahaanikai orders and made them administratively separate. The centralised control of the monkhood was in the hands of a few state-selected representatives (ibid.: 29, 81–82).

Ischii states that the 1962 Sangha act swept away all the democratic provisions of the previous act and concentrated power in the person of the Supreme Patriarch. This created an organisation through which he could control the *sangha* via the Council of Elders, of which he could appoint the majority of members (Ishii 1986: 116). The Sangha Act has been criticised over the years and a new bill has recently been drafted and been under debate. The proposed

Sangha Bill will raise the status of the Supreme Patriarch to that of a symbolic holy leader without executive power. The power of the Sangha Supreme Council will also be reduced in favour of a younger clerical body, the *Maha Kanissorn*. The draft bill is a struggle over power and has given rise to much controversy both between monks and among lay people. The proposed law is criticised for several things. For example, the bill leaves the centralised system of the *sangha* untouched and imposes legal sanctions on the media for publishing anything deemed damaging to Buddhism. Furthermore, there is nothing in the draft bill about gender issues and discrimination towards ascetic women (Ekachai 2002c).

CENTRALISATION OF THE *SANGHA*

Buddhism in Thailand has never been thoroughly homogenous. The existence of wandering (*thudong*) monks, who have never been embedded in the *sangha*, is one example of the complexity and multilayered character of Buddhism (Tiyavanich 1997: 252). Popular forms of Buddhism are not in line with the centralised *sangha*'s aim to cleanse Buddhism of animistic and superstitious elements. Doctrinal Buddhism is based on a notion of a single truth and a single correct spiritual path. It upholds a rationalist view of the world. Phra Dhammapitaka (Prayuth Payuttho), one of the intellectual mainstays of doctrinalist Buddhism, is explicit in his rejection of the widespread popularity of *saiyasaat*, 'superstition', which he claims to be an inferior form of religiosity (Jackson 1999).

The former religious reforms also aimed to rationalise traditional cosmology, and the goal of the state-supported *sangha* was to implement a strict interpretation of the *vinaya* throughout the country.[2] Regional differences in teaching and practice were reduced (Swearer 1999: 202). The complex hierarchical monastic structure was developed, together with procedures for conferring ordination, rules regulating the movement of monks from one monastery to another, records of monks in the temples and how they moved between temples, etc. Thai monks are today formally integrated into this monolithic male *sangha* and there is no admission of women. The presence of *mae chii*s at monasteries is often overlooked. All temples in Thailand report the numbers of monks and novices to the Department of Religious Affairs. Some temples also report the numbers of *mae chii*s living at the temple, while others do not. Therefore it is difficult to estimate their numbers in the country. The *mae chii*s at temples do not possess monastic status and consequently do not receive the same privileges as the monks, and the their financial and material resources are very limited compared to those of the monks.

The acceptance and treatment of the *mae chii*s by the laity in Bangkok differs from the way they are treated in local communities like Ratburi. Tiyavanich says that before or beyond Bangkok's influence, which she dates to before the 1950s, women actively participated in their religious communities as skilled meditators, healers, or teachers and were highly respected by local people. Meditation masters generally held female practitioners in high esteem, considering them comparable to monks (Tiyavanich 1997: 283). The centralising of the *sangha* has no doubt had a detrimental effect on the position of *mae chii*s by accentuating the boundary between the ordained and lay realms. However, there are many examples of well-respected *mae chii*s in Bangkok who are. For example, at the temple Wat Paknam Phasi Charoen in Bangkok, skilled *mae chii*s are still held in high esteem for their healing and meditation skills. Many *mae chii*s at Wat Paknam are likewise respected for their educational knowledge. This temple has the rather unusual policy that *mae chii*s should study. Another uncommon characteristic of this monastery is that neither the *mae chii*s nor the monks go on alms round, which is a normal everyday practice for monks in Thailand. Instead, lay people come to the temple and donate food that the *mae chii*s take care of. The temple is in great need of the *mae chii*s since they are responsible for cooking food for the entire temple community. Wat Paknam has two categories of *mae chii*s. One consists of those with financial assets or disciples who support them financially and therefore they do not have to work in the kitchen. The other category does not have any financial means and cannot pay the fees to the temple. Their only chance for continuing their ordained life at the temple is to work in the kitchen. Both categories of *mae chii* have access to education. However, preparing food for this large community is a demanding and time-consuming task. Therefore, compared to the monks, *mae chii*s who work in the kitchen have less time for studies and meditation practices.

In the forest tradition, many *thudong* masters believed that women were capable of the highest spiritual attainment. Female monastics were referred to as exemplary teachers. Juan, a famous wandering monk, related that he had a vision of an enlightened *bhikkhuni* coming to instruct him. He said she was an *arahat*[3] and she had taught him with much compassion and he was deeply impressed. When he wanted to bow to her, she reminded him of the *vinaya* rule in which the Buddha requires a *bhikkhuni* to bow to a monk, even when the *bhikkhuni* is *arahat* and the monk has been ordained for only a day (Tiyavanich

1997: 286). Tiyavanich reports further that, *thudong* monks generally consider women to have a great capacity for understanding the *dhamma* and to be able to attain high levels of *jhana*[4] and supernatural knowledge. In their wandering lives, *thudong* monks meet both laywomen and *mae chiis* who surpass monks in their meditation. A monk named Lui, in the Northeast of Thailand, once spent the rains' retreat in a cave on a mountain in Kut Bak District in Sakon Nakhon. He was told about two *mae chiis* named Jan and Yau, who were staying at a temple. The villagers believed that they had supernatural powers. After discussing the *dhamma* with the *mae chiis*, the monk said he realised that their understanding of the *dhamma*, derived from meditation practice, was deeper than his (ibid.: 282). It is not only the *thudong* monks who realise women's spiritual capacities. There are numerous other monks and lay people who hold women's spiritual potential in high esteem.

The *sangha* authorities, however, did and still do not show much appreciation of female renunciates. The authorities suppressed the custom of female ascetics going wandering or going on alms rounds. When the Thammayutnikai elders came around to approving *thudong* practice in 1939, their recognition did not extend to *mae chiis*. The *sangha* authorities continued to admonish any monk who took *mae chiis* along on wanderings or pilgrimages (Tiyavanich 1997: 286).

The local monks were also prohibited from using their rich mythology and cosmology in their teachings. Nor were they allowed to continue telling the drama of moral pilgrimage over many lifetimes contained in the Jataka tales of the Buddha's former births (discussed in Chapter 6). Local Buddhism was not considered in line with rationalistic, modern Buddhism, and monks from Bangkok were sent to the countryside in order to control and instruct local monks in their vocation.

THE *MAE CHIIS'* NATIONAL ORGANISATION

Mae chiis, who are scattered all over the country, have traditionally not belonged to a religious congregation. The formation of the Thai Mae Chiis' Institute in 1969 was not directly linked to any global networks. Until then, Thai *mae chiis* lacked a national network and a public representative. In the late 1960s, this lack was recognised by the Thai representatives at an International Buddhist Association meeting. They became aware that they had no one to represent *mae chiis*, but that the *mae chiis* were so lacking in organisation that no one could hope to represent them. That later led the Supreme Patriarch Somdet Phra Ariyawongsaakatayaan to order the secretary of the Mahamakut Education

Council to co-ordinate the *mae chii*s. As a result a meeting of *mae chii*s from various temples and *samnak*s was called to discuss the issue in late August 1969 (Cook 1981: 195). In 1969, the Thai Mae Chiis' Institute, *Sathaaban Mae Chii Thai,* was founded and in 1972 it fell under the patronage of the Thai queen.

The Institute works with the objective of assisting and uniting *mae chii*s from all over the country, and its central goals are to help them develop intellectually and spiritually. Its organisation is modelled upon that of the monks' *sangha*. The Institute is hierarchically organised with offices and heads (*hua naa*) at regional, provincial and district levels. The Institute has introduced rules and regulations for the *mae chii*s that are influenced by the monks' rules. It also promotes the foundation of *mae chii* communities and the streamlining of *mae chii* practice and its efforts have strengthened *mae chii*s as a distinct category and today growing numbers have tasks similar to those of the monks.

The membership of the Institute is voluntary and free of charge, and the number of members varies between 4,000 and 9,000. Both those who stay at temples and those who stay at separate *samnak chii*s can enrol as members of the Institute, but those at *samnak chii*s are not listed in the Department of Religious Affairs' statistics. There are also *mae chii*s who stay at *samnak chii*s or private places without becoming members of the Institute. These *mae chii*s are thus not evident in either the Department of Religious Affairs' statistics or in the Thai Mae Chiis' Institute's figures. This illustrates the difficulties in knowing the actual number of *mae chii*s in Thailand. There are, however, *mae chii*s in all the four regions of Thailand, with the largest percentage living in the central part, but this does not mean that the *mae chii*s living there are from the central region. At my field site in Central Thailand, many of the *mae chii*s originated from the Northeastern provinces. The Northeastern region is considered to be a highly religious part of Thailand with many venerated monks. However, it is also a poor area and not a region considered to have a large number of *mae chii*s (Kabilsingh 1991: 65).

The Institute headquarters are located in a small office at the prestigious royal temple Wat Bowonniwet in Bangkok which is the head monastery for the Thammayut order. No *mae chii*s reside at Wat Bowonniwet; however, the Institute's annual and other meetings are held there. Training courses, practical and religious education and various meetings are all organised at this office. Books, clothes and other necessities for *mae chii*s and *chii phraam*s are also sold there. Ratburi Samnak Chii is a branch of the Thai Mae Chiis' Institute and I had contact with the Institute throughout the fieldwork. The *mae chii*s from Ratburi Samnak Chii took part in various meetings that the Institute initiated.

They were also involved in many of the Institute's activities and I accompanied *mae chii*s to training courses, study trips and other things that the Institute organised.

The Institute has been significant in uniting the *mae chii*s, and forming a *mae chii* identity, distinct from that of lay practitioners. During the first two decades of the Institute's existence, the *mae chii*s experienced troubles with the numerous 'fake *mae chii*s' who were around, especially in urban areas. These women shaved and dressed as *mae chii*s in order to attract donations from people (Cook 1981: 205). This behaviour became a threat to the reputation of serious *mae chii*s, and was a problem that was difficult to come to terms with. It was the Institute's subsequent effort to shape the *mae chii*s into a special category which proved to be instrumental in controlling 'fake *mae chii*s'. Proper ordination procedures, appropriate conduct, religious practice, and education made it easier to distinguish serious *mae chii*s from false ones. The special *mae chii*s' identity card that the Institute issues has also been helpful for identifying *mae chii*s. These are obtainable for *mae chii*s who are members of the Institute and who have been ordained by at least one year. There is also a test to prove that the *mae chii*s know the rules stipulated by the Institute. The different sets of rules are printed in the Mae Chii handbook, which contains, among other things, ordination procedures and careful descriptions of how to dress as a *mae chii* and as *chii phraam* (see Chapter 5).

NEW BUDDHIST MOVEMENTS

In recent decades, Thailand has experienced major changes in all areas of society. The *sangha*'s importance in legitimating political leaders has decreased and the *sangha* is no longer under the strict control of political authorities. The decline of religion, envisioned by earlier secularisation and modernisation theorists, has failed to materialise (McCargo 1997: 67). Religion still plays an important role for Thai people. However, the *sangha* has lost some of its credibility as an upholder of Buddhist practice and people are now looking for morally strict monastics outside the formal Buddhist authority. Monks like Buddhadasa Bhikkhu, the sect Santi Asoke and Wat Phra Dhammakaya have attracted large followings. At the same time *samnak chii*s, independent of monks' temples, began growing in number and more lay people began paying attention to the *mae chii*s' activities.

Buddhadasa Bhikkhu

One of the most important and venerated religious reformers in the second part of the twentieth century was the monk Buddhadasa Bhikkhu (1906–1993). Several *mae chii*s have told me that Buddhadasa's teachings have been an important source of inspiration to them. He integrated modern views and a distinctive forest tradition, and his interpretation of canonical texts attracted not only many *mae chii*s but also an educated following among lay people. His Buddhist interpretations have constituted a contrast to the supernatural formulations of Buddhism that legitimate wealth and power with reference to *kamm*ic explanations. He reconceptualised fundamental Buddhist concepts and, for example, explained Buddhist cosmological ideas by defining heaven and hell as mental states. Further, he described central Buddhist concepts differently from traditional Thai understanding and saw *kamma,* merit, rebirth and *nibbana* as things of the present. Thus, past and future lives become less relevant. The core concept of Buddhadasa's philosophy is the free mind, a mind free of self-centredness. He stated that through a state of mental calmness and mindfulness in every action, we can all achieve *nibbana* in this world. Moreover, Jackson (1988) points out how important it was to Buddhadasa's thinking that lay men and women have access to the same spiritual insights as monks have. Buddhadasa's teaching could be seen as an authorisation of the *mae chii*s as religious persons. His work to restore the Buddha's teaching to what it once was includes recognizing women's right to ordain and their capability of attaining *nibbana.* His admiration for his mother's comprehension of the Buddhist ethics is in line with his work towards peace and equality.

The monk Santikaro Bhikkhu worked closely with Buddhadasa Bhikkhu for almost a decade and he claims that Buddhadasa Bhikkhu's life's work has been to restore the Buddha's teaching to its pristine state. Over the centuries many cultural practices and superstitions have inevitably obscured the essential *dhamma.* The consequences of this reappraisal have been many, including an emphasis on the here-and-now, a rediscovery of the spiritual dimension of everyday life, a bridging of the lay–monastic fracture, greater compatibility with science, greater intellectual rigor, and the reintegration of political and social issues within a Dhammic worldview (Santikaro 1996: 147–148). In his childhood Buddhadasa Bhikkhu recognised three primary influences: his mother, the temple and Nature. Santikaro Bhikkhu says that Buddhadasa's first spiritual guide was his mother. She taught the morality and values that have underpinned all of his later insights and accomplishments. In a Mothers' Day talk on 12 August 1989, Buddhadasa Bhikkhu said that his mother's influence was crucial in the formation of his character. 'Whatever abilities, knowledge, and such I have now – where do they come from? Let me say that they come from my mother most of all' (ibid.: 149).

Buddhadasa developed a role quite independent of the religious hierarchy. His interest in reforming Buddhism ranged far beyond institutional reform to a fundamental and profound rethinking of basic beliefs, values, and practices (King 1996: 402). He provided an articulate defence of an ethic that would foster suppression of personal greed in favour of redistribution of wealth to alleviate suffering more generally. Buddhadasa identified the doctrinal core of Buddhism as being consistent with reason (*heetphon*) and science (*wittjaasaat*). His interpretation of Buddhism resolved the sense of contradiction introduced by modernisation theory, which posited that modernity is incompatible with religion (Jackson 1999).

Buddhadasa's interpretation of the *dhamma* found a large following among urban elites, while also providing an ideological base for Buddhist social activists in the periphery. Both monks and laity who were critical of the establishment and the Buddhist civil religion identified with it. Buddhadasa's doctrine of faith in the ethical teachings of the Buddha as well as in science, reason, modernity and democracy have been attractive to many educated Thais. Many of those involved in the student movement of the 1970s, which was the main force for social change then, found inspiration and guidance in his teaching. The well-known social activist Sulak Sivaraksa was profoundly influenced by his life and work (Santikaro 1996: 182). Buddhadhasa was critical of mainstream Buddhism. In the 1960s and 1970s, he was accused of being a communist, as were many of the wandering *thudong* monks. Buddhadasa lived in the South of Thailand, and was probably saved by living and teaching far from the centre of power in Bangkok and by his increasingly broad, non-politicised popularity (Swearer 1999: 216–17).

A number of well-known *mae chii*s and female *dhamma* teachers have also been deeply influenced by Buddhadasa. One is Upasika Ki Nanayon (known as Acharn Kor Khao-suan-luang, mentioned in Chapter 1) and, more recently, Upasika Ranjuan Indarakamhaeng, a former university lecturer, who has been a resident of Suan Mokkh, Buddhadasa's monastery and meditation centre, for many years and is today one of Thailand's most respected *dhamma* and meditation teachers (Santikaro 1996: 181). Buddhadasa felt that the status of women had been dropping steadily since his youth and that this decline should be reversed. He saw women's important contribution to solving problems in society. He wanted to establish a centre for women who wanted to become *dhamma* mothers (*dhamma-mata*), 'those who give birth through dhamma'. Buddhadasa considered it not yet possible to re-establish the Bhikkhuni Order in Thailand and since the *mae chii*s have limitations, he felt thata new approach was needed. Santikaro says: 'Although he was not in a position to give the *dhamma* mothers the same social status as *bhikkhu*s receive, he believed that material support can be provided so that women are also able to live the homeless life and have spiritual opportunities equal to those of the *bhikkhus*' (ibid.: 185). He envisaged that the *dhamma* Mothers would live a simple life focused on meditation, with some supporting study. He hoped, as the *dhamma* Mothers live up to their name through example and teaching that society will give them the respect they deserve (ibid.: 185). Buddhadasa is held in high esteem by the *mae chii*s. Several of Buddhadasa's disciples, monks and lay people are involved in various training and educational programmes provider especially for the *mae chii*s and organised by INEB (International Network of Engaged Buddhism).

Wat Phra Dhammakaya

Two Buddhist movements, Santi Asoke and Dhammakaya, established in the 1970s, offered alternative interpretations of the relationship between Buddhism and society. These movements enhance the religious role of the Buddhist laity as a means for transcending their disenchantment with modernity. Lay meditation opened new venues for spiritual renewal by endorsing temporary withdrawal from a seemingly materialistic world (Schober 1995: 313).

The Mahaanikai monastery, Wat Paknam Phasi Charoen in Bangkok, had in 1998 one of the largest *mae chii* communities in Thailand with more than 200 *mae chii*s residing there and a large number of *chii phram*s. That temple has long had a reputation for popularising *dhammakaya* meditation. Lay meditation teachers have also become prominent and gained followers among educated people in Bangkok. The creation of the (*samatha-vipassana*) *dhammakaya* meditation technique[5] is credited to Luang Phôô Sot Chantasaro (Phra Mongkon Thepmuni), a monk better known as Luang Phôô Wat Paknam Phasi Charoen. After Luang Phôô Sot died in 1959, his method was perpetuated by some of his followers among whom a *mae chii*, Khun Yai Chan Khonnokyoong has been significant. She was born in 1909 and became a disciple of Luang Phôô Wat Paknam when she was 24 years old. She was successful in her meditation practice and was believed to have reached the highest levels of *dhammakaya*. People admired her for her unique gift of explaining the difficulties in the Buddhist doctrines. She became the leading disciple while Luang Pho Sod was alive and both were believed to have supernatural powers.

She assisted him in high-level *dhammakaya* meditation and became leader of the meditation system, which she helped to propagate further after Luang Phôô Sot's death. The Dhammakaya followers said that she was the only one capable of continuing the teaching of the meditation system. However, there was debate over the chosen successor to the teaching and this led to problems for other meditation masters at Wat Paknam following Luang Phôô Sot's death (Bowers 1996: 52–53).

Khun Yai Chan is an example of a woman who is believed to have attained sacral powers through meditation. It is claimed that the powers of high-level *dhammakaya* meditation have been used to counter the negativity of Mara (the Buddhist personification of evil). At Wat Paknam, high-level meditation was done in a secluded place within the temple. Luang Phôô Sot selected the monks and *mae chii*s who were allowed to participate. They were engaged in high-level meditation 24 hours a day by working in six-hour shifts. The goal was to attack Mara. One example of the positive results of *dhammakaya* meditation concerns the Second World War when Bangkok was bombed. Khun Yai Chan used the powers of high-level *dhammakaya* meditation and it is believed by her followers that she and others were able to keep Wat Paknam and other important areas of Bangkok safe from the falling bombs (ibid.: 26–27).

In 1970 Khun Yai Chan left Wat Paknam, claiming that the temple had lost its direction and no longer represented the true teachings of Luang Phôô Sot (Bowers 1996: 50). She decided to found a meditation centre. She had a group of followers among whom were a university student who later became the Wat Dhammakaya s abbot Phra Dhammachayo. A widow and lay follower, donated land for spiritual use. The temple Wat Phra Dhammakaya opened in 1980. Members of the Council of Elders led the opening ceremony and Princess Mahachakri Sirindhorn laid the foundation stone. Wat Phra Dhammakaya is one of Thailand's largest Buddhist communities.[6] Wat Phra Dhammakaya has centres in almost 60 provinces. The temple has been careful to maintain its standing within the Mahaanikai order of the Thai *sangha*.

Khun Yai Chan's followers at Wat Paknam were primarily young college students. The movement continued to appeal to, and focus its recruitment on, college and university students when Wat Phra Dhammakaya was established in Pathum Thani (Bowers 1996: 54). In the early 1970s Dhammakaya Buddhist University clubs started. The typical Dhammakaya follower was a lay person who combined spiritual retreat at the weekends with work or study in the everyday world during the rest of the week. For these people, Dhammakaya offered religious legitimation for inequalities in wealth since success in the world was held to be a reward for spiritual attainment (Keyes 1999a: 32). The movement has been extraordinarily successful in recruiting followers among members of the Thai middle class comprising university students, technocrats, military, and small-business people. The movement offers its followers concrete methods for attaining spiritual enlightenment in this life and a membership in a pristine Buddhist community that promises to restore the nation's moral life, individual peace, and material success.

Wat Phra Dhammakaya advocates a life-long commitment to ordination and performs lay ordinations for masses of lay devotees. Most Dhammakaya monks complete their secular university training prior to ordination. It is telling to note that in 1999, 289 monks out of 652 possessed a Bachelor's degree and 22 monks a Master's degree, whereas 316 *upasika*s out of 359 held a Bachelor's degree, nine *upasika*s a Master's degree and one a PhD (Dhammakaya Temple, 1999: 26–27). However, the founder, Khun Yai Chan was illiterate. Her ability to understand the highest level of *dhammakaya* meditation is subscribed to her supernatural abilities. She is described as a type of 'merit calculator' by which it is meant that she could determine exactly how much merit, and presumably demerit, one has accumulated through a given act. This could be an explanation for the emphasis that Wat Phra Dhammakaya places on giving.

For a couple of decades Wat Phra Dhammakaya was the fastest growing Buddhist movement in Thailand. The movement attracted the backing of the military and political leaders and was under the royal family's patronage. The Dhammakaya became the controlling influence in the Buddhist Associations of most major Thai universities and sought to restore a Buddhist civil religion which they perceived to be under threat from an increasingly fragmented Thai society (Swearer 1995: 115).

The movement is today criticised for being controlled by the economic and ruling elites and their activities are labelled 'religious consumerism' based on the movement's aggressive recruiting methods and commercial approach. Wat Phra Dhammakaya has raised enormous sums of money over the years, and blamed for of commercialising Buddhism (*phuttha phanit*). Wat Dhammakaya succeeded in attracting well-off followers from all over Thailand, but they did not succeed in creating peace in their own neighbouring area. There was a dispute over land-tenure and compensation between Wat Phra Dhammakaya and nearby land-renting farmers in 1985– 1989. The conflict turned violent when hundreds of farmers invaded the temple, destroyed the Buddha image and declared their intent to set fire to the temple (Fuengfusakul 1998: 40–41).

The Dhammakaya movement is today highly controversial. The temple has been under investigation for having misused the temple funds and the Abbot was suspended because of criminal charges against him and the temple. The commercialisation of Buddhism of Dhammakaya and other temples and monks risks undermining spiritual authority of Buddhism and has become a political issue. The Dhammakaya is also accused of violating the Theravada Buddhist teachings. The influential monk Phra Prayuth Payuttho has written extensively on Buddhism and social issues and is widely regarded as one of the most articulate and insightful of Thailand's philosopher monks. His writings demonstrate that the Dhammakaya claims that *nibbana* is a permanent heaven, are contrary to the understanding of Theravada Buddhism, although the idea is found in some Mahayanist sects. In Theravadin thought that *nibbana* is not understood as a place but as 'a state free of defilement, and being non-self'. Phra Prayuth further shows that the idea of the 'body of *dhamma*' alluded to in the name Dhammakaya is also understood in a Mahayanist rather than a Theravadin way. For these, and other reasons, he argues that Dhammakaya should not be recognised as falling within the Theravadin tradition. Phra Prayuth's criticism carries considerable weight with high-ranking monks in the Thai *sangha's* hierarchy. In April 1999 the *Sangharaat*, the Supreme Patriarch of the Thai Buddhist Sangha, ruled that the abbot of Wat Phra Dhammakaya, Phra Dhammachayo, had violated the disciplinary code by accumulating personal wealth which had been donated to him.

Santi Asoke

The Santi Asoke is a movement that emerged outside of the state bureaucracy and was established in Nakhon Pathom province in Central Thailand in 1975. Santi Asoke (*santi asok*) means 'peace without sorrow' and the sect presents an alternative lifestyle and a new Buddhist vision, replacing traditional rituals with training of the mind through daily work, thrift and discipline. Santi Asoke's main temple is located in Bangkok with branches in Nakhon Pathom, Nakhon Ratchasima, Sisaket, Ubon Ratchathani, Nakhon Sawan and Chiang Mai. They have built centres in Trang, Chaiyaphum, Nakhon Phanom, Udon Thani, Roi Et and Loei (Heikkilä-Horn 2003: 29–31). Santi Asoke differs from Wat Phra Dhammakaya in many respects. However, both movements are interesting from gender perspectives since ascetic women are visible in ways that are uncommon in mainstream Thai Buddhism. Santi Asoke was founded by the Buddhist monk Bodhiraksa, who officially resigned from the state Buddhist order in 1975. Santi Asoke advocates rejection of modern materialism and consumerism. Swearer characterises this religious group as a fundamentalist community critical of the amorality, indulgence in sensual pleasures and materialist greed that it perceives in wider Thai society (Swearer 1991: 670 ff.). The movement has become an alternative, anti-consumerist community. Asoke centres organise training courses for Thai peasants in natural agriculture and Buddhist lifestyle. They produce and sell many products based on herbs and run several vegetarian restaurants. Furthermore, they run a number of schools for primary and secondary students, vocational schools and also an Asoke 'university'.

Those who become followers of the movement, whether lay persons, *sikkhamat*s (ten-precept female ascetics) or ordained monks or novices, are expected to follow a strict regimen based in part on the precepts followed by novices and by lay disciples on Buddhist holy days. Followers are expected to practise moral discipline (*sila*) in all social contexts, to lead a modest way of life informed by agricultural self-reliance and vegetarianism and to reject capitalist consumerism and materialism. Most threatening to the *sangha* was probably Bodhiraksa's action of ordaining monks and novices without being officially designated as having this right. Those activities together with his claim to have attained enlightenment are offences for which a monk can be expelled from the order (see Taylor 1989: 117–18; Keyes 1999a: 24).

Santi Asoke's members distinguish themselves from the mainstream *sangha*. The lay followers wear traditional peasant dress and live in communes of '*dhamma* families' that include monks, *sikkhamat*s and lay people. This eliminates the traditional *vinaya* based on separation of monastic and lay societies as well as status and gender distinctions. The practice is justified by the claim that realisation of the Buddha's spiritual and moral ideals is incumbent equally on all (Swearer 1991: 672). The group rejects formal training in meditation, the chanting of Pali liturgy, merit making and the transfer of merit to deceased relatives, ritual offerings to images of the Buddha and the asceticism of forest monks (see Heikkilä-Horn 1996). Bodhiraksa points to the possibility of a modern Buddhism without the *sangha*.

However, Santi Asoke was set up as an independent Buddhist temple and had serious disagreements with the Thai *sangha* authorities. This led to prosecution of the founder and leader Bodhiraksa; he was brought to court and sentenced to leave the monkhood. In 1989, regional monastic leaders called for Phra Bodhiraksa to be defrocked, and the Thai *sangha* initiated legal proceedings against him for violating the *vinaya* and distorting Buddhist principles (*dhamma*). He was even incarcerated for a period. He escaped formal defrocking after voluntarily changing the colour of his robe from brown to white – the ascetic lay colour that *mae chii*s also wear. However, Santi Asoke survived and Bodhiraksa continues to be recognised by his followers as a person of exceptional merit (*bun baaramii*).

Thousands of volunteers work and live in Asoke centres and up till now more than a hundred monks and about 25 *sikkhamat*s have received ordination in the Asoke group (Heikkilä-Horn 2003). Theoretically it takes one year for a lay man to become a monk, and two years for a lay woman to become a *sikkhamat*. In practice, however, it takes several years to become a *sikkhamat* since the number of *sikkhamat*s is restricted to correspond with the number of the monks. The reasons for the proportional restriction are probably that the leaders of the group do not want the number of the female monastics to exceed the number of monks. If all Asoke lay women were ordained, this would most certainly be the case (Heikkilä-Horn 1996: 37–39).

The *sikkhamat*s' status and position is unique in the Thai Buddhist world and offers an opportunity for women to become part of the ordained realm. In their local community the *sikkhamat*s are awarded ordained status. They wear brown robes and they go on alms rounds every morning. Among the lay women at Santi Asoke there is a group of female temple residents, *upasika*s, who shave their heads and are dressed in white shirts and black sarongs. A woman who wishes to become an *upasika* needs the permission of the head monk Bodhiraksa (ibid.: 40). The *sikkhamat*s have created a category separate from the *mae chii*s. Through the ten Buddhist precepts they have informally entered the ordained, male domain, though they are still under the control of the monks, possess a secondary position at the monastery and remain unrecognised by the Thai *sangha*.

Politicians are attempting to associate themselves with ethical, impeccable Buddhist monks and religious movements in order to secure and maximise their legitimacy. Santi Asoke attracted many influential followers among whom the former Bangkok governor Chamlong Srimuang was one of the most renowned disciples (see McCargo 1997: 78–103). Bodhiraksa's radical move raised fundamental questions about the definition of clerical authority, in particular whether a monk's authority derived from following the Buddha's directives in the scriptures, as Bodhiraksa claimed, or from obeying non-scriptural state laws governing clerical conduct, as the *sangha* hierarchy maintained. Many saw the trial as a conflict between a corrupt *sangha* seeking to uphold its entrenched power and an ethically strict Buddhist renunciate aiming to purify and revitalise the religious order (Jackson 1997: x). The Santi Asoke has also bestowed upon the

Figure 7.1. Sikkhamat Chinda Tangpao at Santi Asoke

*sikkhamat*s a unique position by giving them the ten Buddhist precepts, which grants them the same status as the Buddhist novices. The *sikkhamat*s perform religious tasks that *mae chii*s who live at monks' temples are not entitled to do (Heikkilä-Horn 2000: 79–82).

WEAKENING INSTITUTIONAL BUDDHISM

In the final decades of the twentieth century, Thailand underwent major economic and socio-cultural changes. The role of the monks' order, which has been important for centuries in legitimating the exercise of state power of the Thai kingdom, was also undergoing a process of change. Jackson states that the rapid weakening of politicians' interest in controlling forms of religiosity in Thailand, apart from trying to eradicate monastic corruption or clerical immorality, has permitted the rise of a range of religious movements which, in earlier decades, would have incited political and legal intervention to enforce normative practice and teaching (Jackson 1997: 75).

A decline in institutional Buddhism should not be mistaken for a necessary decline in religiosity. Several of the Buddhist movements at the margins of the *sangha* seek to replace conceptions of religious authority based on social hierarchy obtained through merit-making rituals and the state's role as a patron of religion with communal visions of Buddhism that propose the realisation of enlightenment through the practice of morality. McCargo notes that new religious movements may be regarded as either a manifestation of modernisation or a counter-movement against modernisation (McCargo 1997: 68). Widespread popularity of new religious movements and charismatic monks is on the increase and the movement of 'Engaged Buddhism' has attracted many Thai Buddhists. The term is usually associated with Buddhadasa Bhikkhu and used by the social activist Sulak Sivaraksa.[7]

Thai Buddhism has been reconceptualised by the influential, educated middle class who felt a growing disenchantment with the traditional civic religion (Taylor 1993). Many Thai people are shifting their association to new religious movements at the margins of state control. It is not only new Buddhist movements that attract many Thai people, but also cults such as those associated with the Mahayana *bodhisatta* Kuan-Yin (goddess of compassion) and the former Thai king, Chulalongkorn. Over the last decades, Kuan-Yin (Kwan Im in Thai) has increased in popularity in Thailand, especially among the large population of Sino-Thai descent in the Central and Southern parts of the country (Hamilton 1999). Many of the Thai temples have Kwan Im shrines and in Ratchaburi province there is also a well-attended Kwan Im temple. At Ratburi Samnak Chii, a group of lay people from Bangkok had taken the initiative and got the permission to raise a Kwan Im statue in the middle of a pond on the *samnak chii* compound. In current Thai society, Kwan Im's most important signification arises from her association with vegetarianism, particularly the avoidance of beef and at Ratburi Samnak Chii beef was never prepared. Most of the *mae chii*s at the *samnak chii* did not show any particular interest in this project of raising a Kwan Im statue at the *samnak chii*. One exception was a Sino-Thai *mae chii* who was involved in the preparations and ceremonies that took place while building the platform for the statue and before raising it. I found that many of the *mae chii*s who came from Northeastern Thailand had not been exposed to the practices associated with Kwan Im (see for example Aeusrivongse 1994 and Morris 2000).

The links between the state and organised Buddhism have for centuries been important for upholding legitimacy and power structures. Jackson (1989) has argued that the political importance of Buddhism as a system of legitimating practices and discourses explains the intensification of state control that was exercised over the *sangha* in the last century through a series of efforts to restructure the monkhood in the image of the secular political order. There were also debates over what constituted the correct forms of Buddhist teaching and practice and these tended to follow lines that mirrored broader political and economic divisions within society.

The weakening in politicians' interest in controlling the forms of Buddhist religiosity has proceeded since the 1980s. The state's loosening of its historical grip over expressions of Buddhist religiosity and the decline in the authority and standing of the *sangha* have together fostered the emergence of new religious trends. The rise of a diverse range of movements and cults at the periphery of the state-controlled *sangha* marks a shift in the pattern of relations between Buddhism and secular political authority (Jackson, 1988; 1989, Taylor 1996).

One example of reconfigured relations between political and religious institutions is the involvement of the highly venerated monk Luang Taa Mahaa Bua, who responded to the 1997 economic crisis in Thailand by initiating a fund-raising campaign named *Chuay Chaat* (Help the nation). The campaign was carried out during the time of my fieldwork and involved *mae chii*s and monks as well as lay people. Luang Taa Maha Bua succeeded in reaching out to a great number of Thais and made them give donations that would render them religious merit and at the same time help the nation. The campaign collected donations of more than three tonnes of gold from personal jewellery and about one and a half billion baht (Satithamajit 2001). Luang Taa Maha Bua has been criticised for this involvement in secular matters. However, the many advocates of the campaign justified the interconnection between the state and religion using the metaphor: if the body of the nation is sick, then the spirit or heart (*hua cai*) of the nation, namely religion, is likewise sick. While the institution of Buddhism is seen to be in decline, the search for charismatic spiritual actors means that many individual monks remain important as political opinion leaders.

THE THREAT FROM WITHIN

Regional Buddhism indirectly threatened the authority of Buddhism by representing a danger to the modernisation of Thailand. However, the moral authority of state-dominated Buddhism was not in fact threatened by regional Buddhism. The threat came from inside the *sangha,* since the *sangha* was seriously challenged by several charismatic monks. Monks have been exposed by the media for being involved in various irregularities and this has shaken the Thai Buddhist community and weakened the moral authority of the monks. Cases of monks who have broken their vows of celibacy have been publicly displayed. The famous and popular monk in Chiang Mai, Phra Nikorn, is one example. In 1990, he was taken to court by a woman who claimed he was the father of her child. Another example was the charismatic monk Phra Yantra Amaro Bhikkhu who in 1994 was accused of having sex with four female followers and of fathering one daughter. Phra Bhavana Phuttho, a well-known monk in Nakorn Pathom province, was arrested in 1995 and defrocked on charges of having raped several under-age hill tribe girls who were being cared for at his monastery (Jackson 1997: 81–82). The growing number of scandals is undermining the authority of the *sangha*, and charismatic individual monks at the margin of the official *sangha* are tending to become strong focuses of popular devotion. The growing popularity of individual monks and of female renunciants could be seen as marking a return to the historical emphasis placed on individual ascetics who uphold moral authority.

MORAL AUTHORITY

A morally pure *sangha* is important for lay people, and people who believe that only strict monks can transfer power and contribute to a lay persons' store of religious merit have no reason to support defiled monks. Nor have the followers of reformist Buddhism any interest in monks who do not follow ethical principles. Immaculate ethical actions are thus posited as the source of legitimate secular power and this power is believed to be immanent in ethical action.

The commercialisation of Buddhism is considered to contribute to the declining public respect for organised religion. The commercial activities at temples include, for example, open activities such as trade in blessed amulets and other religious relics. However, some temples are involved in more shady economic businesses, which have added to the questionable activities of institutional Buddhism. As mentioned earlier, Thai newspapers have been filled in recent decades with stories about monks accused of violating the precepts which are the foundation of the moral standing of the *sangha*. The moral integrity of individual monks is of great significance and monks' ethical standards are consequently closely monitored by the laity. Dissatisfaction with the clerics' lack of ethical behaviour and distrust of the established monkhood has led people to search for alternative, undefiled Buddhist movements and religious persons.

People who are believed to 'have merit' or 'have merit and virtue' (*mii bun* or *mii bun baaramii*) are capable of much more effective action than ordinary humans. The *sangha* and the kingship are two offices associated with merit and virtue (Keyes 1999a: 5). Most Thais still hold to the assumption that moral authority is manifested in those having 'merit and virtue'. Today, people in Thailand look to many different sources for moral authority. Most local traditions have valued lay asceticism, although this has varied from region to region. There are many examples of ascetic women, both now and earlier, having 'merit and virtue'. Today, sections of the *mae chii* category are recognised as fields of merit for others (see Chapter 6). For example, the *mae chii*s at Ratburi Samnak Chii have shown that their exemplary lifestyle, education and a willingness to work hard with individual meditative practice as well as sharing their knowledge with the lay community are able to win them the respect of the village laity and other supporters. The increase in lay support for *mae chii*s at *samnak chii*s can partly be explained by the laity's disenchantment with particular monks; this has spurred them to look for worthy Buddhist practitioners. The Ratburi *mae chii*s' strict monastic behaviour, their Buddhist knowledge and their contribution to society have won them a following not only in the village but also in other parts of Thailand.

NOTES

1   King Mongkut was 47 years old, and had been a Buddhist monk for 27 years when he became King Rama IV in 1851. Chulalongkorn was Mongkut's son and succeded his father and reigned until 1910 (Wyatt 1984: 181–212).

2   *Vinaya* (Pali): disciplinary rules for the monastic community, as laid down in the *Vinayapitaka*, a section of the canonical Theravada scriptures.

3   An *arahat* is an enlightened person who has fully attained *nibbana*, one who has reached the highest stage and having completely eradicated all defilements (*kilesa*).

4   *Jhana* means a state of deep mental unification characterised by a total immersion of the mind in its object.

5   *Dhammakaya* meditation involves three meditation techniques: *aloka kasina*, meditation by concentrating on a bright object; *anapanasati*, meditation by concentrating on the motion of breathing, and a part involving a mantra called *buddhanussati*, where the mantra *samma araham* is repeated (Bowers 1996: 12 f.f.)

6   The name of the movement and the *wat* which serves as its headquarters point to the central tenet of the movement, i.e., that the *dhamm*ic 'body' (*kaya*) of the Buddha can be found within the body of every person through meditation (Keyes 1999a: 30).

7   The Vietnamese monk Thich Nhat Hanh used the term in 1963. Sulak Sivaraksa published *A Socially Engaged Buddhism* in 1988. The term has achieved currency within the Buddhist Peace Fellowship, founded in 1978, and the International Network of Engaged Buddhists, founded in 1989.

CHAPTER EIGHT

Mae Chiis' Quest for Education

Religious educational disparities in Thailand are accentuated along gender lines and access to education, both secular and religious, is of crucial importance also for the *mae chii*s. Education has implications for *mae chii*s' religious legitimacy and spiritual fulfilment and their generally low level of education reflects how the schooling system has been in Thailand. Buddhist studies are separated according to gender and religious or lay belonging and there has always been an interplay between the Buddhist institutions and education. Traditionally, education has been the concern of the Buddhist temples and women have not been entitled to enter temple schools. Also the fact that women have not been part of the Thai Buddhist *sangha* has previously limited their access to secular as well as to religious education.

The three well-educated *mae chii*s, whom I have chosen to portray in this chapter, have been of great importance in opening opportunities for the *mae chii*s to study. They all have university degrees and are not representative of most *mae chii*s, who have usually only completed primary education. However, they exemplify the importance of education and commitment in the struggle for providing better prerequisites for Thai *mae chii*s to accomplish their vocation.

In Thailand, Buddhist institutions did play a major role in both secular and religious education. Today secular and religious education are separated and secular education is open to women and men. However, as already noted, educational opportunities have not been available for *mae chii*s as they have for monks. Access to Buddhist and to secondary and higher education has long been an important issue for *mae chii*s and they have facilitated education for *mae chii*s through their own efforts. The national Thai Mae Chiis' Institute plays a central role in providing education and has been involved in the establishment of Dhammacarinii Witthayaa, the school at Ratburi Samnak Chii and also in the recent establishment of Mahapajapati Theri College, the first Buddhist College for women in Thailand. Within the formal Buddhist institutions, *mae chii*s have made some limited progress over the years, but they are segregated and are not only separated out but are also given qualifications distinct from those widely recognised for monks. The Buddhist educational institutions provide Buddhist education for monks that is much more formal and systematic than the education available for *mae chii*s. Obviously, with the lack of opportunities for higher academic training, fewer qualified teachers graduate and in the absence of these, women have less access to religious education, a cycle which is self-perpetuating and which the *mae chii*s try to break.

In most religions, theoretical and scriptural studies have traditionally been men's vocations and women have been excluded from advanced learning and teaching. For example, Hindu women were not allowed to study the Vedas, just as Jewish women were not allowed to study the Torah and Talmud, which were indispensable for becoming a rabbi and for a very long time Christian women had no access to theological faculties and seminaries (King 1989: 43). The problem of gaining access to education is well known to contemporary female Buddhist ascetics. They are often interested in studying and Tsomo (1988) states that there is no justification for asserting that female ascetics lack the interest or ability to develop themselves academically. On the contrary, throughout Buddhist history there are examples of highly learned female ascetics. In countries where female ascetics have access to education, for example in Taiwan and in Burma, they are filling the Buddhist colleges to capacity.

In Thailand, Buddhist studies have been regarded as suitable for monks while meditation has been considered more appropriate for *mae chii*s. The practice of meditation is seen as more of a personal vocation necessary for gaining Buddhist insights but divorced from knowledge achieved through books. Jane Bunnag (1973) found that in contrast to scriptural studies, meditation was regarded as an activity more appropriate not only for *mae chii*s but also for monks who were *saiyasaat* (magical practitioners), or for those monks who carry out the special ascetic practices (*thudong*) associated mainly with forest-dwelling monks.[1] Further she reports that the *sangha* encouraged meditation among laity and *mae chii*s. She describes how monks came from the Buddhist Universities in Bangkok, sent by the Department of Religious Affairs, in order to start meditation classes for *mae chii*s and lay people. Meditation is considered easier than studying *dhamma* by books (ibid.: 54, n. 7). Many *mae chii*s at temples still follow the more lay-oriented and less prestigious activity that meditation constitutes (see for example Cook 1981, Kabilsingh 1991).

THE GENDERED DIVISION OF MEDITATION AND EDUCATION

During the past century, the stress on education increased and emphasis on achievement of accepted standards of learning dominated. The Thai *sangha* became centralised and that implied also enhanced significance of urban centres. Jane Bunnag conducted fieldwork in 1966–67 in Ayutthaya, a province in Central Thailand north of Bangkok. She notes that the institutionalised *dhamma* studies were concentrated in urban centres and the nation-wide ecclesiastical hierarchy tended to be attached to temples in towns (Bunnag 1973: 47). Buddhist studies were placed hierarchically above meditation practice and the power of the *sangha* was centralised in Bangkok and other urban areas. One consequence of modern state Buddhist preference for study over practice was that it devalued local tradition and lay asceticism. Meditation practice was, in principle, open to anyone and in order to recognise the importance of meditation practice the highly respected monk Luang Taa Maha Bua from the Northeastern Thailand compared his meditation tradition to a forest university. Many monks who refrained from studying and devoted themselves to meditation gained great respect for the wisdom that they attained. In regional traditions, there were also prominent women renunciants, but their identities and teachings do not appear in official records because of their preference for meditation practice and their lack of scholastic training (Tiyavanich 1997: 280–81).

The Northeastern Thailand has a national reputation for asceticism and disciplined piety and the region has a higher percentage of forest hermitages than any other region in the country. The ascetic monks who reside in the forest hermitages have achieved renown not only within the region but also nationally. However, despite *mae chiis'* austere practice, they are not usually formally honoured for their skills in meditation.

Thai monks usually devote themselves to learning and scholarship as well as to the discipline of meditation. Some monastic places emphasise either studying or meditation, others combine these two different approaches according to their own distinctive needs, capabilities and traditions. Since *mae chii*s have commonly lacked access to theoretical Buddhist studies, education has been identified as the key means to gain thorough comprehension of the Buddhist teachings and to enhance their position. However, access to education has been difficult for *mae chii*s. Many reported that they had been encouraged to practise meditation but not to study books. One *mae chii* who came from the Northeastern Thailand said that ever since she was young she had understood that studying was closed for her. After finishing primary school, she had wanted to continue to secondary school but her parents could not afford that. She said that meditation had been easy for her compared to studying, and several years later when she had become a *mae chii*, she was solely interested in practising meditation. However, her interest changed and she had gradually become more interested in getting knowledge and being able to share it with others. She said that education had not been easy to attain. Nor had it been easy to find a place to study or to find the financial means needed.

The vast majority of the *mae chii*s that told me about their enthusiasm for meditation said that their aim was to attain *nibbana* and that meditation was the only way to realise that goal. Rather than taking formal courses on Buddhism these *mae chii*s considered that their time was most profitably spent in practising meditation. Therefore, Buddhist education was not considered necessary and some *mae chii*s said that studying books would even be a hindrance to their practice. In order to show that education through books has never been a prerequisite for attaining enlightenment, the *mae chii*s referred to the lack of books and education in the Buddha's time, and noted that this did not prevent people from attaining the highest realisation.

Meditation is thus seen by some as the most important facet of Buddhist practice, while others, in Thailand as elsewhere, maintain that meditation without a correct understanding of the scriptures would not be a proper path. Some of those who favour the latter opinion tend to emphasise study rather than meditation. *Mae chii*s who were ordained at temples and emphasised meditation said that not only the *mae chii*s but also the monks at their temples stressed the importance of meditation practice.

My main fieldsite was at a *samnak chii* with an educational profile; hence it was perhaps natural that most *mae chii*s that I met were eager to educate themselves. Interestingly, many who studied at Ratburi Samnak Chii came from temples in the Northeastern Thailand that emphasised meditation. Commonly, the *mae chii*s were not ambitious about becoming scholars and teachers, but they considered that they needed both secular and religious knowledge in order to achieve profound knowledge and to be an asset to the laity. They expressed an obligation and sincere inclination to thoroughly study the Buddha's teachings. Moreover, they were in general skilful in reciting Buddhist chants and many of them wanted to enhance their knowledge about the meaning of the texts they recited.

The *mae chii*s devote their lives to Buddhism, sacrifice worldly pursuits and material comforts, but most find that the doors to religious advancement are closed to them. They want to develop themselves and many identify education as the key to their improvement. They know that intensive meditation is vital for transforming the mind and they see Buddhist studies as a step in their religious achievement.

THE *SANGHA* AND EDUCATIONAL INEQUALITY

The important role of the Buddhist institutions in education could explain the high degree of literacy in Thailand. However, this has been associated with social and sex-based divisions of knowledge. Both lay women and *mae chiis* in pre-modern Siamese society were excluded from access to text-based knowledge (Keyes1991: 94). Some women in pre-modern urban settings did become literate, but rural women were, almost without exception, illiterate until compulsory primary education was instituted after 1932 when Thailand became a constitutional monarchy (ibid.: 123, n. 3; Pitiyanuwat and Sujiva 2005: passim). Monks assumed a prominent social position commensurate with their monopolisation of knowledge associated with written texts. By contrast, ascetic women with a deep knowledge of meditation have seldom had scholastic training. Nevertheless, some of these ascetic women were held in high esteem by Buddhist teachers as well as by the laity, for instance the late Khun Yai Chan, one of the founders of Wat Phra Dhammakaay (see Chapter 7). She was illiterate but this did not prevent people honouring her for the sacred powers she was believed to have attained through meditation practice. However, in a world of widespread literacy only few individual practitioners without education would be revered.

Before the introduction of Western education, education in Thailand was administered solely by the monasteries and originally designed to inculcate literacy and thus provide access to the Buddhist teachings. Since women were denied the right to become monks, they were deprived of any education. Ordination was not class-specific, it could be temporary and the monastery was equivalent to an Open University where all men could come and go and acquire education. Women were encouraged to be more active economically in order to support the Buddhist order and to gain merit, indirectly through men, in the hope of better rebirth (as a man!) (Tantiwiramanond and Pandey 1991: 16). As already mentioned, men without economic means can acquire education up to a university degree through the *sangha,* an avenue that is closed for women. It is well documented that monks and novices saw ordination as an opportunity to advance in both secular and Buddhist knowledge and used this opportunity actively. Most of those monks and novices who pursue secular qualifications during their time at the city temples are often from other provinces, a pattern we are already familiar with from the research of Bunnag (1973), Tambiah (1976) and Cook (1981).

MAE CHIIS' STUDIES YIELD FEWER CREDITS

The government has standardised Buddhist education. There are three areas of study recognised in the system: Buddhist teachings (*dhamma*), Buddhist philosophy (*Abhiddhamma*), and Pali, the language of the Theravada Buddhist texts. Furthermore, there are three degrees offered in the first two areas, each requiring about a year of study: beginning, intermediate and advanced. In Pali there are nine levels of competency. Ideally, the subjects should be studied together. The lowest level of *dhamma* studies, called *naktham tree,* covers knowledge concerning discipline, basic principles of *dhamma* to be applied in living or teaching, the life of the Buddha, and Buddhist ceremonies and rituals. The two higher levels of study, *naktham tho* and *naktham ek,* go deeper, and include subjects such as meditation. As in other countries where Buddhism is taught, the original Pali texts are transliterated into the local alphabet. Thus, in Thailand, the texts are read in the original language, but written with Thai characters.[2]

The formal recognition of *mae chiis'* educational capabilities is progressing very slowly, though some are now recognised as skilled in the Buddhist teachings. I found that most *mae chiis* did not share the common notion that men were more able in attaining Buddhist knowledge. However, the structure of the Buddhist educational system elevates monks' Buddhist studies and distinguishes their studies from those of women. Thai Buddhist education is organised so that monks' studies belong to the ordained realm and *mae chiis'* studies are placed in the lay realm. Moreover, Thai *mae chiis* have been excluded from the Buddhist universities with the exception of some courses that are open to them. When monks have successfully completed their studies, they are given certificates from the Religious Affairs Department and they also get the respectful title *Phra Maha.* These educational qualifications have been regarded as prerequisites for promotion to administrative positions within the *sangha* as well as for secular positions for monks who leave the monkhood. *Mae chiis,* on the other hand, are given recognition of success in their exams at a secular level, but no formal title or other benefits apply. Further, the courses that monks and *mae chiis* study are given different names. While monks and novices study *naktham* (skilled in *dhamma*) and *parian* courses, *mae chiis* and laity study *thamsüksaa* (*dhamma* studies) and *baaliisüksaa* (Pali studies) even though both courses in Pali are precisely the same. At Ratburi Samnak Chii, both the lay and the ordained versions were used when the *mae chii*s referred to their own studies.

Over the decades, many Thai men have been ordain for a limited period of time while they improved their secular qualifications so they would be entitled to better academic and job opportunities. That was not the case with the *mae chii*s that I interviewed. A *mae chii* who was 24 years and had been ordained ten years, remembered her mother saying before she became a *mae chii*: 'When girls become ordained there is no comfort (*may sabaay*). When boys become ordained everybody is happy. For monks there is a career, they can be teachers, for *mae chii*s there is nothing to expect.' That underlines the radical differences in opportunities that men's and women's ordination carries. Despite the somewhat hesitant attitudes to *mae chii*s' studies, many *mae chii*s considered that it was their duty as *mae chii*s to study Buddhism. Even *mae chii*s who viewed meditation as their prime goal came to Ratburi Samnak Chii for educational reasons. A young *mae chii* who was ordained at a Thammayut temple in Isaan with emphasis on meditation made up her mind about studying after a pilgrimage to India.[3] She said: 'When I was in India, some Thai monks asked me about Buddhism and I could not answer. I felt that I wanted to be able to explain. I decided to study because theory is also important.'

She had received ordination after finishing six years of primary education. She came to Ratburi Samnak Chii with the intention of studying Buddhism, *nak tham*, Pali and *abhidhamma*.[4] In 1998, she had finished the first *nak tham* level of three, and she was also doing secondary-school studies. However, she had not planned to study further at the university. She said that it was difficult to study Pali language at Ratburi Samnak Chii since the time for studying was limited due to the amount of work that had to be carried out. Therefore, she planned to study Pali at another *samnak chii* where it was possible to devote more time to it and she would then finish the courses faster. Her sister had promised to support her financially which was a prerequisite for her. Two years later she had finished her secondary education and the three levels of Buddhist studies at Ratburi Samnak Chii and had, together with another *mae chii*, gone to study Pali at the place she had planned. Her intention was to complete her studies and then go back to her resident temple in Isaan and continue her meditation practice.

Pali has traditionally been the special preserve of the monks. The study of Pali, and hence of the sacred texts, is an integral part of a monk's path of practice of Buddhism. Pali is also associated with the memorisation of the

Pali chants, which form a focus for many of the rituals which monks perform for the laity. Since knowledge of Pali is difficult, the monks who are known to be proficient at it receive the respect of the laity for their scholarship. Anyone who passes the examination for level nine of Pali studies should be able to understand the Buddhist texts in Pali, translate them into Thai and have a detailed understanding of them. In earlier times to be recognised as a 'knowledgeable person' (*bandhit*) required that the person had passed the exam for the highest degree of Buddhist philosophy. It was a government policy that national administrators conferred posts on men who had achieved *bandhit* status, with reference to their knowledge and exemplary behaviour. These men had achieved their education during their period in the monkhood. The tests for the Pali courses are known as 'the Pali exam at Sanaam Luang'.[5] When the exam is given, testing takes place for levels 4–9. Not more than about a hundred monks in the whole country usually take the exam for the ninth level (Suthon 1998).

Older *mae chii*s told me that a few decades ago, when they wanted to study Pali, they had to persuade the senior monks at their temples to give them permission. Lack of incentive was a likely reason for *mae chii*s' low degree of engagement in studying Buddhist scriptures. Nerida Cook reported that when the abbot at Wat Paknam begun to encourage the *mae chii*s to study Pali, more and more *mae chii*s became successful in their studies (Cook 1981: 201). At Ratburi Samnak Chii the *mae chii*s also study Pali and the *samnak chii* offers courses in Pali studies. Several *mae chii*s had passed the exams for intermediate level, but none had yet passed the most advanced level. In 1982 there were four *mae chii*s in Thailand who had completed the ninth level of Pali, in 1998, 12, and in 2004, 20 had achieved the ninth and highest level. Since it was considered extremely difficult to pass the exam for the ninth level, I found that it was encouraging for *mae chii*s that some have proved that they had the capacity to study the same courses as the monks. *Mae chii*s who had accomplished the ninth level were met with respect by the laity, the *mae chii*s and also by monks.

Mae chii Sirivan, a brilliant young *mae chii* who had successfully passed the ninth level of Pali studies seemed to have convinced the monks with her skills and was appointed to teach monks at one of the two monks' universities in Bangkok. On a study trip that I participated in together with *mae chii*s from different *samnak chii*s and monks from the Buddhist University Maha Chulalongkorn, we discussed women's difficulties in gaining access to Buddhist education. The monks said they were in favour of opening the Buddhist

University to women and referred to Mae chii Sirivan as an example of women's capacity to study.

Mae chii Sirivan came from the Northeastern Thailand and she had been ordained since she was 16 years old. She had lived at a big temple in Bangkok for several years and said that she had no intention of returning to Isaan where she was ordained. A monk from her village temple, who had known her since she was a child, sponsored her financially and without his support it would not have been possible for her to study. In March 1998, she went to visit her home town and I made an appointment to meet her in her native city in Isaan. She invited me to visit her family, the monk who supported her and the monks and the *mae chii*s at the temple where she was ordained. Her mother showed me a large picture of her daughter receiving a religious fan from the hand of Princess Somsavali at a ceremony at the Royal temple Wat Bowonniwet. The ceremony was held in 1997 when she had finished the highest level of Pali studies. The monk who had supported her through her studies was very proud of her being the first *mae chii* from Isaan who had passed the ninth level of Pali exam. Besides studying Buddhist subjects she also studied at the Open University, Ramkhamhaeng, and graduated with a BA in 1999. She finished her MA at Thammasat University and was then granted a unique opportunity to study for her PhD at the monks' university, Maha Chulalongkorn, which shows that the monks' university can be opened to individual *mae chii*s.

THE SEPARATION OF MONASTIC AND SECULAR EDUCATION

During the twentieth century, governmental primary schools gradually replaced Buddhist temple schools as centres of traditional education. The establishment of government schools meant that literacy was no longer the prerogative of males only, and females as well as males were given access to schooling. This has been one of the most striking changes in social structure that has come about with the introduction of compulsory education. The separation of state schools from temples has given Thai girls primary schooling of initially four and, later, six years. According to the National Education Act of 1999, compulsory education is to increase to comprise nine years. However, in 1998, secondary education was still out of reach for girls without financial means. In contrast, temple education is still a support for poor boys. As novices, they get free education, board and lodging. As monks, they can go to Buddhist colleges and receive degrees equivalent to those at a secular university. Most graduates quit the monkhood and their degrees enable them to get a good job in lay society (Ekachai 1998). Underprivileged girls have no equivalent safety net. In 1990 Ratburi Samnak Chii opened the first secondary school for impoverished girls; there are few Buddhist *samnak chii*s in Thailand that offer free education to poor rural girls.

The initiative to secularise education in Thailand was taken at the end of the nineteenth century by King Chulalongkorn and his advisors. They established a state-wide educational policy based on the premise that all citizens, regardless of their ethnic origin or class background, should receive the same basic education and that this should be given in Thai, the national language. Since the promulgation of the Primary Education Act of 1921, children have been required to attend school, and since the 1930s the law has been implemented in most communities throughout the kingdom. Missionary and Chinese schools have been forced to follow the state-prescribed curriculum. However, in Northeastern Thailand, the separation of state schools from temples proceeded rather slowly until about the1960s when the government promoted the building of new schools on public land that did not belong to temples (Keyes 1991: 101).

Today the schools in rural communities throughout Thailand have links with the traditional Buddhist schools found in nearly all Thai villages. Initially the government grafted state schools onto traditional monastic schools, but altered the character of the latter by insisting on a curriculum devised for national rather than religious purposes (ibid.: 7). Monks were replaced by trained persons who had taken up teaching as a vocation. The government established teachers' training institutions throughout the country. However, the vocation to teach seemed to become more a role of lay women than for men. While temple schools continued to exist, they were, in fact, unequivocally subordinated to secular schools. At temples, a large number of monks and novices were of an age which corresponded not only to the established male pattern of ordination at a young age, but also reflected the tendency to stay at the temple to receive further education, both monastic and secular. The ages of *mae chii*s at temples did not reflect such established patterns. Moreover, the government made completion of compulsory primary education a prerequisite for entering the temples as a novice monk. In turn, fewer novices went on to become monks and the *sangha* saw its social role as well as its size reduced as a result of the success of the state secular educational system (ibid.: 97). However, in times of economic crisis, temple schools are evidently still important. During 1997 and 1998, 300,000 pupils were forced to drop out of school due to lack of money. A temple-run novice school, Wat Sri Nuam, reported that the number of novices at the temple school increased then by 40 per cent (Ekachai 1998).

The manner in which the state school all but totally replaced the traditional Buddhist monastic school engendered almost no conflict (Keyes1991: 7). The *sangha* leadership remained supportive when the government replaced monk teachers by lay teachers. Educational policy-making and curriculum construction were highly centralised. The government included Buddhist moral instruction as part of the curriculum and monks continue, even today, to be called upon to provide this instruction. Even when monks were teaching only ethics in the new type of school, the fact that most village schools continued to be housed in temple buildings perpetuated the link in villagers' minds between state-supported secular schools and pre-modern monastic schools. The local school was often viewed as an extension of the temple by village monks and lay people alike. Monks have often agreed to help sponsor money-raising projects for schools located in temple areas, thus rendering such fundraisers a form of traditional merit-making, an example of which was related in the previous chapter.

In 1998, Thai girls and boys had equal access to six years of primary education. The primary education programme had initially been for four years. It was in 1977 that the government implemented a national policy to upgrade it from four to six years. In 1998, the school system comprised the six years of primary school (*pratom 1–6*), three years of lower secondary school (*mathayom 1–3*), and three years of upper secondary school (*mathayom 4–6*) prior to higher education. A proposed draft of an Education Bill was endorsed by the cabinet on 23 June, 1998. The National Education Act includes both teaching and learning reforms and among other things it holds that the government should provide 12 years of education for all from primary to secondary level. The draft passed into law in August 1999, but it will take several years to implement it throughout the country.

It was not until the late 1950s and the early 1960s that a plan for university co-ordination and the expansion of higher education to the provincial areas was carried out. All higher-education institutions created until then were government institutions. As the demand for higher education grew, private colleges were established, beginning in 1969. In addition to public and private universities and colleges, there are other post-secondary institutions within the Ministry of Education, the Ministry of Public Health and other ministries (Ketudat and Wichit 1979: 1–10). The system of higher education in Thailand, then, embraces various types of institutions, including universities, colleges and specialised professional training institutions. In 1979, two Open Universities, Ramkhamhaeng and Sukhothai Thammathirat, were established. They provide home-based education through integrated media to participants in rural areas as well as urban centres. Further, Thailand has two Buddhist universities: Maha Chulalongkorn and Mahamakut Rajavidyalai, both situated in Bangkok, with branches in other provinces in Thailand.

PIONEERING *MAE CHII*S

Several *mae chii*s are deeply committed in their work for increasing *mae chii*s' opportunities to study. I have chosen to present three of them who have played important roles in improving educational opportunities for *mae chii*s and young women in Thailand. These three are actively engaged in creating and formalising secondary and higher education for *mae chii*s through the Thai Mae Chiis' Institute, the Dhammacarinii School and the Mahapajapati Theri College. These three pioneers, Khunying Kanitha Wichiencharoen, Khun Mae Prathin Kwan-orn and Mae chii Srisalab Upamai, are all *mae chii*s with university degrees. However they came from very different backgrounds. The key theme that has guided them is social engagement and motivation to work against exploitation of vulnerable girls and young women. All three *mae chii*s have been studying abroad, Khun Mae Prathin and Mae chii Srisalab in India and Mae chii Khunying Kanitha in United States, and their experiences have inspired them to focus on open educational opportunities for ascetic and lay women and girls in Thailand. Mae chii Srisalab was born in the Northeastern Thailand and brought up under poor circumstances. Khun Mae Prathin was from a province in Central Thailand and described her childhood as happy without financial difficulties. Mae chii Khunying Kanitha came from Bangkok and her family was wealthy and of high rank. She had the highest social position among the three *mae chii*s but also with fewest years as an ordained person, which made her religious standing lower than the other two *mae chii*s'. In practical work, the *mae chii*s complemented each other and their different backgrounds and positions turned out to be an advantage in their vocation.

Khun Mae Prathin Kwan-orn

Khun Mae Prathin Kwan-orn was born in a province not far from where Ratburi Samnak Chii is situated. She and her younger brother were their family's only children. Their father was a construction worker and their mother had a shop where she sold a variety of things. Khun Mae Prathin was ordained some 35 years ago when she was 19. She said that it was not common for women to become *mae chii*s and it was unusual that a young woman chose to live a life as a renunciant. When she was a teenager, she suffered from severe headaches and initially sought temporary ordination in order to come to terms with her health problem. But in fact, she wanted to live a spiritual life and said that she wanted freedom. She did not believe that the lay life would meet her needs. She thought that there must be other openings for women than to be 'locked up' in a marriage with the responsibilities of caring for a husband and children. Understanding their daughter's sincere wish to live an ordained life, her parents gave their permission, and Khun Mae was ordained at a temple of both monks and *mae chii*s. These had no contact with each other and a large wall separated the *mae chii*s' dwellings from the monks'. The *mae chii*s were ruled by themselves and they did not have to cook for the monks, otherwise a common task for *mae chii*s at temples in Thailand.

Khun Mae Prathin realised early the importance of education. She started her own secondary education while living at the *samnak chii* where she was ordained. Later on, she went to study Pali in Bangkok. She completed her Bachelor of Arts and thereafter Master of Arts in India. It is still rare that *mae chii*s have the financial means to study. Khun Mae Prathin was supported by her family and by lay followers. When she returned to Thailand, some lay people had donated land for the purpose of building a freestanding *samnak chii*. Khun Mae Prathin and her close friend Khun Mae Sumon, were invited to establish it. These two *mae chii*s had studied together in India and Khun Mae Sumon was one of the very few *mae chii*s in Thailand who had completed a PhD. degree. If they had not had the opportunity to start the *samnak chii*, Khun Mae Prathin said, she would probably have continued her studies.

Mae chii Srisalab Upamai

The *mae chii*s from Wat Paknam Phasi Charoen in Bangkok have played an important role, both for the Thai Mae Chiis' Institute and for the Dhammacarinii School. When the school started, three *mae chii*s from Wat Paknam went to work there. One of these three *mae chii*s was Mae chii Srisalab Upamai who was appointed the principal for the school. When she was ordained about 27 years ago, she was not interested in studying. Her main focus was on meditation. She had meditated regularly since she was 14 years old. At that time she had finished her four years of compulsory education and she spent her days looking after buffaloes. In the evening she went to the temple and meditated together with other practitioners. She said that meditation had become popular and in

Figure 8.1. Khun Mae Prathin Kwan-orn and Mae chii Yuphin Duangjun meeting with families on the application day to the Dhammacarinii School

the evenings the temple was crowded with teenagers who practised meditation. Meditation became an important part of her life and she said she felt happy and she progressed in her practice. She felt that her mind became peaceful and very smooth.

She was 21 when she was ordained at the temple Wat Paknam Phasi Charoen in Bangkok. At that time, she was not especially interested in education. However she had been ordained at the temple of Wat Paknam, which has the unusual policy that every *mae chii*, except the very old ones, have to study. Reluctantly, she started to study the three grades of compulsory Buddhist studies. At the same time she studied lower and, later, the upper secondary school.

Usually monks in Thailand go on alms rounds in the morning, but at Wat Paknam they do not. The lay people donate money or food to the temple and the *mae chii*s at Wat Paknam have to cook food for all monks and *mae chii*s. Mae chii Srisalab was working in the kitchen every day from early morning until noon, and in the afternoon she took classes. She recalled how tired she was during these years. The time for doing homework was very limited. She woke up before 4 o'clock for the morning chant. After that the time before noon was spent cooking. The *mae chii*s also had to attend afternoon chanting and meditation. There was no time for rest during the day so that she usually went to bed late.

When Mae chii Srisalab finished her Buddhist studies, she intended to spend a period in intense meditation. However, some older *mae chii*s at the temple encouraged her to study Pali. Although she was not really interested in further education she fulfilled their wishes. While studying Pali she also started to study for her Bachelor of Arts at the Open University, Ramkamhaeng. At the same time, she was appointed to teach at Wat Paknam Phasi Charoen. After her graduation, she was chosen to be the principal of Dhammacarinii Witthayaa at Ratburi Samnak Chii. For three years, she taught both at Wat Paknam in Bangkok and at Dhammacarinii School at Ratburi Samnak Chii, which involved a considerable amount of time-consuming travelling.

Mae chii Srisalab had gradually become more and more interested in studying. When she was more than 45 years old she went to study for her Master's degree in India where she spent three years in Poona before graduation in 1997. Upon return from India she continued to teach and work at Dhammacarinii School. Today Mae chii Srisalab views studying as the key factor for helping girls and young women in Thailand and she has taken an active role in developing the *mae chiis*' college, Mahapajapati Theri College, together with Mae chii Khunying Kanitha.

Mae chii Khunying Kanitha Wichiencharoen

When Mae Chii Khunying Kanitha was young, it was assumed that she should study and get an education. She attended St Francis Xavier and St Yoseph convent Schools in Bangkok and after that she went on to Thammasat University. She graduated from law school in 1945 and over the next two years she worked with counselling less fortunate women who had suffered many types of abuse and discrimination. In 1948 she travelled to the United States and studied international relations for one year at the American University in Washington, DC, and at Columbia University in New York City. The following year she went to Geneva to study international relations. During a stopover in Paris, she met the future Queen Sirikit, who at that time was the 15-year-old daughter of Thailand's ambassador to France. That meeting was the beginning of a long friendship with the royal family. Many years later, her service to the King and Queen was recognised and she received the title Khunying, the equivalent of the British Dame. She returned to Bangkok in 1949 and started working at the Ministry of Foreign Affairs and for the U.S. Agency for International Development (USAID). In 1953, she went to United States again and this time she studied social welfare at Howard University in Washington, DC. When she returned to Thailand in 1955 her jobs varied from that of supervisor for Standard Vacuum Oil to legal advisor for the Tourist Authority of Thailand; later, she worked in several capacities for the USAID. In 1963, she became executive secretary of the Thai–American Technical Co-operation Association in Bangkok.

Mae chii Khunying Kanitha together with a handful of others, primarily Thai female lawyers, emerged as the country's first women's rights activists. She gave interviews and made speeches in Thailand to achieve equal rights for Thai women. She served as president of the Women Lawyers Association of Thailand from 1961 to 1964 and participated actively in the women's rights movement in Thailand which, by the 1970s, was receiving support, but also criticism, ridicule and insults. In 1974 a group of concerned women and men formed the Status of Women Promotion Group as a vehicle for their movement. Khunying Kanitha served as its president and also as chairperson of the Standing committee on Women and Labour for the National Council of Women. During her travels over the years Mae chii Khunying Kanitha had met with directors of local welfare agencies and NGOs involved in women's rights and she was inspired by their work. In 1981 the Emergency Home I was established in the Dusit area in Bangkok with the co-operation of the Thai Women Lawyers Association and the Girl Guides Association of Thailand, founded by her sister Khunying Kanok Samsen Vil. The shelter overflowed with clients and soon became too small. In 1986, Mae chii Khunying Kanitha opened Emergency Home II and the Children's Home in the Donmuang area on the outskirts of Bangkok, where Emergency Home III was set up later. The shelter expanded constantly and provided education and vocational training programmes. Over the years the association also had to meet the need of taking care of the increasing numbers of women and children who were infected with HIV/AIDS.

Mae chii Khunying Kanitha was ordained in 1993, but even before that she was engaged in the problems of inequality that the *mae chii*s suffered. She started to take up causes for *mae chii*s, whose status, she believed should be promoted. She compared the unegalitarian situation of *mae chii*s' with ordained women in other countries and came to the conclusion that it was obvious that ordained women should have the same rights and functions in religion as the monks. She said: 'But *mae chii*s are second-class citizens who primarily serve the monks. In fact, our women are encouraged to become *mae chii*s so that they can gain merit and be reincarnated as men.' She believed that *mae chii*s could contribute much more to Buddhism and to Thai society than they had been allowed to do. In order to increase the *mae chiis'* educational level she has, together with the Thai Mae Chiis' Institute, initiated the building of a college where *mae chiis* can study religion and philosophy, learn about social work and to be teachers. The *mae chiis'* college is affiliated with the Faculty of Religion and Philosophy at the monks' university, Mahamakut University, and located in Nakorn Ratchasima province.

Khun Mae Prathin, Mae chii Srisalab and Mae chii Khunying Kanitha have devoted themselves to finding ways to provide education for girls and *mae chiis* in Thailand. Their different backgrounds in terms of class, origin, age at ordination and interests display factors that influence educational opportunities for Thai women. These three *mae chiis* did not share an interest in studying when they received ordination. However, later they all identified access to education as one of the most important issues for *mae chiis*. Individual *mae chiis* with the initiative to work for their right to education are essential for realising educational facilities. Support from lay people, from individual monks and institutions that work together in establishing educational centres for *mae chiis* is also indispensable.

DEBATED SOCIAL ENGAGEMENT

Improving the *mae chiis'* educational level has always been a concern for the Thai Mae Chiis' Institute. Access to Buddhist as well as to secondary and higher education have been important issues for the *mae chiis*. Over the years the Institute has organised and been engaged in various training courses and educational programmes which reflect the Institute's dual emphasis on both the religious and secular development of the *mae chiis*. The Institute's engagement in social work has been criticised by those who hold the opinion that monks and *mae chiis* should solely concern themselves with helping people to develop spiritually. *Mae chiis* who are focused on their meditation practice see the training courses that the Institute organises as incompatible with their religious vocation. Most of my informants thought that *mae chiis* should not be involved in lay occupations such as nursing, child care and other similar lay activities that they consider improper vocations for ordained persons. Some *mae chiis* said that they felt that the Institute had been one-sided in stressing the *mae chiis'* social role and they preferred to emphasise the importance of the Institute's engagement in developing the *mae chiis* spiritually. The stress on involvement in social activities and similar work has perhaps been inspired by perceptions of the roles of Christian nuns. It is interesting to note that in comparison with monks who are socially engaged, the *mae chiis*' involvement in the community has a nurturing tone. The *mae chiis*' work has become oriented towards women's activities, whereas monks tend to deal with the community as a whole.

The Institute's programmes are specifically designed to cater for *mae chii*s with little educational background. There is an acceptance of the fact that some women will become *mae chii*s simply in order to be able to have access to the education provided; however, that has always been the case with a certain proportion of monks. Improvements in educational opportunities for *mae chii*s are emphasised by the Institute for several reasons. For example, the *mae chii*s' poor educational background reflects badly on the image of the *mae chii*s themselves, and the Institute strives to improve the *mae chii*s' representation by encouraging them to study. The president of the Institute stated: 'The laity want the *mae chii*s to be educated. The *mae chii*s have to teach others and lay people would not respect the *mae chii*s if they only had knowledge of religion. If we only know *dhamma,* there would be a lack of communication with people.' The Institute also recognises the benefits of giving *mae chii*s some training which would allow them to earn a living should they leave the ordained state. While encouraging Buddhist studies in general and the knowledge of Pali in particular, the Institute hopes to increase the number of *mae chii*s who have levels of religious knowledge equal to that of the monks. That will earn them the respect of the laity as knowledgeable and scholarly religious specialists.

The Institute's capacity to facilitate education has been limited by the fact that it has basically relied on *mae chii*s organising education for themselves. The Institute is dependent on private donations; religious education for women in Thailand is thus largely a private, individual responsibility handicapped by a scarcity of facilities and qualified female instructors. The *mae chii*s also stress the need for opening structured systems of religious education for *mae chii*s. Despite their lack of education, the *mae chii*s might well progress spiritually, but this is not sufficient to allow them to take their rightful places in the religious hierarchy as teachers, administrators, role models, and so forth. Lacking a solid educational foundation themselves, they would have no footing from which to make contributions to the lay community.

The pursuit of secular education and the acquisition of formal qualifications by *mae chii*s are complex questions. At one level, they simply reflect the increasing need of religious specialists to be well educated in secular subjects to maintain the respect of educated laity. This indeed was the argument for the establishment of Buddhist universities for monks, and the same argument could also be applied to the *mae chiis*. At another level, the availability of education for monks has led poorer men to join the *sangha* and thus seek self-advancement within the ranks. Secular education for women has usually, however, the less ambitious role of attempting to teach *mae chiis* only the basic skills suitable to their position.

SAMNAK CHIIS OFFER FREE EDUCATION

The Thai Mae Chiis' Institute had by 1998 established 18 branches scattered all over Thailand; by 2005 the number of branches had increased to 26. Two of the *samnak chii*s run free secondary schools for girls and *mae chii*s and one of them is located at Ratburi Samnak Chii. Khun Mae Prathin, the head *mae chii* of Ratburi Samnak Chii, is also the principal of the school. She had long felt pity for young women who had the chance to study only at primary school and she was strongly committed to the issue of providing education for girls. Khun Mae Prathin said that the educational level has shown to be a crucial factor for both lay and ordained Thai women. She added that after the six years of primary schooling, many underprivileged girls could not afford to continue studying; many girls started working instead in poorly paid jobs while very young. Khun Mae Prathin saw that many young Thai women sought employment in urban areas to help support their families. They had to cope with poor working conditions because they lacked qualifications for better employment. She identified girls' lack of access to further education as a basic problem that had to be dealt with if young women were to be rescued from harsh treatment in factories or recruitment into the sex industry. As soon as she had the opportunity, she decided to dedicate herself to providing secondary education, especially for girls who could not afford to study otherwise.

The initiative to start Ratburi Samnak Chii came from the Thai Mae Chiis' Institute. Khun Mae Sumon and Khun Mae Prathin had made an earlier attempt to start a school for *mae chii*s. At first there were 20 *mae chii*s studying, but only two teachers. The large amount of work and the lack of teachers forced them to close the school. However, they continued with the hard work of constructing buildings on the difficult marshland. While they were building the *saalaa*, the main building at the *samnak chii*, Khun Mae Sumon became severely ill and passed away. Khun Mae Prathin felt she had to continue the work with the help and support of the other *mae chii*s at the *samnak chii*.

Some years later the abbot Luang Phôô Im, from Wat Somanas in Bangkok, suggested starting secondary education at the *samnak chii*. He also wanted to give girls and young women from poor families opportunities similar to those of underprivileged boys and he helped the *samnak chii* to found the school. Khun Mae Prathin was delighted to have a new opportunity to establish a school for girls and *mae chii*s in Thailand. This time they had better conditions. They had buildings, better financial support and more teachers. When the Dhammacarinii School started in 1990, there were ten teachers, and by 1998 there were 15.

The financial resources for starting Dhammacarinii School came from many individual donors who agreed that impoverished girls and women needed more opportunities for education. For the first five years Dhammacarinii School survived on support from the lay community and from individual monks and *mae chii*s. The government gave some financial support to the school in 1995, but due to the 1997 economic crisis in Thailand, the government decided to cut their support drastically, causing considerable economic difficulties for the school.

A *mae chii* who has been of crucial importance for the Dhammacarinii School's existence is Mae chii Yuphin Duangjun. She was also from the temple Wat Paknam Phasi Charoen in Bangkok and she has been an important fund-raiser for the school. Twice a year, in late August and in January, Mae chii Yuphin helped to organise a fund-raising festival, *phaphaa*. As previously mentioned these festivals are commonly arranged at Buddhist temples in Thailand (see Chapter 6). Through her large network of supporters, the school has become known to people in Bangkok and elsewhere. Since the *mae chii*s have to rely on their own ability to finance and run their different projects, networking and co-operation are indispensable.

The school system in Thailand is currently undergoing a process of change and as a result of the National Education Act of 1999 compulsory education is now nine years implying that girls from poor families would have access to free secondary education. In fact, the poor, whether male or female, have more access to secondary schooling as a consequence of these reforms and it is now rare for boys from poor families to seek education through the *sangha*. Dhammacarinii School has increased its numbers and has upgraded its educational standards. The school became a 'formal' school in 2004 and new school buildings were erected. About a hundred students are studying there.

DHAMMACARINII WITTHAYAA

The Dhammacarinii School brochure says that the school has three objectives: to provide and increase the opportunity of impoverished young women to be educated in both academic and *dhamma* studies and practice; to develop the quality of life of young women; and to stimulate and instill in them the importance of one's contribution toward oneself and society: to train young Buddhists to sustain the teaching in the service of the religion and the nation.

Young girls who apply to study at secondary school must have finished primary education, *pathom six* (ages 11 or 12). For most girls at the Dhammacarinii School, this was their only chance to continue their studies. In the school's brochure there is a list of six prerequisites for admission. The first requirement is that it has to be the girl's own wish to continue her studies. Further, she must be without the financial means to study at any other school. She must have finished primary education (*pathom six*), be between 12 and 15 years of age, in good health and not carrying any contagious disease.

The application to the Dhammacarinii School is made personally by the girls and their families on 1 May every year. The girls who are going to study at the secondary school are requested to bring the certificate of their primary education, two copies of their birth certificate and six copies of photos of themselves. They have to be prepared to start living at the school immediately after their admission. The girls' parents have to fill in forms and they also have also to write the name of the person who is going to fetch the girl at the end of the semester, since the girls are not allowed to travel back home alone. In 1998, parents had to pay 1,300 baht (US$34), for clothes, books, etc.[6]

I followed two girls from a Northeastern province in their plans to apply to study at the Dhammacarinii School. The girls were cousins and they had a relative who was a *mae chii* and had studied at the school. The girls' families were poor and said that studying at the Dhammacarinii School was their daughters' only chance to get further education. In January 1998, I went with the girls' aunt to visit their village. I met their families, neighbours, schoolteachers, schoolmates, and the monks at the village temple, where we stayed during our visit. The girls' schoolmates, who could afford the school fees, said that they would study at secondary school in the nearby town. Other girls said that they were going to stay at home helping their parents or trying to find a job. Some families were reluctant to send their children to schools outside the village to obtain more education. They knew that children who obtained further education were likely to find work in an occupation other than farming and would therefore probably leave the village.

Usually, information about the Dhammacarinii School spread through friends, relatives, monks and *mae chii*s at their village temple. An example of the impact that monks can have in promoting study for girls was the Dhammacarinii School in Northern Thailand where most of the students came from the same village in the Northeastern Thailand. This was thanks to a monk who was engaged in the educational situation of girls and arranged for girls in his village to study at the Dhammacarinii School in Lamphun province.

The two cousins that I followed had learnt from their aunt about the possibility of studying at the Dhammacarinii School. She had explained in detail about the school and although it was a long way from their home, she strongly suggested that her nieces should go to Ratburi Samnak Chii and apply for entrance. The *mae chii* said to me that she was worried about what would happen to her nieces if they left school after only finishing primary level. She talked about the difficult situation for girls in the village, that girls married and had children while very young. Later their husbands often left them to take care of the family themselves, which they had great difficulty managing.

The families discussed the school and the prospect of sending the girls so far from home at length. One family said that they actually needed their daughter to stay at home and work at the food stall that they had recently set up. Eventually, however, both families decided to let the girls study at the school. They said they considered schooling important also for girls and the fact that the Dhammacarinii School was a Buddhist school was important. They were reassured by the fact that the school was located at a *samnak chii* and that they appreciated the moral training there.

A few days before the first of May the girls' families rented a truck and went to Ratburi Samnak Chii. About ten people accompanied the girls to the school. It took them more than 20 hours to drive from their province in Isaan. The entrance interviews took place in the *saalaa* and started at 8 o'clock in the morning. The applicants and their families gathered on the ground floor. Three of the leading *mae chii*s carried out the interviews and collected the documents that the girls were requested to bring. The meeting took about two hours. Although Khun Mae Prathin was not among the *mae chii*s who conducted the interviews, she was present in the *saalaa* and talked with the families and answered various questions that they had about the school. People showed her respect, and bowed three times in front of her, in the same way as when they pay respect to the monks. Khun Mae Prathin conducted a ceremony and made a speech. The other leading *mae chii*s at the school also gave talks to the girls and their families. They spoke about the aims of the school and the curriculum and they also explained the rules that the girls had to follow. These were about practical things such as prohibition of using cameras and making phone calls except for urgent calls. They also spoke about the eight Buddhist precepts that both *mae chii*s and students must observe. The *mae chii*s have special additional rules to follow, stipulated by the Thai Mae Chiis' Institute (see Chapter 5) and the students observe nineteen school rules (*rabiab Dhammacarinii*). The school rules concerned daily practices and school standards, including simple politeness, keeping personal dormitory space clean, class attendance and respectful behaviour. The *dhammacarinii*s do not shave their heads, they wear school uniform – a white blouse and a grey or blue skirt – every day except for *wan phra*, the Buddhist holy day, when they wear white.

The secondary school students study at the Dhammacarinii School for two or four years. The academic education includes a common curriculum for high school students in four years (six years in formal schools) based on the requirements of the Non-formal Education Department. During the school's first eight years of existence about 200 students graduated and the school has continued to assist several hundred girls. Besides their secular education, the students also receive a religious education and more than 150 *dhammacarinii*s had by 1998 completed the three grades of Buddhist studies. *Mae chii*s who want to pursue a university education can receive financial support from the *samnak chii* and study at one of the Open Universities. Some *dhammacarinii*s decide to be ordained as *mae chii*s after completing school. However, most of the *dhammacarinii* students leave the *samnak chii* for work and/or further studies at other places. In 1998 some 20 students went to college at their own expense after completing high school at Dhammacarinii Witthayaa. Since 1999 many of the *mae chii*s and some *dhammacariniii*s have continued their higher studies at the newly established *mae chii* college, Mahapajapati Theri college.

The *mae chii*s at the *samnak chii* were either resident or visiting *mae chii*s. During their first period at the *samnak chii*, the young *mae chii*s shared a room with a longstanding *mae chii* who taught them how to behave, receive *dana*, perform alms rounds, recite Buddhist chants, etc. Later they moved in together with other young *mae chii*s and they shared a big room. The older *mae chii*s normally sleep one or two to a room in *mae chiis'* dormitories or in separate buildings. The *dhammacarinii*s live in dormitories with about 13 students to a room. The visiting *mae chii*s lived at the *samnak chii* while they studied and went back to their resident *samnak chii* or temple when they finished their education, which could take up to four years or more. The resident *mae chii*s were usually ordained at Ratburi Samnak Chii and not all of them studied even though the opportunity to study was important in their choice to seek ordination at this particular *samnak chii.*

Access to education was one important reason why Mae chii Mina became a *mae chii* at Ratburi Samnak Chii. She was born in the province, not very far from the *samnak chii* and she was ordained there when she was 25 years old and had been ordained for eight years when I met her. She recounted that after finishing primary school, she had helped her parents with work in the fields, and she cooked and took care of her five younger siblings. She would have liked to continue studying but her parents were not healthy and she said:

> I had to help them and I did not want to bother my parents with my education. Further she said: When I lived with my family I always thought of my parents, sisters and brothers first and I did not think of myself. There was no time for me to study when I was at home because there was always so much work to do. When I was 25 years I was already old and if I had not become a *mae chii* I would not have had a chance to study.

Mae chii Mina was in the first group to study at the Dhammacarinii School and she started with the compulsory Buddhist studies and attended secondary-level classes at the same time. It took her two years to complete the three grades of Buddhist studies and four years to finish secondary school. When she had finished the third grade she was appointed to teach the first grade of Buddhist studies. After finishing secondary school she continued studying at the Open University. She said: 'I do not study because I want to go outside. I study because I want to help Khun Mae to teach.'

Initially the Dhammacarinii School only offered three grades, equivalent to the first part of the secondary education in Thailand. The curriculum later expanded to cover the final three grades of the secondary education. The *mae chii*s who undertake secondary education do not follow exactly the same curriculum as the *dhammacariniis*; they begin with one year of Buddhist studies but otherwise their subjects are the same. The school follows the curriculum that the National Educational Committee has decided upon. The *dhammacariniis*' programme covers three secular grades in two years. Everyone studies six basic subjects: English, Thai, mathematics, social science, science and Buddhism. Successful completion is required for further study in colleges or universities. The girls also study vocational subjects such as typewriting, computer skills, handicrafts, dress-making, nutrition, farming and first aid to enable them to be self-reliant and to earn an honest livelihood. They also learn cooking and gardening which is both a way for the school to cut costs and a

Figure 8.2. Students at Dhammacarinii School at Ratburi Samnak Chii

way to teach these skills. The girls gain first-hand experience through working in the *mae chiis*' gardens. That is part of the instructional program and they mostly work together with the *mae chii*s at the plantations and in the kitchen. The standard academic subjects are tested twice a year by the Non-Formal Education Department of Ministry of Education. The students take all their tests outside the *mae chii* school, together with students from the schools in the district. When they have finished their education they receive a certificate from the Department of Education. The *mae chii*s also have the opportunity to study Pali at the *samnak chii* with a resident *mae chii* who is a well-regarded Pali teacher. During my stay, one *mae chii* reached the sixth level of Pali studies. She was among a group of *mae chii*s who were honoured for their achievement at the Royal temple Wat Bowonniwet in Bangkok.

As mentioned above there has always been a close connection between the *mae chii*s from the temple Wat Paknam in Bangkok and the Dhammacarinii School. *Mae chii*s from Wat Paknam have taught at the school since its opening and they still hold leading positions at the school and during the semesters live there. In recent years resident *mae chii*s, like Mae chii Mina, have also begun to teach at the school. The great demand for teachers has not been fully catered for by the *mae chii*s themselves, and lay teachers come and teach vocational subjects such as dressmaking and typewriting on a voluntary basis.

Despite the many rules that the students have to follow, they do not object to the strict regime. There are usually a few girls who feel homesick and cannot cope with being away from home and they leave the school. However, most of the girls feel at home after a while and when they have acclimatised to the life they seem confident in their role there. What struck me when I first came to the *samnak chii* was the students' extremely polite behaviour towards the teachers. Mae chii Mina said: 'We are training the *dhammacariniis* to be neat and nice. We want them to think about their behaviour and to think about their minds. To train their minds is the most important thing and we cultivate them every day. The rules are significant because they help them to cultivate their minds and their behaviour.'

Teachers in Thailand are classified into two categories, *khruu* and *acaan*. The *khruu*s have a lower position than the *acaan*s, and at the *samnak chii* the *khruu*s were often young teachers. I noticed that the *khruu*s had a closer relationship with the students who often turned to them with various problems. Also, in regular schools in Thailand the students credit teachers with an unquestioned authority. The relationship between teacher and student is one that places great emphasis on the pupil absorbing unquestioningly the knowledge that the teacher dispenses.[7] Most evaluations of teachers are based on the results of examinations; good teachers are expected to have students who pass the exams. Such an expectation leads to an emphasis on cramming for exams under the guidance of teachers. The actual teaching process serves to underscore strongly the authoritarian stance of the teacher towards the students. Pupils are expected to learn through rote memorisation and are not encouraged to ask questions (Keyes 1991: 108). The function of the teacher is not to disseminate his or her interpretation of the texts, much less to encourage students to undertake their own interpretations, but to facilitate the mastery of the knowledge contained in the texts. Lesson plans are not drawn up by teachers on their own initiative, but are provided to teachers in a standard format by educational authorities (ibid.: 112).

HIGHER EDUCATION OPENS FOR *MAE CHII*S

*Mae chii*s have not been entitled to study for Bachelor degrees at the two Buddhist universities in Thailand and there are very few opportunities for them to attain higher education. However, the Buddhist universities are not entirely closed for them: for several decades special educational programmes for *mae* *chii*s and lay people have been offered, including subjects like Pali, English, science, home economics and first aid (Tambiah 1976: 471). Most of my informants who complemented their education after finishing secondary school studied at one of the two Open Universities. Also, an additional opportunity was opened through the government university Mahidol that began to provide monks and *mae chii*s with the opportunity to study for Bachelor degrees in 1998. Private donations used as grants for monks and *mae chii*s made it possible for renunciants to study there. Already in the first year, two *mae chii*s who had finished their secondary education at Ratburi Samnak Chii applied and were accepted at Mahidol University.

Most of the efforts to facilitate opportunities for *mae chii*s to study and develop spiritually are made on individual basis. One example is the prominent *mae chii* Mae chii Sansanee Sthirasuta who is the founder and head of the Sthiradhamma Sthana religious centre and *samnak chii* located on the outskirts of Bangkok. She runs programmes for *mae chii*s with the objective of deepening their understanding of Buddhist practice and to introduce them to applications of Buddhist teaching to social and rural development. Mae chii Sansanee has also many community service projects including an alternative kindergarten and a rehabilitation home for sexually abused women and those with unwanted pregnancies. She teaches university students and other lay people meditation, trains Thai boxers in compassion and positive attitude and offers Sunday *dhamma* activities for families in the area. Her centre is also a meeting place for *mae chii*s from around the country to network and discuss ways of coping with various issues that especially affect them. She also invites *mae chii*s from all over the country who wish to study in Bangkok to live at the *samnak chii*. This is of great help since one of the great difficulties for *mae chii*s seeking higher education is finding housing in the expensive and crowded city.

The scarce opportunities for *mae chii*s to access education have led to discussions among them about opening a Buddhist university for *mae chii*s. Once, there were plans to develop the area at Ratburi Samnak Chii into a fully fledged university for *mae chii*s. They had wanted to offer the *mae chii*s both Buddhist and secular subjects in a similar vein to those now available to monks. However, the plans were never realised and Khun Mae Prathin said that there were no longer any such plans.

The *mae chii*s appreciate studying at *samnak chii*s together with other *mae chii*s. They used the word *isara,* to describe that they felt freer living and studying at the *samnak chii* than living at the temple. One young *mae chii*, who studied at the Dhammacarinii School and was ordained at a temple, related that the head monk had invited her to study together with the novices at the temple school. She said that she studied together with the male novices for a short period of time, but she felt awkward with the monks and therefore applied for entrance to the Dhamacarinii School.

Mae chii Khunying Kanitha, who had always stressed the importance of education, had long wanted to open a college for *mae chii*s. She said she went to the *mae chii*s' meeting before she was ordained and talked with them about her intention to establish a college. She had a vast network among people in influential positions and initially she tried to get the government interested in the issue of the *mae chii*s' poor educational situation. She wrote to the prime minister and asked for his help, and the issue was passed to a committee which was to look into the matter and do something to improve the *mae chii*s' situation. Later she and the head of the Thai Mae Chiis' Institute wrote to the minister of the Department of Religious Affairs and asked him to be their advisor on the committee, and he replied that he was happy to accept.

The plan of establishing a *mae chii*s' college progressed during my period in the field. The Thai Mae Chiis' Institute regularly called the *mae chii*s to meetings about the college. Mae chii Khunying Kanitha had had different suggestions about where the college should be situated. Eventually, a family donated two pieces of land in the Northeastern Thailand, Nakorn Ratchasima province, for the specific purpose of building a college for *mae chii*s. In January 1998, a *mae chii* from Ratburi Samnak Chii and I were visiting a *samnak chii* not far from the donated land. During our visit, Mae chii Khunying Kanitha arrived to see the *mae chii*s and discuss the plan of building a college in the area. Some other *mae chii*s from the province also attended the meeting. In the afternoon of 25 January the donor of the land came to the *samnak chii* and formally handed it over. The donor's family was originally from the area but had lived in Bangkok for many years. Mae chii Khunying Kanitha told me that the man had studied at Thammasat University and had been a student of her husband, Acaan Adul Wichiencharoen.

Over the following months, the Thai Mae Chiis' Institute arranged several meetings on details about the college and the main question was whether the Institute should accept the donated land in Nakorn Ratchasima or not. Some of the *mae chii*s were hesitant about the location because it was in a remote area. If they accepted the land, they would be obliged to fulfil the donor's wish to establish a college, and that would require a lot of work with raising money and finding teachers who wanted to live there. At the end of February, a two-day meeting was held at Ratburi Samnak Chii. The items on the agenda were the *mae chiis'* college and the proposed *Mae Chiis'* Bill (see the next chapter). About 60 *mae chii*s participated in the meeting and 30 provinces were represented. The Sathaaban Mae Chii Thai was represented by its leading *mae chii*s, and a *mae chii* who had had a professional career at the Ministry of Education was also present. The *mae chii*s were divided into smaller working groups. Later, representatives from every small group presented what they had concluded to the large assembly and the issues were discussed thoroughly. The meeting did not arrive at any final decision about the donated land. However, they decided that representatives from the Thai Mae Chiis' Institute should travel to Nakorn Ratchasima and inspect the site.

Three weeks later, on 14 March, a meeting was held in the temple Wat Chana Songkhram in Bangkok. I went to the meeting together with Khun Mae Prathin and some of the other *mae chii*s from Ratburi Samnak Chii. The meeting was well attended with about 35 *mae chii*s present. Most of the participants had been to the previous meeting at Ratburi Samnak Chii. Representatives from the Thai Mae Chiis' Institute had inspected the land and reported that they found it suitable for the college and said that it was not as far away as they had anticipated. The atmosphere at the meeting was positive and the discussions seemed to be constructive. However, still no decision was made. On 7 April, the Thai Mae Chiis' Institute's annual meeting was held in Bangkok. It was a three-day meeting with 348 *mae chii*s from the whole country participating. The day before the annual meeting, *mae chii*s gathered at Wat Bowonniwet to discuss the college. Mae chii Khunying Kanitha was in hospital for treatment and could not attend the meeting, nor was I present. One of my informants who attended the meeting told me that some *mae chii*s had once again questioned the likelihood of being able to raise funds for the college. Since Mae chii Khunying Kanitha was not present, another *mae chii* who strongly approved of the college talked at length about the advantage of accepting the land. The *mae chii*s continued to discuss the college and the meeting arranged at Wat Bowonniwet on 3 May 1998 was crucial for the college project. Forty *mae chii*s met at the temple and they finally decided to accept the land. The leader of the provincial district (*amphoe*) was present at the meeting and he personally donated 20,000 baht to the college. This was exactly the amount the *mae chii*s had to pay to the district for receiving the land. The next issue on the agenda was to give the college a name. The *mae chii*s had different suggestions and they decided to vote. The name that won most votes was Mahapajapati Theri College. Mahapajapati was the Buddha's aunt, foster mother and the first woman to receive ordination as a female Buddhist monk (*bhikkhuni*) (see Chapter 2). *Theri* is a Pali term of

Figure 8.3. The meeting on the 22–23 February 1998, at Ratburi Nunnery

respect used for female ascetics who have either spent many years in the *sangha* or have achieved eminence in wisdom and learning and in spiritual attainment (Ling 1981: 182–183).

Since opening a private college was associated with large costs the *mae chii*s decided to propose that one of the Buddhist Universities, Mahamakut Buddhist University, authorise the *mae chii*s' college. The proposal was adopted by the Mahamakut Buddhist university in November 1998. The college started as a pilot project in May 1999, at the premises of the Association for the Promotion of the Status of Women on the outskirts of Bangkok, the place founded by Mae chii Khunying Kanitha. The *mae chii*s moved it to its permanent site in Nakorn Ratchasima in May 2002. In the first year, 11 *mae chii*s and four lay women studied at the college and they have since accepted about 30 new students every year. In 2005 there were 66 students studying at the college and 35 students have graduated with Bachelor's degree. Since there were not many *mae chii*s qualified to teach, the *mae chii*s who studied were encouraged to prepare themselves to become teachers in the future. The teachers come from the two monks' universities, Mahamakut Buddhist University and Mahachulalongkorn Buddhist University, and from other universities in Bangkok and in Nakhorn Ratchasima province.

Figure 8.4. The *saalaa* at Mahapajapati Theri College, the first *mae chiis'* college in Thailand

The college offers a Bachelor of Arts degree in Buddhism and Philosophy. The Mahamakut Buddhist University is responsible for the curriculum and the president of the *mae chiis'* college is a monk from the Mahamakut Buddhist University. The students at the college study subjects such as the three levels of Buddhism taught at Thai Buddhist universities and temples, Buddhist philosophy and psychology, basics of Pali, mathematics, law, computer skills and English. The college has a socially engaged profile and in their fourth and final year the students teach basic English, mathematics and Buddhism in the local schools in the vicinity of the college.

EDUCATIONAL EXCLUSION – AN OBSTACLE FOR FEMALE ASCETICS

Martha C. Nussbaum (1999) states that nothing is more important to women's life chances than education. That statement, I would say, is true for ascetics as well as for lay women. Research on female ascetics in Asia has shown that difficulties for women to access education are a common feature (see for example: Lekshe Tsomo 1988, 2000; Havnevik 1990; Bartholomeuz 1994; Jaschok and Jingjun 2000; Vallely 2002 and Gutshow 2004). Like the *mae chiis* in Thailand, female ascetics in other countries try to organize education or find

223

Figure 8.5. A *kuti* at Mahapajapati Theri College

ways to educate themselves. Hanna Havnevik relates that monks and lamas in Tibet felt that the reason why they so seldom taught female ascetics was because they were afraid of breaking their vows. Another factor mentioned was that 'nunneries' were unimportant religious institutions and teaching there did not offer much prestige (Havnevik 1990: 119). To meet the growing need among the Tibetan female ascetics there have been attempts to increase the teaching in the 'nunneries'. However, like the situation in other Buddhist countries, the teaching for female ascetics is not as well organized and systematized as that for monks (ibid.: 197). Kim Gutshow notes that the perception in Zangskar is that sending a daughter to the 'nunnery' is something like placing her in an impoverished public university. She may have access to knowledge and peers, which take her far beyond the village life, but she or her parents must pay her way. In contrast, sending a son to the monastery will give him a highly valued monastic education that will secure a comfortable livelihood in cash and kind as well as ample opportunities for privilege and private profit (Gutshow 2000: 112).

Excluding female ascetics from education blocks their way of becoming knowledgeable ordained persons. For both male and female Buddhists, the Buddha is the ultimate paradigm for all constructive modes of human action. It is said that once the Buddha had undergone the sequence of renunciations that enabled his breakthrough to full enlightenment, he had nothing left to give except the *dhamma*, the Buddhist teachings, which are, however, considered the best of offerings. Giving *dhamma* is regarded as a special kind of offering (*dana*) that is considered to go beyond the offering of material goods (*Dhammapada*, verse 354). Participation in acts of giving and receiving is important in monks' and *mae chiis'* religious practice. Giving is considered to be the most effective form of making merit. For the laity, that generally means giving food and other supplies to members of the *sangha* (*amisadana*). For the *sangha*, it may mean the giving of *dhamma* (*dhammadana*) to the laity in the form of sermons, sutra recitations or spiritual advice. However, the gender-based division of education and meditation, in which education is associated with monks and meditation with *mae chiis*, has prevented *mae chiis* from possessing the most prestigious *dana* (*dhammadana*): the *mae chiis* been silenced in that respect.

Teaching Buddhism requires education and monks who have studied Buddhism can deliver speeches. However, the discipline of meditation is needed to reach an understanding of *dhamma* and to acquire wisdom. There are therefore *mae chiis* who have attained profound knowledge by practising meditation and there are also *mae chiis* who have Buddhist knowledge and give Buddhist speeches, but most *mae chiis* have not pursued formal Buddhist studies and have no training in giving *dhamma* talks. In recent times, *mae chiis* have been expected to teach Buddhism; and the more specialised study of the scriptures, which was previously regarded as unnecessary for *mae chiis*, has become essential. Education is associated with a social division of knowledge and contributes to the structuring of the realm of social relations and the relation between the lay and ordained communities. Education legitimates the *mae chiis'* ordained position and is also crucial for the religious practice of fulfilling their vocation towards others. Gaining an unambiguous legal position as renunciants has also been an important issue for *mae chiis* and this is the focus of the next chapter.

NOTES

1   The Thai word *thudong* is derived from the Pali term *dhutanga*, meaning austere practices, of which there are 13 mentioned at various points throughout the *Sutta-pitika* (see Bhikkhu Khantipalo 1965: 10). *Thudong* is, however, most commonly used to refer to those monks who leave the monastery and go on foot to visit the various Buddhist shrines that are scattered throughout the country (see Bunnag 1973: 54).

2   The transliteration system used in Thailand was devised by Somdej Krom Phra Wachirawaan Worarot who was the head of the Thammayut Order during the reign of King Rama V.

3   Thammayut (Thai) is one of the two official sects of Theravada Buddhism in Thailand (see Chapter 6).

4   This *mae chii* referred to the Buddhist subjects by using the 'monks'' terms.

5   The reason that the exam is called 'the Pali exam at Sanaam Luang' is that in the past it was patronised by the king and the exam was conducted in the 'royal field'. The candidate being tested for level nine had to sit in the middle of the testing area facing the examiners and answer the questions; the king would also be present, supervising the examination.

6   A financial crisis hit Thailand in 1997. The value of the Thai baht dropped from about 25 baht to 1 US$ to 38 to 1 in May 1998.

7   This relationship is epitomised in the 'saluting of the teacher' (*wai khruu*). In this ceremony the students symbolically demonstrate their deference to and dependence upon the teacher. According to the custom, teachers can not begin sharing their knowledge until this ceremony has been completed (Keyes 1991: 108).

CHAPTER NINE

Struggles for Legal Recognition

In Thailand, female ascetics (*mae chii*s and *bhiksunis/bhikkhunis*) have created their own religious spaces outside the formal religious structure. Despite the long tradition of *mae chii*s in Thailand, they have not succeeded in achieving formal recognition as religious persons. The Theravada female monks (*bhikkhunis*), who are new in the Thai religious field, have not been formally recognised in their religious role either. These two categories of female ascetics have chosen different ways to deal with the subordinate position that women occupy in the religious field. This chapter focuses on efforts and strategies that female renunciants employ in order to achieve formal legitimation as religious persons. Most of the *mae chii*s that I interviewed had adopted the general opinion that the *bhikkhuni* order was broken and could not be restored. Moreover, the *mae chii*s did not aspire to be part of the *sangha*. This perspective contrasts with those who advocate a *bhikkhuni* order and embrace another widespread notion, holding that the *bhikkhuni* order survived through the *bhiksunis* in China and could therefore continue in the Theravada tradition. The *bhikkhunis* also consider that they have a right to be part of the *sangha*.

As already mentioned in Chapter 2, the *bhikkhuni* order has recently been revived in Sri Lanka and is today the only Theravada country to recognise the female order. The *bhikkhunis* in Thailand aspire to be part of the Thai *sangha*. However, up to now there is no sign that the *bhikkhunis* will be admitted into the Thai Buddhist *sangha*. In Thailand, the *bhikkhuni* issue was not much debated during the period I carried out fieldwork. However, *bhikkhuni* ordination was a theme that I frequently brought up and discussed with the *mae chii*s. A majority of the interviewed *mae chii*s said that they were not interested in receiving *bhikkhuni* ordination. They admired and were inspired by the *bhikkhunis* of ancient times; however, they thought that contemporary *bhikkhuni* ordination would violate the scriptures that say that the *bhikkhuni* order has died out and cannot be reestablished. Most of the *mae chii*s wanted to achieve legal recognition in their capacity as *mae chii*s. In 1998, there was still no Thai woman who had received dual *bhikkhuni* ordination, and women who aspired to receive full ordination had to obtain it from the Mahayana order. During the 1990s some Thai researchers brought up the issue of *bhikkhuni* ordination, but it was not until February 2001, when Acaan Chatsumarn became the first Thai Theravada novice *bhikkhuni,* that *bhikkhuni* ordination became a publicly debated issue in Thailand.

CONTROVERSY OVER A MAE CHIIS' LAW

The *mae chii*s are not fighting to become part of the *sangha,* but they have been struggling for legal recognition as ordained persons. Their ambiguous position between the lay and the religious realms, between the laity and the monks, appears in some respects to be obstructive to their religious vocation.[1] Also, their unclear legal standing is reinforced in Thai law, which does not mention the category of *mae chii* at all. Consequently, the *mae chii*s do not officially exist as a specific legal category. Changing this inequity between monks and *mae chii*s occupied Mae chii Khunying Kanitha ever since she became a *mae chii* in 1993. She had been lobbying for a Mae Chiis' Bill, which would give them legal status and entitle them to financial assistance from the government. However, all *mae chii*s were not convinced that creating a special law would be something positive for them. Over the years, voices had been raised in concern about the risk of power falling into the wrong hands. Opponents referred to problems with the monks' law of 1962, on which the Mae Chiis' Bill was originally modelled. The centralised structure of the *mae chii*s, which was suggested in the proposed bill, has been criticised as being unsuitable for the complex and rapid changes of the modern world (Ekachai 1996).

Some of the controversial issues in the first version of the draft of the Mae Chiis' Bill were compiled by Sanitsuda Ekachai:

*Mae chii*s to be legally recognised as Buddhist clerics, replacing the extinct *bhikkhuni*s.

The government to finance the *mae chii* clergy.

Abbesses to have absolute authority in running *samnak chii*s.

Fund-raising projects must be approved by provincial heads.

*Samnak chii*s must report annually to their governing body and the Religious Affairs Department of the Ministry of Education.

All *mae chii*s' must have and carry identification cards.

The *mae chiis'* governing body would have absolute power to:

Set rules and determine proper dress codes;

Punish impostors and disrobe dissident members;

Elect executive committee members;

Appoint abbesses, and provincial and regional heads.

Own and manage *samnak chii*s not registered as foundations or already supervised by temples.

Approve new *samnak chii*s. (Ekachai 1996)

The 1962 Monks' Bill was imposed on the monks' *sangha* by the military strongman Marshal Sarit Thanarat. That bill centralised the clergy's hierarchical and feudal administration, and entrusted absolute power to the Ecclesiastic Council (ibid.). The Monks' Bill is criticised for violating the democratic principles that were laid down in the Buddhist canonical scripts. For example, the bill overrules the ancient right according to the *vinaya* that any group of five or more monks is free to operate as an independent monk community (ibid.). Like the Monks' Bill, the *mae chiis'* legislation would create an all-powerful governing body with the absolute authority to appoint and defrock members, and to allocate budgets (ibid.). Professor Prawase Wasi has criticised the *mae chiis'* draft bill, saying that he believes that *mae chiis* would lose the potential that comes with their freedom if they are governed by a tight bureaucracy as monks are. Instead of building chains around themselves, he suggests that the *mae chiis* should empower themselves through networking (ibid.).

A monk's view of the Mae Chiis' Bill

The interest that some monks have taken in the process of establishing a *mae chii* law led me to the outspoken American monk Phra Santikaro Bhikkhu. In 1997, he had lived for 17 years in Thailand and been a monk for 12 years.[2] He is a disciple of Buddhadasa Bhikkhu and has played an active role in INEB, the International Network of Engaged Buddhists. Phra Santikaro was frequently invited to speak at Mae chii Sansanee's centre in Bangkok and I met him on some of these occasions. In an interview that I conducted with him, he said that he had taken an interest in the *mae chiis'* situation and in the proposed Mae Chiis' Bill because he found their situation to be unjust. He referred to his many friends who were Catholic and Buddhist female ascetics and he said he was tired of seeing how the female ascetics subordinated themselves to monks. He stated that the female ascetics were as capable as monks and that they practise as hard as monks, or even harder. He found no reason for the subordinating treatment of the *mae chii*s. He said: 'There is a lack of direction among monks. Usually I do not like competition, but I think that if the monks could have some competition from *mae chii*s it would be very good for the monks.'[3]

Phra Santikaro added that he was tired of the corrupt society and the dictatorial organisation of the *sangha*. He considered the Monks' Bill to be bad in many respects and he was also very critical of the draft Mae Chiis' Bill that Mae chii Khunying Kanitha was responsible for. He had gone through the Mae Chiis' Bill carefully together with a friend who had studied the Monks' Bill in detail. They had come to the conclusion that the proposed Mae Chiis' Bill was even worse than the Monks' Bill. Phra Santikaro said that he had not really talked with the *mae chii*s about his views. He explained that *mae chii*s had turned to some monks who were his friends and asked them for advice about the bill. They had asked the monks for help since they did not know how they should handle the draft bill. They felt that Mae chii Khunying Kanitha had simply presented the proposal and would not listen to any critical voices.

Phra Santikaro was invited together with two other monks to the eighth Mae Chiis' Bill's meeting, held on the 2–3 September 1996 at Mae chii Sansanee's centre in Bangkok. Just before he went to the meeting, he studied a book about Buddhist mediation written by John McConnell.[4] He said he found the book interesting, and relevant for conflict resolution. When the *mae chii*s asked Phra Santikaro for his opinion of the bill, he answered that they did not need a bill at all and he advised them to discuss what they really wanted. At the meeting, he suggested that they should form groups and start discussing the content of the bill. Phra Santikaro saw his initiative as a way of letting every *mae chii* voice be heard and at the time of this interview, almost one year after the meeting, the *mae chii*s were still discussing the bill.

Not every *mae chii* was against the draft Mae Chiis' Bill. Some had reacted to the way Mae chii Khunying Kanitha presented the bill. Phra Santikaro's opinion was that everything had gone too fast and the *mae chii*s did not understand the process. Mae chii Khunying Kanitha was the only one who was a lawyer and he said that she should have explained to the *mae chii*s how the process runs so they would have a chance to understand. Therefore, one of the leading *mae chii*s invited an MP to one of the meetings, who then explained the legal process. Mae chii Khunying Kanitha had not attended any of the *mae chii*s' meetings after the eighth gathering, when the *mae chii*s formed the discussion groups. Phra Santikaro said that he was personally against the bill because it would not help the *mae chii*s. He said that Mae chii Khunying Kanitha would like the government to sponsor the *mae chii*s financially but in his opinion the government money was not needed. He feared that the government would use the bill against the *mae chii*s. He said: 'There is a lot of corruption. The government people come with a proposal that you sign a check of 100,000 and they give you 70,000. That is the way it is. It is corrupt.' And he claimed: 'If the *mae chii*s practise the *dhamma* and have good relationships with the monasteries, they will survive. Look at the monasteries, they do not benefit from their bill. Look at the education system for monks. Many of them are only studying for their degree, not for knowledge.' [5]

Agreement on the Mae Chiis' Bill

I had followed Mae chii Khunying Kanitha's work with the Mae Chiis' Bill since 1996, and saw her sadness and disappointment when she was, as she saw it, misjudged and overruled by the monks and *mae chii*s at the eighth Mae Chiis' Bill's meeting in September 1996. It took almost one and a half years until she again participated in the Mae Chiis' Bill's meetings. That meeting was on 22–23 February 1998, and it was held at Ratburi Samnak Chii. The meeting had two items on the agenda: the Mae Chiis' Bill and the *mae chii*s' college (see Chapter 8). Mae chii Sansanee, who arranged the eighth meeting, was invited but not present; no monks were invited to this meeting. It opened in the same manner as all *mae chii*s' meetings, by lighting candles and incense at the Buddha shrine followed by taking refuge in the triple gem, the Buddha, the Dhamma and the Sangha. Mae chii Khunying Kanitha was appointed president of the meeting. The *mae chii*s discussed freely at the meeting. Various problems were reported about communicating the bill to the *mae chii*s all over the country. Every head *mae chii* had been assigned to explain the law but difficulties were recounted concerning the ability of uneducated *mae chii*s of fully comprehending the law. A young, well-educated *mae chii* who lived in Bangkok but who was originally from the Northeast, reported that the *mae chii*s in her area in Isaan devoted most of their time to meditation and did not know anything about the draft law. The meeting discussed the differences between the central parts of Thailand and the other regions.

The *mae chii*s at the meeting formed themselves into working groups which outlined the formulation of the law. The content of the law consisted of a definition of the category *mae chii;* they were particular about distinguishing *mae chii*s from *bhikkhuni*s. Further, the precepts, the *mae chii*s' dress, residence, administration and hierarchical organisation, education, punishment for law violations etc. were dealt with in the bill. The *mae chii*s kept minutes throughout the meeting. The sentiments of willingness to co-operate and to complete the protracted process with the bill permeated the meeting. The outcome of the meeting was a draft for a proposed *mae chiis'* law, which was presented at the annual meeting of the Thai Mae Chiis' Institute at Wat Bowonniwet on 7–9 April 1998.

The annual meetings are open to all *mae chii*s, even for those who are not members of the Institute, and in 1998 the meeting had 348 registered participants. Those who participated in the meeting came from almost all the provinces in Thailand. Every province's head *mae chii* was given the opportunity to report from her district. The annual meeting is the forum for important issues that concern all *mae chii*s. Princess Somsavali attended the meeting, representing the Queen, who is the patron of the Thai Mae Chiis' Institute. The presence of royalty is important for the Thai Mae Chiis' Institute and it attracts many lay donors. At the event, the princess gave white fans to the *mae chii*s who had received high grades in Pali studies, and she also handed over a special brooch to lay people who had donated money to the Institute. A photographer took pictures of everyone receiving gifts from the princess's hand. Later the same day people were able to purchase the photographs. Thirteen monks were also present during the princess's visit. The monks performed a chanting ceremony and received *dana* from the princess. A female MP, Khun Laddawan Wongsinwong talked at length about the importance of education and of achieving legal status for the *mae chii*s.

The Mae Chiis' Bill had been on the agenda of the previous year s annual meeting and this year, the draft of the law was read out loud by the 82-year-old and highly venerated monk Luang Phôô who founded the Thai Mae Chiis Institute. After listening to Luang Phôô, the *mae chii*s formed eight groups according to the region of Thailand from which they came. The groups discussed the law in detail, and every group appointed one person to be a *wittiyakhon* (a critic). Two scholar monks from the monks' universities were invited by the *mae chii*s to assist them if necessary. After discussions and changes of formulations in the draft, the *mae chii*s agreed and finally the Mae Chiis' Bill was passed at the 1998 annual meeting.

Mae chii Khunying Kanitha and the Mae Chiis' Bill

In June 1998, I interviewed Mae chii Khunying Kanitha about the process of making a law for the *mae chii*s. This was almost one year after the interview with Phra Santikaro, after several more Mae Chiis' Bill's meetings and after the *mae chii*s had agreed to send the proposed bill to the Department of Religious

Figure 9.1. *Mae chii*s working on the *mae chii*s' bill at the Thai Nuns' Institute's annual meeting 1998

Affairs at the Ministry of Education. Mae chii Khunying Kanitha recalled her initial intention for the law and the numerous meetings that had taken place before a final draft was sent to the authorities. She said that the object of the law was to support the *mae chii*s and to have them recognised as religious persons in Buddhism, just as the monks and novices are recognised. She explained that the *mae chii*s have the Thai Mae Chiis' Institute, but they cannot be forced to become members of the Institute. Consequently, the rules that the Institute have set up are not compulsory. If there was a *mae chii* law, every *mae chii* would have to obey it. For example, every *mae chii* would have to live in a *samnak chii*. Mae chii Khunying Kanitha said:

> Look at me, I would be illegal. I told the *mae chii*s that you cannot force me to get a licence [ID card], I can stay at home if I want. We should be a *sangha*, we should help each other. We are not only living for ourselves. You help yourself and at the same time you help others. The law will unite the *mae chii*s.

Mae chii Khunying Kanitha explained that up till now the word '*mae chii*' had not been mentioned in any law, not in the civil law and not in the monks' law.

She said that there had not been a word about *mae chii* for hundreds of years, but since Rattanakosin (the era inaugurated by the Chakri dynasty in 1782), Ayutthaya and Sukhothai, the *mae chii*s have always been there in white with shaved heads. She added that despite their lack of legal recognition, they were respected if they behaved well.

The *mae chii*s are scattered around the country and Mae chii Khunying Kanitha said that they need to know exactly how many *mae chii*s there are in the country, where they are and what they need. All the *samnak chii*s should then be registered at the Department of Religious Affairs. The law would make the status of the *mae chii*s clearer. Further, she said that there will be one unit, and every year there would be a national assembly. Each *samnak* would send representatives to attend the meetings. Today about half of the *samnak chii*s in Thailand are members. Mae chii Khunying Kanitha said:

> When we have the law, the *mae chii*s will be under one order, one *Khana Mae Chii Thai. Sathaaban Mae Chii Thai* will be a legal entity like the central government of the *mae chii*s. We will have this law to protect the *mae chii*s and to support the *mae chii*s and to clarify that *mae chii*s are religious members of Buddhism. The way we have proposed the law will give the power to Sathaaban Mae Chii Thai. They have the right to establish rules and things like that.

According to the draft *mae chii*s' law, they must be ordained with an *upachaa* (preceptor) in Thailand, or with a monk who lives abroad. However, the monk must be appointed by the ecclesiastical assembly to be the *upachaa*. Mae chii Khunying Kanitha explained that a proper preceptor is important since it makes the ordination sacred and the monks would not accept the *mae chii*s if they were not correctly ordained. Women who have become *mae chii*s before the *mae chii*s' law was introduced do not have to be ordained again; they can join under the *mae chii*s' law.

The identity cards called *sutiban/bai sutthi* that the Thai Mae Chiis' Institute issues are certificates for the *mae chii*s who are registered with the Institute; the Department of Religious Affairs is the registrar and the district office issues the identity cards. A *mae chii* belongs to the area in which she was born. Of course, to acquire an identity card, the *mae chii*s must know the Thai Mae Chiis' Institute's regulations and the *mae chii*s' rules of conduct. The government would have to provide a budget to support their education and their public activities.

Before Mae chii Khunying Kanitha was ordained she participated in one of the *mae chiis'* meetings and informed them that she planned to become a *mae chii* and that she wanted to do something to help the *mae chiis*. She said:

> When Chuan Lekpai became Prime Minister, I wrote to him and asked him to do something for the *mae chiis*. He asked his secretary to write to the Department of Religious Affairs and to the Ministry of Education and told them to look into the situation of the *mae chiis*. I continued writing letters and they changed government three times, and each time I wrote to the Minister. The first time I wrote alone, but then I asked Khun Mae Lampai, head of The Thai Mae Chiis' Institute to sign it together with me [extract].

Mae chii Khunying Kanitha made the draft for the law in 1996. Even though she had proposed the law and lobbied for it, it was actually made on request from the Department of Religious Affairs which had set up a committee for the purpose of investigating the status of the *mae chiis*. At their first meeting they suggested asking the Supreme Patriarch, *Sangharaat,* to let the '*mae chiis*' order' emanate from him without drawing up a special law for them, but some of the committee members were against this suggestion and adhered to the idea of a law. The department decided to propose a short draft for a Mae Chiis' Bill. Mae chii Khunying Kanitha agreed to write the draft in 1996 and she presented it to the *mae chiis* at The Thai Mae Chiis' Institute's annual meeting the same year. The *mae chiis* accepted the draft when it was presented in 1996 and they met seven times and worked with the contents of the draft. Mae chii Khunying Kanitha said:

> The eighth meeting was at Mae chii Sansanee's place. I do not know who invited the monk Santikaro and the other two monks. These monks told us that the monks got stuck because of the monks' law and they questioned whether the *mae chiis* really needed a law. They said the *mae chiis* did not need a law to be recognised. They said, 'Look at Mae chii Sansanee, you can do as she does.' Mae chii Sansanee has a very nice place, she has money and people accept her. How could every *mae chii* possibly do as she does? Her situation is unique!

It took several years until the Department of Religious Affairs dealt with the proposed Mae Chiis' Bill. Mae chii Khunying Kanitha reminded them regularly. However, the process with the irregularities at Wat Phra Dhammakaya kept the authorities busy. Legal recognition of the *mae chiis* as religious persons would certainly make their position less ambiguous. However, the Thai Mae Chiis' Institute was not challenging the *sangha* authorities and the recognition of *mae chii*s was not going to change their position in relation to the monks. Formal recognition as ordained persons would grant the *mae chii*s increased access to education and greater financial security through the benefits ordained communities receive from the Thai government. However, in March 2003 the Department of Religious Affairs rejected the proposed Mae Chiis' Bill, implying that the *mae chii*s have not yet gained legal recognition and that their position continues to be ambigous. My informants had the impression that the Department of Religious Affairs was unsure of what implications the Mae Chiis' Bill would have. A long time had passed since they submitted the proposed Mae Chiis' Bill and there was no longer any constant pressure from the *mae chii*s on the Department of Religious Affairs to deal with it. At the time of the decision Mae Chii Khunying Kanitha was dead. She had been the one who had had the influential contacts at the department. The *bhikkhuni* issue was under debate at the same time, and my infortants said that the department probably got 'cold feet' and decided to reject the Mae Chiis' Bill. The Department of Religious Affairs told the *mae chii*s to discuss the matter with the *sangha*. To my understanding it would, from a doctrinal perspective, be easier for the Department of Religious Affairs to legitimate the *bhikkhuni*s than the *mae chii*s who have created a new category that falls outside the traditional Buddhist categories of the four groups of lay and ordained persons, *bhikkhuni, bhikkhu, upasaka* and *upasika*. It would be hard to justify an admission of a 'new' submissive category of ascetic women and at the same time reject the traditional *bhikkhuni* order.

THAI WOMEN IN THE *BHIKKHUNI* MOVEMENT

The objective of establishing the *bhikkhuni* order in Thailand might well be conceived as the most obvious way to tackle the inequity in Thai Buddhism. That would be a doctrinal answer to the quest for religious rights and a traditional one in that the *bhikkhuni* order is integral to Buddhism as established by the Buddha. However, the *bhikkhuni* order was apprehended as alien by most of my informants and generally they preferred the idea of reforming the institution of *mae chii*. The striving for establishment of a *bhikkhuni* order would certainly be more threatening to the Buddhist monkhood, since the *bhikkhuni* would demand entrance into the *sangha*. On the other hand, an augmentation of the laicisation of Buddhism that legal recognition of *mae chii*s could represent would similarly be threatening to the *sangha* since that would blur the boundaries between the lay and the ordained realms and this would also weaken the *sangha*'s exclusive authority. The boundary between the two domains, ordained and lay, would perhaps be better maintained if the *sangha* was open for *bhikkhuni*. However, in that case the category of *mae chii* would probably be even more marginalised.

In 1998 there were only four *bhiksuni*s in Thailand. They had received ordination from Mahayana monks abroad and none of them was recognised by the Thai *sangha*. Acaan Chatsumarn had not yet received her *samaneri* ordination and at that time, a dual *bhikkhuni* ordination had never taken place in Thailand.

Over the centuries, the Thai *sangha* has strongly guarded itself from the entry of females. An oft-cited example are the two sisters Sara and Chongdee, who received novice ordination on 28 April, 1928. They were the daughters of Pra Panom Saranarin, a critic of Thai society, who protested against the unfairness of keeping women out of the Buddhist monkhood. Sara and Chondee refused to give up their robes and were arrested. Sara was jailed for eight days and Chongdee for four. After their release, they continued to wear robes and they travelled to different provinces. Sara remained an ordained person for eight years: a *mae chii* for two years, a *samaneri* for four, and a *bhikkhuni* for two years (Kabilsingh 1991: 45–48).[6] That incident inspired the *sangha*'s supreme council to pass an order forbidding any monks to give women novice status or full ordination as monks. The rule was implemented in 1928 and there has been no sign that the Thai *sangha* is likely to annul it.

The first Thai bhikkhuni

Acaan Chatsumarn, now Dhammananda Bhikkhuni, is well known for advocating women's rights to full ordination. She has a vast international network and in 1987, she, together with three *bhiksuni*s, founded the Sakyadhita International Network of Buddhist Women. The female monks were Karma Lekshe Tsomo, Jampa Tsedroen, and Ayya Khema. The first conference on Buddhist female asectics was held in Bodh Gaya in India. Although there have been some councils since the death of the Buddha, this was the first recorded conference on Buddhist women (Tsedroen 1988: 44–52).

Before her ordination, Acaan Chatsumarn had been successful in her profession as professor at one of the leading universities in Thailand. She travelled around the world, but she said that she felt that personal glory or success had lost their value and she wanted to devote her time to Buddhism. However, sickness was one important reason why she made up her mind about seeking ordination. A year prior to her ordination she began suffering from positional vertigo and became severely ill. When she recovered, she decided not to postpone her ordination any longer. Originally, she had planned to seek ordination after her retirement, but she was afraid she would be too old if she waited. Therefore, she sought early retirement from the university in 2000 and she also resigned from Thai television where she had been working with Buddhist programmes for many years (Achakulwisut 2001; *Yasodhara* 2001b: 17). One of the first things she did before the ordination was to file for a divorce. She said: 'My husband had known before we were married that I would follow the Buddha's way one day. Now that my children have grown up and settled down well, my job is done. I have no concern left' (Achakulwisut 2001). In April 2000 she went to Taiwan and received the lay *bodhisattva* precepts as a way to train her mind. Soon afterwards she became a vegetarian. On the first full moon night of the first month of 2001, she received the eight precepts. The day before the next full moon, the day before the Buddhist holy Makha Bucha Day, which occurred on 6 February, she had her head shaved and received novice ordination (ibid.).

Acaan Chatsumarn's novice ordination follows a spiritual heritage from one generation to the next. Her mother, Voramai Kabilsingh was the first fully ordained female monk in Thailand who had received ordination from both the male and the female *sangha*. She was first a *mae chii* for many years and in 1971 she received *bhiksuni* ordination in Taiwan in the Dharmagupta lineage.[7] Acaan Chatsumarn's grandmother, Mae chii Somcheen, Voramai Kabilsingh's mother, was also a Buddhist renunciant. Mae chii Somcheen was descended from Vientiane in Laos. She was widowed with five daughters to take care of when she was only 36. When her daughters were grown up she received *mae chii* ordination and later became the chief *mae chii* at Ganikaphala Temple in central Bangkok (*Yasodhara* 2001a: 5).

The most difficult question for Acaan Chatsumarn was in which tradition she should ask for ordination. She said: 'Ordination was not just for myself; I wanted to be accepted in this country where female ordination has not been accepted for 700 years' (*Yasodhara* 2001b: 17). She considered the Chinese tradition, in which her mother was ordained. However, she said she had learned from her mother's example, who, despite being ordained for several decades and having many supporters, did not have any followers. Acaan Chatsumarn considered the possibility of becoming ordained in the Tibetan lineage with which she had close connection. However, they have only novice ordination with maroon robes and if she were to receive full ordination after two years, she would have to change robes and go to another tradition, which might look strange to the lay people. She looked closely into ordination in Sri Lanka, but at first she thought that it was wrong that the Sri Lankan *bhikkhuni*s started ordaining others when they had only three years standing instead of the 12 years required by the scriptures. Then she read an interview given by the local Sri Lankan monk who was organising ordination, and he said that the Buddha gave permission to alter minor rules, 'If the Sangha so desires'. The Sri Lankan *sangha* granted permission for the *dasa sila mata*s (ten-precept female ascetics) who had 40 years experience as renunciants, but only three years as *bhikkhunis*, to ordain others. This explanation satisfied Acaan Chatsumarn, and she decided to seek novice ordination in Sri Lanka (Achakulwisut 2001).

In February 2003, Dhammananda Samaneri had completed her two years as a novitiate and on 28 of February she received full ordination in Sri Lanka together with three other *samaneri*s, one American and two Burmese. The novice ordination of Acaan Chatsumarn, which was performed in 2001, was recognised by *bhikkhuni*s and five senior male monks from Siyamnikaya, which is a lineage from Ayutthaya, Thailand, and the dominant sect in Sri Lanka. Siamnikaya is the lineage that actually reinstated the Bhikkhu *sangha* in Sri Lanka after it had been wiped out by a Hindu king. Acaan Chatsumarn's higher ordination in 2003 was conducted by 12 senior *bhikkhu*s, and ten senior *bhikkhuni*s. However, the Thai *sangha* persists in not recognising her ordination and her status as a Theravada *bhikkhuni*. Currently Dhammananda Bhikkhuni is the only Thai *bhikkhuni* with higher ordination. There were six novice female monks, *samaneri bhikkhuni*s, and a handful of *bhiksuni*s in Thailand in October 2004 who had received ordination from Mahayana male and female monks abroad.

REACTIONS TO THE THAI WOMEN'S ORDINATION

Initially, there were several attempts to silence Dhammananda Bhikkhuni's ordination which was publicly critized in the press; even her TV interviews were banned. The Thai Journalist Association protested against the cancellations of the programmes, referring to the violation of Thailand's 1997 constitution which guarantees freedom of speech and freedom to practice the religion of one's choice, and the ban was eventually lifted. Additionally, the Religious affairs officials issued threats that her temple would be at risk if it was not properly registered or if they were to find anything unclear in the temple's financial accounts (Ekachai 2001a).

Manas Pharkphoom, director of the Office of the Secretariat of the Sangha Supreme Council, said in an interview that they do not prevent women from

Figure 9.2. Dhammananda Bhikkhuni

receiving ordination in Sri Lanka, but they would not be recognised by the Thai *sangha* as *bhikkhuni*s (Janssen 2001). Phra Dhepidilok, vice-abbot of the leading royal temple Wat Bowonniwet, was quoted in the Thai newspaper *Matichon* saying 'What Dhammananda, or Chatsumarn, is doing is not a way out. She only wants to take revenge for her mother. In her day, her mother also caused a lot of trouble for religion. ... If Chatsumarn had any knowledge of *dhamma* practice and spiritual liberation, she would have known that ordination is unnecessary. Everyone is equal in practising *dhamma*. Forms are not necessary. What matters is the mind' (Ekachai 2001b). The spontaneous question that follows that statement is: if form and ordination are unnecessary, why do men need to become monks?

Today, monks no longer monopolise knowledge of the Buddhist canons and female Buddhist scholars like Dhammananda are equally versed in the Buddhist scriptures and challenge the *sangha*'s authority to interpret the scriptures in ways advantageous to monks. Dhammananda has been accused of destroying Buddhism through her ordination. Her opinion is the opposite. She said that she chose to be ordained because she wanted to carry on the heritage of the Buddha. The Buddha originally taught that female monks were one of the four pillars of Buddhism, along with male monks and lay followers of both sexes. Dhammananda said that she is 'trying to revive the four pillars of Buddhism – *bhikkhus*, (male monks) *bhikkhunis*, (female monks) *upasakas* (laymen) and *upasikas* (lay women) that will sustain the religion into the future' (Achakulwisut 2001). There is probably no room for a specific category of *mae chii* in the order of the four pillars. If the *bhikkhunis* were to be part of the Thai *sangha,* I assume that the *mae chii*s would have to choose between becoming pious female lay *upasikas* or receiving *bhikkhuni* ordination. Dhammananda Bhikkhuni said in an interview on 21 March 2001 at Thammasat University that before her ordination she did not consider *mae chii*s to be 'the right soil' because they were scared. However, when she saw the Dasa Sila Matas in Sri Lanka and their role in the *bhikkhuni* ordination she changed her mind (*Yasodhara* 2001b).

For Dhammananda Samaneri the debate about the continuation of the *bhikkhuni/bhikksuni* lineage is academic. 'What I'm trying to prove is that during the Buddha's time there was no Mahayana or Theravada, and ordination was given to women, period' (Janssen 2001). Without the Thai *sangha*'s approval, Dhammananda has now received full *bhikkhuni* ordination and has started building up a female monks' community in Thailand. Today she gives sermons and teaches Buddhism at her temple in Nakhon Pathom. However, initially she did not collect alms in the mornings since she would then face the threat of being arrested. The lay supporters had invited her to make alms rounds at least once a week and in December 2001, she started to walk on alms rounds in the area around her temple (*Yosodhara* 2002). Dhammananda said: 'I intend to lead my life quietly, be a good monk, set an example and once I have my community of female monks then maybe I'll start talking to the authorities'

(Janssen 2001: 16). 'The spirit of Buddhism is freedom, peace and happiness – and it is for both men and women' (Yasodhara 2001b: 19).

The first bhikkhuni ordination in Thailand

On 10 February 2002 the first Thai woman received dual novice *bhikkhuni* ordination in Thailand. The ordination took place at Dhammananda's temple Songdharmakalyani in Nakhon Pathom. The woman who was ordained was the 56-year-old Mae chii Varangghana Vanavichayen; her ordained name is Dhammarakhita Samaneri. Dhammarakhita had been a *mae chii* for nine years before she became a novice *bhikkhuni*. She had a diploma in business studies from Australia and before she entered the nunhood had worked as a secretary and translator. During her time as *mae chii* she was still married, but in order to be qualified for novice ordination she sought a divorce from her husband. Her two children were supportive of her decision to live a religious life. She said: 'I quit the worldly life because I want to break the chain of lifetimes by practising *dhamma*' (Ekachai 2002a).

The ceremony was conducted in the Sri Lankan tradition. This historic event was an international gathering and the ceremony was presided over by eight *bhikkhunis/bhikksunis* from Sri Lanka, Taiwan, Indonesia and from Thailand. Dhammarakhita's preceptor was the Sri Lankan Bhikkhuni Sadha Sumana who said that the ceremony marked the long religious exchange between Thailand and Sri Lanka. When Sri Lanka's monks' order disappeared in the eleventh century, the Thai *sangha* sent a delegation of monks to re-establish Theravada Buddhism there. Now the Sri Lankan *bhikkhus* and *bhikkhunis* were helping the Thai female renunciants (ibid.).

Dhammarakhita's ordination was not met with the same criticism from senior monks as Dhammananda Samaneri's ordination had one year earlier. The religious establishment was this time openly challenged by the *bhikkhuni* ordination held in Thailand. The Deputy Education Minister Chamlong Krutkhunthod said that the government could not stop the ordination because the monks who performed it belonged to the Sri Lankan Theravada order and not to the Thai Theravada order. According to the Thai constitution's mandate on religious freedom the state cannot intervene unless national security is under threat (Ekachai 2002b). The media's reactions to Dhammarakhita's ordination also indicated a more liberal attitude than a year earlier when Dhammananda had been ordained. Sanitsuda Ekachai reports that *Thai Rath,* the country's largest newspaper, attacked the ordination although the reaction was not shared by most other papers. *Matichon Daily* gave the ordination its full support and welcomed an end to gender discrimination in Thai Buddhism. Also TV talk shows gave a balanced viewpoint on the female *bhikkhuni* ordination (ibid.).

Since October 2002, the *bhikkhuni* issue has been of special interest to the Thai Senate Committee on Women, Youth and Elderly. The board of senators (upper house) set up a sub-committee led by a female senator, Rabiabrat Pongpanit, to investigate the possibility of establishing the *bhikkhuni* order in Thailand. A study group spent six months researching the topic. They found that the *bhikkhuni* order did not defy the principles of Buddhism. Senator Rabiabrat said the ban issued in 1928 by the Supreme Patriarch prohibiting monks from ordaining women as novices or female monks should be revoked because it violated the constitution, which enshrines gender equality and freedom of faith. Senator Rabiabrat and the senatorial sub-committee presented their study to the parliament on the 11 March 2003. The ensuing discussions with representatives of the Sangha council have so far not led to sanctioning of the establishment of a *bhikkhuni* order in Thailand. The deputy prime minister has announced that the *bhikkhuni* issue is not a case for the secular constitution, but he has urged the Sangha's Council of Elders to consider the *bhikkhuni* *sangha*. In February 2004 the National Buddhist Bureau stated in reply to the senate proposal that there can never be *bhikkhuni* ordination in Thailand due to the irretrievable loss in the lineage of Theravada *bhikkhuni* order and lack of a *bhikkhuni* preceptor.

TWO PATHS TOWARDS A COMMON GOAL

Dhammananda Bhikkhuni and Mae chii Khunying Kanitha are here representing two categories of ordained Thai Buddhist women, *bhikkhuni* and *mae chii,* who both strive towards enlightenment and have the common goal of being legally recognised as ordained Buddhist women. These women are actors in their own right, though they operate from different standpoints. Dhammananda Bhikkhuni represents the established Buddhist tradition as being one of the four categories mentioned in the Buddhist canon (*bhikkhu, bhikkhuni, upasaka, upasika*). Her aim is to open the religious realm for Thai women and make it into what the Buddha once prescribed it to be. The *mae chii*s are a response to the lack of a female Buddhist order in Thailand and have developed their own tradition and they try to improve their standing and circumstances within the Thai Buddhist framework. The *mae chii*s have to some extent accepted the Thai understanding of the subordination of female ascetics. The *mae chii*s are not challenging the order as Dhammananda Bhikkhuni has done by going beyond the Thai Buddhist demarcation and repossessing what she considers to be every Buddhist woman's right: to receive female monk ordination. In doing so she confronts the Thai *sangha* and goes against Thai cultural norms for women.

Even though the *mae chii*s have not been in opposition to the *sangha* exclusion of women as the *bhikkhuni*s have been, the *mae chii*s do not passively accept their secondary position. Instead of requesting to be part of the *sangha*, the *mae chii*s have created their own space outside the *sangha*'s sphere of influence and many *mae chii*s have, through the strict monastic lives and knowledge, improved their status. The *mae chii*s are making efforts to improve themselves spiritually and to help others through religious practice, educational programmes etc. Under prevailing circumstances when mainstream society stills consider it inappropriate for women to act as equals to monks, most *mae chii*s refrain from seeking *bhikkhuni* ordination. They seem to think that receiving ordination would be easy but it may be difficult to uphold and to survive as a *bhikkhuni* in a hostile environment. That requires not only courage but also education and financial resources. Most *mae chii*s do not have the means required for becoming pioneering *bhikkhuni*s in Thailand. Without proper training, a *bhikkhuni* community, respect and support from the lay as well as from the monks' community, the *bhikkhuni* path is not considered an alternative for most *mae chii*s.

Dhammananda Bhikkhuni has long been involved in the work of restoring the *bhikkhuni* order and introducing it to Thailand. She stands up for women's rights to exercise the religious vocation that women, according to the Buddha, are qualified for and once obtained thanks to the struggle by the first *bhikkhuni*, Mahapajapati, to establish a *bhikkhuni* order. Dhammananda Bhikkhuni has begun to establish a Thai *bhikkhuni* community and the first *bhikkhuni* ordination has already taken place at Dhammananda Bhikkhuni's temple in Thailand. The *mae chii*s have established numbers of *samnak chii*s in the country and they show that it is possible to live an ordained life and at the same time be beneficial to society. On the individual level, women renunciants do achieve acceptance and veneration from the laity and there are also examples of individual monks who are supportive of female ascetics. The development of self-governed *samnak chii*s is a step towards a more egalitarian religious realm in Thailand. However, on the structural level, both *mae chii*s and *bhikkhuni*s are still excluded from the sources of institutionalised power and prestige.

The current movement to introduce full ordination for Buddhist women involves a significant reconstruction of religious traditions. The global process of gaining legitimation for female monks is effecting changes in attitudes and institutions in various monastic communities. Introducing a *bhikkhuni* order in Thailand entails institutionalising and according official recognition to a female monks' order which would bring about fundamental changes of the *sangha*'s relationship within the nation. Rita Gross argues that there has been a deep contradiction between the theory and practice of Buddhism. She explains that the core Buddhist concepts of egolessness, emptiness, and Buddha nature is beyond ascribed gender differences (Gross 1999: 78–109). But Buddhism, like other religions, has 'one long dismal record of misogyny and sexism' from the eight special rules to the current domination by men of Buddhist institutions. Buddhism needs to be reformed in order to provide women with better education, full ordination and economic support for female ascetics and more female teachers as role models. The Department of Religious Affairs' and the *sangha*'s unwillingness to seriously negotiate women's right to have a legal position as female ascetics clearly shows that the male patriarchy is firmly determined to maintain male power over the formal religious realm in Thailand.

NOTES

1   The *mae chiis*' white robes mark them as affiliated with the laity, while their shaved heads and practice of celibacy connect them with the monks.

2   He has since returned to America and in 2004, he left the monkhood.

3   Interview 17 August 1997.

4   McConnell John A. (1995) *Mindful Mediation: A Handbook for Buddhist Peace-makers*. Bangkok: Buddhist Research Institute, Mahachula Buddhist University Wongsanit Ashram, Foundation for Children.

5   Interview 17 August 1997.

6   The two sisters did not receive dual ordination.

7   Dharmaguptaka is the ordination lineage that leads back to Dharmagupta. Dharmagupta was one or the early Buddhist schools in India and is thought by some scholars to be a forerunner of the Theravada School and by others considered to be a sub-branch of Theravada Buddhism.

CHAPTER TEN

Summary and Conclusions

This anthropological study has addressed the interaction and interconnectedness between religion and gender relations in Thailand and has analysed this through the lens of the *mae chiis'* lives, actions and role in Thai society. Here, religion plays an important role in establishing gender boundaries, and gender differences find expression in religion. The *mae chiis* who are the focus of this study have a long history in Thailand. The category of *mae chii* arose within the religious realm that was, and still is, dominated by male Buddhist monks, *bhikkhus*. The order of female monks, *bhikkhunis*, which elsewhere once offered women similar religious opportunities as to men, never existed in Thailand. However, *mae chiis* have a long history here and to some extent they provide a response to the missing category of female Buddhist monks.

The *mae chiis* have existed in Thailand for centuries, long before the country became a modern nation-state and the Thai Buddhist *sangha* became centralised. The formalisation of Buddhism that accompanied modernisation in Thailand over the last century placed the *mae chiis* firmly outside the *sangha*. The preference that modern state Buddhism gave to the study of Buddhist scriptures rather than the practice of meditation devalued lay asceticism, including the *mae chiis'* practices. Since the study of religious texts was confined to male monks and novices, this avenue was closed to women (Tiyavanich 1997: 280).

The changing reality for contemporary *mae chiis* is related to changes within the broader social and religious landscape. Through four decades of industrialisation, Thailand has experienced major changes in all areas of society. Religion has traditionally played a central role in Thai society and Buddhism is still relevant to most Thai people and intertwined in their daily life. However, modernisation has weakened the role of Buddhism in some areas. For example, temples are no longer the natural centres of education and social life in Thai communities. Furthermore, the *sangha* is no longer under the strict control of politicians and it is less important for the legitimation of political leaders.

People have not necessarily become less religious over the decades. However, many are now looking for new religious affiliations outside the state-sponsored *sangha* (Jackson 1997: 76; Tanabe and Keyes 2002: 8). The *sangha's* central position in Thai society has been eroded in recent decades not only by modernisation but also by the behaviour of some of the famous monks who have been exposed for involvement in sex and corruption scandals. Such irregularities together with the growing commercialisation of Buddhism have led to a crisis of faith in the *sangha* and prompted people to look for worthy Buddhist renunciants outside the formal Buddhist authority. The influential and highly respected monk Buddhadasa Bhikkhu is a monk who has dissociated himself from the *sangha* and gathered a large following. Another example is the Buddhist sect Santi Asoke, which also won people's respect through its strict code of living.

It was in the 1970s, when the Santi Asoke and another Buddhist sect, Wat Phra Dhammakaya, were established, that *samnak chiis* independent of monks' temples began growing in number and more lay people began paying attention to the *mae chiis'* activities. The *mae chiis'* national organisation, the Thai Mae Chiis' Institute, was founded in 1969 and has ever since played an important role in uniting the *mae chiis* and forming a national body that assist in their development. Their position in society is progressing slowly but gaining increasing respect and support from the laity in recent decades. At least some groups of *mae chiis* now enjoy enhanced status. Many individual monks appreciate their practice and support them both financially and educationally. However, most of the *mae chiis* in Thailand still live secluded lives at temples and lack opportunities to develop in their religious vocation.

Ratburi Samnak Chii, where most of the data for this study were collected, is governed by the *mae chiis* themselves. In order to deepen my understanding of the *mae chiis'* lives I spent time at temples and interviewed *mae chiis* living there. It is important to point out that the *mae chiis* at Ratburi Samnak Chii do not represent all *mae chiis* in Thailand. The aim of this study has not been to give a generalised picture of *mae chiis* but to understand contemporary *mae chiis'* lives, activities and performances at *samnak chiis*. The focus has been on the processes of change and the ways in which the *mae chiis* are achieving religious legitimacy.

LIVING ON THE MARGINS

To be a female renunciant in Thailand is going against the prescribed female gender norms. The impropriety of women renouncing the world is expressed in several ways. The discourse concerning female ordination in Thailand phrases female renunciation in terms of failure in life. The degrading way in which *mae chii*s are spoken of inspired me to investigate who these women were who clearly upset many people by their choices and evoke a sense of disorder. I interviewed *mae chii*s at temples and *samnak chii*s and found that they constitute a heterogeneous category, whereas simplified picture of the *mae chii*s often presented in academic literature corresponds with the stereotypical discourse about *mae chii*s in Thai society. However, this picture does not tally with the way that the *mae chii*s whom I met in the field see themselves. I conclude that Thai women's ordination cannot simply be explained away as a sort of 'escape' from old age, poverty, sickness or 'broken hearts', although the recognition of different kinds of suffering is certainly relevant for women who seek ordination. I have emphasized *mae chii*s' own narratives and the reasons that they give for seeking an ordained life. I found that their religious lives cannot be reduced to a 'response to' something or 'because of' something. For most *mae chii*s, religious life is expressed as meaningful in itself.

Thai women who aspire to become *mae chii*s have to be firm in their decision and they usually make strenuous efforts to reach their goal. A celibate, single life is chosen in preference to married life with children, which they consider to be filled with suffering and attachments and to therefore to constitute a hindrance to spiritual development.

By seeking ordination and entry into a religious realm, women cross a gendered boundary and impinge upon what has become a predominantly male domain. From a spiritual viewpoint, gender is downplayed by the *mae chii*s. Most of them are confident in their religious capacity and they do not subscribe to the prevailing notion that the religious path is solely for men. Most of the *mae chii*s that I interviewed saw themselves as ordained religious persons who belong to the religious sphere; lay people legitimate this view.

As demonstrated in this study, the *mae chii*s are agents and creators of meanings and new orders in Thai society. I have considered factors that serve to encourage women within an androgenic religious system to become ordained religious persons. I found that most *mae chii*s overlook the structural inequalities of the religious organisation and find inspiration in the Buddhist scriptures, which assert that women have the same faculties as men to reach the final goal of Buddhism, enlightenment. To support their standpoint, the *mae chii*s refer to the many narratives of female monks, *bhikkhuni,* and lay women who attained *nibbana.* Furthermore, Thai lay women's evident capacity to handle life's challenges without men's assistance inspires the *mae chii*s.

Education has been recognised as pivotal for the ordained state and in recent decades *mae chii*s have begun to address their exclusion from both secular and Buddhist education. Some well-educated women have become ordained and live religious lives as *mae chii*s. However, most *mae chii*s have only four or six years of primary education prior to their ordination. Researchers have tended to attribute the lack of respect granted to *mae chii*s to general Thai assumptions about their lack of knowledge of Buddhism. Since formal religious education has been primarily the prerogative of monks, few *mae chii*s have gained a thorough comprehension of the Buddhist teachings. Consequently they have not been able to fulfil their spiritual potential to the fullest extent and serve as guides for others.

Education has therefore been recognised as essential for the *mae chii*s' development and in 1990, Ratburi Samnak Chii opened the first secondary school for *mae chii*s and underprivileged girls in Thailand. Since the school is also open to lay girls, the *mae chii*s' work with the school has been intertwined in society in a way that is new for them. Their work with the school has given the *mae chii*s credibility and it further legitimates their role in society. The *mae chii*s have taken on an even greater responsibility by establishing a college for themselves and lay women named Mahapajapati Theri College after the first female monk and the Buddha's foster mother, Mahapajapati Bhikkhuni.

Although some mobility is possible in Thai sex/gender system, the *sangha* has been exceptionally persistent in maintaining a male hegemonic structure. The *mae chii*s' long history in Thailand has not granted them formal religious legitimacy. Their secondary standing in the religious field is further confirmed by their lack of support from the Thai government and the Thai *sangha.* The *mae chii*s' ambiguous situation in society can be explained by their lack of legal recognition as ordained persons and this has placed the *mae chii*s in a sort of official limbo. There is no legal category of *mae chii* and they are therefore invisible in the eyes of the authorities. For example, the Ministry of Transport and Communications regard *mae chii*s as lay people and thereby deny them the free transport to which monks are entitled. Ironically, the Ministry of the Interior denies them the right to vote on account of their ordained status, although the law does not recognise the *mae chii*s as clerics. However, the ambiguity of their position makes it open to interpretation (see Douglas 1966). The *mae chii*s have begun to take advantage of their being 'out of place'.

In order to make the *mae chiis'* standing clear and give them legal status as ordained persons, some have striven to introduce a *mae chiis'* law. Proposing a Mae chiis' Bill turned out to be a complex issue and not all *mae chiis* were convinced that it would be meaningful and constructive for them. The draft for the Mae chiis' Bill was modelled on the monks' law, which had been heavily criticised by members of the *sangha*. Those who were against such a law predicted that it would chain the *mae chiis* into a bureaucracy which would hamper their freedom and the potential this implies. The *mae chiis'* law was thoroughly debated during the period of my fieldwork and a draft Mae Chiis' Bill was finally decided upon at the end of my stay in the field. Those who advocate a *mae chiis'* law anticipate that legal recognition as ordained persons and formal belonging within the religious realm, although not in the *sangha* per se, would make their status unambiguous even in legal situations. Moreover, as recognised ordained persons they would be entitled to some financial support from the government. However, the *mae chiis* did not reach their goal. In March 2003 the Department of Religious Affairs rejected the proposed Mae Chiis' Bill.

CREATING RELIGIOUS SPACE

Today, Thai women who want to become ordained have at least two opportunities: either to become a *mae chii* or to become a *bhikkhuni*. Both categories are outside the Thai *sangha*'s realm, demonstrating that female renunciants in Thailand have to create space outside the formal structures, which are solely male. That women-only spaces have also been shown to facilitate autonomy for religious women in other religions, is evident for example in Maria Jaschok's (2000) work on women's mosques in China. Thai *mae chiis* are inspired by, and often refer to, the legacy of the *bhikkhunis* in early Buddhism and the majority of the *mae chiis* whom I interviewed did not aspire to become *bhiksunis*. Although ordination in the Mahayana tradition was the only avenue open to women who wanted to receive female monk ordination. The *mae chiis* considered Mahayana Buddhism and *bhiksuni* alien to Buddhism in Thailand; in fact they regarded ordination in the Mahayana tradition as a conversion from Theravada to Mahayana Buddhism. Moreover, they identified the subordinate position that the female monks hold in relation to the male monks as a disadvantage. The *mae chiis* contrasted the female monks' secondary standing in the *sangha* with their own autonomous and more desirable position, outside the male monks' influence.

The *mae chiis'* attitude towards the Buddhist organisation is in harmony with the older tradition of Buddhism in Thailand which was a grassroots and community-based religion (see Tiyavanich 1997). This stands in contrast to modern centralised state religion, which does not tolerate diversity in Buddhism. Charles F. Keyes argues that after 1976, the hegemonic domination of the centralised *sangha* collapsed and there is no longer a consensus in Thai society about the religious basis of authority (Keyes 1999a: 36). Furthermore, he states that the fragmentation of Buddhism in Thailand that has occured since 1976 has led Thai people to look to many different sources for moral authority. He gives examples of various non-established socially engaged Buddhist movements. I argue that particular groups of *mae chii*s also provide sources for moral authority for lay people.

The *mae chii*s are interested in gaining access to the Pali-based Buddhist education that is promoted by the *sangha*. However, they are not confronting the *sangha* by seeking formal entrance into the congregation. This is in contrast to the *bhikkhuni*s who strive for a rightful place within the *sangha*. If the *sangha* were to accept the *bhikkhuni*s as part of their membership, it is not clear how this would affect the position of the *mae chii*s; it is likely that more *mae chii*s would become interested in seeking *bhikkhuni* ordination if the *sangha* approved of the female monks' order and provided *bhikkhuni* training.

The *mae chiis'* underprivileged situation will not change without their own efforts. Moral conduct, Buddhist practice and Buddhist knowledge are important for their religious status. This study has demonstrated that where the *mae chii*s live, whether at temples or at self-governed *samnak chii*s, is also of crucial significance for their vocation and potential to enhance their religious position. *Mae chii*s who live predominantly as housekeepers for the monks have no chance to develop an ordained identity that contrasts fully with the lay world. Nor do lay people recognise those *mae chii*s as religious alms persons and fields of merit. At temples, they risk to become consumed by household chores and services to the monks and they are then left with limited time for studies and Buddhist practice. Furthermore, they are not entitled to officiate at ceremonies nor allowed to go on alms rounds, which are significant performances marking the ordained state.

The activities and spatial organisation of the *mae chii*s who live at *samnak chii*s separate them from lay life and constitute them as persons belonging to the religious realm. Self-governed *samnak chii*s that provide education, combined with controlled and regulated practices, are fertile grounds for *mae chiis'* spiritual development and vocation as religious specialists. At *samnak chii*s their role has been augmented and broadened to become more analogous to the monks' role. At Ratburi Samnak Chii have become visible in the lay community. Their religious performance, their hard work at the *samnak chii* and strict monastic behaviour have been recognised by the lay people. Not only do they now gain better educational standards; they also earn religious legitimacy. This has not given them formal recognition, but they are granted informal legitimacy as religious specialists. It is in areas in which *samnak chii*s are situated that *mae chii*s achieve increased acceptance by and support from the laity.

I conclude that *mae chii*s at *samnak chii*s, together with the laity, create new orders, and become fields of merit for the lay people. Lay informants claim that they consider that donating to the Ratburi *mae chii*s yields the same merit as donating to monks and they include the *mae chii*s in the daily ritual of alms giving. At *samnak chii*s like Ratburi Samnak Chii, *mae chii*s commonly initiate alms rounds at the request of the lay people living in the neighbourhood who want to make merit by donating food to them. Hence, they have the potential to cross the boundary between the lay and religious realms and be transformed into fields of merit. Impeccable conduct, religious performances and Buddhist knowledge have proved to be requirements for achieving religious legitimacy. Co-operation with monks and lay people are of significance in the recognition of the *mae chii*s' capacities as religious persons.

TRANSCENDING GENDER BOUNDARIES

The often disapproved ordinations of Thai women stand in sharp contrast to men's ordinations, which are highly desirable and expected. Through the monks' ordination, men alter their formal belonging from the lay to the religious sphere, implying that their status is elevated over every lay person. Thai women's ordinations do not result in such an automatic, formal alteration of status, and the religious position of *mae chii*s has to be individually achieved through each woman's own practice.

Like men, women have various reasons for seeking ordination. My informants considered spiritual grounds to be the principal motive for their choice of becoming *mae chii*s, a motive that has generally been downplayed in earlier research. A common reason that young men give for becoming novice monks is to show gratitude to their parents and to transfer religious merit – particularly to their mothers. Women are not expected to become ordained for the sake of their parents. On the contrary, women are expected to remain as lay persons in order to help their parents if necessary. Another contrast is that young men are considered to achieve maturity through ordination while women become mature through motherhood.

The notion that ordination is inappropriate for women makes it difficult for many women who wish to become ordained to get permission from their families. Moreover, the ethnography presented here shows that financial restraints tend to prevent women from becoming ordained rather than forcing them into it, as has been suggested in earlier research.

The *mae chii*s experience their ordination as a clear break with the lay world and as an evidence of their transition into the religious realm. When women go through an ordination ceremony, and say farewell to their families, relatives and friends, they perceive themselves to be entering a new realm in life. They claim that their whole existence changes with ordination and the subsequent training.

At *samnak chii*s, the *mae chii*s embody the monastic code. They control and refine their manners and their lifestyle becomes distinct from lay life. As *mae chii*s, they are forbidden to involve themselves in lay duties and domestic activities such as child-rearing and taking care of sick persons or the elderly. Furthermore, the *mae chii*s do not provide service to lay people other than in matters such as teaching and counselling. The *mae chii*s consider women and men to have the same potential to transcend gender. This notion is supported by both Buddhist and Thai historical sources where gender has a fluid and transformable character. Moreover, the *mae chii*s do not agree with the widespread notion that only men can reach *nibbana* but argue that also women can attain the ultimate Buddhist goal.

Representations of the Thai sex/gender system (cf. Rubin 1975; Jackson and Cook 1999: 4–6) show that sex and gender differences as well as sexual orientation are conflated. Van Esterik (2000) says: 'Thai gender can best be represented as a continuum with permeable boundaries, a system that is in essence non-binary but in conventional language provides conceptual space for a third gender' (ibid.: 202). In Thailand, the sex/gender discourse is non-exclusive and it is possible for people to move in and out of gender categories. The gendered surfaces tell how a person expects to be treated. What is behind the surfaces is private and not communicated (ibid.: 203). The *mae chii*s show that they are female renunciants who live ascetic, celibate lives but lack formal religious legitimacy because of the exclusion from the *sangha* and the religious realm. However, the *mae chii*s' identity is not that of lay persons. They have embodied the monastic code and consider themselves to belong to the religious realm. Although they live a highly regulated life, following the monastic code, they stress the importance of the freedom that ordained life provides. They are liberated from the demands of lay life that, according to them, leads a person further away from the ultimate Buddhist goal.

There are gendered boundaries that are exceptionally difficult to cross. The boundary between the lay and religious realms is one of them. The case of the *mae chii*s demonstrates how it is possible for multiple gender models to co-exist within cultures (cf. Moore 1994: 55–56). The *mae chii*s' entry into a domain that is believed to be male disturbs the normative binary sex/gender discourse which separates men from women by positioning women in the lay realm but men giving access to both the lay and religious spheres. Female renunciants challenge the dichotomy of male/female. However, the binary male/female discourse, with reference to other gender models in the Thai context, has the potential to be transcended.

Buddhism has proved to be both liberating and constraining for Thai women. The Buddhist teachings about non-self and impermanence discourage fixed binary gender identities. However, the structures that have developed in the Thai Buddhist hierarchy, that expel women and deny them formal admission into the religious realm, are due to rigid concepts linking formal religious authority and power with the male gender; they have so far been impossible to transgress, though they are now facing challenge. With their demands for change female renunciants in Thailand are contesting the existing orders. The women portrayed in this book do not passively accept their marginalised position. They are utilising their autonomy and finding ways to create space outside the male hierarchy. This is done with support from lay people and individual monks. The *mae chii*s at *samnak chii*s appreciate the female governance and their serious performance has changed the attitudes of many lay people towards them.

While the *mae chii*s consent and conform to the dominant ideology of women's religious subordination, through their actions they simultaneously cross gender boundaries and oppose the mainstream prevailing notions of women's lay status and religious inferiority. Examining the dynamics of this complexity has been central to this study. The *mae chii*s both adhere to gendered boundaries and erase them. The subtle ways in which they challenge and transcend boundaries give an understanding of how gender boundaries are created in Thai society. The *mae chii*s deserve our serious consideration because they are important links in our understanding of socio-cultural changes and movements in contemporary Buddhist societies.

Glossary

Thai is a tonal language with a number of vowel and consonant sounds not found for instance in English. While Thai has its own phonetic script (derived from ancient Indian scripts via medieval Khmer), there is no generally agreed system for transcribing Thai words by the Roman alphabet. In the present book, the Thai terms are generally transcribed phonetically. The system of translation used here is based on that of Mary Haas (1964) with some modifications. To those who can speak Thai this will still give sufficient information to indicate which words are meant. The Thai words and phrases are translated from standard Thai which distinguishes between five tones; for reasons of simplicity tonal markings are not included whereas vowel length is spelled out. The Theravada and Mahayana Buddhist terms are written in their Pali and Sanskrit forms respectively. The Thai and Pali words are italicised and may take forms for plurals e.g. *mae chii*s or adjectives e.g. *kamm*ic.

Names and titles are romanised according to established conventions, and personal names follow the preferences of the individuals concerned. Many Thai people transcribe their names with the silent characters that are spelled but not pronounced in Thai. It is also common for names derived from Sanskrit and Pali to be spelled as in the original languages, despite the fact that they often have radically different pronunciation in modern Thai.

The orthography of the Pali and Sanskrit words follows the conventions of romanisation but omits all diacritical signs.

abhidhamma (Pali)	literally the 'higher teaching'; the predominantly philosophical and analytical final section of the Tipitaka
amphoe	district
anapanasati (Pali)	mindfulness by concentrating on inhalation and exhalation
anatta (Pali)	not-self, non-ego, 'egolessness' impersonality; the last of the three characteristics of existence
anicca (Pali)	impermanent; the first of the three characteristics of existence

255

anudhammas (Pali)	six precepts that *sikkhamana* observe
arahat (Pali)	enlightened person who has reached the highest stage and completely eradicated all defilements (*kilesa*)
acaan	honorific term for a graduated or honoured teacher or lecturer
baap	wrong, sinful, demerit
baaramii, parami (Pali)	perfection, quality leading to Buddhahood
baht	Thai unit of currency
bandit	learned man, wise person
bhikkhu (Pali) *bhikksu* (Sanskrit) *phikkhu*	male Buddhist monk
bhikkhuni (Pali) *bhiksuni* (Sanskrit) *phikkhuni*	female Buddhist monk
binthabaat, pindapata (Pali)	daily alms round
bodhisatta (Pali), *potihisat*	the Theravada notion of a being destined to attain complete salvation or Buddhahood
bodhisattva (Sanskrit)	Mahayana Buddhist 'saint' who vows not to enter into complete nirvana until all other sentient beings have likewise been saved
boot	the consecrated building in a monastery where important religious ceremonies and rituals are performed
borisut	pure, innocent, virgin
bun, punna (Pali)	Buddhist merit
bun khun	attitude and value of reciprocal obligation, especially to those who have offered assistance parents, teachers, monks, doctors
caga (Pali)	generosity, liberality
cangwat	province
chedi	a pagoda containing relics of the Buddha or of highly respected Buddhist followers.
chii phraam	a woman with 'lay', temporary ordination (without shaving her head)
dana (Pali)	almsgiving, offering, charity, generosity, benevolence, donation, benefaction

danadharma (Sanskrit)	the law of the Indian religious offering
dasa jataka (Pali)	the Buddha's ten last birth stories before his birth as Siddhattha Gotama
dasa sila mata (Pali)	Sri Lankan ten precept female ascetics
dek wat	temple boy
dhamma (Pali)	word with many meanings; here it generally refers to the Buddhist view of the nature of things, the teachings of the Buddha
dhammacarinii (Pali)	Buddhist religious women. The name of the schoolgirls at Ratburi Samnak Chii
dhammakaya (Pali)	the 'truth body' which is said to be identical with ultimate reality
dii	a feminine lesbian
dukkha (Pali)	dissatisfaction, which is one of the three characteristics of existence
garudhamma (Pali)	the eight chief rules for *bhikkhuni*
gatha (Pali, Sanskrit) *khatha*	verse, stanza, magical text, spell
haiphôôn	to bless, wish (someone) happiness and good fortune
hua cai	heart
hua naa	chief, boss
Isaan	Northeast, Northeastern region
isara	freedom
Jataka (Pali) *chadok*	the collection of 547 legendary stories about the former lives of the Buddha
jhana (Pali)	state of deep mental unification characterised by a total immersion of the mind in its object
jivorn (Sanskrit) *civara* (Pali)	monks' outer robe
kam, kamma (Pali)	intentional or volitional actions
karma (Sanskrit)	which bring about moral consequences for the performer
kathoey	originally a hermaphrodite or male or female transvestite or transsexual; today a transgender male
khandha (Pali)	one of the five aggregates or elements which constitute human existence (i.e. 1: *rupa* – materiality, 2: *vedana* – feeling 3: *sanna* – perception 4:

	sankhara – mental factors associated with desire 5: *vinnana* – consciousness)
khreng	to be strict, rigorously observant of precepts, rules; to be devout
khruu	teacher
khun	polite term of address (Mr, Ms or Mrs)
khun mae	honorific for a *mae chii* with high status such as an abbess
khunying	honorific title given to a woman by the King, equivalent to the English Dame
khwaamsuk	happiness
kilet, kilesa (Pali)	moral defilement or impurity which leads to suffering
kuti	*mae chii*'s or monk's living quarters; often a small basic one-room house
lobha (Pali)	greed
lokiya (Pali)	mundane, worldly; associated with the realm of attachment, craving and suffering
lokuttara (Pali)	supramundane, transcendental; associated with *nibbana* or the path leading to the attainment of *nibbana*
luang phôô	venerable father; honorific for a monk with high status, e.g. an abbot
luuksit	follower, pupil or disciple
mae chii	term used for white-robed Buddhist female ascetics in Thailand
mahaanikai	'large order' of monks; term coined after the establishment of the Thammayut order in the nineteenth century
Mahatherasamakhom	Council of Elders, the Thai *sangha* administrative authority
mara (Pali)	Buddhist personification of evil
mathayom	secondary educational level
metta (Pali)	loving kindness
metta songsaan	sympathy for other people
mia nôôy	minor wife, mistress
muubaan	village

nak buat	one who has gone forth, become ordained
nak buat chii	one who has received *mae chii* ordination
nak tham	lower grades in the religious curriculum.
Nang Thoranii *Dharani* (Pali)	Goddess of Earth
niphaan, nibbana (Pali)	permanent extinction of suffering; release from the cycle of rebirth
pali	canonical language of Theravada Buddhism
pabbajja (Pali)	going forth (from home to homelessness)
panca-sila (Pali)	he five Buddhist precepts
panna	wisdom, understanding, knowledge.
parian	a monk with a level of graded Pali exams (the ninth being the highest)
patibat, patipatti (Pali)	meditation practice
paticcasamuppada (Pali)	doctrine of 'dependent origination', explaining the causal relations between ignorance and craving and the arising of suffering and rebirth
pathom	primary school
patimokkha (Pali) *patimok*	the clerical code of conduct for Theravada monks; monks' disciplinary code of 227 precepts
pavarana (Pali)	ecclesiastical ceremony at the end of the rains retreat; monks invite one another to speak of any offences or improper behaviour they have seen, heard or suspected during the rains
pavattini (Pali)	the *bhikkhuni* preceptor
phaa mae chiis'	outer robe, fabric
phaan	tray with pedestal
phaphaa	donation ceremony
phaasin	women's sarong-like wrapped skirt
phansaa, vassa (Pali)	annual three month rainy season retreat
phet	sex/gender
pintoo	food carrier, consisting of a set of containers stacked vertically and strapped together
phra	Buddhist monk
phra maha	respectful title for Buddhist monks

phuttha phanit	commercialising Buddhism
rabiab	rules
rabiab mae chii thai	the *mae chiis*' rules
rakhang	bell
riabrôôy	neat, tidy, polite, well-mannered
rodnaam	dedicate religious merit while pouring water
rôôn	to be hot
saai sin	sacred cotton thread
saalaa	hall, pavilion, wayside shelter, study and merit-making hall, public building, preaching hall, multi-purpose hall
saamlôô	tricycle-cab
sabong	monks' under robe
sai bat tak bat	donate food to monks' and *mae chiis*' alms bowls
saiyasaat	mystical/magical powers
samadhi (Pali)	state of concentration attained through meditation
samanera (Pali)	a male novice Buddhist monk
samaneri (Pali)	a female novice Buddhist monk
samatha (Pali)	a meditative state characterised by a 'single-pointedness' of mind
samnak	hermitage, unofficial *wat* (without ordination hall) usually consisting of *kutis* and an open hall
samnak chii	*mae chiis*' department at a temple, *mae chiis*' self-governed religious 'abode'
samsara (Pali)	phenomenal existence, the cycle of rebirth
sangha (Pali)	the community of Buddhists. *Sangha* can be used just to refer to male monks, or to male and female monks, or can also include lay men and women who have taken the five Buddhist precepts. In Thailand *sangha* refers to the assembly of male monks (*bhikkhu*)
sangharaat *sangharaja* (Sanskrit)	the Supreme Patriarch
sanghati (Pali)	the monks' outer robe

sathaaban mae chii thai	the Thai Mae Chiis' Institute
sekiyadhamma (Pali)	the seventy-five training rules for monastics
Siamnikaya	a Theravada Buddhist lineage from Ayutthaya in Thailand
sikkhamana (Pali)	women who aspire to become *bhikkhuni*. It also refers to the *sikkhamanas'* ordination
sikkhamat	a female ordained ascetic in the Asoke sect
sila (Pali)	virtue, self-discipline, moral training rules
sima (Pali) *sema*	the boundary stones that surround an ordination hall
sok	ripe
stupa (Sanskrit)	a reliquary monument
suatmon	Buddhist chant
suk	resign from the ordained state
tambon	subdistrict (administrative unit above the village level)
tham bun	to perform meritorious deeds
thammadaa	to be normal, common, usual – referring to the reality of things
thammayut	one of the two official sects of Theravada Buddhism in Thailand
thansamay	being modern, modernity
therigatha (Pali)	verses of the female elders; collecting of writings of the elder female ascetics of the early Buddhist community
thila shin	Burmese term for Buddhist female ascetic
thudong, dhutanga (Pali)	austere practices, however most commonly used to refer to those monks who leave the monastery and go on foot to visit the various Buddhist shrines
thôôm a	masculine acting lesbian, from English 'tomboy'
Tipitaka (Pali)	the canonical Theravada scriptures, incorporating the *Vinaya-pitaka*, *Sutta-pitaka* and the *Abidhamma-pitaka*
trong	directly, straight

upachaa	preceptor, or ordinator, the officiating monk at an ordination ceremony, a spiritual teacher
upasaka (Pali)	male lay devotee
upasampada (Pali)	full (or higher) ordination. Ordination ceremony
uposatha (Pali) *uboosot*	observance, the observance of the eight precepts; biweekly recitation of the *Vinaya* rules by a chapter of Buddhist monks, the day for special meetings of the order, and for the recitation of *Patimokkha*. The *uposatha* hall is a consecrated assembly hall, called *'boot'* in Thai
upasika (Pali)	female lay devotee
vassa (Pali)	the annual three-month rainy season retreat; usually between July and October
Vessantara jataka (Pali)	the story of the Buddha's last rebirth prior to his birth as Siddhattha Gotama
vihara (Pali)	literally 'an abode or dwelling place'. Also refers to a place where monks gather for services of chanting
vinaya (Pali) *vinai*	disciplinary rules for the monastic community, as laid down in the *vinaya-pitaka*, a section of the canonical Theravada scriptures
wai	gesture of greeting that shows respect
wan phra	Buddhist day of worship
vipassana (Pali)	insight meditation
wat	Thai Buddhist temple
winjaan	spirit, soul

Bibliography

Achakulwisut, Atiya (2001) 'A path less travelled'. *Bangkok Post,* 17 April.

Aeusrivongse, Nidhi (1994) 'Latthi Phithi Chao Mae Kwan Im [The cult of Kuan Im goddess]'. *Silipa Watthanathan.* 15, 10 (August 1994). pp. 78–106.

Ardener, Edwin (1975) 'Belief and the problem of women and the "problem" revisited'. In Shirley Ardener (ed.), *Perceiving Women.* New York: Halsted Press, pp. 1–27.

Atkinson, Jane Monnig and Shelly Errington (eds) (1990) *Power and Difference: Gender in Island Southeast Asia.* Stanford, California: Stanford University Press.

Barnes, Nancy J. (Schuster) (1987) 'Buddhism'. In Arvind Sharma (ed.), *Women in World Religions.* Albany: State University of New York Press, pp. 105–133.

—— (1996) 'Buddhist women and the nuns' order in Asia'. In Christopher S. Queen and Sallie B. King (eds), *Engaged Buddhism: Buddhist Liberation Movements in Asia.* Albany: State University of New York Press, pp. 259–294.

Bartholomeusz, Tessa (1994) *Women under the Bo Tree: Buddhist Nuns in Sri Lanka.* Cambridge: Cambridge University Press.

Basic Religious Data (1999) Bangkok: Data Statistics and Information Section Planning Division, Department of Religious Affairs, Ministry of Education, January.

Batchelor, Martine (2000) 'Achaan Ranjuan: A Thai lay woman as master teacher'. In Ellison Banks Findly (ed.), *Women's Buddhism, Buddhism's Women: Tradition, Revision, Renewal.* Boston: Wisdom Publication, pp. 156–158.

Bessey, Allan (1990) 'Women and Buddhism in Thailand: A changing identity for religious women'. In *Radical Conservatism: Buddhism in the Contemporary World— Articles in Honour of Bhikkhu Buddhadasa's 84ᵗʰ Birthday Anniversary.* Thai Inter-Religious Commission for Development and International Network of Engaged Buddhists. Bangkok: the Sathirakoses-Nagapradipa Foundation, pp. 311–345.

Bhikkhu Khantipalo (1964) *The Blessings of Pindapata.* Kandy, Ceylon: Buddhist Publication Society.

—— (1965) *With Robes and Bowl.* Kandy, Ceylon: Buddhist Publication Society.

Blackstone, Kathryn R. (1998) *Women in the Footsteps of the Buddha: Struggle for Liberation in the Therigatha.* Richmond, Surrey: Curzon Press.

Boonmongkon, Pimpawun (2004) 'Infertility as gender discourse in Thai society'. In Suwanna Satha-Anand (ed.). *Power, Knowledge and Justice.* Seoul: Ewha Womans University Press, pp. 231–257.

Bowers, Jeffery (1996) *Dhammakaya Meditation in Thai Society.* Bangkok: Chulalongkorn University Press.

Bowie, Katherine A. (1998) 'The alchemy of charity'. *American Anthropologist.* 100 (2), pp. 469–481.

Brown, Sid (2001) *The Journey of One Buddhist Nun: Even Against the Wind.* Albany: State University of New York Press.

Buddhist Monastic code: The Patimokkha Training Rules Translated and Explained. (1993) Bangkok: The Mahamakuta Educational Council, The Buddhist University, Thailand.

Bunnag, Jane (1973) *Buddhist Monk, Buddhist Layman: A Study of Urban Monastic Organisation in Central Thailand.* Cambridge: Cambridge University Press.

Butler, Judith (1993) *Bodies that Matter: On the Discursive Limits of 'Sex'.* New York and London: Routledge.

—— (1999 [1990]) *Gender Trouble: Feminism and the Subversion of Identity.* New York and London: Routledge.

Bynum, Caroline Walker, Steven Harrell and Paula Richman, (eds) (1986) *Gender and Religion: On the Complexity of Symbols.* Boston: Beacon Press.

Cabezon, José Ignacio, (ed.) (1992) *Buddhism, Sexuality, and Gender.* Albany: State University of New York Press.

Chirawatkul, Siriporn (2004) 'Gendered body and health care practice in Thailand'. In Suwanna Satha-Anand (ed.), *Power, Knowledge and Justice.* Seoul: Ewha Womans University Press, pp. 193–229.

Collins, Steven (1982) *Selfless Persons.* Cambridge: Cambridge University Press.

Cook, Nerida (1981) 'The position of nuns in Theravada Buddhism: The parameters of religious recognition'. Canberra: Unpublished MA Thesis, Department of Prehistory and Anthropology, Australian National University, Canberra.

—— (1998) 'Dutiful daughters, estranged sisters: women in Thailand'. In Krishna Sen and Maila Stivens (eds), *Gender and Power in Affluent Asia.* London and New York: Routledge, pp. 250–290.

Davies, Richard B. (1984) *Muang Metaphysics: A Study of Northern Thai Myth and Ritual.* Bangkok: Pandora.

De Silva, Lily (1990) 'Giving in the Pali canon'. In Bhikkhu Bodhi (ed.). *Dana The Practice of Giving: Selected Essays.* Kandy: Buddhist Publication Society, pp. 19–44.

Derrida, Jacques (1992) *Given Time I. Counterfeit Money.* Chicago: University of Chicago Press.

Dhammakaya Temple (1999) *29 years of the Production of Good Men*. Bangkok: Dhammakaya Foundation.

Dhammapada (1996) Translated from Pali by S. Radhakrishnan. Oxford: Oxford University Press.

Douglas, Mary (1966) *Purity and Danger: An Analysis of Concepts of Pollution and Taboo*. London: Routledge and Kegan Paul.

Duangjun, Yuphin (1999) 'Buddhist women and ordination: A comparative study of the status and the attitude of the "Maeji" at Wat Paknam, Phasicharoen in Bangkok and at Danmahamongkol Meditation Center in Kanchanaburi'. Bangkok: Unpublished MA Thesis, Mahidol University, Bangkok. (In Thai.)

Egerton, C. Baptist (1990) *Dana – Gifts and the Blessings of Giving*. Selangor: Majujaya Indah Sdn. Bhd.

Ekachai, Sanitsuda (1996) 'Crusading for nun's right'. *Bangkok Post*, 4 September.

—— (1998) 'Our girls deserve schooling as well'. *Bangkok Post*, 8 October.

—— (2001a) 'The rules are there to be tested'. *Bangkok Post*, 3 May.

—— (2001b) 'What has become of goodwill?' *Bangkok Post*, 17 May.

—— (2002a) 'First Thai woman ordained.' *Bangkok Post*, 11 February.

—— (2002b) 'Clergy lose monopoly to serve our needs'. *Bangkok Post*, 14 February.

—— (2002c) 'Clerics square up over law'. *Bangkok Post*, 4 April.

Falk, Nancy Auer (1980) 'The case of the vanishing nuns: The fruits of ambivalence in ancient Indian Buddhism'. In Nancy Falk and Rita Gross (eds), *Unspoken Worlds: Women's Religious Lives in Non-Western Cultures*. San Francisco: Harper and Row Publishers, pp. 207–223.

Findly, Ellison Banks. (ed.) (2000) *Women's Buddhism, Buddhism's Women: Tradition, Revision, Renewal*. Boston: Wisdom Publication.

Fongkaew, Warunee (2002) 'Gender socialization and female sexuality in Northern Thailand'. In Leonore Manderson and Pranee Liamputtong (eds), *Coming of Age in South and Southeast Asia: Youth, Courtship and Sexuality*. Richmond, Surrey: Curzon Press, pp. 147–164.

Fuengfusakul, Apinya (1998) 'Empire of crystal and utopian commune: Two types of contemporary Theravada reform in Thailand'. *Sojourn* 8 (1), pp. 153–183.

Godelier, Maurice (1999) *The Enigma of the Gift*. Cambridge: Polity Press.

Gombrich, Richard F. (1971) *Buddhist Precept and Practice: Traditional Buddhism in the Rural Highlands of Ceylon*. Oxford: Oxford University Press.

Gombrich, Richard F. and Gananath Obeysekere (1988) *Buddhism Transformed: Religious Change in Sri Lanka*. New Jersey: Princeton University Press.

Gombrich, Richard F. and Margaret Cone (1977) *The Perfect Generosity of Prince Vessantara*. Oxford: Clarendon Press.

Goonatilake, Hema (1997) 'Buddhist nuns' protests, struggle, and the reinterpretation of orthodoxy in Sri Lanka'. In Judy Brink and Joan Mencher (eds), *Mixed Blessings: Gender and Religious Fundamentalism Cross Culturally*. New York: Routledge, pp. 25–39.

Grimes, Ronald L. (ed.) (1996) *Readings in Ritual Studies*. Upper Saddle River, New Jersey: Prentice Hall.

Gross, Rita M. (1993) *Buddhism after Patriarchy: A Feminist History, Analysis, and Reconstruction of Buddhism*. Albany: State University of New York Press.

—— (1999) 'Strategies for a feminist revalorization of Buddhism'. In Arvind Sharma and Katherine K. Young (eds) *Feminism and World Religions*. Albany: State University of New York Press, pp. 78–109.

—— (2001) [1994] 'Buddhism'. In Jean Holm and John Bowker (eds.) *Women in Religion*. London and New York: Continuum, pp. 1–29.

Gutschow, Kim (2000) 'Novice ordination for nuns: The rhetoric and reality of female monasticism in Northwest India'. In Ellison Banks Findly (ed.) *Women's Buddhism, Buddhism's Women: Tradition Revision, Renewal*. Boston: Wisdom Publication, pp. 103–118.

—— (2004) *Being a Buddhist Nun: The Struggle for Enlightenment in the Himalayas*. Cambridge, Massachusetts and London: Harvard University Press.

Haas, Mary R. (1964) *Thai-English Student's Dictionary*. Stanford, California: Stanford University Press.

Hale, Ann. (1984) 'The search for a jural rule: Women in Southeast Asia —the Northern Thai cults in perspective'. *Mankind* 14 (4) (August), pp. 330–338.

Hamilton, Annette (1999) 'Kwan Im, nine emperor gods, and Chinese "spirit" in Southern Thailand'. Paper presented at the Seventh International Conference on Thai Studies, Amsterdam, 4-8 July.

Hanks, Lucian (1962) 'Merit and power in the Thai social order'. *American Anthropologist* 64, pp. 1247–1261.

Hanks, Lucian and Jane R. Hanks (1963) 'Thailand: equality between the sexes'. In Barbara Ward (ed.), *Women in the New Asia*. Paris: UNESCO, pp. 424–451.

Hantrakul, Sukanya (1988) 'Prostitution in Thailand'. In Glen Chandler, Norma Sullivan and Jan Branson, (eds.), *Development and Displacement: Women in Southeast Asia*. Clayton, Australia: Monash Papers on Southeast Asia – No. 18, pp. 115–136.

Harvey, Peter (2000) *An Introduction To Buddhist Ethics: Foundations, Values and Issues*. Cambridge: Cambridge University Press.

Havnevik, Hanna (1990) *Tibetan Buddhist Nuns.* Oslo: Norwegian University Press.

Heikkilä-Horn, Marja-Leena (1996) *Santi Asoke Buddhism and Thai State Response.* Turku: Abo Akademi University Press.

—— (2000) 'The status and values of the Santi Asoke *Sikkhamat*'. In Karma Lekshe Tsomo (ed.), *Innovative Buddhist Women: Swimming Against the Stream.* Richmond, Surrey: Curzon Press, pp. 72–83.

—— (2003) Small is beautiful in Asoke villages . In Marja-Leena Heikkilä-Horn and Rassamee Krisanamis (eds), *Insight Into Santi Asoke.* Bangkok: Fah-aphai Co.Ltd., pp. 25–62.

Holm, Jean and John Bowker (eds) (2001) [1994] *Women in Religion.* London and New York: Continuum.

Holt, John Clifford (1999 [1981]) *Discipline: The Canonical Buddhism of the Vinayapitaka.* Delhi: Motilal Banarsidass Publishers.

Horner, Isaline B. (1990 [1930]) *Women Under Primitive Buddhism: Laywomen and Almswomen.* Delhi: Motilal Banarsidass.

Ischii, Yaneo (1986) *Sangha, State, and Society: Thai Buddhism in History.* Honolulu: University of Hawai'i Press.

Jackson, Peter A. (1988) *Buddhadasa: A Buddhist Thinker for the Modern World.* Bangkok: The Siam Society.

—— (1989) *Buddhism, Legitimation, and Conflict: The Political functions of Urban Thai Buddhism.* Singapore: Institute of Southeast Asian Studies.

—— (1995) *Dear Uncle Go: Male Homosexuality in Thailand.* Bangkok: Bua Luang.

—— (1997) 'Withering centre flourishing margins: Buddhism's changing political roles'. In Kevin Hewison (ed.), *Political Change in Thailand: Democracy and Participation.* London: Routledge, pp. 75–93.

—— (1999) 'Thailand's culture wars: Economic crisis, resurgent rationalist Buddhism and critiques of cults of prosperity'. Paper presented at the Seventh International Conference on Thai Studies, Amsterdam, 4–8 July.

Jackson, Peter A. and Gerard Sullivan (eds) (1999) *Male and Female Homosexualities in Contemporary Thailand.* Chiang Mai: Silkworm Books.

Jackson, Peter A. and Nerida M. Cook (eds) (1999) *Genders and Sexualities in Modern Thailand.* Chiang Mai: Silkworm Books.

Janssen, Peter (2001) 'Thai novice attempts to launch female monkhood'. *Yasodhara* 17 (3,68), pp. 15–16.

Jaschok, Maria and Shui Jingjun. (2000) *The History of Women's Mosques in Chinese Islam: A Mosque of Their Own.* Richmond, Surrey: Curzon Press.

Jones, Gavin W. (1997) 'The "flight from marriage" in Southeast and East Asia'. *Journal of Comparative Family Studies,* 36. 1, pp. 93–119.

Jootla, Susan, Elbaum (1990) 'The practice of giving'. In Bhikkhu Bodhi (ed.), *Dana The Practice of Giving: Selected Essays*. Kandy: Buddhist Publication Society, pp. 4–18.

Kabilsingh, Chatsumarn (1984) *A Comparative Study of Bhikkhuni Patimokkha*. Varanasi, Delhi: Chaukhambha Orientalia.

—— (1988) 'The role of women in Buddhism'. In Karma Lekshe Tsomo (ed.), *Daughters of the Buddha*. Ithaca, New York: Snow Lion Publication, pp. 225–235.

—— (1991) *Thai Women in Buddhism*. Berkeley, California: Parallax Press.

—— (1998) *Women in Buddhism: Questions and answers*. Bangkok: Faculty of Liberal Arts, Thammasat University.

—— (2000) 'Why do Buddhist nuns observe more rules?' *Yasodhara: Newsletter on International Buddhist Women's Activities*. 17 (2) (no. 62), pp. 6–10.

Kapferer, Bruce (1997) *The Feast of the Sorcerer: Practices of Consciousness and Power*. Chicago and London: University of Chicago Press.

Kawanami, Hiroko (2000) 'Theravadin religious women'. In Frank E. Reynolds and Jason A. Carbine (eds), *The Life of Buddhism*. Berkeley, Los Angeles and London: University of California Press, pp. 86–95.

Kepner, Susan Fulop (1996) *The Lioness in Bloom: Modern Thai Fiction about Women*. Berkeley, Los Angeles and London. University of California Press.

Ketudat Sippanondha and Wichit Srisa-an (1979) *Buddhism, Legitimation, and Conflict: The Political Functions of Urban Thai Buddhism*. Singapore: Institute of Southeast Asian Studies.

Keyes, Charles F. (1971) 'Buddhism and national integration in Thailand'. *Journal of Asian Studies*, 30 (3) (May), pp. 551–567.

—— (1984) 'Mother and mistress but never a monk: Buddhist notions of female gender in rural Thailand'. *American Ethnologist* 11 (2), pp. 223–241.

—— (1986) 'Ambiguous gender: Male initiation in a Northern Thai Buddhist society'. In Caroline Walker Bynum, Stevan Harrell and Paula Richman (eds), *Gender and Religion: On the Complexity of Symbols*. Boston: Beacon Press, pp. 66–96.

—— (1987) *Thailand: Buddhist Kingdom as Modern Nation-State*. London: Westview Press.

—— (ed.) (1991) *Reshaping Local Worlds: Formal Education and Cultural Change in Rural Southeast Asia*. Connecticut: Monograph 36/Yale Southeast Asia Studies Yale Center for International and Area Studies.

—— (1999a) 'Buddhism fragmented: Thai Buddhism and political order since the 1970s'. Keynote Address presented at the Seventh International Conference on Thai Studies, Amsterdam, 4–8 July.

—— (1999b) 'Moral authority of the Sangha and modernity in Thailand: Sexual scandals, sectarian, dissent, and political resistance'. In Sulak Sivaraksa, Pipob Udomittipong and Chris Walker (eds), *Socially Engaged Buddhism for the New Millennium*. London: Wisdom Books, pp. 121–147.

Khin Thitsa (1980) *Providence and Prostitution: Image and Reality for Women in Buddhist Thailand*. London: Change International Reports, Women and Society.

Khin Thitsa and Signe Howell (1983) 'Nuns, mediums and prostitutes in Chiangmai: A study of some marginal categories of women'. *Women and Development in Southeast Asia I*. Occasional Paper I. Canterbury: University of Kent.

King, Sallie B. (1996) 'Conclusion: Buddhist social activism'. In Christopher S. Queen and Sallie B. King (eds), *Engaged Buddhism: Buddhist Liberation Movements in Asia*. Albany: State University of New York Press, pp. 321–329.

King, Ursula (1989) *Women and Spirituality: Voices of Protest and Promise*. London: Macmillan Education.

Kirsch, Thomas A. (1975) 'Economy, polity and religion in Thailand'. In William Skinner and Thomas A. Kirsch, *Change and Persistence in Thai Society*. Ithaca: Cornell University Press, pp. 173–196.

—— (1977) 'Complexity in the Thai religious system: an Interpretation'. *Journal of Asian Studies,* 36, pp. 241–266.

—— (1985) 'Text and context: Buddhist sex roles/ culture of gender revisited'. *American Ethnologist* 12 (2), pp. 302–320.

—— (1996 [1982]) 'Buddhism, sex-roles, and the Thai economy'. In Penny Van Esterik (ed.), *Women of Southeast Asia*. Southeast Asia Monograph Series. Dekalb, Illinois: Northern Illinois University, pp. 13–32.

Klausner, William J. (1997) *Thai Culture in Transition*. Bangkok: The Siam Society.

Komin, Suntaree (1992) *Psychology of the Thai People: Values and Behavioural Patterns*. Bangkok: NIDA (National Institute of Development Administration).

Kornfield, Jack (1996, [1977]) *Living Dharma: Teachings of Twelve Buddhist Masters*. Boston and London: Shambhala.

Lang, Karen (1995) 'Shaven heads and loose hair: Buddhist attitudes toward hair and sexuality'. In Howard Eilberg-Schwartz and Wendy Doniger, (eds.), *Off with Her Head! The Denial of Women's Identity in Myth, Religion, and Culture*. Berkeley, Los Angeles and London: University of California Press, pp. 32–52.

Leach, Edmund. R. (1961) *Rethinking Anthropology*. London: Athlone.

Lévi-Strauss, Claude (1969) *The Elementary Structures of Kinship*. Boston: Beacon Press.

Lindberg Falk, Monica (2000a) 'Women in between: Becoming religious persons in Thailand'. In Ellison Banks Findly (ed.) *Women's Buddhism, Buddhism's Women: Tradition, Revision, Renewal*. Boston: Wisdom Publication, pp. 37–57.

—— (2000b) 'Thammacarini Witthaya: The first Buddhist school for girls in Thailand'. In Karma Lekshe Tsomo (ed.) *Innovative Buddhist Women: Swimming Against the Stream* Curzon Press, Richmond, Surrey, pp. 61–71.

—— (2002) 'Making Fields of Merit: Buddhist nuns challenge gendered orders in Thailand'. Unpublished doctoral thesis, Department of Social Anthropology, Göteborg University, Sweden.

Ling, Trevor (1981) *A Dictionary of Buddhism: Indian and Southeast Asian*. Calcutta, New Delhi: K P Bagchi and Company.

Lyttleton, Chris (1999) 'Changing the rules: Shifting bounds of adolescent sexuality in Northeast Thailand'. In Peter A. Jackson and Nerida M. Cook (eds) *Genders and Sexualities in Modern Thailand*. Chiang Mai: Silkworm Books, pp. 165–187.

Manderson, Leonore and Pranee Liamputtong (eds.), (2002) *Coming of Age in South and Southeast Asia: Youth, Courtship and Sexuality*. Richmond, Surrey: Curzon Press.

Mauss, Marcel (1967 [1925]) *The Gift: Forms and Functions of Exchange in Archaic Societies*. London: Cohen and West Ltd.

McCargo, Duncan. (1997). *Chamlong Srimuang and the New Thai Politics*. London: Hurst and Company.

McConnell, John A. (1995) *Mindful Mediation: A Handbook for Buddhist Peacemakers*. Bangkok: Buddhist Research Institute, Mahachula Buddhist University, Wongsanit Ashram, Foundation for Children.

Mills, Mary Beth (1999) *Thai Women in the Global Labor Force: Consuming Desires, Contested Selves*. New Brunswick, New Jersey and London: Rutgers University Press.

Moore, Henrietta L. (1994) *A Passion for Difference: Essays in Anthropology and Gender*. Cambridge: Polity Press.

Morris, Rosalind (1994) 'Three sexes and four sexualities: Redressing the discourses on gender and sexuality in contemporary Thailand'. *Positions* 2 (1), pp. 15–43.

—— (2000) *In the Place of Origins: Modernity and its Mediums in Northern Thailand*. Durham, North Carolina: Duke University Press.

Mueche, Majorie (1992) 'Mother sold food, daughter sells her body: The cultural continuity of prostitution'. *Social Science and Medicine* 35 (7): 891–901.

Murcott, Susan (1991) *The First Buddhist women: Translations and Commentaries on the Therigatha*. Berkeley, California: Parallax Press.

Ven. Nanamoli Thera (trans.) (1992) *The Patimokkha: 227 Fundamental Rules of a Bhikkhu*. Bangkok: Maha Makutrajavidyalaya Press.

Nussbaum, Martha C. (1999) *Sex and Social Justice*. New York: Oxford University Press.

Nyantiloka (1972) *Buddhist Dictionary: Manual of Buddhist Terms and Doctrines.* Colombo, Ceylon: Frewin and Co., Ltd.

Parry, Jonathan (1985) 'The gift, the Indian gift and the "Indian gift"'. *Man* (N.S.) 21, pp. 453–473.

Paul, Diana (1985 [1979]) *Women in Buddhism: Images of the Feminine in Mahayana Tradition.* Berkeley and Los Angeles: University of California Press.

Phongpaichit, Pasuk and Chris Baker (1996) *Thailand's Boom!* Chiang Mai: Silkworm Books.

Pitiyanuwat, Somwung and Sujiva Siridej (2005) *Educaion in Thailand: Policies and Practices in Schools.* Bangkok: Chulalongkorn University Press.

Pruekpongsawalee, Malee (2004) 'The constitutions and legal status of women in family related laws in Thailand: A historical perspective'. In Suwanna Satha-Anand (ed.) *Power, Knowledge and Justice.* Seoul: Ewha Womans University Press, pp. 85–155.

Rabiab patibat khôông sathaaban mae chii thai haeng pratheet thai [Rules of practice of the Thai Mae Chiis' Institute] (1975) Bangkok.

Raheja, Gloria Goodwin (1988) *The Poison in the Gift: Ritual, Prestation, and the Dominant Caste in a North Indian Village.* Chicago: The University of Chicago Press.

Rahula, Walpola (1978 [1959]) *What the Buddha taught.* London and Bedford: Gordon Fraser.

Rubin, Gayle (1975) 'The traffic in women: Notes on the political economy of sex'. In Rayna Reiter (ed.) *Toward an Anthropology of Women.* New York: Monthly Review Press, pp. 157–210.

Santikaro Bhikkhu (1996) 'Buddhadasa Bhikkhu: Life and society through the natural eyes of voidness.' In Christopher S. Queen and Sallie B. King (eds) *Engaged Buddhism: Buddhist Liberation Movements in Asia.* Albany: State University of New York Press, pp. 147–193.

Satha-Anand, Suwanna (ed.) (1999) 'Truth over convention: Feminist interpretations of Buddhism'. In Courtney Howland (ed.) *Religious Fundamentalisms and the Human Rights of Women.* New York: St. Martin's Press, pp. 281–292.

—— (2004) *Power, Knowledge and Justice.* Seoul: Ewha Womans University Press.

Satithamajit, Kosol (2001) 'Revered monk hands over gold, cash to boost reserves: Stresses need for personal sacrifice'. *Bangkok Post* 22 April.

Schrift, Alan D. (ed.) (1997) *The Logic of the Gift: Toward an Ethic of Generosity.* New York: Routledge.

Sharma, Arvind (1977) 'How and why did the women in ancient India become Buddhist nuns?' *Sociological Analysis* 38, pp. 239–251.

—— (ed.) (1987) *Women in World Religions.* Albany: State University of New York Press.

Sharma, Arvind and Katherine K. Young (eds.) (1999) *Feminism and World Religions.* Albany: State University of New York Press.

Schober, Juliane (1995) 'The Theravada Buddhist engagement with modernity in Southeast Asia: Whither the social paradigm of the galactic polity?' *Journal of Southeast Asian Studies* 26 (2), pp. 307–325.

Sered, Susan Starr (1999) 'Woman as symbol and women as agents: Gendered religious discourses and practices'. In Myra Marx Ferree, Judith Lorber and Beth B. Hess, (eds) *Revisioning Gender.* Thousand Oaks, London and New Delhi: Sage, pp. 193–221.

Sinnott, Megan J. (2004) *Toms and Dees: Transgender Identity and Female Same-Sex Relationships in Thailand.* Honolulu: University of Hawai'i Press.

Sivaraksa, Sulak (1988) *A Socially Engaged Buddhism.* Bangkok: Thai Interreligious Commission for Development.

—— (1992) *Seeds of Peace: A Buddhist Vision for Renewing Society.* Berkeley, California: Parallax Press.

Sponberg, Alan (1992) Attitudes towards women and the feminine in early Buddhism . In José Ignacio Cabezon (ed.) *Buddhism, Sexuality and Gender.* Albany: State University of New York Press, pp. 3–36.

Somdet Phra Buddhaghosacariya (1992) *Uposatha Sila: The Eight-Precept Observance.* Bangkok: Mahamakut Foundation, Wat Borvornives Viharn.

Sri Dao Ruang (1996 [1985]) 'Matsii'. In Susan Fulop Kepner (ed.) *The Lioness in Bloom: Modern Thai Fiction about Women.* Berkeley, Los Angeles and London. University of California Press, pp. 95–103.

Strathern, Marilyn (1988) *The Gender of the Gift: Problems with Women and Problems with Society in Melanesia.* Berkeley: University of California Press.

Suthon, Sukphisit (1998) 'The language of the Lord Buddha'. *Bangkok Post,* 3 April.

Suwanbubbha, Parichart (1983) 'A Comparative study of the status and roles of Theravada Buddhist and Roman Catholic nuns: A case study in the community of Bangkok'. Bangkok: Unpublished MA Thesis, Mahidol University, Bangkok.

Suwanna, Satha-Anand (1999) 'Truth over convention: Feminist interpretations of Buddhism'. In Courtney Howland (ed.) *Religious Fundamentalisms and the Human rights of Women.* New York: St. Martin's Press, pp. 281–292.

—— (ed.) (2004) *Power, Knowledge and Justice.* Seoul: Ewha Womans University Press.

Swearer, Donald S. (1976) 'Some observations on new directions in Thai Buddhism'.

In Heinrich DuMoulin (ed.), *Buddhism in the Modern World*. New York: Collier Macmillan.

—— (1991) 'Fundamentalistic movements in Theravada Buddhism'. In Mary E. Marty and R. Scott Appleby (eds) *Fundamentalism's Observed*. Chicago: University of Chicago Press, pp. 628–690.

—— (1995) *The Buddhist World of Southeast Asia*. Albany: State University of New York Press.

—— (1999) 'Centre and periphery: Buddhism and politics in modern Thailand'. In Ian Harris (ed.) *Buddhism and Politics in Twentieth-Century Asia*, London and New York: Pinter, pp. 194–228.

Tambiah, Stanley Jeyaraja (1970) *Buddhism and the Spirit Cults in Northeast Thailand*. Cambridge: Cambridge University Press.

—— (1976) *World Conqueror and World Renouncer: A Study of Buddhism and Polity in Thailand Against a Historical Background*. Cambridge: Cambridge University Press.

Tanabe, Shigeharu (1991) 'Spirits, power and the discourse of female gender: The Phi Meng cult of Northern Thailand.' In Manas Chitkasem and Andrew Turton (eds) *Thai Constructions of Knowledge*. London: School of Oriental and African Studies, University of London, pp. 183–212.

—— and Charles, F. Keyes, eds. (2002) *Cultural Crisis and Social Memory: Modernity and Identity in Thailand and Laos*. London: RoutledgeCurzon.

Tan Acharn Kor Khao-suan-luang (1991) *Looking Inward: Observations on the Art of Meditation*. Kandy, Sri Lanka: Buddhist Publication Society.

Tannenbaum, Nicola (1999) 'Buddhism, prostitution, and sex: Limits on the academic discourse on gender in Thailand'. In Peter A. Jackson, Peter A. and Nerida M. Cook (eds) *Genders and Sexualities in Modern Thailand*. Chiang Mai: Silkworm Books, pp. 243–260.

Tantiwiramanond, Darunee and Shashi Ranjan Pandey (1987) 'The status and role of Thai women in the pre-modern period: A historical and cultural perspective.' *Sojourn* 2 (1), pp. 125–149.

—— (1991) *By Women, for Women: A Study of Women's Organizations in Thailand*. Singapore: Institute of Southeast Asian Studies.

—— (1997) 'New opportunities or new inequalities: Development issues and women's lives in Thailand. In Virada Somswaasdi and Sally Theobalds (eds) *Women, gender relations and develoment in Thai society*. Vol. 1. Chiang Mai: Women Studies Center, Faculty of Social Sciences, Chiang Mai University.

Taylor, James Leslie (1989) 'Contemporary urban Buddhist "cults" and the socio-political order in Thailand.' *Mankind* 19 (2), pp. 112–125.

—— (1993) 'Buddhist revitalization, modernization, and social change in contemporary Thailand.' *Sojourn* 2(1), pp. 125–149.

—— (1996, [1993]) *Forest Monks and the Nation-State: An anthropological and Historical Study in Northeastern Thailand.* Singapore: Institute of Southeast Asian Studies.

Terwiel, Barend Jan (1976) 'A model for the study of Buddhism.' *Journal of Asian Studies,* May, pp. 391–404.

—— (1994) *Monks and Magic: An Analysis of Religious Ceremonies in Central Thailand.* Bangkok: White Lotus.

Tiyavanich, Kamala (1997) *Forest Recollections: Wandering Monks in Twentieth-Century Thailand.* Honolulu: University of Hawai'i Press.

Tsedroen, Jampa (1988) 'The significance of the conference'. In Karma Lekshe Tsomo (ed.) *Sakyadhita: Daughters of the Buddha.* Ithaca, New York: Snow Lion Publication, pp. 31–52.

Tsomo, Karma Lekshe, (ed.) (1988) *Sakyadhita: Daughters of the Buddha.* Ithaca New York: Snow Lion Publications.

Vajirananavarorasa, Somdet Phra Maha Samana Chao Krom Phraya (1989) *Ordination Procedure and the Preliminary Duties of a New Bhikkhu.* Bangkok: Mahamakut Rajavidyalaya Press.

Vallely, Anne (2002) *Guardians of the Transcendent: An Ethnography of a Jain Ascetic Community.* Toronto: University of Toronto Press.

Van Esterik, John (1996 [1982]) 'Women meditation teachers in Thailand'. In Penny Van Esterik, (ed.), *Women of Southeast Asia.* Southeast Asia Monograph Series. Dekalb, Illinois: Northern Illinois University, pp. 33–41.

Van Esterik, Penny (1996 [1982]) *Women of Southeast Asia.* Southeast Asia Monograph Series. Dekalb, Illinois: Northern Illinois University.

—— (2000) *Materializing Thailand.* Oxford: Berg.

Van Gennep, Arnold (1960 [1909]) *The Rites of Passage.* Chicago: University of Chicago Press.

Van Gorkom, Nina (1990) 'Generosity: The inward dimension'. In Bhikkhu Bodhi (ed.) *Dana. The Practice of Giving: Selected Essays.* Kandy: Buddhist Publication Society, pp. 45–58.

Weiner, Annette B. (1992) *Inalienable Possessions: The Paradox of Keeping-While-Giving.* Berkeley: University of California Press.

Whittaker, Andrea (1999) 'Women and capitalist transformation in a Northeastern Thai village'. In Peter A. Jackson and Nerida M. Cook (eds) *Genders and Sexualities in Modern Thailand.* Chiang Mai: Silkworm Books, pp. 43–62.

—— (2000) *Intimate Knowledge: Wimen and their health in NorthEast Thailand*. St Leonards, NSW: Allen & Unwin.

—— (2002) 'Water serpents and staying by the fire: Markers of maturity in a Northeast Thai villlage'. In Leonore Manderson and Pranee Liamputtong (eds) *Coming of Age in South and Southeast Asia: Youth, Courtship and Sexuality*. Richmond, Surrey: Curzon Press, pp. 17–41.

Willis, Janice D. (1985) 'Nuns and benefactresses: The role of women in the development of Buddhism'. In Yvonne Haddad and Ellison Findly (eds) *Women and Religion and Social Change*. Albany: State University of New York Press, pp. 59–83.

Wyatt, David K. (1984) *Thailand A Short History*. New Haven: Yale University Press.

Yasodhara: Newsletter on International Buddhist Women's Activities.

—— (2001a) 'To continue a lineage of ordained women'. 7 (3, 67), pp. 5.

—— (2001b) 'Feel the beauty of the lotus: An interview with Dhammananda'. 17 (3, 68), pp. 17–19.

—— (2002) 'Following the samaneri on an alms round'. 18 (3), pp. 7–10.

Yoddumnern-Attig, Bencha (1992) *Changing Roles and Status of Women in Thailand: A Documentary Assessment*. Bangkok: Institute for Population and Social Research, Mahidol University.

Zwilling, Leonard (1992) Homosexuality as seen in Indian Buddhist texts. In José Ignacio Cabezon (ed.) *Buddhism, Sexuality, and Gender*. Albany: State University of New York Press, pp. 203–214.

Index

of money, 63, 79, 101 n. 3, 113, 136, 154,
161–162, 165, 221, 232
Douglas, Mary, 106, 249
dukkha, 44, 55,62, 69, 76, 80 n. 6, 257. *See
also* suffering

economic crisis, 18, 189, 202, 212
economy, 18, 33, 35, 159
education, 16, 37, 106, 193, 197, 200, 201,
202, 203, 210, 211, 215
access to, 54, 74, 78, 175, 193, 194, 195,
209, 210, 211, 216, 219, 223, 236
higher, 16, 78, 193, 203, 204, 218
secondary, 16, 74, 93, 199, 201, 205, 211,
212, 216, 219, 258
Eight Chief Rules (*garudhamma*), 26, 257
eight precepts. *See* Buddhist precepts
embody, 107, 129, 132, 253
empower, 50, 229
emptiness, 50, 245
enlightenment, 7, 24, 43, 50, 55, 76, 81, 84,
154,183, 185, 188, 196, 225, 243
and gender, 44, 50, 85, 248
equanimity, 143

faith, 43, 54, 67, 68, 69, 79, 139 n. 5, 152,
153, 180, 243, 247
Falk, Nancy, 27, 43, 49
family law, 35, 36
female
Buddhist Order, 25, 44, 87, 243
identity, 34
monks, 9, 10, 26, 29, 30, 42, 43, 52 n.4,
163, 227, 237–239, 241, 243–246, 249–
251, 260. *See also bhikkhuni, bhiksuni*
femininity, 44, 48
fertility, 33, 89, 107, 108
final goal, 8, 42, 81, 100, 113, 248
five precepts. *See* Buddhist precepts
forest tradition, 175, 179
forest-dwelling monks, 172, 194
foundation,
of *samnak chii*s, 103, 153, 177
stone of Wat Phra Dhammakaya, 182
fund-raising ceremony (*phaapaa*), 141, 153,
158, 164–167, 189, 212, 228

garudhamma, 26, 27, 44, 257. *See also* Eight
Chief Rules
gender
categories, 44, 253
differences, 44, 62, 245, 253
discourses, 2, 8, 28, 30, 47, 51, 253, 254
identity, 8, 44, 45, 46, 89, 100, 101, 102,
129, 131, 132, 253
norms, 101, 131, 248
See also Thai sex/gender system
generosity, 19, 140, 141, 143, 144, 145, 153,
154, 157, 256
van Gennep, Arnold, 99
greed, 10, 80 n.4, 81, 141, 145, 152, 154,
180, 185, 258
Gross, Rita, 7, 23, 26, 27, 245
Gutschow, Kim, 106, 108

Havnevik, Hanna, 50, 138, 223, 224
Heikkilä-Horn, Marja-Leena, 6, 184, 185,
186, 188
homosexuality, 47, 48
Horner, Isaline, 24, 26, 27, 42, 87, 88, 163
house blessing ceremony, 132

identity
lay, 8, 45, 96
mae chii, 127, 178
masculine, 34, 46
ordained, 19, 82, 101, 121, 122, 129, 131,
251
sangha, 131
Thai, 9
identity card, 25, 112, 127, 168, 178, 234
impermanence. See *anicca*
inheritance, 36

Jackson, Peter, 46, 47, 171, 173, 174, 179,
180, 186, 188,189, 190, 247, 253
Jataka tales, 143, 145, 168 n. 2, 176, 257,
262

Kabilsingh, Chatsumarn, 9, 16, 25, 30, 40,
41, 87, 107, 128, 136, 137, 177, 194,
237
Kabilsingh, Voramai, 29, 163, 169, 238
kamma (karma), 7, 8, 22, 30, 49, 52, 86,
109, 140, 157, 167, 179, 257

www.ingramcontent.com/pod-product-compliance
Lightning Source LLC
Chambersburg PA
CBHW031411270326
41929CB00010BA/1412